A Forgotten Heritage

Map from C. Golder, John Horst, J. G. Schaal's
Geschichte der Zentral Deutschen Konferenz

A Forgotten Heritage

The German Methodist Church

by
Barbara Dixon

Little Miami Publishing Co.
Milford, Ohio
2011

Little Miami Publishing Co.
P.O. Box 588
Milford, Ohio 45150-0588
www.littlemiamibooks.com

Copyright ©2011 by Barbara Dixon . All rights reserved. No part of this book may be reproduced or transmitted in any form or by any means, electronic or mechanical, including photocopying, recording or by any information storage and retrieval system without written permission from the author, except for the inclusion of brief quotations in a review.

Printed in the United States of America on acid-free paper.

ISBN-13: 978-1-932250-96-1
ISBN-10: 1-932250-96-4

Library of Congress Control Number: 2011928623

DEDICATION

This book, and the many years of research that went into it, is dedicated to my grandfather and grandmother, the Rev. Theodore Rudin and Otillia Weidmann Rudin, and my great grandparents, the Rev. J. C. Weidmann and Katherine Ribbe Weidmann. Together, their careers spanned much of the German Methodist mission from its inception to its demise in the 1930s.

Otillia Weidmann Rudin and Rev. Theodore Rudin.

Reverend John C. Weidmann
COURTESY OF THE
CINCINNATI MUSEUM CENTER– CINCINNATI HISTORICAL SOCIETY LIBRARY

Contents

Preface **ix**

PART ONE **1**

THE GERMAN METHODIST EPISCOPAL CHURCHES
IN THE CINCINNATI DISTRICT

Chapter 1 *Eastern Indiana Churches in the Cincinnati District* **3**

Chapter 2 *Indianapolis and Some Western Indiana Churches* **17**

Chapter 3 *Cincinnati Area Churches in the Cincinnati District* **27**

Chapter 4 *Northern Kentucky Churches in the Cincinnati District* **43**

Chapter 5 *Southwestern Ohio German M. E. Churches* **53**

Chapter 6 *German M. E. Churches in South Central Ohio* **63**

PART TWO **85**

THE GERMAN METHODIST EPISCOPAL CHURCHES
IN THE LOUISVILLE DISTRICT

Chapter 7 *Churches in the Louisville Area* **87**

Chapter 8 *Churches in the Seymour Area and Areas South* **99**

Chapter 9	*Southwestern Indiana German Churches*	*117*
Chapter 10	*German M. E. Churches in Southern Indiana*	*137*
Chapter 11	*More German M. E. Churches in Southwestern Indiana*	*143*
Chapter 12	*Other Churches in the Louisville District*	*165*

Part Three   171

The German Methodist Episcopal Churches in the Michigan District

Chapter 13	*Western Michigan Grand Rapids*	*173*
Chapter 14	*Detroit Area German Methodist Churches*	*185*
Chapter 15	*Central Michigan Churches*	*193*
Chapter 16	*Michigan's "Thumb" and Adjacent Area*	*209*
Chapter 17	*Churches in Other States*	*219*

Part IV   253

The German Methodist Episcopal Churches in the North Ohio District

Chapter 18	*Lake Erie Area*	*255*
Chapter 19	*Central Ohio*	*279*
Chapter 20	*Northeastern Ohio*	*323*
Chapter 21	*Southeastern Ohio*	*327*
Chapter 22	*Churches East of Ohio*	*349*
	Acknowledgments	*359*
	Glossary of Terms	*361*
	Bibliography	*363*
	Index	*377*
	About the Author	*401*

Preface

WILHELM NAST STARTED THE GERMAN METHODIST EPISCOPAL CHURCH in the 1830s by traveling throughout the Midwest United States ministering to German-speaking settlers of the Methodist Episcopal persuasion. His mission was difficult at first because he traveled by horseback through all kinds of weather and did not always find a friendly welcome. Eventually, due to the influx of German immigrants in the late 1840s, his mission flourished and the church had its heyday in the late nineteenth and early twentieth centuries. When the arrival of newcomers from Germany slowed and the German Americans became acclimated to their new country, the need for German-speaking churches dwindled. In the early 1930s the German M. E. Church was absorbed by the English-speaking Methodist church.

The subject sparked my interest because my grandfather, Theodore Rudin, was a German Methodist minister from 1898 until 1934. He pastored churches at Sandusky, Hannibal, Galion, and Cincinnati, Ohio; New Albany and Holland Indiana; and Louisville, Kentucky; and in his capacity as a minister visited many other churches in the Central German Conference. Although I remember my grandfather, I was too young to know about his interesting life, so it was a revelation to relive his experiences and thoughts through the diaries that he kept for more than forty years from 1898 to 1943. He commented not simply on his daily life, but on world events, church activities, the weather, and so on. Some comments were quite acerbic and some of his views would be less than politically correct today.

I visited many sites of German Methodist churches in the Central German Conference. I discovered that some had long since become dust but some still flourish in other incarnations, having been updated and remodeled. Some church histories have been reverently preserved on historical tablets outside the church; while others require backtracking through yellowed city directories and area histories to find any evidence of their existence and location. A good starting place (even if you don't read German) is *Geschichte der Zentral Deutschen Konferenz* by C. Golder, John Horst, and J. G. Schaal (Cincinnati, Ohio: Jennings & Graham, n.d.), which I found in the rare book section at the Hamilton County Main Library in Cincinnati. This book lists all the churches in the Conference at the time of its publication which was about 1907. There are also photographs of many of the church buildings. You may be able to even glean an address from the entry. Hereafter I will just refer to this book as the *Geschichte.* A translation of part of the *Geschichte* is *Ministers and Churches of the Central German Conference* by Julie Overton (Heritage House, 1975). She lists all the G.M.E. churches in each of the then-existing four districts and gives a short history of many. County histories are another good source. Also, local historical societies, the local history room of the public library, the United Methodist Church in the location being researched or the state United Methodist Archives at Ohio Wesleyan in Delaware, Ohio, the archives at Depauw University in Greencastle, Indiana, the archives in West Michigan at Adrian College in Adrian or at Albion College in Albion, Michigan (Detroit District). For other details on specific sources, please refer to the bibliography. Sometimes in the course of my research, I came across a knowledgeable person by accident, who was willing to tell me everything he or she knew and would sometimes even look up information that I could not otherwise have found. Some were their church's historian; others were recommended to me by pastors, librarians, or church secretaries. The internet also provided some church histories, such as Brown Street United Methodist Church in Lafayette, Indiana, for example. The United Methodist Archives listed above should all have copies of the *Minutes of the Annual Conferences* which include the minutes of the Central German Conference. These give the facts and figures of the German churches for any given year from 1864 to 1933.

My book tells the history of the German Methodist churches up to the present, when applicable; and, in excerpts from his diaries, my grandfather will tell what it was like from his unique perspective. The result is a compelling glimpse at "the way it was" during the era of German Methodism, covering everything from the cost of installing electric lights to sermon topics of the day, descriptions of various church groups to the perils of driving a horse and buggy. World War I had a significant impact on the church and its members and is reflected in many church histories, as well as grandfather's diaries. One hundred years ago a country preacher (who served as many as four churches) typically earned about two hundred dollars a year. Time and the economy have marched forward, but the cares and concerns of yesterday, as reflected in church histories and grandfather's diaries, still sound surprisingly the same, even in our high-tech, fast-paced world of the twenty first century.

Wilkommen! Join me on a leisurely stroll through yesterday.

PART I

The German Methodist Episcopal Churches in the Cincinnati District

The Cincinnati District included a wide range of churches from Terre Haute and Lafayette, Indiana, in the west to Ironton and Pomeroy, Ohio, in the east. Covington and Newport, Kentucky, also belonged to the district and Dayton and Springfield, Ohio, were the northernmost sites.

CHAPTER 1

Eastern Indiana Churches in the Cincinnati District

Batesville, Indiana, Circuit

German Methodism came to Laughery Township on September 12, 1845, according to old German records. The circuit of preaching places emanated from the Lawrenceburg Mission and was under the jurisdiction of the Ohio Conference of the German Methodist Episcopal Church. Christian Wyttenbach was the first preacher. He had his hands full as at one time there were as many as fourteen preaching points, or sites, in the area. Below is one list of churches (or preaching places) and their contributions to the pastor's salary.

1.	Salt Creek	$10.75
2.	Huntersville	$2.50
3.	Laugher	$17.60
4.	Layhery (?)	$8.37 1/2
5.	Pipe Creek	$9.16
6.	Pennsylvaniaburg	$8.80
7.	Stegner's School	$18.65
8.	Mailand	$8.55
9.	Franklin Church	$6.85
10.	South Hogan	$13.87 1/2

In addition, $17.56 was raised at quarterly meetings which made the pastor's yearly salary a total of $123.17.

The mission later became known as the the Pennsylvaniaburg Mission and finally, in 1861, as the Batesville Circuit.[1]

Batesville Circuit—Batesville German M. E. Church

The German M. E. church in Batesville was founded in 1870 and a brick meet-

Batesville, Indiana, church, currently United Methodist

ing place was erected near the Methodist Cemetery in 1871 on Mulberry Street. In 1889 a new building was built at Park and South streets. By 1918 preaching in German was discontinued due to the anti-German sentiments during World War I and the church changed its name to First M. E. Church. In 1926 the English M. E. church, Wesley Chapel, merged with First Church. In 1934 Wesley Chapel was moved to the site of the former German church and became an addition uniting the two literally. You can see both buildings at the Park and South streets location as the church is still being used as a United Methodist church.[2]

Many of the small preaching points associated at one time or another with Batesville were only operative for a few years. It is difficult to find any information about many of them. In some cases, names have been changed—for example, Pennsylvaniaburg is now known as Penntown.

Batesville Circuit—Pennington Church

The Pennington church, now Zion UMC, is located at the intersection of 330S and 550E, two gravel roads in Salt Creek Township a mile and a half south of Smith's Crossing. The congregation met in an old schoolhouse until the church was built about 1866. The church shared a pastor with Batesville from 1910 to 1927 and had services every second Sunday afternoon. Most sermons were in German until the World War I period when the name was officially changed from the German Methodist Episcopal Church to the First Methodist Episcopal Church.[3] An educational room was completed in 1960, a vestibule added in 1964 and a kitchen and bathroom constructed in 1975.[4]

Present Zion UMC in southeastern Indiana, formerly known as German Methodist Episcopal Church, First M.E. Church, and Pennington Church.

Batesville Circuit—Laughery German M. E. Church

The Laughery German M. E. Church was located in Laughery Township at Baseline Road and 1300N. It was organized in 1845 and the building was built in 1850. By 1910, the church was no longer active and all that is left to mark the spot today is the cemetery.[5]

In 1925 my grandfather Theodore Rudin served as pastor of Second (German) Church in Cincinnati. He related his experiences at Batesville where he attended a district conference in May.

Monday, May 18

Went to Batesville this afternoon to attend our District Conference. A number of the Brethren were on the train including Bro. Werner. We arrived at our destination at about half past four. Bro. Lageman was at the station to greet us and assign us to our hosts. Dr. Enderis and I are the guests of Mr. Edward Zierer, who is an insurance agent and undertaker, and apparently is quite well-to-do. This evening Dr. Moeller preached a good sermon on John 20:20–21.

Tuesday, May 19

At the close of last night's meeting the Epworth League tendered us preachers a reception. Bro. Benz preached the communion sermon on Rom. 12:1–3. Bro. E. A. Rodeheffer was made secretary of the Conference and I was made chairman of the Messenger Committee and appointed reporter for the *Western*. Bro. Roesner is reporter for the *Apologete*. Dr. Morlock made a few introductory remarks. This afternoon Bro. Beal read an excellent paper on "The Value of the Modern Translations of the Old and New Testaments."

Wednesday, May 20

Last night Rev. E. Henke, Superintendent of the Old Folk's Home at Quincy, Illinois, preached. His text was Luke 24:31. It was a good sermon though it did not appeal to Dr. Enderis. Took a long walk with Bro. Benz after dinner. Bro. Nocka led the devotions yesterday and gave a very good talk. Father Severinghaus led the devotions this morning. Bro. Beuscher read his paper: "Divine and Human Agencies in Evangelism." I think he handled his subject pretty well.

Bishop Nicholson came in while we were having some singing and praying. When I came on the platform to read my review, the Bishop shook hands with me. Dr. Bucher and others said my essay was a fine piece. The Bishop also commended it.

Thursday, May 21

Left Batesville at 6:28 this morning. Bro. Roesner followed me yesterday with a review: "The Character of Paul" by Jefferson. It was a good piece of work. In the afternoon Bro. Edelmaier read a paper on "How to Coordinate the Several organizations of the Local Church so they function as a Unit." It was a vigorous presentation of deplorable conditions prevailing in nearly every church. In the evening Bishop Nicholson spoke to us on "World Service." The more I see of Bishop N., the better I like him. The afternoon devotions were conducted by Dr. Nast.

Friday, May 22

Must say that I enjoyed the District Meeting. Batesville is quite a nice place, and we have a nice congregation there. There are people in it with a good education and they evidently are much interested in their church. They have a vested choir and a woman is the leader, Mrs. Gelvin; also, a fine male quartette. Two small country appointments are connected with Batesville. By the way, our host told us that Bro. L. is the poorest preacher they have ever had in so far as preaching is concerned. They are often ashamed of him on account of his faulty language; he uses no

Lawrenceburg, Indiana, German M.E. now remodeled into Zerbe Law Offices.

notes, does not stick to his text and at one time preaches 15 minutes and at another, 50, and he is quite tactless, so Mr. Zierer told us. He is a good mixer, however, and a sincere Christian, he admitted.[6]

Lawrenceburg, Indiana

Rev. Adam Miller, pastor of the First German Church in Cincinnati, brought German Methodism to Lawrenceburg on April 11, 1839. A few weeks later William Nast followed and formed a class of ten people. The Germans met in

Plaque on the former Lawrenceburg German M.E. building.

Hamline Chapel, then on Walnut Street. In 1842 the German Methodists erected a two-story church building on what was then East Liberty Street. The street has since been renamed Center Street.[7] There is some disagreement about when and where the first church was built. A publication by the Lawrenceburg Historical Society, Incorporated, says that the congregation rented a two-story brick building on East Center Street in 1842 and then built a "substantial and commodious" church building on West Center Street in 1860. A parsonage was also erected at this time. In 1845 the Lawrenceburg church also became a station, rather than being on a circuit with other churches.[8] A county history relates that the first church was built in 1842 on Market Street and, later, on Center Street. The "substantial and commodious" building was built for eight thousand dollars.[9]

In the 1840s the church had forty members with 120 attendees. The pastor's salary was $225 a year. A new Lawrenceburg church, built in 1860, featured a flower garden and a potato patch in the backyard.

Author C. H. Wesler in the *Lawrenceburg Press*, painted a picture of how the singing in the German M. E. church was done. At first, the pastor would read a line and then the congregation would sing that line. This procedure continued until the whole hymn was sung. In 1866 a song book with notes and the first verse of each song came out. In 1888 another song book was published, this one having the first verse printed under the notes and successive verses below. Wesler added that there was no organ prelude. The pastor gave the number of the song; then read all the verses. After that the organ played and the singing began.[10]

Wesler also described the lighting and heating in the church. The congregation used coal oil or kerosene lamps, some of which had handles so they could be carried from place to place. Seven-foot-tall pillars were at the end of every third row along the center aisle of the church. At the top of these pillars were cast iron platforms where glass bowl lamps stood. Along the outer walls lamps in tin receptacles with adjustable reflectors hung. The janitor, who earned a salary of about forty dollars a year, did the trimming of the wicks, filling of the lamps and cleaning the lamp chimneys. The church had four wood-burning stoves upstairs for heating. The twenty-four-inch logs had to be carried up a flight of stairs which had a sharp turn. The Sunday school rooms downstairs had two similar stoves. The cast iron potbelly stoves, which burned coal, were a later improvement. This also required the carrying up of coal and the lugging down of ash.[11]

In 1925, a new furnace was installed. The church closed for three years and the congregation met elsewhere while redecorating and improvements were done. It reopened on January 20, 1926. Rev. A. F. Zarwell rededicated the church with a Union Prayer Meeting, a gathering involving other churches. Then in 1927 the German church was given up and the property deeded to the Fraternal Order of Eagles.[12]

The old church building still stands on Center Street and now houses the Zerbe Law Offices. When the Eagles vacated the building in 1976, People's National Bank took over and used the building for storage. In 1992 it passed to the Zerbe Law Offices.

Lawrenceville, Indiana, Circuit

There were a number of small German M. E. churches in the area of Dearborn and Ripley counties. Some existed for only a short time and merit only a sentence or two in the county histories. Others existed in towns long gone or geographical designations that are no longer known. The *Geschichte* mentions the following places: Aurora, Milan, Newpoint, Brookville, Pennsylvaniaburg (also known as Penntown), Pennington, Laughery, Lawrenceburg, and Batesville. The latter two became stations and the remainder went on the Lawrenceville Circuit which was originally called Laughery Mission.[14]

Lawrenceville Circuit—Penntown German M. E. Church

Penntown or Pennsylvaniaburg was the oldest town in Ripley County's Adams Township, although there is nothing much left of it now. German settlers began coming into the area in the 1830s and in the 1840s a German M. E. church was started. It took over a building that had been used by the English Methodists, but the Germans eventually moved to the Lawrenceville area.[15] A little more information is found in the *History of Adams Township* which says the "little frame church" was east of Penntown. A private individual bought the building when the German congregation moved to Lawrenceville. The building was torn down and its materials used in building a house. A small cemetery marks the original site.[16]

Lawrenceville Circuit—Lawrenceville German M. E. Church

Lawrenceville is a town that has seen more prosperous days. About the only thing left to mark the site of the German M. E. Church is a cemetery. A surviving cement slab may have been the doorstep. The Baptists had erected the original building which was then purchased by the German congregation in 1856.[17] It is hard to tell how long the Lawrenceville church lasted as, down through the years, it shifted to and from the Batesville Circuit and the Lawrenceville Circuit. It no longer shows up in conference records after 1928.

Lawrenceville Circuit—Milan German M. E. Church

The Milan area was also the site of a German M. E. church on the Lawrenceville Circuit. Little information can be found about it today. The congregation formed in 1845 at a place called Brunt's Corner which was about three miles north of Old Milan. Shortly after this, the English-speaking Methodists decided to build a church at Old Milan and the German group joined them in this effort in 1851.[18]

According to the records of the Central German Conference, the Milan church was on a circuit with another German church (unnamed) from 1864 to 1870.[19] It was combined with Aurora until 1881, after which it was no longer mentioned in the records.[20] This seems to conflict with the above information about the Germans and the English-speaking Methodists forming a church together. Perhaps, however, the Germans had separate meetings in this church in their own language.

Lawrenceville Circuit—Aurora

The Aurora church was another whose history has been largely lost to the ravages of time. The church building was located on Fifth Street on lot no. 204 and is shown on the 1875 Atlas map of Aurora. The Baptists originally built the church and then, in 1879 it was used by the Christian Church. At present, there is a private home on the site at 108 Fifth Street.[21] According to Central German Conference records, the Aurora church was on a circuit with Lawrenceburg from 1865 until 1871.[22] It was transferred to Milan in 1871, along with another church at Creslan (I have not been able to locate Creslan on any map or find any other reference to it). In 1882 it was listed on a circuit with Dillsboro until 1886.[23] Then it was switched back to Lawrenceburg from 1887 until 1890 when it was dropped from the records.[24]

Lawrenceville Circuit—Dillsboro German Methodist

Dillsboro was home to another small German church. A county history published in 1885 related that the German Methodists held services "some thirty odd years ago" at the old Methodist church situated at the Cole Cemetery. The German group later bought the house of worship and used its materials to build their church at the town of Farmer's Retreat.[25] There is a map (originally in an 1875 atlas) in *A Tale of Two Townships* that shows the church location in Farmer's Retreat. The church was located between a store/restaurant on the Bosse property and a store and post office on the Opp property.[26] Conference records show Dillsboro paired with Aurora from 1882 until 1886 and then no more mention of it is made.[27]

Lawrenceville Circuit—Chesterville German M. E. Church

The Chesterville German M. E. congregation met in a small, frame building a half mile south of the town. The county history, published in 1885, noted that it had disbanded.[28] The Chesterville German M. E. Church is never mentioned in conference records, so it was most likely one of those anonymous numbers listed as a church on the Lawrenceville Circuit.

The location of the Chesterville church is shown on the Sparta Township map in the *1875 Atlas of Dearborn County, Indiana*. It was at the corner of what is now called Longbranch Road and another road which I was unable to find. Back then it may have been a small dirt road which has disappeared in the last 125 years. There is no sign of a building today that might have been the small church on Longbranch Road.[29]

Lawrenceville Circuit—Brookville German M. E. Church

In Brookville, around 1845, the German Methodists worshipped in private homes. The Price family donated lot no. 27 on Fourth Street to the German M. E. Church trustees as a building site, and in 1849, a church was erected. A school also met in the new church building and, while the courthouse was being built, the church functioned as a court room. In 1865 the group disbanded and, in 1896, they sold the building to the United Brethren church.[30] After 1914, the Church of the Nazarene bought the old church and in 1970 the Franklin County Senior Citizens became its owners.[31] There is no building at the site at present.

Two other small churches were also apparently associated with Brookville. I could find nothing to confirm the existence of one at Peppertown in Franklin County, either in the local history room at Brookville or in what remains of the town. The other, reported to be at Enochsburg, actually seems to have been located at St. Maurice in Decatur County. It may have been used by both English- and German-speaking Methodists and was built about 1842. Anthony Charles donated the land for the brick building. Two preachers mentioned as serving there were Reverand Kiesting or Kiesling (probably Rev. John Kisling) and Reverand Gommel. The church was abandoned in the 1870s and by the 1960s Anthony Moorman had bought the land. All that remains is a small cemetery.[32]

Madison, Indiana, German M.E. now serves a different congregation.

Madison, Indiana, Circuit

In the early 1840s, John Kisling brought German Methodism to Madison, Indiana. Kisling came from a farm near Greensburg and was responsible for starting the German congregations in Lawrenceburg and many of the towns along the Ohio River including Aurora, Madison, Jeffersonville, New Albany, Huntingburg, and Evansville.

Madison Circuit—Madison German M. E. Church

In 1844 Rev. Peter Schmucker helped fourteen congregants organize the Madison church. They first met in a building called the Upper Seminary and soon their number increased to one hundred. In 1847 the group spent two thousand dollars to erect a church on Second Street. Two additions were later added. The thriving church was moved from the Central German Conference to the Indiana Conference in 1899 during the pastorate of Rev. G. H. Fritchie who preached both in English and German to prepare the church for the transition.[33] The name of the church was apparently changed to Grace M. E. about the time it joined the Indiana Conference. Later, membership fell off and the church disbanded with most members joining Trinity Methodist in Madison. For a while, the old G.M.E. building was home to the Barnard Art Memorial and housed a

Zoar UMC in Hanover, Indiana, was formerly German Methodist.

number of sculpture works.[34] Faith Covenant now meets in the building and has once more claimed it as a church.

Madison Circuit—Hanover (Zoar)

There was also a German M. E. church in Hanover, Indiana, on the Madison Circuit. John David Schmidlapp, who saw a need for a worship service in his native tongue, offered his home as a meeting place. Soon the new congregation erected a log building to serve as a church. In 1858 a larger building was needed, therefore, Thomas and Mary Ramsey sold some land in Section 3, Township 3, Range 3 for this purpose. Originally, the church was just the German Methodist Church but at the beginning of the twentieth century became Zoar Methodist Church. Services gradually switched from German to English and the church left the Central German Conference to join the English-speaking conference.

A fire destroyed the building in 1904 but a new church was built on the old foundation in 1905. The old building had featured two brass chandeliers which were saved and converted to electricity when installed in the new church. In 1955 Zoar Church added a kitchen and Sunday school rooms. The congregation purchased an electric organ in 1957 and also refurbished the original communion set and baptismal bowl. Zoar became a two-point charge with West Madison in 1973 and a mobile home became the parsonage.[35] The Zoar UMC is located on Zoar Church Road, Madison, IN 47250.

Switzerland County, Indiana

A German M. E. Church was rumored to have been in Posey Township in Switzerland County. The notation then says, "This does not appear to have been a separate congregation, but was rather the result of conversions from missionary work by Methodists." I'm not sure what that means, but I have found no other mention of the Posey Township church.[36]

Notes

1. *The Centennial of Methodism in Laughery Township (1845–1945)*, pamphlet, Ind.; *The Seventy-Fifth Anniversary of the First Methodist Church Batesville, Indiana 1870–1945* (Batesville, Ind.: Batesville UMC, 1945), 8.
2. *Ripley County History*, vol. 2 (Ripley Co., Ind.: Ripley County Historical Society, 1993), 107–108.
3. Ibid., 105.
4. Church History Summary, Church Record Survey, The Archives of Indiana United Methodism, Depauw University, Greencastle, Ind., 1977.
5. *Ripley County History*, 107.
6. Theodore Rudin, Diaries, 1925, author's collection.
7. C. H. Wesler, "History of German M. E. Church in Lawrenceburg," *Lawrenceburg (Indiana) Press*, August 20, 1953.
8. Lawrenceburg Historical Society, Inc., *History of Lawrenceburg, Indiana* (Lawrenceburg, Ind.: 1953).
9. *History of Dearborn and Ohio Counties, Indiana* (Chicago: F. E. Weakley & Co. Publishers, 1885) 276.
10. Wesler, "History of German M. E. Church."
11. Ibid.
12. Lawrenceburg Historical Society, Inc., *History of Lawrenceburg, Indiana.*
13. Historic Lawrenceburg Foundation plaque outside of Zerbe Law Offices, Lawrenceburg, Indiana.
14. C. Golder, John H. Horst, and J. G. Schaal, *Geschichte der Zentral Deutschen Konferenz* (Cincinnati, Ohio: Jennings & Graham, n.d.) 342.
15. Ripley County History Book Committee, comp., et al., *Ripley County History 1818–1988* (Dallas: Taylor Publishing Co., 1989), 27.
16. Harold L. Freeland, *History of Adams Township* (Sunman, Ind.: 1950), 7.
17. *History of Dearborn and Ohio Counties*, 597.
18. *Ripley County History 1818–1988*, 79.
19. *Minutes of the Annual Conferences* (New York: Carlton & Porter 1864–67, Carlton and Lanahan 1868–70).
20. *Minutes of the Annual Conferences* (New York: Phillips & Hunt, 1881), 227.
21. *Aurora Sesquicentennial* Historical Committee, ed. Aurora Sesquicentennial, Aurora, Indiana, 1959, 46.
22. *Minutes of the Annual Conferences*, 1865–1867 and 1868–1871.
23. Ibid., 1882–1886.
24. Ibid., 1887–1888 and 1889–1890.
25. *History of Dearborn and Ohio Counties*, 513–14.
26. Alan F. Smith, *A Tale of Two Townships* (Vevay, Ind.: Venage Press, 1996), 45.
27. *Minutes of the Annual Conferences*, 1882–1886.
28. *History of Dearborn and Ohio Counties*, 563.
29. *Atlas of Dearborn County, Indiana* (Philadelphia: Lake, Griffing & Stevenson, 1875), 43.
30. August J. Feitel, *History of Franklin County, Indiana* (Indianapolis, Ind.: B.F. Bowen & Company, Inc., 1915), 434–35.
31. Herschel L.. Phillips, "Brookville United Methodist Church, 1883–1983," *177 Years of Methodism, 1806–1983* (Brookville, Ind.: Whitewater Publications, 1983), 7.

32. Decatur County Historical Society, *Decatur County History* (Dallas.: printer Taylor Publishing, 1984), 82.

33. Rev. R. M. Barnes, D.D., and Rev. W. W. Snyder, A.M., "Grace Church," in *Historic Sketches of the M. E. Church in Madison, Ind.* (Madison, Ind.: The Courier Company, Printer and Binders 1906), 80–81.

34. "Grace Church" *The Madison Daily Herald* (Madison, Ind.), Monday, June 21, 1897.

35. *Zoar Methodist Church 1858–1983: 125 Year Celebration*, (anniversary bulletin) Zoar, Hanover, Indiana, 1983.

36. Robert W. Scott, "The Religious Landscape in Southern Indiana in the Nineteenth Century," *MyIndianaHome.net*, myindianahome.net/gen/jeff/records/church/religions (accessed 2003).

CHAPTER 2

Indianapolis and Some Western Indiana Churches

Indianapolis, Indiana

There were four German M. E. churches in Indianapolis: First Church, Second Church, Third Church, and Nippert Memorial Chapel. A fifth church, the German M. E. Church of New Palestine (a town east of Indianapolis) was most often served by the pastor of Second Church. Unlike some of the other big cities, it is very difficult to find a trace of the former German churches in Indianapolis. Some information is available on First Church and Nippert Memorial, but I found nothing on Second and Third churches. I expected the Palestine church to be even more of a challenge, being a country church, but I was surprised to find its present-day counterpart still thriving. The pastor there was very cordial and helpful, giving me a history booklet and a church cookbook.

Indianapolis—First German Methodist Episcopal Church

German Methodist preaching began in Indianapolis in 1846 when nineteen-year-old Louis Nippert came to town and began preaching on the Circle. The first people to show interest were the Stump and Druckses families who became the first members of the German M. E. church in the city. William Nast and Rev. Charles Bauer also preached, but the congregation was mostly led by local leaders and Reverend Sedelmeyer from Brownstown until 1849. Rev. Konrad Muth was the first permanent pastor and, under his pastorship a lot on Ohio Street between New Jersey and East streets was purchased. The German church met in a schoolhouse on New Jersey Street and in the courthouse, before the dedication of their new building in 1851.

By the late 1860s the congregation saw the need for a larger church home. They sold the old building for six thousand dollars and it became a German school. A new building was erected on the corner of East New York and New

Jersey streets. When the lower floor of the church was ready in 1869, the congregation moved in. The entire church structure was finished and dedicated in April 1871. During World War I, in response to anti-German sentiment, the name was changed from First German to New Jersey Street Methodist Episcopal Church.[1] At the time of its centennial celebration in 1946, the New Jersey Street building had stood for seventy-seven years and was one of the oldest Methodist churches in the city.[2]

In 1953 trustees decided to merge with Arlington Place Methodist Church and the former German Church was put up for sale with the asking price of one hundred thousand dollars. The two churches renamed their new congregation Immanuel and erected a building and parsonage at Thirty-second and Catherwood streets.[3]

Although the building on New Jersey Street is long gone, the centennial pamphlet describes the architecture as Gothic in style with one tall spire. The red brick walls were overlaid with waterproof concrete. The main entrance on New Jersey Street had a tile floor installed by one of the members. The street level housed Sunday school rooms; while the sanctuary was located on the second floor. The sanctuary was adorned with windows of cathedral glass. In 1946 the entire church was redecorated.[4]

Indianapolis—Second German Methodist Episcopal Church

All of the other German M. E. churches in Indianapolis had their roots in First Church and started as missions from there. The Second German M. E. was founded in 1873 at Prospect and Spruce streets. It later was named the Prospect Street M. E. Church.[5] Prospect Street Church was still a going concern at the time of the disbandment of the Central German Conference and had eighty-three members.

Indianapolis—Third German Methodist Episcopal Church

In 1891 a second mission church was begun at the corner of Church and Morris streets and, until 1896, was served by the pastor of First Church.[6] In that year the church got its own pastor until 1903 when it was again paired with another church. This time Nippert was its partner and, the following year, Second Church. In 1907, it again became associated with First Church until it was eventually absorbed by that church around 1911.

Indianapolis—Nippert Memorial Chapel

A third mission church, the Fourth German M. E. church, was started in 1893 but was soon renamed the Nippert Memorial Methodist Church. Located at East Tenth Street and Keystone Avenue, it was named in honor of Louis Nippert who first brought Methodist preaching to the Germans of Indianapolis. Reverand Nippert preached the dedication sermon for the new church named for him.[7] In the early 1920s the Nippert church again rejoined First Church which had taken the name New Jersey Street M. E. Tenth Street M. E. Church purchased the property and planned to convert the building into a community house.[8]

Wayne Guthrie, columnist for the *Indianapolis News*, described an interesting sidebar to the Nippert church's fate. Eventually, Tenth Street Church tore down the old German church but kept some of its furnishings including a beautiful stained glass window. In the early 1950s a chapel was planned for the campgrounds at Santa Claus, Indiana. Through the offices of Rev. J. Borcherding, his grandson Dr. Frank Greer, Judge Alfred K. Nippert of Cincinnati, and Mrs. Fred Hamp, the window was obtained from East Tenth Street Church and became an integral part of the chapel at the campground.[9] So at least a part of the old church lives on into the present.

In 1900 the annual Central German Conference meeting was held in Indianapolis and grandfather Rudin attended it, as all the pastors were expected to. Following are his remarks about the conference and Indianapolis:

Monday, September 3

Left Sandusky for the seat of the Conference on the 7 AM train. Arrived at Indianapolis safe, sound, dirty and hot at 4:15.

Tried to do some studying in the train but did not much feel like it. At Tipton I partook of a magnificent dinner consisting of coffee, sandwiches and pie. Found the Denzlers, my hosts, without much trouble. Mr. D. is foreman in the panhandle shops. Mrs. D. is quite talkative while her husband is rather quiet. They have four children—two boys and two girls. Denzlers are of Swiss parentage.

Tuesday, September 4

Got up early this morning and did some studying and finished my Aufsatz. Edwin took me to the church. The examining committee was present and also all those who were to show what they still knew of the contents of the books they were expected to have studied during the year. We were given ten questions on each book and I did not find any of them hard. A little after three, I was done with my examination and felt splendid in consequence. Met Beyer, Borneman, Harrer and several others that I knew years ago. Pa [J. C. Weidmann, his father-in-law] came around in the afternoon. When I got to Denzlers I found Mr. Bockstahler there. He's quite humorous. Went to church in the evening.

Wednesday, September 5

Bishop Earl Cranston opened the 37th annual session of the Central German Conference at 9 o'clock this morning. He read the 42 and part of the 43rd chapter of Isaiah very impressively. His opening address was full of Christian spirit. The Central German Conference is much larger than the East German Conference. There seems to be more brotherly feeling toward each other among its members, too.

Thursday, September 6

When E. E. Mueller's name was read off by the Bishop this morning the P. E. announced that charges were preferred against him. A committee of thirteen ministers were hereupon appointed to try the case. Revs. G. E. Hiller and J. C. Weidmann were nominated as attorneys for the church and the accused selected John Meyer and J. J. Pink as his defenders. There is hardly any doubt that he will be found guilty. Father and I had dinner with Mr. Biltimeier. It was so awfully warm that we had to dispense with all convention and eat with our coats off. Pa presided at the evening meeting and he made a good presiding officer. B. F. Beal, W. A. Schruff and A. F. Schumann spoke. A chorus of about 100 voices consisting of young ladies and gentlemen and children, provided singing assisted by the orchestra all under the direction of Bro. Hamp.

Friday, September 7

The hot weather is still with us. It is really almost unbearable. It seems to me the Conference ought to be held at least two weeks later. Four young men were recommended for elder's orders this morning. The Bishop gave them a good talk, the burden of which was that a minister of the Gospel must have moral courage, must stand up for the right at all times and under all circumstances. He emphasized that that man is great and splendid who dares to oppose the people when they are in the wrong. The man must lead the people and not the people, the man. In the afternoon a memorial service was held in remembrance of departed members of the Conference. In the evening I went with the Denzlers to hear Rev. George Mitter preach the Missionary sermon.

Saturday, September 8

Dr. A. B. Leonard spoke at this morning's session. His topic was Missions. He had nothing good to say about the American occupation of the Philippines and Porto Rico. This evening all the candidates for ordination met at the Bishop's stopping place to receive instructions concerning tomorrow's ordeal.

Sunday, September 9

Denzlers went to their own church while I went to the First Church and heard the Bishop. It wasn't a sermon really that the Bishop preached, but a talk on the condition of China and the necessity of missionary work there. In the afternoon I was ordained as a local deacon. It was a solemn moment for me. I can now perform all ministerial duties. Two others were ordained with me, while four were ordained as elders. In the evening, communion was celebrated and Dr. Golder preached.

Monday, September 10

The conference session closed shortly after 12. It was thought at first that we would not be done until this evening but the bishop hurried up the business. I have been reappointed to Sandusky and am glad of it. I feel sorry for those who have to move, at least as far as the moving concerned. I have enough yet from a year ago. Left Indianapolis for Berea on the 2:55 train of the Big Four Road. Arrived at Berea shortly before 10. It was a quick run.

Friday, October 5

Received word from Pa this morning that E. E. Mueller has been arrested for forgery. He took up $600 in a bank in Marine City and forged the names of five men. This is awful! But one sin begets another. It is sad indeed that a minister of the Gospel should fall so deep.[10]

New Palestine, Indiana

Tradition has it that the peripatetic Rev. Johannnes Kisling first preached in the German language here, perhaps as early as 1827. However, he officially became missionary to the Germans when he joined the Southwestern Indiana Conference in 1838. Others, including Rev. Ludwig (Louis) Nippert and John Barth also preached in New Palestine. In 1851 the German Methodist Episcopal Church officially organized with fourteen members. A church was built the next year near the old school ground.

Many new members joined the flock during a revival in 1878. In this same year, the church underwent a renovation from foundation to bell tower. The

New PalestineUnited Methodist Church.
The descendent of the local German Methodist Church.

Rev. John Zarwell, of Second Church in Indianapolis, delivered the sermon for the forty-fifth anniversary of the church held in 1896. At noon a bounteous dinner was enjoyed in Schreiber's Hall. Visiting and reminiscing comprised the afternoon activities followed by the Epworth League of Second Church giving the evening service of addresses, declamations, and songs.

According to conference records, New Palestine was on a circuit with Second Church from 1891 to 1904.[11] By 1904, the English language had all but replaced the German in everyday conversation and descendants of the German settlers preferred to worship in English. Thus the German church united with the English-speaking Methodists and Max Herrlich bought the old German property.

In the 1960s it became necessary to either remodel the church on Mill Street (where the German congregation united with the English one) or build a new building. The congregation decided to go with the latter and purchased ten acres on Gem Road where ground was broken for the new church on June 12, 1966. The cornerstone was laid a year later in 1967 with consecration services following on September 24, 1967. Total cost of the building, furnishings, and landscaping came to $261,000. By 1978, a fellowship hall, kitchen, and classrooms were added. The church held a 150th anniversary celebration in 1980 paying homage to both its English- and German-speaking founders.[12] To check out current activities at the New Palestine UMC go to their Web site at www.npumc.com.

Lafayette, Indiana

The Brown Street United Methodist Church began in 1851 when the conference sent Rev. Christoph Keller to start a mission to the German-speaking peoples of Lafayette. Fourteen of the twenty-seven probationers became full members in the spring of 1852. Not long after, Rev. John Barth served as regular pastor with the salary of two hundred dollars per year. At this time, the fledgling church met in the basement of the Fifth Street Methodist Episcopal Church.

In 1858 the congregation purchased land for a church and parsonage at the corner of Brown and Ninth streets.[13] A one-story, frame building which was heated with stoves and had gas lights was erected. The basement served as a cellar to hold fuel and for a storage area for the pastor.[14] The cost for church building and parsonage totaled four thousand dollars.[15]

By 1885 the congregation had outgrown their building and work was started on a new church which was dedicated on October 15, 1885. The next year the annual conference of the Central German Conference took place in the Lafayette church and Dr. William Nast preached his Jubilee Fiftieth Anniversary sermon.

In 1874 the Women's Foreign Missionary Society began as one of the first of the women's groups serving the church. Their projects included supporting the education of a Korean girl, packing boxes of supplies to send to missionary families and canning fruits and jellies for the Home Hospital. The women formed the Ladies Aid Society in 1887 which took care of needs closer to home. They held suppers, bazaars, or other fundraisers to help pay for renovations to the parsonage such as painting, decorating, or new rugs. The Coffee Circle was for socializing, as well as work, and met in the homes of members. In the 1920s, the pastor's wife, Mrs. Dangle, started the Quilters' Group. The members met in various homes, and their projects included mending socks for orphans, tying comforters, and quilting, which became their main focus of interest. In 1940 the Ladies Aid and the Missionary Society combined to form the Women's Society of Christian Service and proceeded to carry on their various good works.

Sunday school was a very important church function and a number of classes flourished. Some of the original classes were the Philathea Class, the Loyal Leaguers, the DULKs, the Progressives, the Standbys, and Fidelity. Later on the Golden Band Class, a group of young married people was quite active.[16]

Music was always important to the German people and played a big part in their worship services. In early days the church had a Reed organ until 1905 when a Hinners organ was installed. On January 1, 1906, at the dedication service, Mr. Hinners gave a recital on the new organ. Choir was another important musical feature and met to practice on Thursday evenings after prayer service.[17]

Brown Street Epworth League, organized in 1889, was the second chapter in the Central German Conference to form. In 1901 the group hosted the Epworth League Convention of the Cincinnati District. In the 1940s Epworth League became known as United Methodist Youth Fellowship.[18] Two anticipated yearly events were the Fourth of July picnic and the Christmas program. The picnic was held at Battle Ground north of Lafayette and the celebrants were transported there in open street cars. The children in the convoy loved to chant:

Who are we? Who are we?
We are the members
of the German M. E.

Not only were delicious picnic goodies enjoyed, but a program for young and old was planned with contests, concessions, worship, and patriotic services. The Christmas program was held on Christmas night rather than Christmas Eve. It was the culmination of an eventful family day that, appropriately, ended with a church service. Christmas music and recitations by the children composed the service itself, all given in the presence of a towering Christmas tree.[19]

As with many German Methodist churches, the Lafayette church underwent a name change during World War I and became Brown Street Methodist Episcopal Church. Shortly after, in 1919, English took over as the primary language in the church. In the 1960s, more change came to Brown Street when it became parent to a new church northeast of Lafayette. Thirty-one attended the first service which was held in a tent. By December 1968, the new building for Heritage UMC was ready for occupancy. At present, both the mother church and her offspring are fully functional churches with an abundance of activities for all.[20]

To learn more, visit Brown Street's website at www.brownstreetumc.org or Heritages's at www.gbgm.org/heritage-lafayette/.

Terre Haute, Indiana

Bishop James (of the Ohio Conference) sent Rev. Konrad Muth to the Terre Haute area in the 1850s. Soon after, eight preparatory members affiliated and the church organized in February 1851. The first church building was actually built for the Presbyterians, but was purchased by the newly formed German M. E. congregation in 1851. A parsonage was built in 1856. At this time, Terre Haute was on a circuit with the Indiana missions in Poland and Greencastle. By 1879, the congregation had outgrown the church on Mulberry (between Fourth and Fifth streets) and a lot was purchased at the corner of Fifth and Mulberry. The completed church was dedicated in April 1883 while a new parsonage had been built a year earlier. The church adopted the name of Calvary Methodist in the early 1900s.[21]

The founder, Rev. Konrad Muth, wrote a brief history of the early church and commented,

> Besides my field of activity in Terre Haute, I also preached on six more fields and at the end of an activity of two years we had 86 members in our district. Still today, I thank the Lord for his mercy, for the 86 members were thoroughly converted to God and remained faithful to the church. God also liked to appoint two preachers and five preacher women into His vineyard. So much for preacher Muth.[22]

Later, in the early 1950s, extensive renovations were made under the guidance of Rev. Theodore Grob. He was bothered by the fact that many of the older parishioners couldn't attend church because of the formidable flight of steps they had to climb to get to the second story sanctuary. Eventually, his dream of a more accessible church was realized. The renovations included a beautiful chapel at street level with two splendid walnut pulpits, French gray walls with white ceiling, woodwork and columns. The comfortable old pews from the old chapel were installed along with a marble font which had been imported from Italy 110 years previously. A fine rose tapestry hung behind the pulpits and brass candlesticks and a cross adorned the altar, these having been donated by members of the Grob family.[23] Alas, the venerable old church did not make it into the twenty-first century. When I visited the site, it was not to be seen, probably torn down for an expansion of the nearby Indiana State University.

According to conference records, Terre Haute and Greencastle were paired on a circuit from 1864 to 1867.[24] Then Terre Haute and Poland were together in 1868 and 1869. In 1869 and 1870 four churches are enumerated (but not named) as being on the circuit. Greencastle was back on the circuit in 1870 and 1871.[25] Terre Haute is listed by itself until 1876. From 1876 through 1881 two churches were listed as being on the Terre Haute circuit, but the second is unnamed. After that, Terre Haute is again alone.[26] Unfortunately, I haven't been able to find out anything about the Greencastle and Poland churches.

Notes

1. "New Jersey Street M. E. Church Had Inception in Days of Mexican War," *Indianapolis News*, February 14, 1931.
2. "Century to be Marked by German Methodists," *Indianapolis Star*, October 6, 1946.
3. "Church Sale Sought for $100,000," *Indianapolis News*, September 26, 1953.
4. *One Hundred Years . . . A Century of Christian Service*, centennial pamphlet for First German Church (Indianapolis: October 6, 1946).
5. *One Hundred Years*
6. Golder, Horst & Schaal, *Geschichte*, 336.
7. Ibid., 336.
8. "Site of Community House and Gymnasium," *Indianapolis* (Indiana) *News*, September 22, 1922.
9. Wayne Guthrie, "New Chapel Will Have Old Window," *Indianapolis News*, 1955.
10. Rudin, Diaries, 1900.
11. *Minutes of the Annual Conferences*, 1891–1895 and 1896–1904.
12. *150th Anniversary, 1830–1980, New Palestine United Methodist Church*, anniversary booklet (New Palestine, Ind.: 1980).
13. Ruth Sinks, *History of Brown Street Methodist Church,* centennial program (Lafayette, Ind.: Brown Street Methodist Church, 1951).
14. "Brown Street Methodist Church Centennial Celebration Historical Reading," read at bicentennial celebration (Lafayette, Ind.: November 27, 1951).
15. Sinks, *History of Brown Street Methodist Church*.
16. "Historical Reading."
17. Sinks, *History of Brown Street Methodist Church*.
18. "Historical Reading."
19. Sinks, *History of Brown Street Methodist Church*.
20. "The History of Brown Street United Methodist Church," http://gbgm-churches.gbgm-umc.org/brownstreetin/history.htm)
21. "Some Types of Early Buildings in Terre Haute—XXIV," article, Community Affairs file, Vigo County Public Library, Terre Haute, Indiana.
22. Konrad Muth, *German Methodist Episcopal Church*, trans. Mario G. Pelli for The Archives of Indiana Methodism, Depauw University, Greencastle, Indiana, 1962.
23. "New Chapel Represents Realization of Theodore Grob's 30-Year Dream," (article, Community Affairs File, Vigo County Public Library, Terre Haute, Indiana, 1953)
24. *Minutes of the Annual Conferences*, 1864–1867.
25. Ibid., 1868–1871.
26. Ibid., 1876–1878 and 1879–1890.

CHAPTER 3

Cincinnati Area Churches in the Cincinnati District

Cincinnati, Ohio

There were several German M. E. churches in the Cincinnati area, including the "Mother Church" of German Methodism founded by Wilhelm Nast, the "Father of German Methodism." Second Church, Third Church, and Spring Grove no longer exist, but First Church (as Nast-Trinity) and Walnut Hills (as Hyde Park Bethlehem) are with us still; and Mt. Auburn, as Mt. Auburn United Methodist Church, just recently closed down. Also, I've included Mt. Healthy German M. E. in this section. There was a wealth of information on some of the churches such as Third Church, Walnut Hills and First Church. On the other hand, there was very little on Second Church except in handwritten German.

Cincinnati—First German M. E. Church

Cincinnati's First German is the very first German Methodist church in the world. William Nast, a professor at Kenyon College, was appointed in 1835 to minister to the German immigrants in Cincinnati. After overcoming many obstacles, including finding an appropriate meeting place and facing opposition from unchurched Germans (who loved their beer whereas the Methodists espoused temperance), he formed a congregation in 1838. For a while they met in a little chapel on Vine Street between Fourth and Fifth streets, which was known as Burke's Chapel. They put effort into collecting funds door to door and, finally, in 1841, erected a church building. This building was two stories with the lower floor for Sunday school and two rooms in back to provide a home for the caretaker. The present building was completed in 1881.

The First German Church was renamed Nast Memorial in 1938 at its one hundredth anniversary. Later in 1958, Trinity Church united with Nast and the name became Nast-Trinity Church.

The church has had a long record of community service from those first days when William Nast and others preached to the German population. The German Methodist Episcopal Home Mission Society of Cincinnati was founded in 1871 at the church. The Emanuel Community Center, adjacent to the church, was dedicated in 1924 to serve the peoples of the "Over the Rhine" district. Emanuel Center, through the church, provided day care, housing for young men and women, clubs for all, social services, and athletic activities.[1]

Even in the twenty-first century, Nast-Trinity continues to serve the neighborhood, although it has changed from German to Appalachian to African American and Hispanic. Sundays begin with a breakfast of, for example, coffee, orange juice, and scrambled eggs followed by devotions, worship, and fellowship. Traditional Methodist songs are sung as well as spirituals and more contemporary music.[2] Nast-Trinity has a website that relates its history as well as giving present services and activities. Go to www.nasttrinity.org.

Cincinnati—Second Church

Rev. John Barth was the force behind the founding of Second Church. With members of First Church, he met in Friedrick Krieg's house on Everett Street to lay the groundwork for the new German church. Soon, the church that was founded on November 1, 1846, could claim thirteen members who were eager to build a church building. This structure took form on Everett Street between Cutter and Linn streets. The lot cost $1,850 and the building, $600. Not five years went by before the congregation had outgrown the building and, on May 19, 1851, plans for a new church were established at the cost of $4,000.[3] A renovation took place in 1882, further modernizing the place of worship.[4]

The *Geschichte* states that many Germans living in the western part of the city (in an area known as "Texas") belonged to First Church but desired a church closer to home. William Hartmann and his wife, along with others, hosted prayer meetings and services in their homes until Jacob Rothweiler came to establish a congregation in 1846. John Barth replaced him after only a few weeks. Barth oversaw the building of the first church which was twenty-eight-by-fifty feet in size and made of wood. It was replaced in 1851 by a two-story brick building measuring seventy-by-forty feet.

A melodeon, acquired in 1869, provided music until a pipe organ was purchased in 1901. A literature society was founded during J. B. Schaal's tenure and a Ladies Aid organized when F. L. Nagler was pastor. Other organizations were the Youth Society and Mission Union.[5]

Not much is recorded about Second church after the *Geschichte* entry in 1907. Grandfather Rudin served as pastor from 1920 to 1925. At the beginning of his tenure he noted that there were 136 full members and 15 probationers. He commented, "This does not look very encouraging."[6] Nevertheless, he organized a committee to plan a Diamond Jubilee for the church which took place on November 27, 1921. A number of former pastors spoke at this event

Nast-Trinity United Methodist Church, the "mother" of all German Methodist Episcopal churches in the United States of America.

including Dr. George Guth, Reverends Kaletsch, Rogatzky, Beuscher, Wahl, and Dr. Albert Nast who spoke on the history of German Methodism.[7]

When my grandfather was moved to Louisville in 1925, Rev. P. C. Phillipp replaced him at Second Church. In 1929 Rev. Phillipp is listed as pastor of both Second Church and Spring Grove. In 1930 Second Church is no longer listed as an active church.[8] Grandpa reported in his 1930 diary that an African-American congregation was then using the Second Church building.[9]

Cincinnati—Mt. Auburn German Methodist Episcopal Church

The Mt. Auburn congregation started meeting in 1854 as a mission Sunday school. They met in the afternoon at the English-speaking Mt. Auburn Methodist Church. The majority of this group were members of Third Church but lived "on the hill" (meaning Mt. Auburn as one of Cincinnati's "seven hills"). The Tatgenhorst family hosted prayer meetings in their home which later became the Mt. Auburn German Church's parsonage. This original group was short-lived, but as the Mt. Auburn community grew, a German church became a more feasible idea.

Auburn Avenue United Methodist Church, until recently an active church, was founded as Mt. Auburn German Methodist.

In 1885 the revived group rented a store at 2622 Vine Street which became their chapel. Five years later, thirty-nine members of Third Church transferred to the newly reborn Mt. Auburn German Methodist Church under the pastorship of Rev. John Oetjen. Soon the group bought a lot at Euclid and Corry streets, but before a building effort was started they were able to purchase the English-speaking Methodist church at McMillan Street and Auburn Avenue. The German group paid $14,500 for the church but the English church offered a donation of $2,000. The lot that had been purchased earlier was sold and the Germans were able to put up $6,000 in cash with the remainder being in notes.

This transaction spurred significant membership growth and there were soon 210 members with a Sunday school of approximately 150. A Ladies Aid, an Epworth League, a Junior League, and a "Helping Hand" Missionary Society organized not long after.[10] The church continued services in German for more than a quarter of a century, but gradually shifted to the English language.

Meanwhile, the English Methodist Church, which had moved to its new building on Maplewood Avenue, also continued to flourish. They celebrated their centennial in 1952 by building a new parsonage and remodeling the sanctuary. Shortly after that, in 1957, the sanctuary was destroyed by fire. The homeless congregation was welcomed back to its original home in the former

German church and the two ultimately merged.[11]

Sadly, the former German church didn't make it very far into the twenty-first century. In December 2004, it was put on the auction block due to declining membership. Auctioneer Brent Semple said (in referring to the Mt. Auburn church and another), "Because of how beautiful they are, I just hope they would be kept as churches by whoever buys them."[12]

Cincinnati—Spring Grove German Methodist Episcopal Church

In 1856 a number of German families lived in the Brighton District near the stockyards. R. A. W. Bruehl felt the rough life of gambling, drinking, and fighting in that area was a bad influence on children and sought to remedy this. He organized a Sunday school in a two-room building on Brighton Street. The class, supported by the Ladies Home Mission Society, outgrew this space in 1859 and moved to Benkenstein Hall.

In the meantime, Blanchard Chapel was built in 1863 with a donation from Mr. Blanchard and a five-hundred-dollar donation from Mr. Benkenstein. One-third of the Blanchard donation of one thousand dollars, was to go to the German work.

In the same year, the Sunday school began to suffer when Mr. Breuhl was frequently out of town due to his employment. The class work eventually ceased that year, at which time there were 230 members.[13]

In 1864, Rev. H. G. Lich organized a German mission in Raper Chapel at Elm and Findlay streets. In 1866, he took on Blanchard Chapel, as well. At this time the Ladies Home Mission Society footed the bill for his salary. A problem arose, however, when he was only able to use Raper Chapel for Sunday evening services. Attendance fell off and this mission, too, was given up.

In 1871 the problem was solved by transferring the Raper Chapel attendees to First German Church, which was nearby. Blanchard Chapel then became a separate German Methodist mission with Rev. Christian Golder as its first pastor. The church then prospered and ended the year with a Sunday school of 100 children and a congregation of 40. Sunday evening services were the most popular with 125 to 150 attendees. Many of the people in the congregation, however, didn't stay for long. Hoping to better themselves with new jobs and better homes, they moved on and the church never achieved a large congregation.

The pastor found that he often had a chore in addition to preaching and ministering to his flock. Often herds of cattle were driven past the church on the way to the nearby stockyards. On cold winter days some animals would bolt and head for the shelter of the church building. The pastor then had to play "cowboy" to keep them from invading the sanctuary, sometimes calling on the police for extra help.[14]

By 1896 Blanchard Chapel was known as the Fourth German Methodist Episcopal Church. Though growth was slow, in 1917 during the pastorate of Rev. Herman Rogatzky, the church was remodeled. Two memorial windows were installed: Christ the Good Shepherd and Christ Knocking at the Door.

More change was wrought in 1921 when the English language was introduced in song books and the minutes were taken in English.

In 1931 York Street Church (English speaking) joined a circuit with Spring Grove, both being served by the same pastor. A new challenge faced the former German church in 1937 when flood waters from Mill Creek invaded the church. When York Street Church closed in 1944, their altar table and baptismal fount found a new home at Spring Grove. Chimes were installed in 1947 and in 1951 the sanctuary was painted, a new rug purchased, and spotlights installed for the picture, *The Head of Christ*.

In 1956 the church received word that it was to fall victim to the I-75 Expressway and would be torn down. The final service was held on June 7, 1959. At that time, there were 159 active members with a Sunday school of 50. Members transferred to the following churches: Fairmount, State Avenue, Lindenwald, Wesley Chapel, Nast-Trinity, and Northside. The money gained from the sale of the church was to be used for a new church in Finneytown and equipment from the old church to be stored until needed.[15]

Cincinnati—Third German Methodist Episcopal Church

Third German Church had its roots in First Church (Nast Trinity) and was founded by its pastor, Rev. J. H. Bahrenberg, in 1849. He first organized a Sunday school on Buckeye Street (now named Clifton Avenue) in that year. In 1850, Third Church became a reality with almost all its members coming from First Church. It became a separate charge that same year with Rev. A. Ahrens as the first pastor. Hoping to attract more members, an English Sunday school was started, but failed for lack of interest. By 1855 the church had a nice little library with 362 German books and 567 English books.[16]

The church remained a "mission" meaning that part of the pastor's salary was paid by the conference. In 1857, under the pastorship of Rev. Conrad Gahn, Third Church became a station. In 1861, a parsonage at the corner of Milton and Young streets was completed for $1,891.24.[17]

Third Church produced two offspring. In 1891, the Auburn Avenue German M. E. Church was organized, with sixty of Third Church's members helping to start it. Later, in 1908, the City Mission, Day Nursery, and Clinic had its birth in the Third Church building. This mission later moved to First Church and became the Emmanuel Community Center.[18]

In 1894 a new church building was erected not far away at McMicken and Lang streets. The church, whose architect was Samuel A. Hanaford, was dedicated on May 13, 1894, on Pentecost Sunday. The cost, including the building site, was more than $32,000. A debt of $10,000 remained but that was all but wiped out when almost $7,000 was pledged on the day of dedication.[19] Elsewhere in the microfilm records it states that the total cost was $34,000 of which $13,000 remained to be paid.[20]

Some activities the church sponsored through the years included the Immanuel Young People's Society, which was the first group founded for young people in a German church. Camp meetings were held at Epworth Heights in Clermont County until the German part of the campgrounds, including the chapel and auditorium, burned down.[21] The Tajenhorst sisters hosted a "prayer and edification hour" starting in November 1889. In that year, a school in needlework for "small girls" was also organized. The class met from 9:00 a.m. until 11:30 a.m. on Saturdays and was free. The girls learned how to gain their salvation while being instructed in needlework.[22]

In 1912 the old Buckeye Street church, which had been vacated when the new building at Lang and McMicken was occupied, was given a farewell. For several years it had been used by the German Mission Society. The Cincinnati Board of Education needed the site to build a school and offered $10,950 for the plot. The price was accepted and the old church was eventually torn down. Rothenberg School now sits on the site.[23]

In later years, two fires devastated Third Church (whose name had been changed to Asbury Third). In January 1957, twelve fire companies battled a blaze that caused fifty thousand dollars worth of damage. It was later discovered that four boys were responsible for the blaze.[24] In February 1971, another blaze hit the basement of the church, then owned by the Wesley United Methodist Church on Fifth Street. Arson was suspected, as shortly before the fire started, a church member found a door open in the building. There were plans to raze the old Third Church building anyway, so a new building could be built on the site for the Wesley United Methodist Church.[25]

My grandfather Theodore Rudin described the annual conference of the Central German Conference held at Third Church in September 1903. He was coming from his first pastorate in Sandusky, Ohio, and was not yet fully ordained—thus the examination he referred to. Pastors were housed in the private homes of congregation members of Third Church. Grandfather stayed at the Wehmann home along with another pastor.

Tuesday September 8

Till and John accompanied me to the station yesterday. Met Bros. Pullmann and Rogatzky on the train between Springfield and Cincinnati. Gave Mr. Pullman my report. The Big Four Railroad is about the dirtiest road I have ever traveled. The ridewas anything but pleasant. Arrived in Cincinnati at about 8 last night. The Misses Ida and Emma Wehmann were waiting for me. Received a cordial reception and a good supper. Got up early this morning and studied some. Miss Ida took me to the church. Believe I got through my examination all right.

Wednesday September 9

Went downtown with Ida and Emma . . . to witness the Fall Festival pageant. It was fine but not as fine as I expected. The floats were beautiful enough, but the escorts were cheap. The long wait made us tired and we were glad to get out of the big crowds and home. The conference opened this morning with Bishop J. M. Walden. . . . Was surprised by Fred Mueller nominating me one of the assistant statistical secretaries. I'm in for work again now and this puts sight seeing out of the question. Have also been put on the memorial committee.

Thursday September 10

Was glad to see Mr. Seher yesterday. He left Sandusky Monday night and arrived at Cincinnati on Tuesday morning. Last night's meeting was held in the interest of German Wallace College.[later, Baldwin-Wallace College in Berea, Ohio]. Magdanz, Lamy and I were advanced to the fourth year this morning, having successfully passed our examinations. My average was 93, but it would have been larger had not Baur only given me 70 in Sacred History. Magdanz was treated no better. Schruff said my sermon was very good and gave me 90. Lamy got 83 and Magdanz 80. The lay conference organized this afternoon.

Friday September 11

The meeting last night was held in the interest of the Conference claimants. This evening was devoted to the orphans and deaconesses. About a dozen deaconesses were consecrated.

Saturday September 12

Somehow I cannot take our deaconesses serious, as I would the Catholic sisters. Our deaconesses do not really make much of a sacrifice. If they can make a good match, most of them get married. With the Catholic sisters it is different: they really break with the world and give up every earthly thing. I don't blame our deaconesses if they get married, but then there ought to be less said about their sacrifices. On the whole they seem to have a very good time of it. There were two conference sessions today. It was thought that the business would be finished tonight but it was not. The lay conference was received by the Conference this morning. Speeches were made.

Sunday September 13

In connection with some remarks that the bishop made yesterday, he said that he found the Swiss to be the most honest, polite people he ever met. [Grandpa was born in Basel, Switzerland] To the class which was taken into full connection, he said: You must preach a positive Gospel with no ring of uncertainty in it. We are sinners lost, but we must be saved and can be saved now. That now ought to influence our preaching. We must preach conversion as sanctification begun. This afternoon the deacons and elders were ordained and afterwards a memorial service held. I read the memoir of Bro. Klockseim.

Monday September 14

Max Dieterle preached the missionary sermon last night. It was really a good sermon but the delivery was slow and tiresome. Bro. D. ought to have a little more fire. Attended Race St. Sunday School yesterday. Was unexpectedly called on to make a speech which I did in a way. The Conference adjourned this morning. The next one is to be held at Louisville. I have been reappointed to Sandusky. Took the 2:00 PM train for home. Met Bro. Pullmann at the station. He told me that I would get $50 increase in salary from both mission treasuries. That's good!

Wednesday September 16

Cincinnati is quite a city and I rather like it. The neighborhood of the church, however, is anything but attractive. To get to the church from our stopping place, we had to climb down steep hills. It was hot and tiresome work down or up. Race Street church has a much nicer location. The pavements and sidewalks of some of the streets are in a disgraceful condition. On the whole, however, I would prefer to live in Cincinnati rather than Pittsburg. Did not see near as much of the town as I would have liked, being tied down by my work as assistant statistical secretary. I never had an idea that the statistical secretary and his helpers had so much work. Wehmanns are nice people and did all they could to make Giesen's and my stay pleasant. They live in a nice house on a nice street. Giesen proved himself quite a nice sort, but I think he gives his wife more work than I do mine. He does not seem to think of keeping things orderly.[26]

Cincinnati—Walnut Hills German Methodist Episcopal Church

Walnut Hills German M. E. Church moved around quite a bit and later underwent a name change to Bethlehem Methodist Church. In the 1880s many German families moved into the Walnut Hills area of Cincinnati and the need was seen for the establishment of a German M. E. church there. Rev. John C. Marting, City Missionary, helped organize the Walnut Hills church in 1886. The church first held meetings in Hewitt Chapel on Dexter Avenue. When that location was no longer available, the Hartmann family opened their home for Sunday and Friday night services. Trustees and stewards, elected in December 1886, soon located a building lot on the southwest corner of Hackberry and Fairfax avenues. The lot cost seven thousand dollars, but two forty-foot lots were parceled off from this and sold for thirty-six hundred dollars. On March 17, 1887, the building of a church facility commenced on the remaining seventy-foot lot. The cornerstone was laid on March 27 and on July 17, 1887, the church was dedicated in 95-degree weather. The total cost of building and lot was eight thousand dollars.[27] A parsonage was built on Hackberry Street, behind the church in 1888. Some renovations were performed in 1902 which included raising up the church and constructing a spacious ground floor, adding a Sunday School room, altering the sanctuary, and adding a colored window and pipe organ.[28]

During World War I, evening services were conducted in English rather than German. In 1923 German language services were dropped entirely and the church became Bethlehem Methodist Episcopal Church. Membership was 210.

Hyde Park Bethlehem—the Bethlehem part was formerly Walnut Hills German Methodist Episcopal.

An addition to the church had been added earlier, but in the 1920s it was necessary to have a new building. The congregation laid a cornerstone for the new building on Woodburn Avenue near Fairfax and the new $250,000 church was dedicated on May 30, 1925.

Bethlehem Church grew again on March 9, 1930, when the Madison Avenue Methodist Church merged with it. This church had organized in 1889 and their church building erected in 1891. In 1933 Bethlehem became a member of the Cincinnati District of the Ohio Conference when the Central German Conference dissolved.

Many activities grew out of the merged church. An orchestra formed which played to accompany the Sunday school singing and also gave special performances. Epworth League was active throughout the 1930s giving plays and attending District Institutes. The Jones Brotherhood (which originated in the old Madison Avenue Church) sponsored turkey dinners at Thanksgiving to finance a project called the Oral Week Day School of Religious Education. The Sunday school continued to grow requiring the remodeling of rooms on the lower level. Boy Scout and Girl Scout troops also met at the church as well as a girls' champion basketball team.

After World War II, the neighborhood went through some changes. People moved to the suburbs, older members died and membership decreased. It became necessary to merge with another church to keep Bethlehem going. On September 17, 1967, the Bethlehem congregation held its last service in the Woodburn Avenue building and on September 24 joined with the North Hyde Park Church at Madison Road and Hyde Park Avenue. The newly merged church became Hyde Park Bethlehem.

The church building for Hyde Park Bethlehem had been at the Madison Road location for more than fifty years. It was dedicated as the Hyde Park Methodist Protestant Church on November 8, 1908. In 1937, the Methodist Protestant denomination merged with the Methodist Episcopal church and became known simply as Methodist.[29]

The Madison Road church had been known for its beauty since its construction in 1908. It was made of stone with a bell tower and even then had some beautiful stained glass windows. At that time Madison Road was a dirt track with a street car line running from Cincinnati to the other end of Oakley, which was the end of the line. It is told that the motorman of a "Trolley Car Birthday Party" stopped the car to show the children the stained glass window of "The Good Shepherd" saying "Look, children, at the beautiful picture of Jesus. See how lovingly He cares for His sheep. That's the way He loves you."[30]

The Walnut Hills German church had a number of cherished stained glass windows which were eventually moved to the Madison Road church. These included a window of Jesus Blessing the Children which was at the front of the old church and given by the Baum family. Another window, a gift by the Hartman family, shows Jesus saving Peter when he tried to walk on the water. A Nativity window was sponsored by the Widmer family. A window in memory of Rev. Louis Nippert, an important German M. E. pastor, is that of the Good Shepherd.

A Crucifixion window, located in the chapel, was presented by the Emmich family. Another window from the German church was that of the Risen Christ shown with Mary Magdalene in the Garden.[31]

Cincinnati—Mt. Healthy (Mt. Pleasant) German M. E. Church

Mt. Healthy (or Mt. Pleasant, as it was known then) became the site of a German M. E. church in the early 1850s. In 1849 some German families from Cincinnati moved to the community and began meeting in each others' homes. Soon William Borcherding, a lay preacher from Everett Street (Second German

Mt. Healthy UMC founded as a German Methodist church.

M. E.) began preaching there. By 1852 the Mt. Pleasant Mission was included in the annual conference appointments.

There is some disagreement about when the first church building was dedicated. It was apparently built in 1850 and probably dedicated in 1852. The first building was about thirty-three-by-twenty-seven feet and erected on a lot purchased for two hundred dollars. After the Central German Conference came into being, the church was put on a circuit with Hamilton in 1867. In 1870 it was paired with the Spring Grove or Blanchard church. In 1875, it was put back with Hamilton but by 1887, it had grown enough to be made a station.

In 1891, the original building was sold for $50 and moved to the corner of Compton Road and Elizabeth Street where it was used as a home. A new building designed by Otto Steinbrecher was built in 1891 and dedicated on November 15, 1891. The cost of the new structure was $3,700. A church bell weighing twelve hundred pounds and costing $375 was one of its features. There were sixty-one members at that time. In 1907, a site for a parsonage was purchased for $500. The construction of the parsonage was completed in March 1909 at a total cost (including the lot) of $3,000. About this time, the Mt. Healthy church was no longer listed in the Central German Conference, no doubt having switched conferences due to the decline of the use of the German language.[32]

In 1949 the church was again feeling growing pains and began the process of building another church structure which was completed in 1955. An educational wing was added in 1962, after a purchase of additional land on Compton Road. In 1968 when the Evangelical United Brethren church merged with the Methodist, making the new denomination United Methodist, there were two Mt. Healthy United Methodist churches across the street from each other. They both concluded that a name change was in order. The former E.U.B. became Heritage United Methodist while the former German M. E. church became Epworth United Methodist.[33]

In 2001 the two Mt. Healthy United Methodist churches became one. Rev. Jocelyn Roper was appointed by the bishop to both churches with the task to promote a merger.[34]

Grandpa Rudin visited Mt. Healthy twice in the spring of 1904, the first time for a district meeting and later on one of his collection trips.

Wednesday, April 20

Bornemann and I are housed and taken care of by Kruses, who are a young couple with three children. The language problem was discussed today. Bro. Horst is in favor of preaching English but most of the others are against it. Took part in the discussion of this all important question. Burke preaching this evening. Otto Giesen read the scripture lesson and I opened the service with the reading of the hymn and prayer.

Thursday, April 21

Bro. Kaletsch and Bro. Roser debated the question this afternoon: Resolved, that the time limit be reestablished. Bro. K. had the affirmative and Bro. R., the negative. The question was put to a vote resulting in 14 for and 7 against the going back to the time limit. Bro. Roser is quite a humorist and story teller. Bro. Schimmelpfennig read a timely paper on "Is our church in danger of nationalistic tendencies?" Bro. S. showed plainly that it is and Bro. H. seconded him.

Friday, April 22

The district meeting closed last night. I enjoyed it but I think ours will be a better one. The Mt. Healthy people have a nice little church but they do not seem to be very prompt. None of the evening meetings could be begun on time. Left our hosts this morning. They made our stay as pleasant as possible. Visited the Apologete and Haus and Herd offices this afternoon. Met Dr. Golder and Bro. Cramer. Went through the printing, binding, etc. rooms and saw pretty much the whole of our Book Concern.

Grandpa arrived, again, at the Kruse's on May 10 after a stopover in Dayton. He came by way of the interurban line which took about three hours.

Wednesday, May 11

Did a lot of traveling today, beginning early this morning and winding up shortly before the meeting tonight. Bro. S. and I went up hill and down, climbed over fences and walked through nearly dried up creeks in quest of contributions for the collection. Had pretty good success. We dined at Muellers and supped at H. Bax's. Preached to about thirty this evening and collected $13.75. Spoke with great freedom and had good attention. Went home with Bro. Schantzenbacher. He lives quite a distance from the church and farms in a small way. The members are very much scattered and it is a job to visit them. Enjoyed my long walk as it was through beautiful country.

Thursday, May 12

Had dinner with S———s, they having specially invited me. Mr. S. was once a drunkard, but was saved by the grace of God. S———s are great talkers and apt to make one tired. Bro. Schantzenbacher told they are quite conceited and therefore cause more or less trouble. Despite this, I had a fairly good time. Did some more hustling this afternoon. Had supper with Herbolts, who lived on a farm. My collection at Mt. Healthy amounts to $34.25 which is better than last year. Bro. S. has been very obliging to run around with me as much as he did. He is not an educated man, having been taken from the work bench to preach the Gospel.[35]

Notes

1. History booklet of Nast and Trinity churches (Cincinnati, Ohio: 1985).
2. Denise Smith Amos, "Church also a haven," *Cincinnati Enquirer*, November 3, 2001.
3. "Kirchen Jubilaum," *Freie Presse*, Nippert Collection, box 2–54, folder 20, Cincinnati Historical Society Library Archives, Ohio.
4. Untitled article, *Commercial* (Cincinnati, Ohio) *Tribune*, 1896, Nippert Collection, box 2–54, folder 20, Cincinnati Historical Society Library Archives, Ohio.
5. Golder, Horst, and Schaal, *Geschichte*, 325–27.
6. Rudin, Diaries, September 30, 1920.
7. Ibid., September 27–28, 1921.
8. *Minutes of the Annual Conferences*, 1929, 1930.
9. Rudin, Diaries, 1930.
10. Mrs. J. J. Koerner, "Our History," *Auburn Methodist Church Sixtieth Anniversary*, 1950, box 2–54, folder 3, Nippert Collection, Cincinnati Historical Society Library Archives, Ohio.
11. Clyde W. Park, "Historical Statement," box 2–54, folder 2, Nippert Collection, Cincinnati Historical Society Library Archives, Ohio.
12. Kevin Aldridge, "God's houses for Sale," *Cincinnati Enquirer*, December 1, 2004 (section A).
13. Handwritten history (Spring Grove Church), n.d., box 2–55, folder 5, Nippert Collection, Cincinnati Historical Society Library Archives, Ohio.
14. M. A. Beck, "The Spring Grove Avenue Methodist Church, Cincinnati, Ohio," box 2–55, folder 3, n.d., Nippert Collection, Cincinnati Historical Society Library Archives, Ohio.
15. "Spring Grove Methodist Church," Cincinnati, Ohio, box 2–55, folder 8, 1959, Nippert Collection, Cincinnati Historical Society Library Archives, Ohio.
16. Edwin C. Walley, *History of Third German Church*, 1934, Public Library of Cincinnati and Hamilton County; Cincinnati, Ohio, microfilm, 15–18, MF929.377178E132p1987.
17. Theodore Baur, *Historical Record*, (Loc. Cit., 1873, microfilm), 5–6.
18. Walley, *History of Third German Church.*
19. "Conference Year 1893–1894," (Loc. Cit., microfilm), 23.
20. Theodore Baur, *Fiftieth Jubilee*, (Loc. Cit., microfilm), 1899, 30.
21. Ibid., 29.
22. J. G. Schaal, report. (Loc. Cit., microfilm), 9–10.
23. "An Interesting Farewell Observance," (Third German Church) (Loc. Cit., microfilm), July 10, 1912, 1.
24. "Church Fire Loss $50,000," *Cincinnati Times-Star*, January, 21, 1957, (second front page) 3.
25. "Arson squad probes church basement fire," *Cincinnati Enquirer*, February 20, 1971, A1.
26. Rudin, Diaries, 1903.
27. *Anniversary Celebrations, Hyde Park Bethlehem United Methodist Church, 1981–1988*, anniversary booklet (Cincinnati, Ohio: 1988).
28. Golder, Horst, and Schaal, *Geschichte*, 329.
29. *Anniversary Celebrations.*

30. Frances Pope and Edna Holle, *Our Memorial Stained Glass Windows, Hyde Park—Bethlehem United Methodist Church*, Public Library of Cincinnati and Hamilton County (Cincinnati, Ohio, 1974), 5.

31. Pope and Holle, *Memorial Stained Glass Windows*, 10–16.

32. *History of Mt. Healthy Methodism*, History of Epworth United Methodist Church (Cincinnati, Ohio: 1974).

33. "Merger," *West Ohio News Worthington, Ohio: The West Ohio Conference of The United Methodist Church*, February, 22, 2002.

34. Rudin, Diaries, 1904.

CHAPTER 4

Northern Kentucky Churches in the Cincinnati District

Covington, Kentucky—Immanuel German M. E. Church

A pamphlet on the one hundredth anniversary of Immanuel German M.E. Church says, "This is the glorious story of a church conceived in the devout hearts of a humble group of emigrant people who, having first erected a shrine to God in their own hearts, built an earthly tabernacle to glorify his name."[1] Peter Cartwright attended the general conference in 1836 where he met Dr. Nast and Rev. Ludwig Jacoby. He quoted Reverend Jacoby on converting the Germans:

> They will not support the work of the gospel until they are thoroughly converted . . . first you have to get them converted in the head because their thinking is wrong—they are stubborn, selfish, willful and sinful. Next you have to get them converted in their heart because their affections are wrong—they love money, possessions and things of this world. Then you have to get them converted in the purse, because they have a tendency to be stingy. But if you get a German converted like that, he will make a good Methodist and he will stick.[2]

Meetings were first held in 1842 in homes and in 1848 Frederick Dohrmann proposed forming a church. A frame chapel on Craig Street was bought from the Baptists and, in 1849, Christian Vogel became the first pastor. The Sunday School formed in 1853 with five church members and fifteen children. The church treated the town of Covington to its first Christmas tree. Member Timothy Heineman and his brother crossed the Ohio River in a skiff and cut a small evergreen tree that they found at the foot of Price Hill. They made the return trip by ferry and carried the tree to the church where members adorned it with popcorn garlands, gilded walnuts, springerle and candles.

From 1849 to 1855, the Newport and Covington churches were on the

Covington, Kentucky, Immanuel German M. E., now abandoned.

same circuit. Both continued to grow and, by 1855, were large enough to each support their own pastor. Rev. Karl Kessinger was appointed as the first full-time pastor of the Covington German Methodist Episcopal Church.[3]

In 1866 there was a need for a larger, newer place of worship and a parcel of land was bought at the corner of Tenth and Russell streets for twenty-five hundred dollars. The cornerstone was laid on July 11, 1869, and the lower room was dedicated on January 2, 1870. Because of some financial setbacks, the remainder of the church was not finished until February 20, 1876.[4] The total cost was twenty-seven thousand dollars with thirty-one hundred collected, forty-one hundred from the sale of the old church, two thousand from the Sunday school and seventeen thousand from the congregation. In 1886 a house next to the church was acquired for a parsonage.[5] The church was given the name Immanuel Church sometime in the 1880s.[6]

Renovations took place in 1890 to the upper room of the church and in 1893 to the Sunday school room. During Reverend Schimmelpfennig's pastorate another facelifting was done for thirteen hundred dollars. Immanuel became the proud owner of a new pipe organ during Reverend Horst's tenure. An outlay of thirty-seven hundred dollars covered the cost of the organ plus additional improvements made to the church and parsonage.[7]

A Sunday school started in 1853 with 5 members and grew to 518 members by 1915. Sophia Guth organized the Ladies Aid in 1882. This organization was a bulwark financially, spiritually, and socially and was known for its annual turkey dinner. The Epworth League began in 1900 with 35 members. Some missionary groups founded were the Tabitha Missionary Society in 1893, the King's Heralds in 1909 and Light Bearers in 1913 (both children's groups), the Standard Bearers for young adults in 1914, and the Women's Home Missionary Society in 1921. The men organized the Men's Club which later became Immanuel Brotherhood in 1915.[8]

In the 1940s a need was seen for a newer, larger church building in a new location, as many of the members had moved to the suburbs. A site was found on Dixie Highway in Lakeside Park, and on June 10, 1949, ground was broken for the new building.[9] In 1950 the congregation moved to 2564 Dixie Highway to the new Immanuel church building. The old building at Tenth and Russell is still standing, as of this writing. In 1960 Armstrong Cork was listed at that address, but at present the building seems to be empty.

The new church building was accomplished in three phases. Fellowship Hall on the Garden Level was completed first, and this is where the congregation first worshiped. On September 17, 1950, a parade formed at the old church and proceeded to the new one "with all flags flying." George Taglauer, chairman of the board of trustees, carried a flame (symbolizing the Holy Spirit) from the altar of the old church to the altar of the new one. In June 1955, the cornerstone was laid for the sanctuary which was completed in 1956. An educational wing was constructed in 1964. All debts were paid and funds were next raised for a Wicks Pipe Organ which was dedicated on May 7, 1973.[10]

In the 1990s, more space was needed due to rapid growth, therefore, it was determined that the new facility needed meeting rooms, a multipurpose area, a new kitchen, music area, and an elevator to make all three floors accessible. The nineteen-hundred-square-foot facility was constructed on the north side of the building and opened on March 21, 1998, as Wesley Hall. Immanuel now has five Sunday worship services including a contemporary one and one in Spanish.[11]

The Covington Immanuel church was one of Grandpa's stops on another collection tour in 1904. Here are his comments:

Saturday, April 16

Left Jeffersonville this morning. My train was nearly an hour overdue at Cincinnati, for which reason I took dinner at a restaurant. Went to Covington and found Schimmelpfennig's without any trouble. Feel somewhat sick on the stomach this evening, caused doubtless by my restaurant dinner.

Sunday April 17

Had the honor of sleeping with Bro. S. Has the pastor of the rich Covington congregation no spare bed? Went to Sunday School and taught Bro. Dickhaut's class, also spoke to the school and felt myself quite at home. Over 200 were in the Sunday School. Preached to a large audience. My collection amounted to $90.[12]

To find out more about Immanuel today, go to their website at: www.immanuelumc.org.

Covington Immanuel's congregation moved to Lakeside Park, Kentucky, and built their present church.

Newport, Kentucky—Salem German M. E.

German Methodism came to Newport, Kentucky, in 1847, brought by those across the river in Cincinnati at the First German M. E. on Race Street. The Newport group first met in the old courthouse where meetings were held by class leaders from Cincinnati. In 1848 Rev. Peter B. Becker took charge as the first minister when the church was organized as part of the Newport and Covington Mission.

The first meeting place owned by the congregation was a small frame building on what is now Sixth Street (formerly Todd Street). This building was erected for the cost of seven hundred dollars. By 1854 the congregation again felt growing pains and purchased a lot at the corner of Seventh Street (then Mayo) and Orchard Street for fifteen hundred dollars. The next year the new brick building was completed to the tune of five thousand dollars. The old one on Sixth Street was sold for six hundred dollars. The church membership grew rapidly during the next twenty years and, after the Civil War many revivals were held. Conference records show a membership of 93 in 1864 with an increase to 208 by 1875.[13]

In 1881 the congregation purchased a site at the corner of York and Eighth (Ringgold), for nine thousand dollars. A cornerstone was laid on July 4, 1882, and the building completed on June 24, 1883, for a cost of thirty-three thousand. A new parsonage was also built at this time for thirty-six hundred dollars. The Ladies Aid Society organized in 1881 with seventy-two members followed by the Woman's Home Missionary Society in 1885 with forty-one members. The choir had its origins in the "Singing School" formed at the previous church building, but actually became a choir when the move was made to the new church.

In 1896 the church of 335 members underwent one renovation with another following in 1905. During the pastorate of Rev. Richard Plueddemann (1905–1907), the English language prevailed and evening services ceased being delivered in German. A few years later, during World War I, the German language was set aside completely. Salem proved its loyalty by sending twenty-six young men into military service. In 1918, the church was again redecorated and the Sunday school rooms equipped. The annual conference was held at Salem in September 1923 while the church celebrated its diamond anniversary. In 1926 more redecorating was done which included new carpet for the sanctuary. The need for a Sunday school building was apparent and one was erected on the west side of the building for a cost of $5,287. When the Central German Conference dissolved in 1933, Salem joined the Kentucky Conference.

Anyone who has lived in the Ohio Valley has heard of the 1937 flood. In that year, Salem Church provided a refuge for 130 African-American women and children for seventeen days. One room became a hospital supervised by a Salem member who was a nurse. Food supplied by the Red Cross was cooked and served by members for the refugees.[14]

The second Salem German M. E. building in Newport, Kentucky. The first one is no longer standing.

In the early 1940s World War II reared its ugly head and the constituents of Salem again answered the call to arms. The church's service banner bore forty-three stars representing members or constituents from Salem. The church newsletter, which served as a connection between the service people and home and was given the Hebrew name MIZPAH meaning "The Lord watch between me and thee when we are absent one from another."

Between the 100th anniversary and the 130th, more renovations took place. This included painting both the church and parsonage and adding more classrooms in the basement. Also, the Tiffany-stained glass windows were repaired and releaded and the steeple and tower completely renovated. An anonymous typewritten history says: "We like to feel our Tower with its beautiful cross is a beacon of the Christian faith and that Salem is a Light House offering hope and faith in the future of our country."[15]

By 1986 the church was destined for a new life. A tornado struck the build-

Newport's third Salem building now used as a theatre.

ing and sent the steeple crashing into the street. The tower plunged through the roof and second floor, ending up in the basement. A diminished congregation could not afford the costly repairs and chose to unite with Grace Methodist on Sixth Street and put the stately brick building up for sale.[16] The Footlighters, a community theatre group, was delighted to find the church and, with the help of grants plus its own money, bought the building for sixty-five thousand dollars. The group proceeded to renovate and transform the building from a church into the Stained Glass Theatre. On the second floor a stage was erected with seating for 165. The first floor featured an art gallery and a dance studio. A two-story staircase, ordered by the fire code, was added behind the stage and cost almost as much as the building itself.[17]

A distinctive feature of the church is the stained glass windows of Tiffany glass. The iron fence around the church property, erected in 1883, came from German ironworks in Cincinnati and was styled by the Germans. In 1905 a new pipe organ was installed and is still in use. It is one of three imported from Germany and is the oldest in this country. A Steinway Baby Grand piano was purchased in 1859 and was one of the first three thousand pianos made in this country. The steeple, which survived a 1906 tornado, was topped with a Celtic cross (unusual for a German church). A Celtic cross also adorns the front of the doorway.[18]

Grandpa Rudin was quite familiar with Salem Church, being pastor at Second Church in Cincinnati from late 1920 to 1925. Maybe that is why he had so few comments on the church itself. In 1923 he and my grandmother (Till) attended the annual conference held there, which I will let his words describe below:

Tuesday, September 4

Till and I went to Newport this evening. The church was pretty well filled and Bishop Henderson gave one of his fiery addresses. Bros. Phillip and Knauf came home with us. [These two pastors stayed with them during the Conference]

Wednesday, September 5

The Conference was opened . . . with a Communion Service . . . followed by the memorial service. Bro. Edelmaier gave the memorial address which was a very good one. After the organization of the Conference, Dr. Ralph E. Diffendorfer spoke on "Our World Service Program." He was followed by Dr. M. R. Burrows . . . on "Saving America through Our New Home Missions." These men did their level best to pump Centenary enthusiasm into us. This afternoon the Preachers' Aid Society met. This evening Bishop W. P. Thirfield spoke on Mexico. He was fine. He was followed by Dr. J. Garland Perm. Dr. F. W. Mueller followed with an illustrated lecture on the early beginnings of German Mission work.

Thursday September 6

We surely got our share of "talking to" yesterday! It was Centenary to the right of us, Centenary to the left of us, etc. all day. This morning heard the reports of the District Superintendents. I liked Bro. Holtkamp's best. Dr. Koch made hardly any reference to the Community House in Cincinnati. After the morning session I went home, walking across the Newport bridge and did some shopping. Till attended the anniversary of the WFMS and the WHMS in the Newport Church. Miss Lebeus was one of the speakers. She expects to go back to China soon. Dr. J. B. Hingeley spoke in behalf of the Conference claimants. Dr. A. J. Loeppert followed with a talk on Epworth League work and Dr. Mueller again showed pictures.

Friday September 7

I was on the program for the closing prayer last night. Dr. Mueller concluded his illustrated lectures this evening. They were very interesting and the pictures were remarkably fine. The Men and Boys Banquet was held tonight. There were several speakers, including the Bishop and Dr. Stair, and all did well. Dr. Nast is out for Dr. Bucher and Dr. Koch as delegates to the General Conference, but there is a movement among the preachers not to vote for detached men. Dr. N. seems specially anxious to have Dr. B. in. Dr. Hugo W. Georgi of Germany spoke on the work in Germany and conditions in the Ruhr. One wonders how long yet will God permit the French to go on in their devilish work.

Saturday September 8

Last night Dr. J. G. Schaal and Bishop Henderson were the speakers. Dr. S. remains as young as ever. The 60th anniversary of the Central German Conference was commemorated.... Dr. Schaal came into the Conference 3 years after its organization. Of the original members, only one remains: Louis Miller. This morning the junior laymen and laymen were received by the conference. Theodore Weiler is president of the junior laymen. Edmund Huber and Charles Waller have been elected lay delegates to the General Conference and Oscar Rogatzky and F. W. Mueller are the ministerial delegates. Everybody is talking about appointments but nobody knows anything. This afternoon the Conference had an autoride to the grave of Dr. William Nast and other points of interest.

Monday September 10

Yesterday the ordination service took place in Newport and the Bishop gave his usual invitation to young people to enter any kind of Christian service.... A lap lunch was served by the Newport ladies. This evening Dr. R. W. Harrup of the Kentucky Conference was the fascinating speaker. He spied me in the audience and came up to me to shake hands and have a pleasant word. I had no idea that he still remembered me. He is a fine man all around. The Conference came to a close after six this afternoon appointments were held up almost to the last moment. It was the longest Conference session I have ever attended.

Tuesday September 11

Bro. Knauff left us yesterday ... and Bro. Phillipp last night. Bro. Werner spent last night with us and left us this morning.... Well, the "talkfest" is over for a talkfest it was! So many speeches I have never heard at any Conference. Apparently all the preachers were glad to get away from the bombardment of oratory.[19]

Notes

1. C. Albert Schroetter, "The Story of Immanuel Methodist Church," in *One Hundredth Anniversary Immanuel Methodist Church*, Covington, Kentucky, 1949, 1.
2. William M. Pope, "The History of the Immanuel United Methodist Church," 2551 Dixie Highway, Lakeside Park, Kentucky, May 15, 1984.
3. Pope, "The History of the Immanuel United Methodist Church."
4. Schroetter, "The Story of Immanuel Methodist Church," 2.
5. Golder, Horst, and Schaal, *Geschichte*, 330.
6. Schroetter, "The Story of Immanuel Methodist Church," 2.
7. Golder, Horst, and Schaal, *Geschichte*, 330–31.
8. Pope, "The History of the Immanuel United Methodist Church," 2–3.
9. Schroetter, "The Story of Immanuel Methodist Church," 1, 2, 6.
10. Pope, "The History of the Immanuel United Methodist Church," 4.
11. Addenda to Pope's essay.
12. Rudin, Diaries, 1904.
13. *Minutes of the Annual Conferences*, 1875, 258.
14. *History and Program, The Ninetieth Anniversary of the Salem Methodist Episcopal Church*, church history (Newport, Ky.: 1938), 9–31.
15. "History," (typewritten history) Salem Gemeinde and Salem United Methodist Church 1876–1982 folder, Campbell County Historical Society, Alexandria, Ky.
16. Gene Franzen, "Tornado ended church function," *Cincinnati Enquirer*, November 5, 2000 (Now & Then column).
17. Toni Cashnelli, "Holy Resurrections," *Cincinnati Magazine* 31 (March 1998).
18. "History—Salem United Methodist Church," article, Salem 1876–1982 folder, Campbell County Historical Society.
19. Rudin, Diaries, 1923.

CHAPTER 5

Southwestern Ohio German M. E. Churches

Dayton, Ohio—Van Buren Street German M. E.

The first German Methodist Episcopal church in Dayton began in 1840 with meetings in the old courthouse, thanks to the influence of Philippina Metzgar Fischbach.[1] In 1843, a one story brick building was erected at Jackson and Sixth streets. Toward the end of the Civil War a lot was purchased at Clay and Van Buren streets where another church building was constructed for fourteen thousand dollars. The new church was brick, also, but two stories high and forty-five by seventy-five feet in area.[2]

Due to damage from the 1913 flood, the church underwent some remodeling that year. The outer walls were coated with cement and the first floor, where the Sunday school met, was raised. The basement depth was increased several feet to allow additional space for social rooms.

Church records show many organizations connected with the church. Sunday school was one of the earliest organized. Men paid twenty-five cents for dues and women, twelve and a half cents. Certain standards were expected of the scholars including promptness in arriving for class, standing for hymns, kneeling for prayers, and quiet during prayers. The members always anticipated the Sunday school picnic with excitement. Sometimes a procession led the members to the fairgrounds, or another location, where a program was held before the picnic. When the event fell on the Fourth of July, the Declaration of Independence was read, hymns sung, and speeches made. Then the group played games, ate their picnic dinners, and drank the lemonade made by a special committee. In 1867 lemons cost $2.10 a dozen and sugar cost $0.20 a pound, so lemonade was not cheap.

Another group at the Van Buren Street church was the Christian Sister Association, founded in 1876. Meetings were in the evening and focused on religious writings. In 1877 the group funded half of the expense for gas lights

Beautifully preserved Van Buren Street German M. E. in Dayton, Ohio, which now a private home.

in the church. The Point Club was another women's group whose purpose was to encourage good fellowship.

The Christian Young Peoples' Society started in 1885 and met the first Tuesday of the month. Yearly dues were fifty cents for men and twenty-five cents for women. This group performed a cantata which raised $70.69 for purchasing Sunday school song books. Eventually, the group became the Epworth League. The author of the church history noted, however, that the former group was revived in 1939.[3]

The church lasted until 1965 when the building became the Van Buren Methodist Community Center through 1975. The address was listed as 100 Van Buren in city directories. At present the building is no longer a church but has been beautifully restored as a private home. The engraved cornerstone on the front of the building tells of its origin in German.

Another collection trip brought my grandfather to Dayton, Ohio, in 1904.

Saturday May 7

Left for Dayton this noon and arrived at 6:12 this evening. Did not enjoy the trip much: it was too warm to feel comfortable and the smoke and dust that came in the open windows was anything but pleasant.

Sunday May 8

Bro. Bach has . . . a good Sunday School, but he says that he has not much to say in its management. Taught class and spoke to the school. Preached to fairly good audiences morning and evening. Mr. B. told me that some staid away on account of the collection. It is the reputation of this congregation that it is rather selfish and and uncharitable. They have no heart for others and even what they do for themselves they do grumblingly. My collection thus far amounts to $29. I expect, however, to bring it up to about $35. Attended the Epworth League meeting tonight. One of the lady members conducted it. They seem to have a promising lot of young people here.

Monday May 9

Visited Wienefelds and had dinner there. Mr. W. is well to do, 80 years old and quite feeble. Bro. Bach told me that he led a bad life in the days of his strength and that he now suffers the consequences. He was all the time a church member and gave great offense but he had money and was quite liberal and was therefore not dropped. He is still one of the best paying members. He gave me $5 for the collection after I prayed with him.

Tuesday May 10

Visited the Panorama of the Battle of Gettysburg. . . . It is situated near the Soldiers' Home and is quite realistic. Visited the public library last night. It is much better than the one at Sandusky and contains many German publications. Took a walk this morning. Dayton is really as fine a town as one would wish. It seemed to me that all the women of the town—rich and poor, old and young—were out marketing. All carried baskets and seemed to find pleasure in it. Left . . . Dayton going by traction to Mt. Healthy. It is a ride of nearly 3 hours. Had a splitting headache when I arrived at Kruse's which moderated later.[4]

Greenville/Piqua, Ohio, Circuit

Greenville/Piqua Circuit—Greenville German Methodist Church

In 1852 William Floerke started the Greenville congregation which was considered one of the oldest in the conference. Originally, the church met at nearby Wakefield until a frame church was constructed on Ash Street in 1856.[5] The church cost $900 and a year later a parsonage was built for $350.[6]

Greenville and Piqua were always on the same circuit and at various times Sidney, Ohio, and Richmond, Indiana, were also on this circuit. *The History of Darke County, Ohio*, says of Greenville, "It is generally recognized that this congregation will discontinue or merge with the First M. E. church within a few years."[7] The *Geschichte* notes that the church had the greatest number of members in its eightieth year after which membership began to fall off due to the decrease in German immigration. They did, however, have a very active Ladies

Aid which made it their mission to take care of and improve church property.[8] According to conference records, it hung on until 1921 after which it no longer appears in the records.[9]

Greenville/Piqua Circuit—Piqua German M. E. Church

In 1857 Rev. William Ahrens organized the German M. E. Church in Piqua.[10] The small-frame building was constructed in 1866 during the pastorship of Paul Brodbeck. It later became known as the Wayne Street M. E. Church as it stood at the corner of Wayne and Young streets.[11] It stood empty during the 1950s until the Assembly of God used the building, but then was razed in the 1960s and is now the site of a parking lot for a supermarket.

Greenville/Piqua Circuit—Sidney German M. E. Church

Sidney, Ohio, also had a German M. E. church which was part of the Greenville Mission from 1875 until the early 1890s. The Sidney church originally was served from New Knoxville, Ohio, and was founded in 1853 by Rev. F. Schimmelpfennig.[12] In 1891 the church united with the English Methodist Episcopal. The building, at the corner of Ohio Avenue and South Street, was sold in 1895 to the German Baptist church for twenty-two hundred dollars.[13] The Sidney church is no longer standing.

Greenville/Piqua Circuit—Richmond, Indiana, German M. E. Church

The Richmond, Indiana, German M. E. church was founded in 1860 and the thirteen members met in the home of a Mr. Fiske who lived on South Seventh Street. The congregation erected a church building in 1861 at Sixth and B streets. The church disbanded after a year but reorganized in 1871. At that time a brick building, costing five thousand dollars was raised at B and Seventh streets. The congregation was never very large being only 13 in 1871.[14] Before joining the Greenville circuit, it was served from the Hamilton and Dayton circuits. The church disbanded for good in 1893[15] and neither building remains.

On his collection trip in 1903, my grandfather made a stop in Greenville and Piqua. Max Dieterle was the pastor at that time.

Wednesday, November 11

> Took the 8 AM train of the Cincinnati and Northern railroad for Greenville. It was a rich country we passed through, much different than old "Kaintuck." Bro. Dieterle awaited me at Greenville and handed me a letter from Till. All are well at home and John is having a good time. I do so long to see my darling boy again! Bro. D. has a nice family. His wife is pleasant and sociable. Bro. D. is quite a good writer but not much of a preacher. He has a well equipped study on the second floor. That is what I ought to have, a study. . . . I can lock myself into. Thus far I have not not seen as fine a library as mine.

Thursday, November 12

I have $14 from Greenville. Hardly expected that much. Took the Pennsylvania Railroad to Piqua where we arrived . . . after 12:00. We put up at Meinders where Dieterle usually stops. Attended a meeting of the Frauenverein and had the honor of opening it with prayer and . . . the Scriptures. It was not such an elaborate affair as at Chillicothe but all seemed to enjoy themselves. The meeting was conducted about as our ladies are wont to do.

Friday, November 13

Had a good meeting last night, though it was small. The Piqua people have a really fine little church of which they can be proud. It has beautiful stained glass windows and fine interior appointments. There can hardly be a finer church of its size in the conference.

Saturday, November 14

On the invitation of the president, I addressed the Epworth League. It isn't much of a league, but still is better than ours. Left Piqua this morning and arrived at Hamilton shortly before 1:00. Had lunch at Dayton in the Union Station. It cost me 30 cents and consisted of two thin sandwiches and a cup of coffee. I won't do that again.[16]

Hamilton, Ohio—Grace Methodist Church

In the 1830s a small group of German residents began meeting in their homes for prayer and worship. Dr. William Nast often visited them to preach. In 1838 the group formally became a congregation and was put on a three-point charge which included Mt. Healthy and Richmond, Indiana. The meeting place was moved to the county courthouse and then to First Methodist Church of Hamilton. The congregation officially became a German M. E. church in 1854 and joined the Ohio Conference. Their first church building was a former English Lutheran church on North C Street.[17] Although most sources agree on the 1854 date as the official beginning, other sources say 1843[18] or 1853.[19] In 1864 the Central German Conference was formed and the Hamilton church as well as all other German M. E. churches in the area became part of it. By 1888 the church had grown enough to become a "station" rather than be on a circuit with other churches.

During the pastorate of William E. Nocka, the church acquired a parsonage on Liberty Avenue and land on South Front Street. In 1906 the cornerstone was laid at 320 South Front Street and the church was dedicated in May 1907. The new building featured "beautiful stained art glass windows."[20]

As the German population assimilated, there was less need for services in German. In 1933 when the Central German Conference dissolved, the church took the name of Grace Methodist Church.

The next big change came in 1949, when the congregation decided to move out of the central city to the west side of Hamilton. They purchased four and a half acres on West Main Street. In 1953 the Payne Chapel AME church expressed interest in purchasing Grace Church on South Front Street. They subsequently bought the Front Street property in 1954 for forty-seven thousand dollars.[21] The new Grace Methodist at 1200 Main Street was consecrated in September 1956.

In October 1954 Grace Methodist observed its one hundredth anniversary with a special service and music. The celebrants enjoyed a dinner and an informal program in the afternoon. In the old German tradition, a hymn sing was held and former German pastor Henry Maag spoke on "Looking Backward" while current pastor Rev. Hughey Jones gave a talk on "Looking Forward."[22]

Both the old church on South Front Street (now Payne Chapel AME) and the new one on Main are still standing. The original building on C Street is gone. To learn about the church as it is today, go to its Web site at www.graceumchamilton.org.

After his stop at the Greenville/Piqua circuit, Grandpa Rudin headed to Hamilton via Dayton. The pastor at Hamilton was H. E. Wulzen. Since this was in 1903, they were still meeting in the old church on C Street.

Saturday, November 14

Bro. Wulzen was at the station in Hamilton. He is a kindly old gentleman, only he seems to have his mind so much on money and investments. My stomach is giving me considerable trouble again.

Sunday, November 15

Got up early feeling somewhat better than yesterday. Did not eat much breakfast, as I wanted to keep myself in good condition for the day. The Hamilton church is an old fashioned edifice, but kept in good condition. Addressed the Sunday School by request of Bro. Schneider, the Superintendent. He is also local preacher and a rather conceited one Bro. Wulzen told me, though quite harmless. Conceit seems to be the weak spot in nearly all local preachers. Preached to a pretty large audience and believe I did fairly well. Bro. W. has quite a number of men in his congregation. That is what I ought to have in Sandusky.

Monday, November 16

Bro. W. told me ... not to expect a big collection. Bro. Mayer reached a high water mark two years ago that was $30 while last year it was only $25. Well, I have received over $35! Congratulations are in order! Wesley Wulzen was in the Philippines as a volunteer in the army. He showed me a lot of relics, among them a murderous-looking bolo which he found in an abandoned house. He also has a Philippines bugle. He seems to be giving his parents much concern as he is careless and unreliable. The army is a poor school for many young men. Left Hamilton early this morning by trolley for Dayton where I took The Big Four for Cleveland.

Hamilton, Ohio's German M. E. church (second building), now Payne Chapel A.M.E.

Hamilton, Ohio's Grace UMC (third building), now an active U.M.C.

Tuesday November 17

Made the journey from Dayton to Cleveland in a parlor car and enjoyed it. It cost me 75 cents extra but was well worth the price. I liked the Wulzens. They live in their own house which they built a few years ago and where they intend to end their days.[23]

Notes

1. "History of Van Buren Street Methodist Church," 1940, folder 21, Box 2-56, Nippert Collection.
2. *The History of Montgomery County, Ohio* (Chicago: W. H. Beers & Co., 1882), 654.
3. "History of Van Buren Street Methodist Church."
4. Rudin, Diaries, 1904.
5. Golder, Horst, and Schaal, *Geschichte*, 333.
6. *The History of Darke County* (Chicago: W. H. Beers & Co. 1880), 436.
7. Frazier E. Wilson, *History of Darke County, Ohio*, vol. 1, (Milford, Ohio: 1914), 210.
8. Golder, Horst, and Schaal, *Geschichte*, 333.
9. *Minutes of the Annual Conferences*, 1924.
10. Golder, Horst, and Schaal, *Geschichte*, 334.
11. "Senior English Class of Piqua High School 1929," *Piqua as it is Today* (Piqua High School, Piqua, Ohio 1929).
12. Golder, Horst, and Schaal, *Geschichte*, 334.
13. *A History of Methodism in Sidney, Ohio*, (privately published, 1989), 201.
14. *History of Wayne County, Indiana* (Chicago: Inter-State Publishing Co., 1884), 132.
15. Golder, Horst, and Schaal, *Geschichte*, 334.
16. Rudin, Diaries, 1903.
17. K. Maag, *History of Grace Methodist Church*, church history (Hamilton, Ohio: 1961), 1.
18. *A History and Biographical Cyclopaedia of Butler County Ohio* (Cincinnati, Ohio: Western Biographical Publishing Co. 1882), 350.
19. *Centennial History of Butler County, Ohio,* (Indianapolis, Ind: B. F. Bowen 1905), 174.
20. Maag, *History of Grace Methodist Church*, 1.
21. Ibid., 2.
22. Ibid., 2-3.
23. Rudin, Diaries, 1923.

CHAPTER 6

German M. E. Churches in South Central Ohio

Chillicothe, Ohio, Circuit

In 1840 George A. Breunig was appointed to the Scioto Circuit to minister to the German Methodists of that area. Thomas Orr and Samuel Ewing from the Western Charge and Eastern Charge, respectively, located a site for the newly formed congregation, and a house was purchased to serve as a meeting place. In 1850 Dr. Nast and Bishop James dedicated the newly erected building on Mulberry Street (at what is now 89 South Mulberry).[1] The building and property cost about six thousand dollars and there was seating for three hundred to four hundred people, ample for the 175 members.[2] The congregation disbanded in 1915, having dwindled to 35, and its members joined other Methodist congregations. The German building is still standing, however, and now being used by the Mulberry Street Wesleyan Church. If you look up below the peak of the roof you can see the keystone with the name in both German and English.

Chillicothe Circuit—Greenfield

There were two other churches on the Chillicothe circuit at one time. One of these was located in Greenfield, Ohio. About 1854, a number of German families, having trouble understanding the English services at the First Methodist Church, decided to have a German-speaking church. They met in an unused school in the three hundred block of Mirabeau Street. When their membership increased to forty, in 1873, the school was razed and a brick church erected. Eventually, by 1894, there was no longer a need for German language services and membership declined. The church disbanded and the building was put to use as the first steam laundry in the town.[3]

64 / A FORGOTTEN HERITAGE: THE GERMAN METHODIST CHURCH

Former German M. E. in Chillicothe, Ohio, now used by another denomination.

Chillicothe Circuit—Waverly German M. E. Church

The German M. E. Church in Waverly, Ohio, was also on the Chillicothe circuit at various times. The church was organized in 1850 and a building erected on Market Street, as well a parsonage at Second and Market streets. It appeared first in conference records in 1865 as a station, but later, in 1869 was on a circuit with Greenfield. In 1884 Waverly and Greenfield joined the Chillicothe Circuit. In September of 1900 a fire damaged the German church.[4] It was last mentioned in conference records in 1901 and, as it had only twenty-five members at this point, most of them probably joined other churches.[5]

In 1903 while my grandfather was at his first pastorate in Sandusky, Ohio, he was sent on some sort of collecting trip to various churches in Ohio. During this time he visited the German Methodist Church in Chillicothe. My grandmother's uncle, Peter Ribbe, was living there and grandpa visited him at the same time. Following are excerpts from his diary. The pastor at Chillicothe in 1903 was William Andree.

Wednesday, November 4

> Arrived at Chillicothe at 9:37 this morning. Bro. Andree awaited me at the station which is quite a distance from his house. Received a cordial reception by his wife, and a German dinner. Called on Mr. Ribbe and Mr. Wiedler this afternoon. Uncle Pete is a nice looking and interesting

man. He is in the shoe business and seems to be prosperous. Preached to a small audience tonight and did poorly. The pulpit was a low, old-fashioned table and I could barely see my notes.

Thursday November 5

After church last night Mr. Ribbe took me to his house to see his wife and son George. Cousin George lives in cozy rooms above his father's store. He and his wife seem to be a happy couple. Made . . . calls with Bro. Andree and this evening attended a "Kaffetrink" of the Frauenverein.

Friday November 6

That Kaffeetrink last evening was quite an elaborate affair and the ladies made $21 as a result. . . . The Chillicothe ladies could give our ladies a few pointers. Bro. A. and I got on politics this morning. He is one of those fanatics who sees nothing good outside of the Republican Party. According to him all Democrats are unmitigated scoundrels and all Republicans models of honesty and ability.

Saturday November 7

Bro. A's vision is rather narrow and he becomes easily excited. Yesterday's tilt, however, was good-natured and no damage was done. Uncle Pete is a Democrat, which is to his credit. Chillicothe has given me $16 in cash and subscriptions which is very good for this congregation. Left Chillicothe this morning.[6]

Ironton, Ohio, Circuit and the Furnaces

All sources agree that the German M. E. Church in Ironton had its roots in the "Furnace Mission" which was organized in 1860. There were many small iron smelting furnaces in that southern Ohio area north of Ironton known as the Hanging Rock Iron Region. In many cases, small communities grew up around them founded by German iron working immigrants. This was viewed as a ripe spot to send mission preachers from the German M. E. church. The circuit was officially known as the Lawrence Furnace Circuit and included the following communities: Lawrence, Pinegrove, Jackson, Mt. Vernon, Centre, Clinton, Hanging Rock, Monroe, Washington, Etna, New Castle, Zion, Little Scioto, Bloomfield, Webster, Waverly, and Jefferson.[7] Some of these communities developed into towns; some, like Jefferson, Bloomfield and Washington, seem to be townships. At any rate, I could find no record of actual church buildings in most of them, so meetings were probably held in homes or schools, and congregations, no doubt, were small.

Many of the furnaces shut down in the early 1870s and their German workers moved to Ironton. In 1873, the Ironton German M. E. Church was organized

Immanuel UMC in Ironton, Ohio, formerly German Methodist.

and first met in a small brick church on Fifth Street near Washington. The present church and parsonage were built at Fifth and Monroe streets in 1884. At some point in its history, the church was given the name Immanuel, but none of several sources pinpoints when this occurred. Toward the end of the nineteenth century members became dissatisfied with the services conducted in German. In 1904 there was a German service in the morning and an English one in the evening. The church officially joined the Ohio Conference of the Methodist Episcopal Church in 1909, leaving their German heritage behind.

The church building has seen a few changes through the years. The entrance was originally on Monroe Street but moved to Fifth Street in 1905. At that same time a number of beautiful stained-glass windows were added. A large window on the Monroe Street side shows the Good Shepherd and was made in Germany. A large rose window is on the east side and fourteen memorial windows complete the display.[8]

The church was also famous for a tradition that started in 1915, a donut bake that, for awhile, was a regular monthly feature. On an average day the Ladies Aid Society sold 150 dozen for thirty-five cents a dozen. The recipe was a well-kept secret for many years but because the church no longer does the donut project, the ladies group decided to share the recipe.[9]

Immanuel's address is 801 South Fifth Street, Ironton, OH, 45638.

Ironton Circuit—Zion Church—Slocum

Two members of the Lawrence Furnace Circuit survived the dissolution to become churches in their own rights. Waverly joined the Chillicothe Circuit and has already been discussed. Zion, which was located at Slocum east of Portsmouth, was on the Portsmouth Circuit until about 1883. Zion church was described as being frame and measuring twenty-eight-by-forty feet. Rev. John Phetzing founded the church and a Mr. Leger built it in 1858. Rev. John Bier officiated at the dedication in September of 1858.[10] Zion was transferred to the Ironton Circuit and shared the same pastor as Immanuel from 1883 until 1904, when it was briefly transferred back to the Portsmouth Circuit. In conference records, Zion is only listed with Portsmouth for two years.[11] Possibly, it transferred out of the Central German Conference to the Ohio Conference of English-speaking Methodist churches. At any rate, in 1917 Zion Methodist merged with Wheelersburg M. E. Church. In 1926 the newly combined congregation built a brick church for the cost of sixty thousand dollars. The merged church celebrated its 125th anniversary in 1947. In 1985 the church had a membership of seven hundred.[12]

A Scioto County history reports a German M. E. church on Dogwood Ridge in Porter Township which was organized in 1855 under Rev. John Phetzing. Rev. John Bier dedicated the first church there in the same year it was built—1858. The article commented that there were about one hundred members and it also had an Epworth League.[13] Since Slocum is in Porter Township, this appears to be the same as Zion. When I contacted Wheelersburg church, they knew very little about Zion's history, saying they had no old records from it.

Grandpa Rudin described his visit to the Slocum church in his 1903 diary.

Saturday November 7

Left Portsmouth on the 2:10 train, arriving at Slocum a half hour later. Brueckner was at the station and took me to his house. Had supper with him and his newly made wife. Am stopping with a family by the name of Schmidt.

Sunday November 8

Bro. Brueckner and his wife called for me and . . . we went to church which is quite distant. The Sunday School is about like the one at Lacarne, only that it is more English. Preached to an attentive audience, my topic being "Prayer." Bro. and Mrs. B. were guests of Schmidts at dinner and at supper. Preached to a good audience in English this evening. My collection amounts to $14. Last year it was $19 but so much could not be expected this year, as several members have moved away and also $38 has to be raised for the preacher's moving expenses.

Monday November 9

Called on Brueckner this morning and had dinner with him. The parsonage is the old farmhouse of the Schmidts and is quite secluded. Mrs. B. is apparently older than her husband and was a teacher. She is pleasant to everybody, but appears to be so because she thinks she has to. She seems quite inexperienced, but no doubt she will be somewhat wiser a year hence.

Tuesday November 10

The country . . . here is fine but rather lonely. The Cincinnati district meeting was held here last summer. Left my kind hosts. Brueckner accompanied me to Portsmouth where he intended to buy some furniture. Crossed over to South Portsmouth and took the 2:50 train of the Chesapeake and Ohio Railroad for Cincinnati.[14]

Just a note here about the pastor at Slocum. For several years from 1896 to 1904 two pastors are listed on the Ironton Circuit. One evidently served at Portsmouth and the other at Slocum. The latter was probably one who was just starting in his career or someone who was superannuated. William Brueckner was just starting out and was at Slocum only that year.[15]

Pomeroy, Ohio, Circuit

At the founding of the Central German Conference, this circuit was made up of four churches—Pomeroy, Chester, Nease Settlement, and Orange. In 1879 conference records showed three churches on the circuit and in 1885 there were four again. By 1889 two were listed until 1906 when the circuit was down to one church, Bethany, in Pomeroy.[16] About this time, German M. E. meetings were held in the Forest Run area in a schoolhouse. The pastor at Pomeroy, Rev. C. J. Schweitzer was instrumental in getting a church built there in 1915. By 1919 there were again two churches on the Pomeroy Circuit—Bethany and Forest Run.

Pomeroy Circuit—Chester

Henry Koeneke came to Chester, Ohio, to preach in 1840 and encouraged brothers John and William Geyer to attend a Methodist camp meeting at Marietta where they were converted. Reverend Koeneke organized a class at Chester in 1841 and made John Geyer class leader. John eventually became a licensed preacher and began preaching from his home, as well as in the surrounding region, thus founding the Chester Circuit.[17] There is little information of the years between then and 1950. In 1950, a small kitchen and additional space in the sanctuary enlarged the building. Two stained-glass windows were removed to accomplish this and put into storage, but, unfortunately, a fire later destroyed them. In 1976 an educational section, restrooms, a larger kitchen, a storage room, and a ramp increased the church's size. In 1978, aluminum sid-

Pomeroy, Ohio, German M. E. Church, later named Bethany M. E., now merged with another church.

ing was added to the original section of the building.[18] The Chester church is still active as the Chester United Methodist Church on Main Street, Chester, OH, 45720.

Pomeroy Circuit—Pomeroy Methodist Church (Bethany)

After helping build the church in Chester, William Geyer moved from his farm at Nease Settlement to Pomeroy to live while he built the church there in 1846. The circuit was for a while called Chester Circuit but since the pastors lived in Pomeroy it was renamed the Pomeroy Circuit. In the early years there were five churches on the circuit: Pomeroy, Chester, Nease Settlement, Orange, and Genheimer Church at Pine Grove.[19]

In 1897, a six thousand dollars brick structure replaced the frame church at Pomeroy. The building was seventy-by-thirty-two feet and included a Sunday School and social room. Rev. William Andree performed the dedication ceremony for the church on February 28, 1898, while Dr. Christian Golder preached the dedicatory sermon.[20]

On May 1, 1943, the former German church (whose name was changed to Bethany during World War I) and Simpson Methodist Church of Pomeroy joined together as one church known as United Methodist Church of Pomeroy. For a time, both church buildings were used—the former Simpson church for

*Pomeroy Circuit German M.E. at Chester, Ohio,
is still an active UMC church.*

services and the former Bethany for Youth fellowship and the women's organization. The parsonage on Mulberry Avenue was kept as the parsonage of the united church and the other house was rented out.[21] Eventually, the Simpson building took over all activities and in 1958 Trinity Church bought the Bethany building. Trinity and Bethany, being next door to each other, were connected by a passageway and Bethany was used as an educational facility. In 1971 history repeated itself and the Pomeroy United Methodist Church and the Chester church once again found themselves on the same circuit served by the same pastor.[22]

In checking addresses via the Hometown Locator site, I discovered a church listed at Nease Settlement on Roy Jones Road. It was not listed on the United Methodist website, so I don't know if it is or was Methodist but it was the only church listed at that site.[23]

Pomeroy Circuit—Forest Run German M. E.

Forest Run German M. E. church was a comparative latecomer to the Central German Conference. In the early nineteen hundreds, some of the German-speaking residents in the area of Forest Run met in a schoolhouse for services. Rev. C. J. Schweitzer of the Pomeroy church encouraged them to build a church. With donations, hard work, help from the Central German Conference and faith in God, the work was completed and the new church dedicated on November 7, 1915. For several years, the Forest Run and Pomeroy churches formed a circuit until Bethany and Simpson churches of Pomeroy united. Then Forest Run church joined the Racine circuit where it remained for twenty years. At present, it is part of the Sycamore charge. In 1953 the church became the proud owner of an electric organ. Some changes to the building were made such as putting the entrance to the side of the vestibule and installing a modern kitchen.[24] The church, located on Forest Run Road near Minersville Road, celebrated its eighty-fifth anniversary in October of 2000.

A third church on the Pomeroy Circuit, Forest Run UMC, began as a German M.E.

Pomeroy Circuit—Orange German M. E. Church

The Orange German M. E. Church was somewhere in Orange Township (I've not been able to find an exact location). It was given a brief mention in a history and atlas which commented that it had twenty members.[25] I looked for the Genheimer Church but was barely able to find Pine Grove, let alone the church. It's possible that these congregations met in homes or schools and were too small to be viable.

In 1904 Grandfather Rudin stopped in Pomeroy on a collection trip. He had the following to say:

Friday, May 13

From Chillicothe on the country is quite rugged and in places romantic. Found a warm welcome and a good supper at Burkles. A strike is on among the miners . . . and everything is at a standstill. The collection will no doubt be affected on this account.

Saturday May 14

Pomeroy is a queer looking town and I do not think I would like to live in it. It is all steep hills and the only comfortable street is along the river front. Burkle is not at all in love with his appointment. He likes neither the place nor the people. The hills are too high and the people stingy and the parsonage unhealthy. Mrs. B. was sick 9 weeks and has not even yet fully recovered. We climbed several hills which made B. puff while it did not affect me at all. Also, visited a coal mine and salt manufactory. It was interesting, but I was sorry not to see the miners at work. A Bro. Stief is foreman of the salt works. We met him and he was quite communicative.

Sunday May 15

Had good audiences in both the . . . services. Felt very much like preaching and do not think I preached as well anywhere on my trip, but nevertheless, my collections were small, amounting to $21. Burkle thinks he can bring it up to $25. On top of it all, someone threw in a leaden dollar. Burkle told the congregation about it this evening. Spoke to the Epworth League this evening. They seem to have a nice set of young people here. Christened Burkle's baby.[26]

Portsmouth, Ohio, German M. E.

Rev. Peter Schmucker first brought German Methodist services to Portsmouth in 1844. The first gatherings met in the homes of Stephen Brodbeck and Daniel Emrich, but not long after, services were held in an old schoolhouse on Lower Fourth Street. Portsmouth joined the circuit served by Rev. John Hoppen which also included Piketon, Waverly, Beaver, and West Union, Ohio, and Maysville, Kentucky. Soon a lot was purchased on West Fourth Street between Market and Jefferson streets and a two-story building of brick erected. This building cost thirteen hundred dollars and served as both home for the pastor (first floor) and church (second floor).[27] The church was thirty-by-forty feet and cost twelve hundred dollars "exclusive of the labor and material furnished by members of the congregation, which amounted to considerable."[28] On April 9, 1848, the church was dedicated and free of all debt. Money left over purchased a small piece of land at the back of the church lot.

By 1860 the congregation had expanded enough to need a larger home. A lot at the southeast corner of Fourth and Washington streets was purchased for sixteen hundred dollars. The new German M. E. church finally was dedicated on July 18, 1869, work having been delayed by the Civil War. The new two-story brick church cost twenty-four thousand dollars and could seat four hundred people. It had stone trim and a tower with two-toned bells given by Vincent Brodbeck and Henry Marting.[29] Another source says the church was actually completed in 1867. It also reported that the cost was thirty-one thousand dollars "with subsequent improvements." In 1916 the church was still in use.[30]

The larger church continued to grow and in 1883 the Concordia Society was organized for the young people. This group preceded the later-formed group, the Epworth League. The Concordia Society helped the church greatly, contributing to renovations after the flood of 1884 and also to the purchase of the church's first pipe organ in 1894. This group also was instrumental in the building of the Franklin Avenue church.

After another flood in 1913, it was clear that a move to a new location was necessary and the church fathers began to examine residential property. The lot at the corner of Franklin Avenue and Logan Street proved to be satisfactory and was purchased in 1915 from Charles Grassman for five thousand dollars. Dr. F. H. Williams also sold the church some additional land. Ground breaking took place on April 2, 1916, with two hundred members each turning over a shovelful. The cornerstone from the Fourth Street Church was incorporated into the basement wall of the new church. The dedication celebration lasted for eight days and included a service in German by former pastor Rev. H. Grentszenberg. Former pastors, bishops, and officials of the Central German Conference performed the other services and Bishop Theodore Henderson gave the dedicatory sermon on May 20, 1916. The new church building and land came to a total of $46,325 which was completely paid off with cash and pledges before the dedication.[31]

Before the new church was built, the question of language arose. Many felt that switching to all English services would attract new people to the church. Finally, those who favored the change to the English language won out.[32]

On Thanksgiving Day, 1919, the church acquired a new Austin electric pipe organ. The bells from Fourth Street Church still peeled, but from their new home in the Franklin Avenue tower. The congregation in the Portsmouth church became the largest in the Central German Conference and by 1924 could boast of having 573 members.

Many groups flourished in the church. Boy Scout and Cub Scout troops were chartered in 1929 and a Drum and Bugle Corps organized. The ladies of the church first formed a "Mite Society" in 1867 which grew into the Woman's Foreign Missionary Society. A Home Missionary Society and then mission groups for children and young people, including the King's Heralds, Home

Franklin AvenueUMC began as a German M. E. church and recently merged with other Portsmouth, Ohio, churches to form Cornerstone United Methodist Church.

Guards, Little Light Bearers, the Queen Esthers, and the Standard Bearers soon appeared. The Ladies Aid, with eighty-five members, replaced many of these groups in 1933 and at present, the United Methodist Women carry on the torch of service. The Sunday school also thrived and in the 1920s more than one thousand belonged.

Portsmouth and the German Methodist Church were both affected by the 1937 flood. The Red Cross set up emergency headquarters in the church and provided meals for flood refugees. On Sunday, January 24 the nearly three thousand people seeking refuge consumed one hundred twenty gallons of soup. Food, clothing, cots, boots and medical equipment were stored in various rooms. The switchboard and a radio station were upstairs, as well as Red Cross meeting rooms. The sanctuary held those made homeless by the flood and was also a typhoid inoculation center. Both rescue workers and homeless found sanctuary in the church until February 18.

The two-week centennial celebration in 1944 began with a worship service on September 24 followed by services held nightly from October 1 to October 8 with guest ministers speaking. Bishop Francis J. McConnell preached the opening service and an organ concert and Sunday school program were also on the agenda.

Improvements were made to the kitchen and Christian education rooms in 1956. In 1959 a new parsonage was purchased on Franklin Boulevard to replace the one on Baird Avenue. A complete remodeling of the sanctuary was finished in 1975. In the years between 1985 and 1994 many more changes or

Cornerstone UMC in downtown Portsmouth, Ohio.

improvements were made including the purchase of a church bus, the installation of an elevator, air-conditioning, new parking lot, front steps and hand rail, security system, new lighting, painting, and a computer system.

The church has founded or contributed to many mission activities including "Loaves and Fishes," a meal program participated in by many of the area churches. The church has also been involved in helping a local food pantry, a senior nutrition program, the Battered Women Task Force, the Pastoral Counseling Center, Meals on Wheels, and others. Children's ministries are important and one such program was Alleluia, a Christian education program meeting each Tuesday which featured worship, Bible study, and music. This group has assisted in the CROP Walk, "Wings of the Morning" and the Giving Tree. Youth at the church also participate in UMYF which has a toy sale for low income parents. Youth go to a nursing home once a month to do a worship service and also join other UMC churches in a Cluster Camp.

Music has always been a big part of the church with choirs for adults and youth, two children's choirs (the Rainbow Choir for preschool through first grade and the Alleluia Choir for second through fifth grade) and, also, a hand bell choir. A Children's Summer Music Workshop was founded at Franklin Avenue in 1972 and is still going strong, although it is now housed at another church. This program provides free instruction in instrumental and vocal music to the neighborhood children.

To quote Dr. Albert Marting (pastor from 1913 to 1920),

> God placed us on a hilltop—a church not to be hid. The Lower Fourth Street Church was a humble place, but men found God there. Up a little farther, men still found God. A step higher, and still men find God on the hilltop.[33]

On Easter Sunday, 2005, Franklin Avenue UMC left the hilltop to merge with Wesley, First and Findlay Street UMCs to become Cornerstone United Methodist Church at 808 Offnere Street, Portsmouth, Ohio. Five years of planning preceded the union of the churches and their move to the modern new facility which takes up an entire block near downtown Portsmouth. The former German Methodist church contributed its long tradition of community involvement and outreach to the merger. As the four churches became one, a lot of excitement and energy was generated as new programs and ideas blended with old traditions.

In the early years of the Portsmouth German M. E. church, several other churches in nearby towns were associated with it. I named these before at the beginning of the Portsmouth article and I wish I could tell you more about them. The Waverly church was by itself when the Central German Conference was founded and later was on the Chillicothe Circuit. For more information, see Chillicothe. The West Union (also referred to as Westheim) was actually located in Oak Grove north of West Union. I will deal with it and others on the West Union Circuit at the end of this section. Another church associated with Portsmouth, at times, was Zion in Slocum. It was paired with Portsmouth until 1884 and then put on the Ironton charge. Again in 1905, it was joined with Portsmouth for about two years. For more about Zion, look under Ironton. I have been unable to find any information on Piketon, Beaver, and Maysville. I am guessing they were very small and might have not lasted to the time when the Central German Conference came into being.

On his 1903 collection tour, Grandpa Rudin made a stop at Portsmouth. This was when the church was still at Fourth and Washington streets.

Saturday October 31

> Took the 10:20 train of the Short Line and arrived at Columbus at 2:00 almost starved. I had forgotten the fine lunch Till had put up for which I felt like kicking myself. Had a very unsatisfactory dinner at Columbus

for which I paid a quarter. Left at 4:10 on the Norfolk Western Railroad, after having had some supper. Had to pay the full fare $3—this road not being in the Central Passenger Association. Arrived at Portsmouth at 7:45. Bro. Werner and his young daughter were awaiting me.

Sunday November 1

Bro. Werner's family consists of himself, his wife and three children. He believes in being on time, for we got to Sunday School some time before it began. He made me acquainted with a number of people. Taught a boys' class whose teacher was absent, and addressed the school in English. This church is more English than German. Preached to a large audience my "Hewn Cisterns" sermon. Took a walk with Bro. Werner this afternoon. He took me to the church to show me their fine organ and then to the banks of the Ohio. Addressed the Epworth League this evening and preached to a large audience.

Monday November 2

My audience last night was mostly composed of young people. Preached in English and felt no embarrassment. The only thing that worried me was the prayer, but I got through that much better than I expected. The young people here are well behaved and intelligent. . . . Thus far I have received $49 in cash and subscriptions. Made several calls with Bro. Werner. Visited sister Locher who lives in darktown. She is sandwiched in between darkies, but she says they are good neighbors.

Tuesday November 3

Nice weather, no doubt Republican weather. Bro. W. is a Republican and Portsmouth also belongs to the GOP. I notice the town has plenty of saloons and lots of loafers standing in front of them. We called on someone yesterday who is a Prohibitionist and he is the first Proh. I have seen since leaving New Rochelle. He was quite a curiosity to me. Visited Mrs. Jahraus . . . the widow of one of our former ministers. She and her invalid daughter live in the old church, in the same rooms where Till was born when Pa was . . . at Portsmouth. By the way, Pa built the new church at P.

Wednesday November 4

I enjoyed my stay at Werners. Mrs. W. is quite sociable and does lots of visiting. Bro. W. is methodical in his work and has a very businesslike study.[34]

In 1920 Grandpa paid another visit to Portsmouth, this time for the annual conference. This took place during the church's Diamond Jubilee and was at the Franklin Avenue church.

Monday September 6

This morning I got up at 2:30 and at 3:00 Alfred Wellemeyer and I left Holland for Portsmouth. At Cincinnati we met Bro. Lamy and his son

John who also expects to join the Conference on probation. Arrived at Portsmouth a little after 10 PM. Was glad to get to bed at nearly 12.

Tuesday September 7

Had a good night's rest. Got to the church in good time, but the candidates for examination were very slow to arrive, some not showing up at all. Bro. Rogatzky was pretty much put out. . . . Was through with my work at 12. Albert Marting's church is a fine church indeed. It has a social hall, kitchen, basketball room, baptistery, Sunday School classrooms, etc. A Bro. Bremer showed me around. We had dinner in the church. This afternoon Dr. Enderis, Herman Rogatzky, Charlie Miller, Paul Philipp and I went to see a ball game between the St. Louis National League team and The "All Stars" of Portsmouth. The League team won 6 to 1. This evening Bro. Brueckner preached on "The Conversion of the Ministry and the Ministry of Conversion."

Wednesday September 8

Bro. Borneman made the opening prayer last night and I prayed at the close. The regular business session of the Conference began this morning with Bishop Henderson in the chair. After the Lord's Supper, a Memorial service was held. This afternoon there was a meeting of the Preachers' Aid Society. The funds of our society are growing. . . . There is talk of many changes, but that is the talk at every Conference. This evening the Portsmouth church celebrated its diamond jubilee.

Thursday September 9

Last night Bro. Werner . . . presided, and Bro. Schruff preached the sermon. Bro. S. spoke mostly of the "Pioneer Days" of the old church, and was quite amusing at times. Yesterday morning the Bishop gave us a long talk on "The Church of the Messiah," and this morning he spoke on the "Church of Pentecost." This afternoon Bro. Maag and I took a walk to town, which is quite a distance. . . . Got back in time to take in part of the Combined Anniversaries of the Women's Home and Foreign Missionary Societies. Mrs. Brueckner presided. She seems to feel as much at home on the platform as does her husband. This evening Rev. W. E. Bancroft, missionary in India, was the principal speaker.

Friday September 10

The mayor of Portsmouth was introduced and made a few remarks. Jake Hauswald and Will Schwaninger are here. Bro. H. told me they want a change in New Albany.

Saturday September 11

Last night the Diamond Jubilee of Baldwin-Wallace College was celebrated. Bishop Henderson spoke and Dr. A. B. Storms gave an illustrated lecture on the work of the college. Last evening Dr. Koch said he had me slated for Second Church in Cincinnati, and Bro. Dangel is to go to Holland. The Bishop is speeding up the . . . business, so he omitted his usual morning address. Alfred Wellemeyer and John Lamy were admitted on trial this morning. This afternoon I went to town to do some shopping and the Conference came . . . to a close at about 9 PM.

Sunday September 12

Went to Sunday School. The different classes were taught by visiting ministers. Bro. Brueckner taught the "Everyman's" class of of which Schaenzlin and I were members. They have a fine Sunday School orchestra but the pieces they played were of the theatrical kind. Albert Marting led the singing. There was frequent hand clapping and altogether little spirituality. Heard the Bishop preach. His text was: "Know ye not that ye are the temple of God?" Was surprised to see so many empty seats. Even a Bishop does not seem to pull in Portsmouth. Bro. Schaenzlin and I enjoyed a good chicken dinner at Griver's, her son-in-law also being a guest. This afternoon Otto Haueter and others were consecrated elders, and the Bishop made his usual appeal for life service volunteers.

Monday September 13

Bro. S. and I got up at 3 AM and left for the . . . station. A lot of ministers were waiting for their trains. Took the 4:10 for Cincinnati, arriving at 7:25. The Louisville train left at 8:15 and arrived at about noon. Alfred and I took dinner at a restaurant and then "killed" time. The first thing John and Rosmarie said when I entered the door was: "Are we going to move?" And when I answered yes they were overjoyed.

Tuesday September 14

The appointments were read at the close of the meeting Sunday. Many changes were made. I go to Second Church, Cincinnati, Dangel goes to Holland, Miller to Wheeling, Plueddeman to Huntingburg, Edelmaier to New Albany, Roesner to Fourth Street Evansville and Werner to Nashville. Bro. Phillip takes Lamy's place and Schruff goes to Marietta. I will have a salary of $1500. Our children are delighted about going to the city. This afternoon we began packing and hope to...leave by next Wednesday or Thursday.

Wednesday September 15

Schaenzlin and I had a good home during the Conference. Mrs. Griver has been a widow for many years and she and her youngest daughter live together. Miss Bertha is in the choir and has a very pleasing voice. Charlie Severinghaus is the new preacher of the Portsmouth church and Mrs. G. told us he will not have an easy time. Sold my horse and buggy to Bro. Dangel for $130 and am glad I'm rid of that worry.[35]

For more contemporary news of Cornerstone UMC, go to their website at www.cornerstoneofportsmouth.org.

West Union, Ohio, Circuit

West Union Circuit—Oak Grove German M. E. Church

The West Union (also called Westheim) German M. E. church which started out on the Portsmouth Circuit, organized in Tiffin township in 1843 and was called the Oak Grove German M. E. Church. The first pastor was Rev. John Baer. A log church was built in 1845, but by 1880 the congregation had dwindled to eight or ten members.[36] In the early 1880s, it was on a four-point circuit with Higginsport, Fairview, and Ripley, but after 1885 that circuit dropped to three churches which seems to point to the disbandment of Oak Grove.[37] There is a small graveyard on route 247 north of West Union which marks the site of the church.

West Union Circuit—Fairview German M. E. Church

In 1864, the Central German Conference listed four churches on the West Union Circuit. One closely related to the Oakgrove church was the German M. E. church in Fairview in Liberty Township. I say closely related because some of the grave stones in the Oak Grove cemetery bore names that were also mentioned in conjunction with the Fairview Church. The church was built in 1853[38] and seems to have been dropped from conference records by 1895.[39] Not much is left of the town of Fairview except one or two houses and a frame church. I have not been able to find out if that church was originally the German one although the location on the map seems to be the same.

West Union Circuit—Liggett Chapel

Liggett Chapel, the German M. E. church of Ripley, Ohio, seems to have lasted until 1888. There was not much material on it and it appears to have been used or connected with several denominations. The Disciples' Church apparently used Liggett Chapel about 1864 and then found they couldn't afford the rent which ended their meetings.[40] Another source claimed that an African American group used the Chapel located at, what is now, 122 North Second Street from 1852 to 1888.[41] There is a deed on file at the Recorder's Office in Georgetown that shows that the building was owned by the trustees of the German Methodist Episcopal Church of Ripley, Ohio until 1889. On August 12, 1889, it was sold to Elmer E. Galbreath for seven hundred dollars.[42]

West Union Circuit—Wesley Chapel

The fourth church on the circuit (organized in 1856) was Wesley Chapel at Higginsport, Ohio. It grew out of a Methodist Episcopal class that started meeting in 1839. In 1857 a frame building was erected measuring twenty-six-by-thirty-eight feet costing nine hundred dollars including the purchase of the lot.[43] The German M. E. Church, which was later used as a store, occupied the corner opposite the Christian Church.[44] According to a deed in the Recorder's Office the property was sold to A. L. Hite on September 3, 1913. The property was described as "Being the 38 feet from and by 82-1/2 feet deep off of the west portion of the south one half of In-lot no. 73 in the incorporated village of Higginsport, Brown County" Mr. Hite paid $207.50 for the old church.[45] Wesley Chapel ceased being listed by the Central German Conference records after 1895. At that time there were only two churches on the circuit which had a total membership of thirty-four.[46]

NOTES

1. James B. Casari, et al., *Chillicothe, Ohio 1796–1996: Ohio's First Capital* (Jackson, Ohio: Ross County Historical Society, printed by Jackson Publishing Co., 1995) D6.

2. *History of Ross and Highland Counties Ohio* (Cleveland: Williams Bros. Publishers, n.d.), 179.

3. "Greenfield Methodist is a Pillar of Community," *Times-Gazette* Greenfield Bicentennial Edition, Greenfield, Ohio, July 14, 1999.

4. C. O. Langebrake, ed., *Chronology of Events in the History of Grace United Methodist Church*, (church history) Waverly, Ohio, 1988.

5. *Minutes of the Annual Conferences*, 1901, 421.

6. Rudin, Diaries, 1903.

7. Golder, Horst, and Schaal, *Geschichte*, 338.

8. Ruth Wisenberger, "A Brief History of Immanuel United Methodist Church formerly known as German Methodist Episcopal Church," in *The History of Immanuel United Methodist Church*, Ironton, Ohio 1997.

9. Donna Segal, "Church's recipe for delicious doughnuts no longer secret," *Indianapolis Star*, January 9, 1985.

10. *History of Lower Scioto Valley* (Chicago: Inter State Publishing Company, 1884), 319.

11. *Minutes of the Annual Conferences*, 1905, 405.

12. June Stinth, "Wheelersburg United Methodist Church," in *A History of Scioto County, Ohio*, (Dallas, Tex.: Portsmouth Area Recognition Society, Taylor Publishing Company, 1986), 145.

13. Nelson W. Evans, *A History of Scioto County, Ohio* (Portsmouth, Ohio: Nelson W. Evans, 1903), 393.

14. Rudin, Diaries, 1903.

15. *Minutes of the Annual Conferences*, 1903, 374.

16. Ibid., 1879; 1885, 368; 1889, 428; and 1906, 657.

17. Golder, Horst, and Schaal, *Geschichte*, 344.

18. Meigs County Historical Society, *Meigs County, Ohio* (Paoli, Pa.: Taylor Publishing Co., 1979).

19. Rev. Nobel Rompel, "Historical Highlights of the Former Churches," *Greetings*, Pomeroy, Ohio, 1943 (Spring Issue).

20. Maye Crary Mora, "Meigs County's Early Religious Heritage," paper presented to Meigs County Pioneer and Historical Society by Return Jonathan Meigs Chapter, Daughters of the American Revolution (Meigs, Co, Ohio: 1976).

21. Rompel, "Historical Highlights of the Former Churches."

22. Mora, "Meigs County's Early Religious Heritage."

23. www.ohio.hometownlocator.com (Meigs County)

24. Meigs County Historical Society, *Meigs County, Ohio*, 30.

25. "Meigs County Ohio," *Hardesty's Historical and Geographical Encyclopedia* (Toledo: H. H. Hardesty & Co. Publishers, 1883), 290.

26. Rudin, Diaries, 1904.

27. *Franklin Avenue United Methodist Church*, 150th anniversary booklet, Portsmouth, Ohio 1994, 2–3.

28. Eugene B. Willard, ed., *Standard History of Hanging Rock Iron Region of Ohio* (Chicago: The Lewis Publishing Company, 1916), 197.

29. *Franklin Avenue United Methodist Church*, 3.
30. Willard, *Standard History*, 197.
31. *Franklin Avenue United Methodist Church*, 5.
32. Willard, *Standard History*, 198.
33. *Franklin Avenue United Methodist Church*, 7–13.
34. Rudin, Diaries, 1903.
35. Ibid., 1920.
36. *Caldwell's Illustrated Historical Atlas* (Newark, Ohio: J. A. Caldwell, 1797–1880), 37.
37. *Minutes of the Annual Conferences*, 1885, 368; and 1886, 385.
38. *A History of Adams County, Ohio* (West Union, Ohio: E. B. Stivers, 1900), 435.
39. *Minutes of the Annual Conferences*, 1895, 288–89.
40. *History of Brown County*, (Chicago: W. H. Beers & Co., 1883), 421.
41. Richard Zachman, *Historic Homes of Ripley*, Ripley, Ohio, 1976.
42. Recorder's Office, Georgetown, Brown County, Ohio, handwritten deed (no number) for Ripley German M.E. Church.
43. *History of Brown County*, 466.
44. Carl N. Thompson, comp., *Historical Collections of Brown County, Ohio* (Piqua, Ohio: Hammer Graphics, Inc., 1969), 141.
45. Recorder's Office, Georgetown, deed #12681 (for Higginsport German M.E. Church).
46. *Minutes of the Annual Conferences*, 1895, 445; and 1896, 471–72.

PART II

The German Methodist Episcopal Churches in the Louisville District

Like the Cincinnati District, the Louisville District also covered a large territory and included churches in southwestern Illinois and Tennessee. However, the majority of the churches under its jurisdiction were in southern and central Indiana.

CHAPTER 7

Churches in the Louisville Area

Louisville, Kentucky

German Methodism came to Louisville in the fall of 1840 when the Kentucky Conference sent Rev. Peter Schmucker to minister to the Germans there. He preached first in private homes, schoolhouses, and even market places. In the spring of 1841, a Presbyterian church on Hancock Street let him use their facility for his preaching and Sunday school. The first German M. E. church formally organized early that year and by late 1841 reported ninety-three members.[1]

There were four German Methodist congregations founded in the city of Louisville. The first, which was organized in 1841, was Market Street German Methodist, followed by Jefferson Street in 1848. Breckinridge Street Church started as a mission in 1868 and Eighteenth Street was the last to be established, in 1890.

Louisville—Market Street Church

Peter Schmucker preached in Louisville in 1840 and by 1841 had gathered 93 full members. His house of worship was a schoolhouse until the congregation built their first church on Clay Street between Market and Jefferson in 1842.[2] It was a one-story building (which cost $1,365.87) on a lot thirty-five-by-sixty-five feet long.[3] In 1859 the Market Street Church was enlarged and a second story added.[4] The congregation continued to grow, starting other missions in the city. Finally, it was necessary to build a new church for Market Street to accommodate the expanded congregation. The church fathers purchased a lot for $6,631 at Market and Hancock streets and constructed a "magnificent" two-story facility with a parsonage adjacent for the amount of $28,000. By 1882 the membership claimed three hundred.[5]

Several great revivals increased the membership of the church including one during the pastorate of Rev. Andrew Graessle which brought forty new members. Another revival during the tenure of Rev. John H. Horst converted eighty-four individuals.

Improvements were made including new furnaces, electricity, art glass windows, and a Pilcher Pipe Organ. In 1916 a social hall was built costing nine thousand dollars. In 1929, many donations enabled the church to perform other improvements, renovations, and work on the parsonage which totaled twenty-eight thousand dollars. Market Street hosted the annual conference for the sixth time in 1935 and did some more renovations, including a new furnace. Preparations and renovations at this time came to five thousand dollars. Membership in 1940 amounted to 462.

The Market Street Church was affected by the 1937 flood, as were many downtown buildings in towns along the Ohio River. The church was described as "down" along the river, but was sufficiently high enough not to be endangered by the flood waters. The social hall and parish house were havens for those forced from their homes. Mrs. Jacob Frank (the church social worker), Miss Pearl Weiler, and others gave comfort to those who sought refuge at the church.

At the founding of Market Street Church, all services were in German and this held true at the fiftieth anniversary, as well. At the seventy-fifth, everything was in English except for two hymns sung in German. As the years passed, the church gradually changed from ministering to the German population to extending their care to "all kinds of white folks with all kinds of backgrounds and antecedents."[6]

The Sunday school was one of the most important organizations of the church and in 1842 Charles Gabel served at the first superintendent. At that time there were 42 class members and 9 teachers. In 1940 the enrollment was 561 under the superintendency of Charles W. Hitt. Another early group was the Ladies Aid, founded in 1867. The primary purpose of this organization was parsonage upkeep and this was done with a monthly payment of dues at ten cents per person. Gradually, the group evolved into more of a social group which continued to support the pastor and the spiritual life of the church. The Woman's Foreign Missionary Society organized in 1886 and supported missionaries, schools and churches with dues and special contributions. Later, the Home Missionary Society was founded during the pastorate of Dr. Timothy Speckmann. This group ministered to foreigners and other peoples as well as schools and orphanages in this country. A separate Orphans' Society supported the Children's Home in Berea, Ohio. Epworth League made its appearance in 1890 and continued to serve the young people of the church until it was replaced by the Youth Division of the Board of Christian Education. All youth from age twelve to twenty-three were invited to participate. The men's group, Wesley Brotherhood, organized in 1897 and had 32 members at the time the constitution was adopted in 1898. The monthly meetings focused on business, literary, and social subjects. They sponsored the annual fish fry, a big yearly event. Market Street's Wesley Brotherhood was the third oldest to be founded in the United States.[7]

Market Street Church is no longer standing. That location was in the heart of downtown Louisville and, no doubt, the land became too valuable to use as a church.

Louisville—Jefferson Street German Methodist

The next church to appear on the scene was the Jefferson Street German Methodist. Rev. H. Henke founded it in 1848 with a nucleus of members from the Market Street Church. Their first meeting place was a warehouse at Market and Twelfth streets. In 1850 their church at Madison and Twelfth streets was consecrated. Later, in 1878, they sold this building to the "colored Presbyterians" and built a new church and parsonage at Seventeenth and Jefferson streets.[8]

The Jefferson Street Church also started a new church about seven miles from town in 1867. This church was out towards Jacob's Park and pastors of the Jefferson Street Church would preach there Sunday afternoons. After about forty years, work was abandoned at this site.[9] No amount of searching uncovered any more information on this church or its specific location.

The Jefferson Street church building at Seventeenth and Jefferson streets is still there, but now is the House of God Testament Temple.

Louisville—Breckinridge Street Church

Breckinridge church began as a mission from Market Street Church in 1868. A chapel was erected next to a parsonage at Breckinridge and Clay streets in 1871, all of which cost $3,860. Seventeen members of Market Street Church formed the nucleus for the new church which formally organized in 1874. The start was rather rocky, however, as the church work was discontinued in 1881 but then reorganized in 1887.[10]

During the heyday of Breckinridge, a new building was erected in 1891 for the cost of twelve thousand dollars. A decline came after that and many of the members returned to the Market Street Church and reduced the membership by half. However, there was still a parsonage built which cost two thousand dollars and the church claimed 100 members with the Sunday school totaling about 135.[11]

Later, Breckinridge was on a circuit with Eighteenth Street Church. When my grandfather, Theodore Rudin, became pastor at Eighteenth Street in 1925, he had a student minister to help him pastor Breckinridge. The church continued to struggle, however, so in July of 1927 at the quarterly conference, the sentiment was for disbanding. This was done several months later and the remaining members affiliated with other churches.[12]

Former Jefferson Street German ME of Louisville, Kentucky, now House of God.

Louisville—Eighteenth Street German M. E.

Very little information is given on this church in the *Geschichte* and none in *History of the Ohio Falls Cities*. . . . The latter was published before the church was founded in the 1890s. Eighteenth Street Church sprang from a series of prayer meetings and then became a mission under the guidance of H. Wulzen. The church was built at the corner of Eighteenth Street and Euclid Avenue, consecrated in 1891 and, soon after, a parsonage erected.[13]

Another source says that Breckinridge's pastor, Rev. J. J. Baechtold originated the prayer meetings which were so successful that a mission was started. The group rented a house and held Sunday school and services there. By 1912,

The Eighteenth Street German ME, aka Second Church, now Sweet Leaf Primitive Baptist Church.

Eighteenth Street Church claimed 70 members. A few years later, the Jefferson Street Church congregation merged with Eighteenth Street, bringing membership to 122.[14]

As mentioned previously, my grandfather, Theodore Rudin, was appointed pastor at Eighteenth Street in 1925. He served there until 1933 when the Central German Conference dissolved. He retired from the ministry at the same time. Since he kept voluminous diaries, I'll draw some additional history from his writings.

My grandparents arrived at their new post on Friday, September 18, 1925, and my grandfather wrote his impression of their new home.

> It is quite out of repairs and needs paint badly. However, we like the arrangement of the rooms and there is breathing space around the house and we can see the sky. There is also a nice garden with two peach trees, 1 plum tree, a grape arbor and grass and flowers. The house contains a really nice bathroom, a water heater and electric lighting. The Ladies Aid had the dining room papered and the parlor is also to receive new paper.

He reported that he had to appear in court to get his ministerial license which cost $1.50. At the quarterly conference, held on October 3, 1925, his salary was set at seventeen hundred dollars for the year. Eighteenth Street Church would raise twelve hundred; Breckinridge, eleven hundred; and four hundred dollars would be realized from the rent of the Breckinridge parsonage. (These figures don't add up to the salary of seventeen hundred dollars, but they are the figures in grandpa's diary. Probably some of it was for his assistant's salary and maybe for other expenses as well.) Grandfather had a young student assistant named Glen Wingerter. The first two months at the new appointment were spent calling on church members and getting to know them. Grandfather was favorably impressed.

During the second year of his tenure there, Breckinridge Church was disbanded. This presented a problem salarywise, but the Eighteenth Street Church board agreed to pay fourteen hundred dollars and the rest would be made up from City Mission funds. During that same year, on Sunday, November 6, 1927, the church basement caught fire. Fortunately, the firemen kept it confined to the basement except for one corner where it broke through to the main floor. It was thought that an overheated furnace was the culprit. The board decided to enlarge the basement when repairs were made. During repairs, Sunday school met in various homes and the preaching service was held in the primary department room of the church. The church had its formal reopening on December 18, 1927. Grandfather reported,

> There was a fine attendance in all the services. The choir and the male chorus rendered special music and I had Bro. Huber give a short talk on the renovation. After church most of the people went to the basement to see how it looked. All seemed to be pleased with the improvements. . . . This was a red letter day.

Improvements included the enlarging of the basement area, refinishing of benches, new furnace, new carpeting and rebinding of the pulpit hymnal.

The last annual conference of the Central German Conference was held in 1933 in Cincinnati. Grandfather had spent eight years at Eighteenth Street Church and, according to his diaries, they had been good years where he had been able to accomplish good things for the church with little strife. He had hoped to do one more year at Louisville, but he and two others were retired. He was assigned to Flint, Michigan, as "supply" (as they referred to it). His last Sunday was September 3, 1933, and he recorded, "Addressed the Sunday School and preached to a large congregation. Felt in good form, though at times my feelings nearly overcame me."[15]

Eighteenth Street Church (which grandpa always referred to as "Second Church"), continued serving the community for at least another quarter of a century. I remember visiting there with my mother in the 1950s. Now the building is Sweet Leaf Primitive Baptist Church.

New Albany, Indiana

The church at New Albany (which eventually was called Calvary) began in the 1840s. At that time, the German Methodist preachers John Kisling and John

*New Albany, Indiana, First German ME,
later an African Methodist Episcopal church.*

Hofer came to the area and held meetings. Soon, a Sunday school class was formed and, at the 1845 quarterly meeting at Charlestown, Indiana, Rev. Konrad Muth was assigned to New Albany. For a salary of $125 a year, Reverend Muth held services in homes and later in the engine house on Fourth Street. Mrs. Mary Coleman related that when she was a child, members got so enthusiastic in their worship that a section of the floor gave way![16]

The congregation erected a frame church, thirty-by-forty feet, in 1850 which cost $1,140.[17] A second, larger church was built on the same lot and was forty feet wide and seventy feet long. It was brick with high ceilings and "comfortable furnishings." This church is now being used by an African-American congregation, Bethel A. M. E. Church.

The third church was built in 1890 and caused quite a stir in New Albany with its tall spire and large auditorium. When the first service was held, the entire congregation met at the old church and marched in procession to the new one. Disaster struck in 1929, however, when a fire erupted in the building. Fortunately, most of the damage was confined to the steeple. Repairs were made but it was decided not to replace the steeple.[18] (My grandfather noted in his 1929 diary that damage was estimated to have been ten thousand dollars) Later, in 1937, Calvary survived the flood of that year but suffered seven thousand dollars worth of damage.[19]

In 1955 a Seventh Day Adventist church purchased the Calvary building and most of its inner furnishings were brought to Centenary Methodist. A room in Centenary was set aside as Calvary Chapel and all the old furnishings were erected there, so part of Calvary Church still lives on.[20] Centenary's website is www.centenary-na,org.

Jeffersonville, Indiana

Rev. Konrad Muth was the organizer of the Jeffersonville church, as well as the one in New Albany. Although founded in 1845, the first church building was not built until 1857. This first building was erected on Locust Street while Jeffersonville was still on a circuit with Charlestown and a church in Louisville. By the early 1870s the congregation had already outgrown the church and purchased a lot on Maple Street for twenty-five hundred dollars. A few years later the cornerstone for the new building was laid on September 1, 1877, and the dedication followed on July 14, 1878. Rev. Jacob Bockstahler supervised the building program which cost seven thousand dollars. Two years later, a parsonage was built on the same lot. The total value of the property was estimated at ten thousand dollars.[21]

The church eventually became more English than German and, after World War I, dropped the German language entirely. At some point, the name was also changed to Maple Street Methodist Church.[22] The church acquired a beautiful pipe organ in 1908.[23]

The 1937 flood hit Maple Street Church hard. The flood waters raised the floor in the sanctuary which then fell down into the basement. The dwindling congregation could not afford the extensive and expensive repairs. The conference suggested disbanding with the congregation seeking new church homes elsewhere in the city. Many people joined with Wall Street M. E. The Seventh Day Adventists eventually renovated the Maple Street building and it is now their home.[24] The website for Wall Street UMC is www.gbgm-umc.org/wall-stumc/.

On the 1904 collection tour, Grandpa visited both the New Albany church and the one in Jeffersonville. Following are his remarks about the churches.

> Saturday April 9
>
> Left Sandusky at six this morning. At Springfield, where there was a lynching a short time ago, I lunched. Saw the ruins of buildings . . . burned by the mob. Had just time to make the train for New Albany. Evidences of floods were everywhere apparent along the railroad and in many places the land was still under water. Vegetation is farther advanced down this way than it is at Sandusky. Some trees are already in blossom. Arrived at New Albany on time and was taken in tow by B. Miller. Had a good supper and warm welcome at the parsonage.
>
> Sunday April 10

*Jeffersonville, Indiana, Maple Street German ME,
now a Seventh Day Adventist church*

Taught a class of intelligent middle-aged ladies and enjoyed it. Bro. M. has a truly fine Sunday School but it is conducted entirely in English, excepting the reading of the secretary's report. Preached to a large audience. My topic was: "Peace like a river and righteousness as the waves of the sea." Got acquainted with quite a number of people, some of whom knew Till [Grandma—her father pastored there when she was a girl] and wished me to extend their greetings to her.

Monday April 11

The Jeffersonville church appears to be larger than the one at New Albany but it is in bad repair. The N. A. church is fine. It is in good condition, has a fine new organ and many large and small beautiful stained glass windows. Bro. M.'s appointment is to all appearances a desirable one. The people are nearly all well-to-do and educated and loyal to their church.[25]

Charlestown Circuit

German M. E. churches were also located at Charlestown and Otisco.

Charlestown Circuit—Charlestown

The German church at Charlestown was built about 1835 from materials of an older church which had been on the site. The Charlestown church seems to have died out early on, before the twentieth century.

Charlestown Circuit—Otisco German Church

Otisco seems to be the same church as the one located at Helzer's Settlement (also known as Holzer, Helser, and Hoelzer). In the *History of the Ohio Falls Cities* it is described as a log house, twenty-by-forty feet, built in 1858. A Rev. John Helser was the guiding light of this church.[26] A personal letter from a woman who lives in the area, dates the log church as starting in 1847 or 1849.[27] The *Geschichte* says that Johannes Holzer and his family and "others in the neighborhood" built a brick church which at the time of the writing of the *Geschichte* was sixty years old. It also stated that it was the only church in the area still using the German language.

Emmanuel UMC, formerly a German ME church near Otisco, Indiana.

The Otisco church had been served from the Charlestown Circuit, the Bradford Circuit and in 1895 was paired with Eighteenth Street Church in Louisville. In 1906 Otisco joined the circuit with Jeffersonville.[28]

In 1910 the church left the Central German Conference to join the Indiana Conference. The new charge became the Otisco Charge and consisted of the Otisco church, New Bethel, and Pleasant Ridge.[29] At some point the former German church took the name Emmanuel.

The church, which is still being used today, is called Emmanuel United Methodist Church and is located in Oregon Township of Clark County, Indiana, on Old State Road 3. There is a sizable cemetery next to it.

Notes

1. L. A. Williams & Co. *History of the Ohio Falls Cities and their Counties*, vol. 1, (Cleveland: L.A. Williams & Co., 1882), 48.
2. Golder, Horst, and Schaal, *Geschichte*, 358.
3. "Historical Sketch," Souvenir and Program *The Centennial Celebration Market Street Methodist Church*, 1940, folder 27, box 2–57, Nippert Collection, Cincinnati Historical Society Library Archives, Ohio (hereafter cited as "Historical Sketch," Nippert Collection).
4. Golder, Horst, and Schaal, *Geschichte*, 358.
5. Williams, *History of the Ohio Falls Cities*, 45–46.
6. "Historical Sketch," Nippert Collection
7. Ibid.
8. Golder, Horst, and Schaal, *Geschichte*, 361.
9. "The History of German Methodism in Louisville and Vicinity" (typed history, author unknown) folder 25, box 2–57, Nippert Collection, Cincinnati Historical Society Library Archives, Ohio (hereafter cited as "History of German Methodism," Nippert Collection).
10. Golder, Horst, and Schaal, *Geschichte*, 360.
11. "History of German Methodism," Nippert Collection.
12. Rudin, Diaries, 1925–27.
13. Golder, Horst, and Schaal, *Geschichte*, 360–61.
14. "History of German Methodism," Nippert Collection.
15. "Calvary Methodist Church Centennial to be Celebrated in New Albany Sunday," March 8, 1945, Calvary Methodist file, Churches, New Albany Public Library, New Albany, Indiana.
16. "History of German Methodism," Nippert Collection.
17. "Calvary Methodist Church Centennial."
18. "Fire, Flood and Time Defied by 100-Year-Old Calvary," *Times*, Calvary Methodist file, Churches, New Albany Public Library, New Albany, Indiana.
19. *Centenary*, Centenary United Methodist Church, New Albany, Indiana, www.centenary-na.org.
20. "History of German Methodism," Nippert Collection.
21. Margaret Sweeney, *Faction, Fiction and Folklore of Southern Indiana* (New York: Vantage Press 1967), 154.
22. Lewis C. Baird, *Baird's 1909 History of Clark County, Indiana* (Indianapolis: B. F. Bowen & Company 1909), 258.
23. *Wall Street United Methodist Church*, 190th anniversary publication (Jeffersonville, Ind.: c.1997), 9.
24. Rudin, Diaries, 1924.
25. Williams, *History of the Ohio Falls Cities*, 372.
26. Sharon O'Bryan to author, 2003.
27. Golder, Horst, and Schaal, *Geschichte*, 361.
28. O'Bryan to author, 2003.

CHAPTER 8

Churches in the Seymour Area and Areas South

Seymour, Indiana, Circuit

Many small congregations in the area owed their start to the camp meetings sponsored by the German Methodists. These were usually held in midsummer in a grove near the Baumgart schoolhouse on County Road 500E southwest of Seymour. People from as far away as Cincinnati and Louisville attended these meetings.[1]

The Seymour Circuit in its prime contained fifteen preaching sites. Some lasted only a short time, while others were joined to other circuits. From 1874 to 1908 the circuit was composed of three churches (St. Paul's, St. Peter's and Trinity).[2] Seymour Trinity Church is the only one still active.

Seymour Circuit—St. Peter's (Ackeret Chapel)

Rev. John Kisling began preaching at Rockford in 1840 and formed a congregation from a group of men "living on the river bank." It is unclear whether or not they actually erected a church building at Rockford. Soon after, another congregation organized near Reddington.[3]

Conrad Ackeret, a Swiss immigrant, was instrumental in founding the church at Reddington. He and his wife provided an acre of land and also furnished the logs for it. The church was completed in 1860 and named St. Peter's. Until 1896, the language of choice in the church service was German. Then both English and German were used until 1905 when German was dropped altogether. The church was remodeled in 1905 and in the middle of the next decade left the Central German Conference to join the Indiana Conference. At that point the church took the name of Ackeret's Chapel. The church was still active in 1960 when it celebrated its one hundredth anniversary.[4] At this writing, the building is still standing but no longer in use as a church. There is evi-

*St. Peter's German ME, aka Ackeret Chapel, near Reddington, Indiana.
This building is no longer in use.*

dence of remodeling in progress on the exterior, so perhaps it is being retooled as a residence.

Seymour Circuit—St. John's German M. E.

German settlers first arrived in Jackson County before 1838. They soon desired a place of worship and founded the first one at the village of Sauers where St. John's Lutheran Church is now located about five miles southwest of Seymour. At first the congregation was multidenominational but after about ten years it became more Lutheran with the arrival of the first permanent pastor, Rev. George Sauer.

Not long after, Methodist preaching began about two and a half miles north of the Lutheran St. John's. The original church was a log building which was replaced by a frame one in 1856. At that time, it was named St. John's Methodist Church. A campground was also located on the church property.[5]

An interesting story is told about an incident at St. John's during the Civil War. During services one Sunday in July, a group of horsemen interrupted the proceedings to announce that Morgan's raiders were approaching. The horsemen were intent on pursuing the rebel band and driving them back across the Ohio River. They commandeered the worshipers' horses and resumed the chase. Once their object was accomplished they brought the borrowed horses back to the church and returned them to their rightful owners.[6]

St. John's was active until sometime in the 1870s. The church hosted many district meetings which required the families of the congregation to have overnight guests frequently. Members felt a more centrally located church was needed, so St. Paul's was built about two and a half miles closer to Seymour.[7] The people of St. John's eventually united with St. Paul's, though camp meetings were still held on the property of the old church. The St. John's building was moved to the St. Paul property about 1877.[8] The trustees of the church sold the land to Fred Vondielingen.[9]

Seymour Circuit—St. Paul's German M. E.

According to George Kasting's recollections, St. Paul's was built about 1850, four miles southwest of Seymour. This gentleman reports being the Sunday school superintendent at age sixteen and also serving as the janitor. He does not give dates but, it would seem that this was in the latter half of the nineteenth century. He commented that his janitor's position paid him $7.50 a year as opposed to the standard rate of fifteen dollars a year.[10]

Another source claims that the St. Paul Church was founded about 1870 in Jackson Township on 600E Road. The land was leased by the church from George Pfaffenberger. The frame building was set on a brick foundation near a beech grove which provided shade for the building and hitching posts for the horses. The building was in use from 1870 to 1910. The pastor was based at Seymour and preached at St. Paul's on Sunday afternoons, alternating with St. Peter's. Attendance at rural churches fell off and more people gravitated to the one in Seymour, when automobiles became more common.[11]

According to Mr. Kasting, the church building was last used about 1910 when a fire destroyed the Pfaffenberger home and they used the church as living quarters until their new house was built.[12] The building is no longer standing. According to Clifton Caddell, the only thing that marks its location are some bricks from the foundation. The beech grove is also gone.[13]

Seymour Circuit—Trinity German M. E.

In 1864 Louis Schneck organized a Sunday school in Seymour and three years later a church was built at the corner of Bruce and Poplar streets.[14] This church measured thirty-by-forty feet when built, but was remodeled in 1884. After the remodeling, which cost three thousand dollars, it could seat three hundred people.[15] In 1912 the country church of St. Paul's united with its sister city. No mention is made of when St. Peter's (Ackeret's Chapel) joined with the Seymour church. In 1918, the church took the name of Trinity.[16]

The first parsonage was located near St. John's and the campground about six miles southwest of Seymour and was used by the pastor who ministered to the entire circuit. I couldn't find any date for the construction of this first parsonage. It was sold in 1868 when a second one was built beside the church in Seymour at the corner of Bruce and Poplar streets. Another larger and more modern parsonage was built in 1908 at the same location.[17]

Trinity UMC, formerly First German ME, Seymour, Indiana.

Trinity suffered growing pains in the 1920s and a parcel of ground was given by Mrs. Louise Schneck Graessle for a new church to be built. The groundbreaking was May 24, 1922, the cornerstone was placed in August and the church dedicated on December 2, 1923.

In 1933, Trinity became a member of the Indiana Conference when the Central German Conference disbanded. In 1939, when the Methodist Protestant and Methodist Episcopal South denominations merged with the Methodist Episcopal church, Trinity dropped the "Episcopal" and became just Trinity Methodist. In 1969, the Evangelical Brethren churches joined the Methodist fold, and Trinity became Trinity United Methodist Church.

One unique feature of Trinity was a radio ministry which began in 1950. On Sundays the church service was broadcast over WJCD in the Seymour area. The program's time was from 11:00 a.m. to 11:30 a.m.[18]

Trinity Church is still going strong in Seymour at its location on Brown Street between Carter and South Chestnuts streets.

Seymour Circuit—Jennings County German M. E.

There was also a German Methodist Church in Jennings County which I assume was on the Seymour Circuit. There is not much available information about it. The church land was donated by George Wetzel and services began in 1870. Preaching there ceased around 1895 and the property was purchased by Frank Schwartz. The building was demolished in the 1940s.[19]

Both Grandpa and Grandma attended the annual conference held in Seymour in August 1927. At this time they were serving Eighteenth Street Church in Louisville (Grandpa usually refers to this as Second Church as the original

Second Church in Louisville was no longer in existence). Following are Grandpa's views of the Seymour Conference:

Wednesday August 24

It was raining when we arrived at Seymour last evening. Arrived at the church in time for the evening service. Dr. John Huber preached his semi-centennial sermon based on Rom. 1:16: "I am not ashamed, etc." and it was a truly wonderful sermon. Dr. Morlock presided and made his usual remarks. Bro. Moeller's "Words of Welcome" were quite witty. Bro. Knauf responded. Our hosts were in bed when we arrived. The Conference session was opened this morning by Bishop Charles Wesley Burns. After the Lord's Supper, the annual memorial service was held, Dr. Nast being the chairman. Bro. Bauman lost his brief case containing his report and other important papers. Drs. Morlock and Brickner read their reports.

Thursday August 25

Took a walk with Bro. Roesner after dinner. He told me that the Armory Ave. Church (Second Church in Cincinnati) would probably disband in a year. The Mutual Preachers' Aid Society met and later Dr. F. C. Eiselen, President of Garrett Biblical Institute, lectured on "The Supreme Need." Last night was "Institution Night" and Rev. G. F. Hausser, Prof. F. Schaub and Dr. A. B. Storms, were the speakers. Bro. Bauman's brief case was found so he could read his report this morning. Bishop Burns is a hustler, and he does not waste any time making unnecessary speeches. The WFMS meeting this afternoon was presided over by Mrs. Brickner.

Friday August 26

Last night was "Our Country's Night." A representative of the Board of Temperance, Prohibition and Public Morals was the speaker and F. W. Mueller gave an illustrated lecture on "Home Field Tasks." Before supper yesterday Till and I took a walk. Till is meeting a lot of friends and enjoys every minute here. Dr. Otto Melle, of Germany led devotions this morning. He gave a fine address on religious conditions in Germany. A. J. Bucher, F. W. Mueller and William Brickner were elected delegates to General Conference. Dr. Eiselen gave his last lecture this afternoon on "Ancient and Modern Prophets."

Saturday August 27

Till and I went to town . . . to buy a present for Helen-Elizabeth, the granddaughter of our hosts. This afternoon the Rotary Club of Seymour gave the preachers and their wives and the lay delegates an auto ride, after which the Conference session resumed and concluded at about 5:00. This evening the Conference Fellowship supper was held. F. W. Mueller was the toastmaster and enjoyed himself. Timothy Speckman and Dr. W. S. Bovard were the speakers.

Sunday August 28

The Seymour people gave a fine concert last night. The spacious church was packed. Mr. Don A. Bollinger is an accomplished organist and the organ with the chimes is a beautiful instrument. Till and I attended the Sunday School session. During the Sunday School hour the Veterans of the Cross held an old time love feast in the Trinity Men's Room. Bro. Oetgen had the meeting in charge. The Bishop preached a great sermon on Heb. 3:1, his topic being "Christ Jesus." He calls our present civilization machine-minded and motor-driven. This afternoon Theodore Grob was ordained. This evening the Bishop preached again and then read the appointments. Joe Schmidt and his mother were visitors . . . and took us home in their auto after church.

Tuesday August 30

Bishop Burns preached on Mark 14:5 Sunday night. There was "standing room only" and the Bishop was . . . feeling fine. He dwelt . . . on the words: "It might have been sold." He deprecated attaching a money value to religion. How much will religion cost me, and how much will I get out of it? The Bishop is a fine man, whole-souled, approachable, genial and not in the least "stuck up." He was old fashioned-like and spiritual, and he joined in all the singing like . . . us common ordinary people. And his voice could be heard, too. Am certainly glad that I do not have to move.

Wednesday August 31

The folks we stopped with at Conference were very nice. They own a grocery and are apparently well fixed. They did all they could to make it pleasant for us, and we felt very much at home. . . . Mr. Ireland said when we left Sunday night: "Don't forget, our house is always open to you whenever you come to Seymour."[20]

White Creek, Indiana, Circuit

Preaching was first held in this area in 1844 in people's homes until a group of seven families built a small log church in 1850.[21] At this time the church belonged to the Rockford Circuit, but later was joined to Seymour. More changes were wrought and the White Creek and Bedford Circuit formed in 1870 consisting of White Creek, Bedford, Salt Creek (Spraytown), Columbia, Vallonia, and St. John's. Later the circuit contained only White Creek and Spraytown.[22]

White Creek Circuit—White Creek Church

The congregation at White Creek soon outgrew the little log church and in

White Creek UMC at White Creek, Indiana, began as a German ME.

1872 a new frame building, forty-by-sixty feet was built. This had a tower with a bell and an "Amen" corner. The cost of sixteen thousand dollars was paid by the congregation which claimed 133 members by 1880.

In 1903 the church was ready for some remodeling. Not long after, in 1916, a fire caused by an exploding carbide light system, destroyed the building. Nothing was saved except the benches, pulpit, and the organ. The story is told that the pastor, Reverend Bockstahler, who was a large man, yanked the pews free and members, Walter and Alfred Behrman, threw them out the window. Reverend Bockstahler presided over the building of a new church which is still being used. This church, which was dedicated on December 3, 1916, cost forty-five hundred dollars and all the members helped with the construction.

During the rebuilding, church services were held in the parsonage which had been built in 1884 on two acres across from the church. The parsonage property consisted of a house with six rooms, a study, cellar, and back porch and included a small barn, a chicken house, and a wood shed. A pastor's salary was small, but they also had a cow, some chickens, a large garden, and fruit trees, as well as a horse and buggy. Members often presented gifts of food, wood, and feed for livestock.[23] (It is implied here that the cow, chickens, etc. came with the parsonage at no cost to the preacher. Maybe that was true at White Creek, but I know my grandfather had to buy his chickens and horse and buggy at his country charge of Holland, Indiana.)

In 1933 the church became part of the Indiana Conference. Since then, changes have included enlarging the basement in 1953 and installing a new furnace. A small storage building was erected for lawn mowers and other items. A new addition on the east side of the church was built in 1975–76 providing a large Sunday school room and two small ones plus a hall, restrooms, and a storage closet. The basement was again enlarged and another furnace installed.

The parsonage and some other buildings were destroyed by fire in 1963. This land was then made into a recreation area with a shelter house, concrete slabs for basketball and volleyball, and swings. At this time, the pastor, Ross Wallace, had his own house, so a new parsonage was not needed.[24]

The White Creek history booklet has some interesting financial data. Records prior to 1920 were apparently lost, but the pastor's salary in that year was $134 which included utilities and travel. The historian noted that today's (1984) budget was forty times larger than the one for 1920. In 1920 the most generous contributor gave thirty dollars for the year. In 1983, some of the members contributed that much each week.

The earliest Sunday school records were from 1914. Sunday school originally was held in German, but no mention is made of when the use of English superseded the German. A program was held on Christmas Eve in the early years, but more recently has been on the Sunday before Christmas. Another big event was the Sunday school picnic in August. It lasted from noon to evening and was similar to a fair with booths that sold food, drinks and handmade articles. Games and contests were held and in the evening a program was given with a flatbed wagon serving as a stage. The Sunday school also sponsored a Memorial Day supper. It was started as a "penny supper," each item of the cafeteria-style meal costing a specified number of pennies. It costs more today but is still a good time to visit with friends and visit the nearby cemetery.

The first Bible school was held in July of 1966. It was two weeks long and was held in the evenings from 6:30 to 8:00. By the 1980s the classes had been shortened to one week. The 1983 session was memorable as it was on the history of the Methodist Church and the students learned about all the Methodist founders and pioneers. On the Sunday after the session, the students held an old-time camp meeting with everyone dressing in old-fashioned clothes. A "pitch-in dinner" was enjoyed and then a "wax museum" featured where the youth portrayed some of the early Methodist pioneers.

The women of White Creek M. E. organized the Ladies Aid in 1930. The first meeting was held in Mrs. George Winkenhofer's home and, thereafter, meetings were held in other members' homes. The women quilted at the meetings and in the winter months held all-day meetings where they quilted and enjoyed a covered dish luncheon. Other activities were food sales, bazaars, serving at dinners and sales, and helping at the annual Sunday school picnic. Another women's group was the Foreign Missionary Society. In 1940, the Women's Society of Christian Service was formed which united all the women's organizations. This organization, as well as previous ones, was instrumental in helping with repair to the parsonage and the upkeep of the church building. Some projects included improving the church kitchen, purchasing song books and hymnals and sprucing up the Sunday school rooms. In 1968, there was another name change when the Methodist churches became United Methodist, the women's group became United Methodist Women.

The first youth organization activity recorded was in 1890 when the young people made a white quilt and charged church and community members ten cents each to have their names embroidered in red thread on it. The quilt was then auctioned for fifty dollars. Epworth League was formed in 1927 and met every two weeks in members' homes. A fairly consistent agenda was an opening prayer, singing at least three songs, a lesson, business meeting, and closing with the Epworth League Benediction. Dues were one dollar a year. Projects included ice cream socials, banquets, and pie suppers, among other events. The group helped the church by contributing four dollars toward janitorial services and money for a carpet in the church. This group also underwent a name change and became United Methodist Youth Fellowship. Activities were similar to the Epworth League but additional projects were undertaken such as retreats, car washes, sports activities, sponsoring Easter egg hunts, and sponsoring a Haitian child and a seminary student in Honduras. A Junior U.M.Y.F. for children from nine to thirteen was organized in 1976 (there had been one previously in the 1960s). The group engaged in other activities such as camping, roller skating, and swimming, as well as more serious pursuits such as learning the Beatitudes, memory verses, memorizing the names of the books of the Bible, and playing Bible baseball. They contributed to the church by doing monthly cleaning chores, preparing Easter treats for younger children and making a bulletin board, to name a few activities. A group of children called the Creek Bankers presented musicals for the church. They came by their name from their first musical which was called "Down by the Creek Bank" and presented for Mother's Day in 1983.

The White Creek history publication is one of the most thorough I've seen, especially for a small church (or maybe *because* it is a small church). The final section is devoted to stories and anecdotes members contributed. I'll include one of my favorites here.

> Rev. S—— was a small, very slender man. His wife was a heavy lady. Everybody traveled with a horse and buggy. The front wheels were smaller than the rear wheels. They [some young boys] put the large wheels on the side of the buggy where Rev. S. sat and the smaller wheels on the side his wife sat. This made it appear that his heavier wife made the buggy lean over to her side.

Grandfather Rudin went to White Creek for a district conference in 1929. The following is a description of the conference and his opinion:

> Monday April 22
>
> A little after 8 this morning Bro. Huber and his wife and I set out for White Creek . . . to attend the District Conference. We stopped at a relative of his a few miles from White Creek, a Mrs. Naffe and her son—

prosperous farmers. We had a fine chicken dinner and remained until after supper. Hubers will stop with Naffes til the close of the District Meeting. Bro. Schaefer preached a good sermon . . . on hope. He is pastor of the Nast Memorial Church in Cincinnati. After the sermon we celebrated the Lord's Supper. Bro. Winkenhofer, the pastor, made an amusing speech of welcome to which Dr. Morlock responded. Bro. Schaefer and I are guests of Bro. Frank H. Woehrman and his wife. We remained up quite late.

Tuesday April 23

I felt well rested this morning, but Bro. S. said that he had dreamed all night. We had a good farmer's breakfast consisting of ham and eggs and other things that farmers are accustomed to have on the table. The meeting had begun when we arrived at the church. Dr. Morlock managed to side-track the report of the District Missions, and I suppose he felt relieved when no one called for it. Carl Allinger again acted as secretary. After the business meeting my paper . . . followed. It was very well received, several of the brethren telling me how much they enjoyed it. Dr. Cramer was especially profuse in praise of my work. Bro. Schreiber followed. His topic was "The Pastor's Devotional Life." His work was well done. Yesterday afternoon we had two papers, one by Carl Allinger entitled "The Minimum Equipment for a Rural Church" and one by O. C. Haas, "The Program of a Rural Church." The first one was a rather poor piece of work. The second was somewhat better. A round table was conducted by Rev. C. A. Shake, pastor of the English M. E. church in Seymour. He talked to beat the band and said nothing. He made me tired.

Wednesday April 24

Last night Charlie Miller preached a really good sermon on "Lo, I am with you alway." Dr. Cramer spoke to us . . . on the proposed memorial for Dr. Riemenschneider. It is really remarkable what a poor speaker he is. This morning Bro. Roessner gave his paper on "Developing Worship Programs." It was . . . very good. . . . Bro. A. H. Mueller read a paper on "Church Music and Worship." It was an elaborate view of some of the hymns in our hymnal. In the afternoon, Bro. Albert Smith, a young man, tried to tell us something on "Is the World Changing?" The question was beyond him and his work sounded like a college essay. Dr. Enderis brought the last paper, "Fundamentals that Abide." In the evening Dr. J. A. Diekmann held forth. He was in good form and interesting.

Thursday April 25

This morning Bro. Woehrman took me to Naffes. We left Naffes . . . before 9 and got home before 12 . . . I greatly enjoyed the District Conference. There was the best of feeling among the Brethren. Our hosts were nice and excellent meals were served. The White Creek people have a pretty nice church. The Woehrmans were very nice and did all they could to make it pleasant for Bro. Schaefer and me. Bro. Winkenhofer, pastor of the White Creek church, is a local preacher, and he seems to be doing good work.[25]

White Creek UMC is at 6730 West 930 South, Columbus, Indiana, 47201.

White Creek Circuit—Bobtown

A church at Bobtown (southeast of White Creek, in Jackson County) was connected with White Creek for a while. A Sunday school was organized there in the early 1900s and met at the schoolhouse. A man came from North Vernon to supervise the Sunday school and brought a fold-up organ to provide the music. The source didn't say whether this was taught in German or English. In the afternoon, the White Creek pastor came by horse and buggy and preached. The Bobtown connection lasted until 1920 when it was given up.[26]

Spraytown Free Methodist near Spraytown, Indiana, had its origins in Salt Creek German ME.

White Creek Circuit—Spraytown

Spraytown was also referred to as Salt Creek and was paired with the White Creek Church. That circuit consisted of other meeting places at Bedford, Columbia, Vallonia, and St. John's, as well.[27] The earliest recorded date for the Spraytown church was 1862. The congregation built a frame church in 1900 which was located "in the northwest corner (or side) of S.R. 58, where the highway makes a sharp turn from east to north, and diagonally across from county roads 950N and 175W junction."[28] Many English-speaking people soon joined, but the German church did not preach the doctrine of Sanctification which bothered some people. In 1917, a group broke away and started holding meetings in a tent. Soon, the Spraytown Free Methodist Church was officially organized in September 1917 and a new church dedicated in October 1930. Ina L. Cochran, an Evangelist from Lawrenceville, Illinois, was the first pastor.[29]

A map in the Spraytown church history shows the location of the German, as well as the Free Methodist Church, and notes that the German M. E. Church was razed in 1931.[30]

White Creek Circuit—Columbia and Vallonia

These were listed as being on the White Creek Circuit but no other information was found on them.[31] Possibly, the congregations met in each members' homes and were not large enough to support a church building.

Bedford, Indiana, Circuit

German Methodism came to Bedford in 1869 and in 1870 Bedford joined the Seymour Circuit.[32] In 1874 Bedford and White Creek combined as a circuit. Bedford remained on this circuit until 1889 when it and Washington, Indiana, were briefly paired. In 1891 Bedford was by itself and remained that way until 1912 when it was briefly paired with White Creek again. From 1916 to 1923 it was on its own again, but then was paired with Seymour for three years. By 1927 it no longer is listed with the Central German Conference.[33] The Bedford congregation was never very large—fluctuating between fifty and seventy-five members. The *Geschichte* describes it as "small but lively. Small, it would stoutly remain, the Germans are few here and many do not want to be German any more."[34]

A newspaper article reports that the Bedford Germans first met in a house at Eighteenth and E streets but later worshiped in a schoolhouse on G Street until 1891. At that time, a church building was erected on Eighteenth between G and H streets. In 1918 the German language services were joined with services in English. By 1922 the use of German was dropped altogether. In 1928, the church switched from the Central German Conference to the Indiana Conference and a year later took the name of Grace Methodist Episcopal.

In 1951 there was a need for a new church so a building fund was started. Four years later, Miss Marguerite Reath presented a lot to the church and a new building was erected. A parsonage was built in 1894 and was enlarged in 1929. In the 1960s, the church purchased more land from Miss Reath and planned to build an addition on the building.[35]

The address of Grace UMC is 1730 H Street, Bedford, IN, 47421.

Grace UMC in Bedford, Indiana, began life as the German Methodist Episcopal Church until the name change in 1929.

Bradford, Indiana, Circuit

The area around Central Barren and Bradford was first served from Charlestown. The German Methodist preaching began in 1845 and soon a church was built which was later replaced by a larger one in 1857. At this time, the area was served from New Albany but in 1863 the Bradford Circuit was organized and included the main church at Bradford and, later, ones at New Salisbury and Pultight.[36]

Another source says that a church was first organized at Central Barren in 1851 and was known as the Zoar congregation. Another congregation at Fishers Settlement was the Emmanuel Congregation. Near New Albany a congregation known as the "Knobs" was organized. Lastly, the Zion Congregation was formed southeast of Corydon in 1849 in an area called the "Sinks." This mission was referred to as the "Barrens" because of the lack of trees growing in the area. In 1863, the Bradford Circuit included churches at Middletown (probably the Sinks], Charlestown, Nobs (the Knobs), and Helzer Settlement (see Otisco).[37]

Bradford Circuit—Central Barren German M. E. (Zoar)

The Zoar congregation's first home was a log building which may also have been a school. In 1856 Paul Biegler (Beuchler) deeded land to the trustees of the M. E. church and a frame building was constructed. Several land transfers are cited, but it is unclear whether other church buildings were built on these sites. Some of the land was used as a cemetery.

Present-day Central Barren UMC began as a German ME church.

Services were held in German until 1909 when the congregation decided to have one service a month in English. Over the next two decades the English services were increased until only one per month was in German. Many people who had belonged to former German-speaking churches enjoyed coming for the German services. Finally, in 1924, the switch to English was finalized when Zoar moved from the Central German Conference to the South Indiana Conference.

In 1892 a new church building was built at the crossroads in Central Barren and the church at the cemetery was abandoned. It was later torn down and a smaller building constructed for cemetery use. A fourth church was built in 1974 with the first service held in December 1974.[38]

A parsonage was built in 1875 until a modern one of Bedford limestone took its place in 1949. The new parsonage cost seventeen thousand dollars and was dedicated in October 1950 during the ministry of Rev. Robert W. Rogers.

The Zoar Sunday School was formed in April 1873 with sixty-seven charter members. The first year, German Bibles and primers for the children were used for study. The next year a quarterly publication called the *Bibleforscher* was used. The Sunday school collection for that first year amounted to $27.24 with expenses of $6.00. A hundred years later, the Sunday school consisted of ten classes and helped support a pastor in India.

In 1874 a singing society was formed "to promote better individual singing." A German brass band, which was very successful and won a number of prizes at various celebrations, evolved from this society. At one time, Zoar sent a decorated float, which was constructed on the chassis of a farm wagon and drawn by six horses, to a local celebration. Singers and children rode the float while a blue and white banner proclaiming "Zoar Sunday School" was carried in front. The "Queen" was a young woman who carried the banner at the head of the parade. Two boys held silk ribbon streamers which flowed from the banner. The German band and singers followed the float. A German star cornet band was revived in 1900 and many members were sons of the previous band's members. A church orchestra functioned for a time in 1927. The church acquired an electric organ in the 1950s.

The Ladies' Aid at Zoar was organized in 1921 and made it their purpose to take care of the parsonage and help the church. In 1940, when the group became the Woman's Society of Christian Service, they added the goals of helping to support Christian work around the world and "to develop the spiritual life and to study the needs of the world." At the end of May 1951, the group sent $786 to the conference for missionary work and contributed $115 to the local church.[39]

You will find Central Barren UMC at 11170 Highway 135 Northeast, New Salisbury, IN 47161.

Bradford Circuit—New Salisbury (St. Stephens)

In March 1873 the south half of lot 14 in New Salisbury plus the NE quarter of Section 29, Township 2, Range 4 was deeded to representatives of the Methodist Episcopal Church. The land was to be used as a "place of Divine Worship." This land, purchased from St. Stephen's Evangelical Lutheran Church, cost the Methodists $350.[40]

Bradford Circuit—Zion ("the Sinks," Detricks M. E.)

This congregation, near New Middleton southeast of Corydon, was organized in 1849 as Zion.[41] In 1852 a half acre of land from the northwest corner of the northwest quarter of Section 12, Township 4, Range 4 was purchased by the trustees in order to build their church. This parcel of land is next to the New Middletown and Lanesville Road in Webster Township. There is little known about the church itself except that it was German and actually stood just over the township line in Franklin Township. The congregation was reportedly not very strong and eventually its people joined other churches. The building was torn down and all that exists today is the cemetery. There is a discrepancy over the exact location as another source says it was in northeast Webster Township rather than northwest.[43]

Bradford Circuit—Emmanuel (Fishers Settlement, Pultight)

The Emmanuel (also, Emanuel in some sources) church was also known as the Fishers Settlement congregation and later as Pultight. It is mentioned as being part of the Bradford Circuit in 1851 but no mention is made of when it was actually founded.[44] The church was active as a United Methodist Church until fairly recently and the cemetery adjacent to it is still being used. The building is still standing and is located in Clark County, Wood Township, west of Borden on the Washington County line.[45] Pultight was the name of the nearest post

Another Emmanuel UMC, now closed, in Clark County, Indiana, near the settlement of Pultight.

office and was so called because when travel was by horse, their harnesses were "pulled tight" in order to get through the muddy roads.[46]

NOTES

1. C. S. Mercer, "Death Claims Pioneer of Jackson Township" (obituary), Seymour, Indiana,1914. (copy of article sent to me with no source, date, etc.)
2. Golder, Horst, and Schaal, *Geschichte*, 368.
3. Loren W. Noblitt, *A History of Jackson County Churches, 1815–1997* (Brownstown, Indiana: Jackson County Historical Society, 1997), 173.
4. "Ackeret's Chapel Methodist Church Has Celebration for 100th Birthday," newspaper article from unknown newspaper (Seymour, Ind.: 1960).
5. Clifton E. Caddell, "German Speaking Settlers in Jackson County," unpublished typed article, (Jackson County, Indiana, n.d.), .2–3.
6. "Churches of Seventy Years Ago Lacked All the Modern Comforts," local newspaper article quoting resident Fred Nieman (Seymour, Ind.: 1922).
7. Mary Miller letter to Barbara Dixon, 2003.
8. "Churches of Seventy years ago,"
9. Caddell, "German Speaking Settlers," 3.
10. George Kasting, notes, 1973, 1.
11. Caddell, "German Speaking Settlers," 4.
12. Kasting, notes, 1–2.
13. Caddell, "German Speaking Settlers," 4.
14. Loren Noblitt, *The Composite History of Jackson County, Indiana, 1816–1988* (Paducah, Ky.: Turner Publishing Company 1988).
15. Kasting, notes, 3.
16. Noblitt, *Composite History*
17. Kasting, notes, 2.
18. Noblitt, *Composite History*
19. Jennings County Historical Society, *Jennings County, Indiana 1816–1999* (Paducah, Ky.: Turner Publishing Co., 1999), 81.
20. Rudin, Diaries, 1927.
21. *White Creek United Methodist Church, 1846–1984*, church history (Columbus, Ind.: 1984), 6.
22. Golder, Horst, and Schaal, *Geschichte*, 369–70.
23. *White Creek*, 8–9
24. Ibid., 15–16.
25. Rudin, Diaries, 1929.
26. *White Creek*, 27, 31–33, 35–36, 37–44, 50–57, 68, 11.
27. Golder, Horst, and Schaal, *Geschichte*, 369.
28. *History of the Spraytown Free Methodist Church*, church history (Seymour, Ind.: Spraytown Free Methodist Church, 1983), 3.
29. Ibid., 3–6.
30. Ibid., 2
31. Golder, Horst, and Schaal, *Geschichte*, 369.
32. Ibid., 349.
33. *Minutes of the Annual Conferences*, 1927, 586.
34. Golder, Horst, and Schaal, *Geschichte*, 349.
35. "Grace Methodists Are Planning Expansion at their New Church," newspaper article, Bedford, Indiana, 1963, 1–2.
36. Golder, Horst and Schaal, *Geschichte*, 352.

37. *History of the Church*, history of the Central Barren UMC, Central Barren, Indiana, 1970s?.

38. *Central Barren, Zoar and St. Stephen*, (history of some of the churches of the Bradford Circuit, Indiana 1970s(?).

39. *History of the Church*.

40. "Zoar and St. Stephen Churches," (a history of the two churches).

41. Frances Quebbeman, *Celebrate 125 Years Central Barren United Methodist Church*, church anniversary booklet (Central Barren, Ind.: 1976).

42. Catherine Kelley Summers, *Harrison County, Indiana Churches* (Harrison County, Ind.: 1989), 149.

43. Frederick P. Griffin, *Harrison County, Indiana Cemeteries*, vol. 3, 1971, 1.

44. *History of the Church*.

45. Clark County Indiana Cemeteries, www.rootsweb.com/~incccpc/emmanuelcemwood, 2003.

46. Lois Mauk, e-mail to Barbara Dixon, loismauk@insightbb.com, 2003.

CHAPTER 9

Southwestern Indiana German Churches

Mt. Vernon, Indiana, Circuit

Mt. Vernon Circuit—St. Paul's

There are various discrepancies in the story of the founding and early history of the Mt. Vernon German M. E. Church. I'll present below what the various sources say ending with the research of the historian of the First United Methodist Church of Mt. Vernon. She cites her sources including deed books and page numbers.

The peripatetic Peter Schmucker started the German Methodist church at Mt. Vernon in 1843 At that time it was part of the Evansville Mission which included Evansville, Mt. Vernon, and Marrs Circuit.[1] Services were first held in private homes, but later were in a brick church built to serve all the denominations. In 1854 the German congregation bought the building of the English-speaking Methodists which was on Fourth Street between Walnut and Mulberry. The German congregation paid four hundred dollars for their new church.[2]

Another source says the church was founded in 1850 and built at Fourth and Locust streets.[3] At any rate, the church was named St. Paul's [not to be confused with St. Paul's on the nearby Marrs Circuit]. In 1883 the Mt. Vernon church became a station with only a country church joined to it. At that time, the pastor's annual salary was six hundred dollars.[4]

In a letter, Sue Goff, historian for Mt. Vernon's First United Methodist Church, quotes some facts and figures on the German church with sources to back her up.

> The former church [English Methodist Episcopal] was then sold to the German Methodist Church for $1,200.00. The copy of the deed—Book V at page 109—shows that only 1/2 of the property was sold to the Ger-

man Church, with the other 1/2 being sold to an individual. There has been no way to verify the buildings on each lot sold. I question if the church and parsonage was on the lot sold to the German Church, and the other lot was vacant. Or if the German church purchased only the church, and the small shed out back, and the parsonage was on the lot sold to the individual. However, at the same time, the German Church sold a home, located at 715 Walnut Street, to the Methodist Episcopal Church. I have no way of knowing how the German Church had been using this home. There is no mention of where they were holding their services. Perhaps in the Walnut Street home?[5]

Goff goes on to say that in 1889 the German Methodists built a new church and parsonage on the southeast corner of Fourth and Locust streets. With the disbanding of the Central German Conference in 1933, St. Paul's considered a merger with First Methodist Episcopal Church. During the winter of 1932–33, a fire which destroyed St. Paul's parsonage finalized the decision. After the merger, the St. Paul's building was used as a parish house for church gatherings and meetings. It was then sold to the Church of Christ in 1944.[6] At a later date the Church of Christ sold the old German M. E. property to Shell Oil which then tore down the building and erected a gas station.[7]

First UMC has a website at www.firstumcmv.com.

Mt. Vernon Circuit—Zoar German M. E.

Mt. Vernon's St. Paul's was paired with one other church after 1883. This was Zoar German Methodist Episcopal Church which was located in the country southwest of Mt. Vernon. This church dates back to the 1840s and has gone through several name changes since that time. At first there was a small church of unknown denomination called "The Community Church" or "Union Church." In the time of the formation of the Central German Conference, this church joined Mt. Vernon on a circuit.[8]

There seems to be some differences of opinion about the origins of the church. A newspaper article states that in 1875 a half acre of land belonging to Henry and Percilla Zenor and John and Mary Dunn was deeded to John Dunn, Jacob Hass, Hiram Woods, Charles Carson, and Charles Sussick for building a nondenominational church. This building came to be known as "the log church" and was located in Black Township in Posey County. The article goes on to say that after several years, the congregation decided it would be better to affiliate with a denomination and as the German Methodists were in the majority, German Methodism became the denomination. The church then joined the circuit of the the Mt. Vernon German M. E. Church and shared its pastor.[9]

In 1902 a new building was needed, so a church which was forty-by-thirty feet with fourteen-foot walls and an arched ceiling was built. A tower stood at the southeast corner and the building had a brick foundation and shingle roof. By December 1902, notes and donations were given by several members and everything was paid in full. The final cost amounted to $1,679.62. The church was dedicated on May 10, 1903, and named Zoar. Many special items were purchased for the church including a bell from Sears, Roebuck costing $40.50 and weighing 450 pounds, pews of yellow pine for $112.00, the pulpit for $12.00 and a pulpit Bible for $3.50. Lightening rods were installed in 1919 and a signboard in 1924.

During the life of the church, music was an important feature, so several organists served the church through the years. Zoar had a pedal organ, which was later destroyed in the 1937 flood. This was replaced by an electric organ donated by St. Paul's Church. Around 1927 Mrs. Carl Weiss started an orchestra which functioned for several years.

The use of the German language was discontinued by 1918. In 1928 Zoar church celebrated twenty-five years in the same building. After the 1933 dissolution of the Central German Conference, Mt. Vernon's St. Paul Church merged with First Methodist. Zoar then joined the Mt. Vernon Methodist Episcopal Parish making nine churches in this parish .

Zoar church was one of many churches affected by the flood of 1937. Several in that area were completely destroyed. Zoar suffered a great deal of damage including the loss of many furnishings and damage to plaster and paint from the six feet of water that invaded it.[10]

> Pews were hanging out the windows, the piano ruined. Bibles and Hymn books scattered everywhere, but with the help of everyone things were put back in order again.[11]

In the 1940s the church was connected to electricity. During that time Zoar underwent another name change from Methodist Episcopal to just Zoar Methodist when the M. E. Church South merged with the M. E. church. The Mt. Vernon Parish became two parishes namely, North Mt. Vernon Parish and South Mt. Vernon Parish of which Zoar was a part. The South parish had its parsonage next to the other church in the circuit, Black's Chapel.

The usual Methodist organizations were a part of Zoar. In 1902 a Sisters' Union was founded which later became the Ladies Aid. The Women's Society of Christian Service replaced the Ladies Aid in the 1940s. Epworth League and the Standard Bearers became the Methodist Youth Fellowship. This group served both churches in the parish. Vacation Bible school was started in 1945.

In 1951 a four-room educational unit was added to the church and oil burning stoves were installed for heating. In 1953, two outbuildings were erected. In the midfifties the church needed new pews so the intermediate Sunday school class started a pew fund by contributing spending money, selling glow candles, having food sales and taking up offerings for that purpose. Other classes followed suit and by 1960 enough money had accumulated so the pews could be ordered. The thirteen ten foot-long pews and three six-foot ones came to $1,361.60. At the same time the interior of the church was redecorated and all the old plastering and old flues were removed and the woodwork refinished. The men also installed new hardwood floors and the women helped with this and also provided food. In 1965 the WSCS paid for carpeting for the aisles and front of the church and for electric fans. Two new gas furnaces were added in 1966.

A Heritage Day Sunday was held on August 30, 1970, for Black's Chapel and Zoar UMC. Those from Black's Chapel were the guests at Zoar for a combined Sunday school and worship service. Both churches took part in a pageant held in the afternoon. The festivities started out in the German language in recognition of the origins of Zoar, and then switched to English. The heritage celebration attracted about three hundred people.[12]

In 1975 Zoar United Methodist Church combined with Faith UMC in Mt. Vernon. Faith was formerly Evangelical United Brethren. 13. As of this writing, it has been remodeled into a private home.

Grandfather Rudin visited both churches on the Mt. Vernon circuit when he was giving the Stereopticon lecture "Black Diamonds" in 1918.

Saturday May 25

We took the 4:00 car to Mt. Vernon and arrived at about 5:00. Bro. Edelmaier was waiting for us. After supper he took us around the country in his auto. Gave my lecture in the country church, also called Zoar.

Sunday May 26

Attended the Sunday School session in our Mt. Vernon church. The superintendent asked me to address the school, which I did. Preached to a fairly good house and felt in fine form. This afternoon we went out to Zoar, where I addressed the school and preached to a good crowd. After the service we went to some farmer's place where there was to be a farewell to a young man who is to go into the army. We were served strawberries, cake and popcorn. Was glad to get back to Mt. Vernon. Lectured this evening. There was a pretty good house, the English M. E. preacher also being present.[14]

Marrs, Indiana, Circuit

Marrs (or Mars) Circuit consisted of three country churches—St. John's at Caborn, St. Paul's, and St. Peter's. At first the latter two churches were part of the Mt. Vernon Circuit but when Mt. Vernon became a station, they formed a circuit of their own. The area (known as St. Philips) received Rev. John Strauch in 1845 as the first preacher of German Methodism.[15]

Another source says that the Indiana Conference formed the Evansville German Mission in 1842 appointing Peter Schmucker, Henry Koeneke, and Konrad Muth to preach the Gospel. These men founded a German M. E. Society in Posey County and held meetings in members' homes. After St. Peter's Church was built, it became a member of the Mt. Vernon Circuit along with St.

Three churches on the German Marrs Circuit west of Evansville, Indiana, are all still active. Pictured here is St. John's UMC.

Paul's and the Mt. Vernon church. In 1863 the Mt. Vernon church became independent and St. Peter's and St. Paul's became the Marrs Circuit. In 1887 when St. John's at Caborn was built, it too, joined the Marrs Circuit. The three churches remained together until 1906 when St. John's became a station.[16]

Marrs Circuit—St. John's

German Methodist meetings were held in the Caborn area as early as the 1850s, sometimes in homes and sometimes in the English M. E. church. Other times people walked the six or eight miles to St. Philip's to attend St. Peter's. St. John's church was built at Caborn in 1887 under the pastorship of Rev. Jacob Bockstahler.[17]

St. John's joined the Marrs Circuit soon after being built, making the circuit a three-point charge until 1906 when St. John's became a station. In 1930 St. John's and St. Peter's were again joined as a charge and remained together until 1939. At that time, St. John's once more separated from the charge and St. Peter's and St. Paul's became the circuit. In 1991 St. John's again joined with St. Peter's under the same pastor and St. Paul's was served from Evansville.[18]

The most striking thing you notice when approaching St. John's is the cross on the peak of the steeple. The cross is actually an anchor which seems a bit odd to see so far from any large body of water. I'm sure there must be a story behind this choice, but I've not found it yet.

Continuing with the particulars of St. John's—Charles Sanders erected the first building which was dedicated in the fall of 1887. The site of the building consisted of one and three-fifths acres purchased from Catherine Caborn for $240.00. Subscriptions of $1,008.75 were collected for the building of the church. A parsonage site was purchased in 1903 for the sum of $75.00. In 1906 when St. John's became a station, a new parsonage was built. In 1930, fire destroyed this parsonage and another was built that summer. Part of the land for the cemetery (five and one-tenth acres) was obtained for $470.00 in 1895 and later, for the sum of $1.00, more land was purchased for this use in 1931.

In the beginning, the church was lit with kerosene lamps on metal brackets attached to the window frames. A little later carbide gas lights were used. These had the disadvantage of being very fragile and often disintegrated. Following these lights, came a Delco generator and glass battery which provided electricity. A drawback to this system was that the generator had to be used frequently to keep the batteries charged. Finally, electric lines came to the area in 1937 and the church connected to this system.

Two wood- and coal-burning stoves, one in the front and one at the back of the church, provided heating. Later a coal furnace replaced the stoves and, still later, an oil furnace was installed.

The usual organizations grew up in the church. Sunday school was a part of the church from the beginning. The Ladies Aid followed soon after, evolving into the Women's Society of Christian Service and then its present-day counterpart, United Methodist Women. The young peoples' group, the Epworth League, was founded in 1894. At one time St. John's had a band which played for various functions including the annual picnic. The church also had a bowling team which brought home several trophies.

The annual church picnic was a tradition for many years and went back to the horse and buggy days when people would arrive with baskets of food. A grove of trees to the north of the church furnished a place for these festivities. Later, chicken dinners contributed a substantial part of the church operating funds. Amusements included ice cream stands, soda pop stands, a country store, and a fish pond for the children. The country store offered such things as canned goods, baked goods, and knickknacks. Later, Burgoo suppers replaced the picnic and fish fries and also helped to raise funds.[19]

In 1987 St. John's celebrated its one-hundredth anniversary with the theme "Anchor in the Community" (referring to the symbol atop the steeple). The celebration began with the pastor emulating his circuit rider predecessors, riding a horse to church. His family followed in an 1885 vintage buggy. The Twenty-third psalm was recited in German and German hymns followed. Reminisces, special music and a rededication completed the program. A picnic and old fashioned ice cream social followed. The cornerstone was opened and a men's quartet from Newburgh provided a concert.[20]

Histories of St. John's are online at www.posey.genwebsite.org/documents and, also, at www.rootsweb.ancestry.com/~inposey3/stjohnumc.

Marrs Circuit—St. Peter's

In 1844 a board of trustees convened to purchase land to build St. Peter's church. Marcus and Prudence Sherwood sold them an acre of land at Princeton and Diamond Island roads for five dollars. In 1845 a simple log church was built, having no floor nor pews, and people sat on the ground to hear the pastor, Rev. J. Strauch. This church lasted until 1857 when a fire destroyed it. North of the church, a log catechism school was erected. A parsonage was needed, so George Schnur sold the trustees five acres of land adjacent to the church for thirty dollars. A school, also built on the land, served the tuition students who were taught in German.

A brick church was built in 1857 during the pastorate of Rev. M. Schnuerle. The bricks for construction were made at the site and water was hauled from a nearby creek by oxen team. The bricks were then cured by fire which almost led to disaster one night. The men tending the fire fell asleep and forgot to watch the bricks, which almost caused their ruin. The church was built with a partition which ran through the middle and separated the women's seating from the men's. The pulpit in the front of the church was a raised area about three feet high and twelve wide. Two stoves at the sides of the room provided heat. Oil lamps furnished light—one on each wall and one hanging from the ceiling in the middle.

A new frame parsonage replaced the log one in 1874. Some church remodeling done between 1885 and 1889, included a vestibule and a steeple. Mule power hauled the steeple's bell into place. The vestibule became the area mail distribution center. Each family had its own shelf and after the pastor picked up the mail at the post office each week, he placed it on the shelves. Each Sunday

St. Peter's UMC, formerly of the Marrs Circuit.

morning the families could look forward to picking up their mail as well as attending church.

A third parsonage was built in 1906 using some of the good lumber from the second parsonage. This was a joint venture of St. Peter's and St. Paul's, St. Peter's contributing two thirds of the wherewithal and St. Paul's contributing a third. The total raised was $1,424.72 and the actual cost was $1,394.54.

As in all the German churches, there was an eventual need to phase out the German and replace it with English. Rev. W. J. G. Bockstahler began this in 1930 by giving five minute sermons in English. He gradually increased the length until half of the sermon time was English. English hymns were also introduced at this time necessitating the purchase of hymn books in English. When Rev. O. E. Killion was appointed in 1939, all of the service switched abruptly to English as he could neither speak nor understand German.

Paying the pastor in those days was always a tricky problem common in most churches. The trustees were responsible for raising funds for this and many times pastors did not receive their full salary. Usually a fundraiser of some sort was held or trustees made the rounds to the various members asking for funds. In 1939 the Reverend Killion started the church envelope system which helped alleviate this problem.

In 1944 the Indiana Conference assessed St. Peter's $640 to go toward relief for the war-torn countries overseas. The congregation also collected food and clothing to send to Europe. Many church members had served in the armed forces during the conflict, as they had during World War I.

In 1947 Mrs. Lena Maier sold a little more than eight acres of land to the church for the sum of $1,068.00. Two years later, St. Peter's and St. Paul's did some remodeling of their parsonage installing an oil furnace and a modern bathroom for the cost of $1,512.67. A barn on the grounds of St. Peter's Church was revamped into a recreation center in 1949. Stalls and haylofts were removed and a floor, windows, and a door were added. Materials came to $300.00 and labor was donated. A class composed of members of both St. Peter's and St. Paul's, the New Endeavor Class, spearheaded the recreation center project.

The St. Peter's Campmeeting Association was founded in 1950 under the guidance of Rev. W. H. McGowan. For awhile meetings were held in tents during the month of July. Then in 1953 St. Peter's had a chance to purchase the abandoned Greathouse Methodist Church in Mt. Vernon. For the sum of $231, the deal was made and the lumber from the Mt. Vernon church was used to build a Tabernacle on the St. Peter's campgrounds. The building was used for this purpose until 1962.

Throughout the years, many organizations grew out of the St. Peter's congregation. Sunday school classes are one of the most important of these. The New Endeavor Class, mentioned previously, was made up of members of both St. Peter's and St. Paul's in an effort to draw them closer together. Another class was the Kum-Join-Us class. A Ladies Aid, started in 1916, went through the usual changes, became the Women's Society of Christian Service in 1939, and then the United Methodist Women in 1968. The men's group, the Methodist Men of St. Peter's Church, was founded in March 1955 and chartered in July 1955. A Boy Scout troop was organized in 1963. During a thirty-year period from 1963 to 1993, 193 boys participated, with 20 going on to become Eagle Scouts. St. Peter's sponsored a number of Girl Scout workshops and activities and then in 1993, began supporting a Cadet Girl Scout troop.

A Centennial Service to commemorate the founding of St. Peter's was held in 1944. Old German hymns opened the service. The history committee gave the history and former pastors delivered comments and greetings.

In 1957 a second Centennial Service was held celebrating the church building which had been in use for a hundred years. The theme again stressed the German heritage of the church with German hymns, a devotional in German, and a choir singing German hymns. The following year the last service was conducted in this building and members prepared to continue their worship in a new building.

In the early 1950s it was apparent that a new church facility was needed, but could they, financially, swing it? A Sunday Morning Coin Drill for the building fund was started. Every Sunday morning children and adults filed past a miniature church building on the altar railing and dropped in their money. Within six years $1,711.48 was raised. Still, there were doubts as to whether a new church building was financially feasible, so a twenty-four-hour prayer vigil was held asking for guidance. After that, the members decided to go ahead with the project and start on the first unit of construction. In 1956 the first unit was finished and formally opened. At this point, the new building was used for educational and social activity while the old church still served as a house of worship. By June 1958 the building debt of $22,853.57 was paid in full, thanks to bequests, special offerings, the coin drill, and building fund envelopes.

In July 1958 the second phase of the building was started and was completed by November. The consecration service was held in the new building on December 7, 1958. One of the features of the new building was a Memorial Window honoring the former pastors and members when the church was in the Central German Conference. The window incorporated old Christian symbols that had been in the windows of the 1857 church building and had been imported from Switzerland.

A new parsonage (number four) was built in 1968 of the same stone used for the church. The old parsonage was dismantled and sold. Other changes or improvements continued into the 1990s and included refurnishing the church lounge by the Kum-Join-Us Class, a new heating and air-conditioning unit for the church, a new roof, storage room, carpeting, handicapped facilities, new front entrance, and many more. In 1988 twenty stained-glass windows costing $28,948.97 were installed as memorials. These were made in Louisville, Kentucky, at the Louisville Art Glass Studio and dedicated on June 26, 1988.

In 1994, 150 years of church service was celebrated during the pastorate of

Dr. Michael Rynkiewich. At that time, the church counted 130 members and a Sunday school enrollment of 74.[21]

Marrs Circuit—St. Paul's German M. E. Church

St. Paul's German M. E. Church was founded during the same timeframe as St. Peter's and joined the Mt. Vernon Circuit in the 1840s. When the Mt. Vernon church left the circuit, St. Peter's and St. Paul's formed the Marrs Circuit in 1863. When St. John's in Caborn was built in 1887, Marrs became a three-point charge. St. Paul's and St. Peter's were connected in many ways including sharing the building and expenses of the parsonage constructed in 1906. In 1930 St. Paul's left the Marrs Circuit and was served from Evansville for nine years. In 1939, St. Paul's was once again joined with St. Peter's. This arrangement lasted until 1991 when St. Paul's again left the charge to be served from Evansville.[22]

German M. E. preaching began in the St. Philips area in 1843. In 1845, as related earlier, Rev. John Strauch came and preached in the area. Other preachers followed including Rev. Frederick Heitmeyer who related the perils of the circuit rider.

> One time I came to a flooded section and succeeded in reaching a bridge and then the approaches were swept away. I saw nothing but water. . . . I used my goad on the horse and plunged into the water. After floundering around, his feet struck ground and carried me out on dry land. . . . I saw I was on an island. I dismounted and knelt down and prayed the Lord to show me the way out. I again mounted my horse and found an easy way out and reached my appointment at Boonville on time.[23]

The German Methodist trustees bought one and a half acres of land for five dollars from Lewis Sirkle in 1844 for a church. The trustees were Nicholas Hahn, John Adam Hahn, Christian Morlock, Simeon Grell, and John Rogue. Camp meetings were held in a tent until it burned. Basket meetings were started in 1873 and held for several years after.

In 1911 the church acquired more land described as "a strip of land 6 rods wide along the north side and 2 rods wide along the south side of the original 1 1/2 acres." where a new building was soon erected. In 1952 a basement was constructed for this building and in 1956 rooms for a Sunday school were added.

Church quarterly meetings were always important functions. The presiding elder, later called district superintendent, was in charge of the meetings. They generally consisted of four services. First, the presiding elder gave a sermon and then presided over the business session. On Sunday morning communion followed a soul-stirring sermon. After Sunday dinner the meeting resumed with a love feast. The congregants consumed bread and water, gave testimonies on how the Lord had blessed their lives and sang hymns. A fourth service was held that evening and those that lived some distance from the church were fed by the locals before attending the service.

St. Paul's UMC, third member of the old Marrs Circuit.

Several interesting anecdotes are connected with St. Paul's history. One involved Rev. H. E. Wulzen who served from 1893 to 1897.

> One Saturday afternoon when snow was on the ground he was driving ... here to give catechism instruction and his horse became frightened at a snowman that the school children had made ... at the school house. The horse turned around and threw the buggy over and spilled him and some of his scholars out. Nevertheless, he filled his appointment. 24.

The German settlers could be very hospitable to people they felt a kinship to and likewise were not too friendly to people they considered strangers. Rev. J. H. Lukemeyer who served from 1879 to 1882 found this out during his travels.

> One evening when tired [he] stopped at a home and asked if he could stay all night. He told them if they had no spare bed he could sleep on the floor and he would be glad to do this if only his horse would be fed. He spoke in English and the man told him he would have to consult his wife. She said "no." Their conversation had been in high German. When the man came from the house to tell the wife's answer, the Reverend spoke in high German. Then the man went to the house to consult his wife. They then talked in low German. The Reverend could hear their conversation and when the man returned the Reverend began to talk in low German. The man was overjoyed and called "Oh Mother, he speaks low German." She answered "Have him come in at once." They had an

enjoyable evening together. On leaving the next morning they had the Reverend promise to stop with them every time he came in that neighborhood.[25]

The three churches of the Marrs Circuit are still active today. St. Paul's is located at 5301 South St. Philip's Road west of Evansville; St. Peter's is also on South St. Philip's Road at 2810; and St. John's is at 4101 West Caborn Road, Mt. Vernon.

Grandpa Rudin visited the churches of the Marr's Circuit in the April of 1915. This was on the occasion of the District Meeting held there.

Tuesday April 6

Met Bro. Werner at Huntingburg and we took the 8:15 train to Evansville where we arrived at about 10:00. We dined at a restaurant and visited stores and walked the streets till 2:00. At the electric car station met a number of brethren. It took us about a half hour to get to the nearest station to Marrs, St. Phillips. Our host, Bro. Grossman met us with his auto. The District Meeting was opened by Bro. Treuschel at about 3:00. Bro. Maag was elected secretary and after some preliminary business, Bro. Tanner read his paper: "Evangelistic Meetings in the Light of Holy Scripture."

Wednesday April 7

Got to bed late last night. Bro. Edelmaier preached a pretty good sermon last night. By the way, he "sports" an auto! Quite some business was transacted this morning. It was decided to petition the bishop and the conference at the next session for a reduction of the Conference to three districts. Bro. Becker read his paper: "The Attitude of our Lord towards the Holy Scriptures." The paper was well received. This morning Bro. Grossman took us over to St. Peter's church, where the parsonage is located. Bro. Tanner lives amid ideal surroundings. Bro. Treuschel is stopping with Bro. Tanner and he showed us the church.

Thursday April 8

Bro. Treuschel's paper . . . was "The Leading of the Holy Spirit." The paper was recommended for publication. Bro. Werner followed with the topic: "Why is Avarice a Root of all Evil?" Bro. Weiler conducted the morning devotion, turning it into a testimony meeting which was evidently enjoyed by all. I read my paper: "Inspiration and Interpretation of the Holy Scriptures." It was well received, even the District Superintendent saying that it was "very good." Bro. Weiler read "The Nature, the Problem and the Aim of the Church of Christ." Dr. Horst and Bro. Schruff criticized it severely for its pre-millennial views.

Friday April 9

Last evening after supper Bro. Grossman took us to Caborn in his auto. Bro. Ackermann is pastor there. We visited the church and the parsonage. Bro. A. seems to have a nice field of labor and he is still in the chicken business. Left for home early this morning and arrived at Holland at a little after 11:00. Yesterday afternoon Bro. Braun read his paper on "The Doctrine of the Last Things According to the Prophet Daniel." Again it was Dr. Horst and Bro. Schruff who criticized severely and for the same reasons that they criticized Bro. Weiler's paper.

Saturday April 10

We had some pretty heavy showers today. Old Bro. Sevringhaus is going to move to Seymour and Bro. Schruff does not like it at all. Well, there will be one mischief maker less in New Albany. The Marrs people have quite a nice little church and a pretty good choir for such a small congregation. Grossmans, our hosts, treated us very nice and did all they could to make it pleasant for us.[26]

Evansville, Indiana

Evansville—First Church (Fourth Street M. E.)

The German Methodists in the Evansville area organized First Church in 1842. They built a church building four years later costing thirteen thousand dollars at the corner of Vine and Fourth streets in what is now downtown Evansville. Twenty two years later the original building was replaced by a brick structure for the cost of about thirty-six thousand dollars.[27]

According to another history, the first meetings were held at an inn where the innkeeper was converted and became one of the charter members. After that, meetings were held in a school. The first church was built on Vine Street and later replaced by a fire department at that site.[28]

Another county history gives some more precise figures on the costs of the buildings. The first German M. E. church building, built in 1846, cost $1263 and the second building—"a commodious brick structure"—was erected for the cost of $34,621. The lot was originally the first graveyard in Evansville. The Fourth Street Church was one of "the largest and finest German Methodist churches in the United States" at the time of its dedication.[29]

Throughout the years, Fourth Street Church promoted many educational, social, and musical programs. The Sunday school was established in the 1850s and twenty years after that, a "Day School" was founded which was attended by many people wanting to learn the German language. The Sunday school also supported an orchestra which provided music on Sunday mornings.

The Ladies Aid was organized in the 1870s and originally called a Mite Society. As in many churches, it was the custom to have the pastor's wife as president. The group met in the homes of members and sometimes meetings were held in the evenings so husbands could attend, but late afternoon meetings were the norm. A Men's Club was created in the late 1920s or early '30s.

First German of Evansville, Indiana, also called Fourth Street ME, now, after several mergers, is Methodist Temple.

The Women's Foreign Missionary Society was established in 1907 and, until 1922, meetings were held every three months. Their purpose was to help missionaries abroad and the group also helped with the education of a boy in India. A Home Missionary Society was also organized but later evolved into a Business Women's Club. This group helped pay the salary of a parish worker. Missionary work was also supported by the Sunday school and individuals.

Other church organizations included the Epworth League which received its charter in 1890. An "Intermediate League" was organized in the 1920s. Both groups encouraged leadership abilities in the young people of the church. Boy Scout and Girl Scout troops were also supported by the church. Another group for youth was the Boy Choir. Junior Church was organized in the early 1930s with the aim of making good church-goers of the young people.[30]

In the 1930s, after the demise of the Central German Conference, Fourth Street Methodist had a decline in membership and felt it expedient to join with another church. It was decided to affiliate with Bayard Park Methodist. Fourth Street church held its last service in the old building on Palm Sunday, 1937. On Easter Sunday the churches held their first united service. Land was purchased at Lincoln and Kelsey streets in 1941 and, due to delays caused by the war, the groundbreaking was held in January 1949. In the summer of 1950, the name of the combined congregations was officially changed to the Methodist Temple and the first service was held in the new building on July 2, 1950.[31]

Vanderburgh County wanted the Fourth Street property and church trustees agreed to sell it for forty-five thousand dollars. This was put in a trust fund to be used for another church building or to be used by the conference. The memorial windows were given to a church in Dale, Indiana, and the pipe organ was stored at the Goodwill building, but then perished in a fire.[32] The church building was used as an annex for the courthouse until it was eventually razed and the land used as a parking lot. One of the bells from the bell tower found a home at the Methodist Temple. The Fourth Street pulpit also went to Methodist Temple to be used in the chapel. Two candle stands were made from spindles of the old altar rail and two sliver-plated goblets and patens for Communion also went to Methodist Temple.[33]

For additional information on Methodist Temple go to their website at www.methodisttemple.com.

Evansville—Second Church (Bethlehem)

There was a need for a German Church on the west side of the city, so Rev. Heinrich Lich of First Church began preaching to the people there during the week. In 1886 Rev. J. C. Speckmann started a mission, meeting in English churches for Sunday school and church. A church was built on West Indiana Street in 1887 and a parsonage followed the next year.[34]

Reverend Speckmann pastored the church on West Indiana Street which cost fourteen hundred dollars and was described as a "small, neat frame structure."[35] Many of its early members came from First Church since Second Church was closer to their homes.[36] In 1907 Second Church claimed 110 members, a thriving Sunday school, a youth league and a women's society. At one time it was on a circuit with Salem north of Evansville.

Later the church was renamed Bethlehem Methodist Episcopal Church. The address of the building was 2214 West Indiana Street.[37]

Evansville—Chapel on Read Street

There is little I could find on this chapel—not even its official name. The *Geschichte* refers to it as a "mission chapel" which was built at the corner of Read and Delaware streets in 1890. It was later sold as it did not thrive as expected.[38] The chapel was not assigned a preacher but was ministered to by the other German M. E. pastors and laymen who served there during the week.[39]

Evansville—Salem German M. E. Church

A group of German Methodists began meeting in 1846 in a schoolhouse in German Township. Rev. Peter Schmucker led the group which founded the Salem German Methodist Episcopal Church. Four years later, under the leadership of Reverend Fusz, a small church building was constructed. Many of the members, however, lived in Center Township in an area known as *die Schweiz* which is now Highland or Kratzville. They wanted a church closer to their homes and so sold the German Township building in 1863. While a new building was

Salem UMC was founded as Salem Kirche in 1887 north of Evansville.

being erected, services were held in the nearby home of Christian Laubscher.[40] There is still a Salem Methodist Cemetery where the church was located in German Township. There are only a few gravestones left at the Meier Road location to mark where the first Salem church was based.[41]

Circuit riding ministers, who also served Boonville, Henderson (Kentucky), and Mt. Vernon, presided at Salem from 1863 to 1872. Rev. Jacob Bockstahler was received as the first resident pastor in 1872.

Under the leadership of Rev. J. C. Speckman in 1886, Salem made plans to build its third building and the dedication followed in the spring of 1888. A historical sketch describes part of the ceremony.

> The procession was led by Rev. J. C. Speckman with Hettie Yokel at his side and Albert Schroetter just behind her. Hettie was given first place for having memorized the most Bible verses during the year. Albert lost out by one verse.[42]

All the children of the church had saved nickels and dimes which they contributed for the new church bell.

The first vacation Bible school was held when Rev. J. J. Bockstahler came to Salem in 1888. The school curriculum covered Bible study, catechism, music, translations of English and German, and games. This first vacation Bible school concluded with a party at Mrs. Simon Laubscher's. The first Ladies Aid was founded by Reverand Floerke and his wife about 1898. Rev. C. E. Ploch, who returned to Salem in 1918, started an envelope system of giving.

Additions and changes to the church property included a parsonage, which was acquired in 1893; a furnace, which was installed for $273.40 in 1912; and a community hall, which was finished in 1918 for $2,126.00. The parsonage burned in 1915 and was replaced that same year. In 1923 eleven acres of land adjoining the church property was purchased. In 1926 electricity came to Salem and electric lights replaced the gas ones. A playground was also added that year to keep the children amused. In 1927 the hall was enlarged with new classrooms added, a new furnace, and running water for the kitchen.

There was a reorganization of church groups after the disbanding of the German Conference and, later, the union of various Methodist conferences. The young People's group became Methodist Youth Fellowship and the Women's Society of Christian Service replaced the Ladies' Aid and other women's groups.

In 1944 more renovation was done which included installing new heating facilities in both the church and parsonage. The interiors of the church and community hall were both refurbished.[43]

Salem Church is still going strong in the twenty-first century. It is located at 6311 Kratzville Road, Evansville, Indiana, 47710 and has gone through additional rebuildings and renovations since 1946. It has preserved some of its German heritage with plaques and markers detailing highlights of its history.

For more information, try the Web site at www.evansvillesalem.org.

Evansville—Blue Grass (Salem Circuit)

There was a church known as Blue Grass Church at Hookerville which was on a circuit with Salem from 1884 to 1907 after which it was then sold to the Evangelicals.[44] The church weakened because of the older members dying and younger ones "becoming indifferent."[45]

Evansville—Independence (Salem Circuit)

The Independence or West Side Church was also linked to Salem. Salem helped build this church in 1886 and was connected with it until 1894.[46]

When Grandpa Rudin was pastor at Holland, Indiana, he also had the opportunity to visit other southern Indiana churches, either for district meetings or other functions. In 1918 he visited several to give a stereopticon lecture called "Black Diamonds" on behalf of the Freedman's Aid Society.

Thursday May 23

> Started out on my lecture trip this morning, taking John (his son) with me. Artus Hufnagel took us to Huntingburg where we boarded the 12:50 train for Evansville. We arrived at about 3:00 and put up at Bro. Werner's. Received a cordial welcome. When we were about ready to give the lecture this evening, we found that the electric light bulb had broken in transit. Fortunately, Bro. Werner was able to get the YMCA machine, and we were able to give the lecture before about 60 people.

Friday May 24

Neither John nor I slept well last night as it was very warm. This morning we ran around from store to store to see about a bulb and succeeded in getting one that would do. After the show John and I went to Baurs, where we had a good supper. Bro. Baur's church is a rather cheap looking affair and his congregation is small. [This is probably Second Church he is referring to.] Gave the lecture to a small crowd. John was my operator.

Saturday May 25

Bro. Baur has two sons in the service and another expects to be employed in Washington. John and I visited the business section of Evansville and did some shopping and sightseeing. John said he would like to live in Evansville, and I confess the town looks prosperous and attractive except for the smoke and soot. This was another hot day and in such weather I prefer Holland.

Monday May 27

Took the 10:00 car for Evansville and got to Werners' about 11:00. [The preceding day had been spent in Mt. Vernon giving the lecture.] Passed a restless night on account of the heat and was glad to get up this morning. We took the 7:00 train for Huntingburg, arriving about 9:00. Am glad to be home again. The parsonage of First Church, Evansville, is almost like a prison.[47]

Notes

1. Goodspeed Publishing Co., *History of Posey County, Indiana* (Chicago: The Goodspeed Publishing Co. 1886), 277.
2. John C. Leffel, ed. *History of Posey County* (Chicago: Standard Publishing Company, 1913), 133, 134.
3. Richard Topper, "Churches Yesterday & Today," *175th Birthday 1816–1991* (souvenir booklet), Mt. Vernon, Ind.: c. 1991, 55.
4. Goodspeed, *History of Posey County, Indiana*, 278.
5. Sue Goff to Barbara Dixon, 2003.
6. See note 5.
7. Rev. August Binder, *Churches: Posey County*, Mt. Vernon: self published, 1988.
8. *History of the Community Church from the 1840s to September 1970*, (church history), Mt. Vernon, Ind.: 1970.
9. "Our Religious Heritage, Zoar United Methodist Church," *Mt. Vernon Democrat*, Mt. Vernon, Indiana, July 4, 1976.
10. *History of the Community Church*.
11. "Our Religious Heritage."
12. *History of the Community Church*.
13. August E. Binder, notebook on Posey County churches 1987, 38.
14. Rudin, Diaries, 1918.
15. Golder, Horst, and Schaal, *Geschichte*, 362–63.
16. *St. Peters United Methodist Church*, church history, (Posey County, Ind.: c.1994).
17. Golder, Horst, and Schaal, *Geschichte*, 362–53.
18. *St. Peters United Methodist Church*.
19. Herman Becker, Viola Hartmann, and Laverne Seifert, *An Anchor in the Community*, St. John's Centennial booklet (Caborn, Ind.: 1987).
20. "Caborn to celebrate 100 years," *Mount Vernon* (Indiana) *Democrat*, July 9, 1987.
21. *St. Peters United Methodist Church*.
22. Ibid.
23. Edward D. Grossman, *The History of St. Paul's Church*, church history, Evansville, Ind.: 1994.
24. Grossman., *The History of St. Paul's Church*.
25. Ibid.
26. Rudin, Diaries, 1915.
27. Joseph P. Elliott, *A History of Evansville and Vanderburgh County, Indiana* (Evansville, Indiana: Keller Publishing Company 1897), 244.
28. Alice Hoelscher, *History of Fourth Street M.E., 1843 to 1933,* church history, (Evansville, Ind.: 1933), 1.
29. *History of Vanderburgh County, Indiana* (Madison, Wisconsin: .Brant & Fuller, 1889), 283.
30. Hoelscher, *History of Fourth Street M.E.*, 4–6.
31. Bob Shepherd, "A brief chronology of Methodist Temple," www.methodisttemple.evansville.net/history , 2000, 1–2.
32. Hoelscher, *History of Fourth Street M.E.*, 8.
33. Vivian M. Taylor letter to Barbara Dixon, 2003.
34. Golder, Horst, and Schaal, *Geschichte*, 355.

35. *History of Vanderburgh County, Indiana*, 234.
36. Hoelscher, *History of Fourth Street M.E.*, 6.
37. Taylor, 5.
38. Golder, Horst, and Schaal, *Geschichte*, 354.
39. Hoelscher, *History of Fourth Street M.E.*, 6.
40. "Historical Sketch of Salem Methodist Church," *Centennial Celebration 1846–1946*, Evansville, Ind.: 1946.
41. www.ingenweb.org/invanderburgh/cemeteries/salemumethcem.htm
42. "Historical Sketch."
43. Ibid.
44. Ibid.
45. Golder, Horst, and Schaal, *Geschichte*, 366.
46. "Historical Sketch."
47. Rudin, Diaries, 1918.

CHAPTER 10

German M. E. Churches in Southern Indiana

Boonville, Indiana, Circuit

The Boonville Circuit was originally part of the Evansville Mission which was started in 1843 when Henry Koeneke and Konrad Muth came to the area to preach. Boonville became a circuit in its own right in 1847. At one time the Boonville Mission included Boonville, Newburgh, Huntingburg, Bretz's Settlement, Cannelton, Oil Creek, Haysville, Jasper, Santa Claus, Rockport, Millersburg, Salem, and Henderson, Kentucky.[1] Another source gives the composition of the mission as Boonville, Newburgh, Huntingburgh, Bretzes Settlement, Troy, Rome, Haysville, and Jasper.[2] Later, the circuit was reduced to three preaching sites.[3]

Boonville Circuit—German M. E.

A congregation was organized at Boonville in 1856 and a church built in 1858 for the cost of eleven thousand dollars.[4] Another source claims the cost was five hundred dollars. In 1871, the congregation added a new roof for one hundred dollars and, in 1880, a new steeple graced the tower.[5] A historical atlas shows the German church located on Fourth Street between Walnut and Elm streets.[6]

Boonville Circuit—Ebenezer German M. E.

A group of Germans founded a settlement about 1838 east of Boonville where all were Lutheran. However, the people became unhappy with their pastor (allegedly, because of his drinking and immorality) and when two German Methodist missionaries arrived on the scene in 1843, they organized a congregation of that denomination. They built a church in 1847.

I could find no more information about Ebenezer until 1968. At that time a special quarterly conference was called to discuss selling the parsonage. They agreed to set the price at eight thousand dollars. If this amount were realized; five thousand would be placed in a Savings Certificate and three thousand in a savings account with Boonville Savings Association. Interest from these accounts would go toward the cemetery upkeep.[7]

On May 4, 1977, another meeting was held with the district superintendent to discuss closing and selling the church building. The attendees decided that proceeds from the sale would go to cemetery upkeep and that before the sale, members would be allowed to take items they had donated. The last Sunday service was held on June 12, 1977.[8]

Ebenezer church was located in the country about three miles east of Boonville on Route 62. The church is gone but there is a cemetery and a wood shelter where the church bell is on display.

Boonville Circuit—Emanuel German M. E.

Emanuel Church was located north of Ebenezer on Tennyson Road. There is nothing left there now except a cemetery which is also known as Roth Cemetery. The only mention of Emanuel says that the building was bought for two hundred dollars in 1872.[9]

Boonville Circuit—Newburgh German M. E.

The trustees of the German Methodist Church in Newburgh bought a piece of land from A. M. Phelps in 1853 on which they erected a small red brick building. Membership was never very large, so the congregation eventually united with the Evangelical Church. In September 1885 the building at 405 Jefferson Street was sold to the town to be used as a school for the Negro community. The school was consolidated with the Newburgh schools in 1958 and the property sold to the Carson family. Mr. Carson used the building for his antique car collection, until the 1970s when he leased it to Electronics' Research INC as storage space.[10] In 2009 when I tried to go to this website, it no longer worked. Perhaps it has been changed—you might put in Warrick County, Indiana, and try your luck.

The old church/school building still stands but in much need of repair. The Women's Club of Newburgh put up a plaque which has some of the above information on it.

Cannelton and Tell City, Indiana, Circuit

There were four German M. E. churches on a circuit in Perry County, Indiana. In 1847 services were first held in homes and schoolhouses at Rome and Cannelton by Rev. Frederick Heller. In 1849 a class was begun at Oil Township

The Newburgh, Indiana, German ME is the only building on the Boonville Circuit to survive to the present. From 1885 to 1950 it served as a grade school for African American children.

(which later became Oriole). A latecomer to the circuit was Tell City which built a church under the leadership of Rev. Jacob Allinger in 1886.[11]

Cannelton Circuit—Cannelton German M. E.

The church at Cannelton was built in 1855 during the pastorate of Rev. Karl F. Heitmeyer and cost fifteen hundred dollars At a later date the frame church was remodeled and a steeple erected. A parsonage was built during the tenure of Reverend Schnuerle.[12] The *Geschichte* has a conflicting report stating that Friedrich Becker was the pastor who first organized the circuit of Cannelton, Rome, and Oil Creek and he was also pastor at the time the church was built. A parsonage, costing five hundred dollars was erected in 1859.[13] The German M. E. Church at the corner of Taylor and Seventh streets, continued to serve the German speaking populace until 1914. At that time, membership dropped off due to assimilation and there was an "experimental consolidation" with the English-speaking Methodists. This group had a frame church on Fifth Street between Taylor and Congress.[14] During the 1930s the old German church was used by the Free Methodists.[15] The building still exists but is now used commercially.

Cannelton Circuit—Rome (German Ridge)

Methodist meetings were held in the late 1830s in Tobin Township in an area called German Ridge where a number of German families had settled. By 1838 a German Methodist class had formed which joined the large circuit out of Boonville but later became part of the Huntingburg Mission. The first church was a log structure built under the pastorate of Rev. Konrad Muth. It was about three miles from Rome above Bear Creek and gave a view of the Ohio River in the distance. In 1873 a frame building replaced the original structure.[16]

Another source notes that church services were first held in the log schoolhouse at German Ridge until the congregation built a twenty-five by thirty-five foot log church on ground donated by John and Katherine Block. In the 1870s the log church, pastored by Rev. Louis Miller, was burned by "an enemy of the society" and then replaced by a frame building in 1871. In 1903, under pastor Elmer Roessner, renovations were completed which included a hall and a steeple. In the 1930s the church building was still used for Sunday school and infrequent services.[17]

Cannelton Circuit—Oil Creek (Oriole, Zoar) German M. E.

In 1849 a German M. E. class was started in Oil Township and joined the two others as part of the Huntingburg Mission. In 1853, the Cannelton Mission was created and Rev. Friedrich Becker served as pastor to the three churches. It was under his pastorate that the first German M. E. church was built at Oil Creek.

In 1864 a second log church was built and in 1875 land was deeded to the church trustees for a graveyard. The deeds refer to "Zoar Church" which was apparently the name of the Oil Creek church. Land for a campground near Oriole was purchased and each summer was the site of uplifting camp meetings. Eventually, about 1914, the German Church united with the Oriole Methodist Church.[18]

Unfortunately, the old Zoar Church was abandoned and eventually collapsed and disappeared.[19]

Cannelton Circuit—Tell City German M. E.

The German M. E. Church at Tell City was the last of the four on the circuit to be organized. Preaching was held infrequently by Revs. Daniel Stoll and J. J. Baechtold until 1886 when a church was erected under the pastorate of Rev. Jacob Allinger. Although I could not find much information on the Tell City church, it evidently outlasted the others as a German M. E. church. It was two years after the other three had merged with nearby English Methodist churches that the Tell City church finally did the same. During this time it was served from Santa Claus by Revs. William Weiler and Louis Ackerman.[20]

It was interesting to note that the First Methodist Church (English speaking) grew out of the German M. E. church. It was founded in 1891 at a revival held at the German church. Evidently, there were both German and English

Sunday school classes held around this time, emanating from the German Church. The English speakers met in the Gatchel home on Fourth Street for Sunday school and Sunday evening services were in the Roehm residence. In 1892, the English formally organized their own church.[21]

Find more about First UMC at www.tellcityfirstumc.org.

First UMC of Tell City, Indiana, came from a merger of the German ME and the English ME churches.

Notes

1. Golder, Horst, and Schaal, *Geschichte*, 349–50.
2. *History of Warrick, Spencer and Perry Counties* (Chicago: Goodspeed Bros. & Co., Publishers, 1885), 128.
3. Golder, Horst, and Schaal, *Geschichte*, 350.
4. Ibid., 350.
5. *History of Warrick*, 128.
6. *An Illustrated Historical Atlas* (Warick Co., Ind., Philadelphia: D. J. Lake & Co., 1880).
7. Quarterly conference minutes, August 11, 1968, on file at Boonville Public Library, Booneville, Ind.
8. Minutes from meeting with District Superintendent, May 4, 1977, on file at Boonville Public Library, Booneville, Ind.
9. *History of Warrick*, 128.
10. http://us-gen.org/in/warrick/cemeteries/germanmethchurch.htm. [Note: This Web site was accessed several years ago and no longer works. I have not been able to find the information cited elsewhere.]
11. James Mosby, "German Methodism in Perry County," *A Living History of Perry County*, www.perrycountyindiana.org/history/methodism, 2.
12. *History of Warrick*, 122–23.
13. Golder, Horst, and Schaal, *Geschichte*, 351.
14. Thomas James De la Hunt, *Perry County, A History* (Indianapolis: The W. K. Stewart Company, 1916), 84.
15. Mosby, "German Methodism in Perry County," 1.
16. Dela Hunt, *Perry County, A History*, 84.
17. Mosby, "German Methodism in Perry County," 2.
18. Ibid., 1–3.
19. Rev. Bill Reid to author, 2004.
20. Mosby, "German Methodism in Perry County," 2.
21. "Our Church History, 1892–1976," *First United Methodist Church* (Tell City, Ind.: The Swiss Printers, Inc., 1976), 3.

CHAPTER 11

More German M. E. Churches in Southwestern Indiana

Huntingburg, Indiana, Circuit

German Methodism began in Dubois County when Revs. Henry Koeneke and Konrad Muth came to the Evansville area to spread the word. In October of 1843 they were invited to preach in the house of H. H. Fenneman near Huntingburg. By 1845 German Methodism had also made an appearance near the Pike County line where Zoar Church was eventually founded. Preaching was also done in the vicinity of Holland where Central Church was later erected. These preaching places started under under the Evansville Circuit but by 1848 the Huntingburg Mission was created. The churches (or preaching sites) embraced by this mission were Boonville, Huntingburg, Central, Zoar, Bretz Settlement, Haysville, Jasper, Troy, and Rome.[1] Some of these have been covered in other chapters—this chapter will deal with the churches at Huntingburg, Holland, Zoar and Santa Claus.

Huntingburg Circuit—Huntingburg German M. E.

Rev. C. F. Heitmeyer collected the funds for the first German M. E. at Huntingburg which was built in 1850. The frame building stood on Geiger Street near Fifth and measured twenty-two-by-thirty-five feet. The Rev. J. H. Lukemeyer was the first to serve the new church. He and his family needed a place to live and, as there was no parsonage, found lodging in an empty one-room barrel factory. This provided enough room for a bed, table, two chairs, and a cradle.[2] Another source describes Lukemeyer's residence as "an old copper-workshop." The quarters were so cramped that at bedtime, when the trundle bed was pulled out for the children, the cradle had to be put on the table.[3]

A Sunday school was started in 1850 and soon could boast of "a president, secretary, seven teachers, twenty-three scholars, and sixty-three bound books."

Huntingburg, Indiana, UMC, formerly German ME.

At the end of 1850, Reverend Lukemeyer had added fifty members to the eight-point Huntingburg Circuit. In 1852 the second quarterly conference decided to built a parsonage which it accomplished for the sum of $470.10. Growth continued until it was necessary to build a church between Huntingburg and Holland. A thirty-by-forty-foot building was erected on the Feldwish-Kuck farm and was called Central Church.

The circuit continued to be reorganized due to growth in all its churches, and eventually, consisted of Huntingburg, Central (Holland), and Zoar. In 1862 a new church became necessary and a brick edifice was built on Main Street between Fourth and Fifth. The church was dedicated in June 1866 and cost $3,593.67.

In 1866 the parsonage also underwent some changes. An addition was added onto it, but by 1885 it was clear that a new parsonage was needed. A frame home was built which adjoined the church.

In 1901 the churches at Huntingburg, Holland, and Zoar celebrated the fiftieth anniversary of the Huntingburg circuit. In 1908 Huntingburg became independent while Holland and Zoar remained together as a charge.

During the second decade of the twentieth century the German language services gradually gave way to English. The church took the name of Main Street Methodist Church. A building fund was set up to build a larger church to better serve the community. During World War I materials and labor were scarce, but money continued to accrue. In 1922 twenty-five more people joined the church as a result of a revival making the time ripe for building a new church. On July 23, 1922, the final service was held and the next day the old church was taken down. The brick of the old church was cleaned and used in the foundation and basement of the new building. The congregation met in Salem Church while the building progressed.

During these same years, various groups formed the Ladies Aid Society, the Women's Foreign Missionary Society, and the Epworth League.

The cornerstone of the new building was laid in October 1922. Many delays followed due to railroad strikes and labor shortages, but, at last, the building was completed and on September 2, 1923, was dedicated. The Friday before the dedication, the congregation, visiting pastors and guests were invited to a banquet in the new dining area. A special service for the young people of Huntingburg, Holland, Zoar, and Santa Claus was held at nine o'clock on Sunday morning. Bishop Theodore Henderson preached the dedicatory sermon at the 10:00 a.m. service. In the afternoon at 2:30 p.m. a union service was held for all the churches in the area. At 7:30 p.m. in the evening the choirs of the Main Street Church and Salem gave a cantata, "The Great Light."

The red-brick building had Bedford stone trim and six Doric columns of white stone in the front. The forty-by-sixty-foot sanctuary had stained glass windows and accommodated five hundred people. There was a choir loft and behind the sanctuary was an area for the Sunday school and midweek services. This section could be opened up to give additional seating for 150 people. The basement featured a gymnasium with a balcony for spectators and also a kitchen and dining room. There were also two classrooms and two restrooms.

In 1931 the Main Street Church held its eightieth anniversary celebration. Several former pastors came back to speak at the event. The church ended its eightieth year with a membership of 216, a Sunday School of 320, an Epworth League, and nine other church-sponsored groups.[4]

Leaping from 1931 to the twenty first century—the church is now called Huntingburg UMC and is located at 416 North Main Street, Huntingburg, IN 47542. Its website is www.huntingburgumc.com.

Huntingburg Circuit—Holland Central German M. E.

The church in Holland had its origins in the Evansville and Boonville missions. In 1851 this latter mission was divided into the Boonville and Huntingburg missions. At that time, Huntingburg Mission included Huntingburg, Zoar, Santa Claus, Cannelton, Rome, Rome Settlement, and Oil Creek. In 1852 the mission was split again and covered Huntingburg, Zoar, Santa Claus, and Center.

The Central Church (at Center), which later became Holland German M. E., was dedicated on October 1859. The 1856 April quarterly conference (held at the William Kuck home) decided to build a brick church in the center of the preaching area. William Kuck donated the land and the bricks were made on the H. H. Fenneman farm to the south. The location of the church was near "Bob's field" which was land cleared by Bob Bolin who later went west. The church building was thirty-by-forty feet long and constructed of brick. Most of the work was done by its members.

Holland, Indiana, UMC, which began as Central German ME.

Central Church continued to grow in membership, partly due to camp meetings which were held at the Evangelical Maple Grove Campground and later at Zoar.

The quarterly conference of May 1879 decided to build a new church to replace Central Church and locate it in the town of Holland. At the February 1880 quarterly meeting, a frame church was planned for a lot on the eastern side of Holland. Bro. Kunz, who had laid out the lots of the town, donated land for the church. The building was forty-by-sixty feet long, and eighteen feet tall costing $2,771.83. The church had a steeple which featured a 642-pound bronze bell from the I. T. Verdin Company of Cincinnati. Not long after completion, the little brick church at the "Center" was torn down and the land reverted back to the former owner.

The new church building was short-lived, being demolished by a wind storm in 1883. The November 1883 quarterly conference decided to rebuild and another church thirty-six-by-sixty feet was erected at the cost of $2,000. In 1900 a Sunday school annex was added for the cost of $510. In 1904 a new Hinners & Albertson pipe organ was purchased for the church for eleven hundred dollars and installed in a small room added onto the east side of the church. Ed Kunz was the first organist.

The fifty year jubilee was held in 1906 during the pastorate of W. J. G. Bockstahler. At this time the total membership of the three churches in the circuit was 383. During this fifty-year period a total of $29,362 had been paid in salary for the preacher, missions had received $8,000 and other causes, $1,200.

More building was done in 1907 when the need for a parsonage was apparent and the resulting new parsonage was appraised at eighteen hundred dollars. In 1908, Huntingburg became a station with its own pastor, and Holland and Zoar remained together as a charge. Some other changes to the church building included a new steel furnace in 1912 and the first electric lights and a new coat of paint in 1914. The Epworth League purchased a quadruple silver communion set in 1918 and the community cup was no longer used.[5]

During the second decade of the twentieth century, things were not always easy for a German preacher. As I've mentioned earlier, this was the time when many German M. E. churches gave up preaching in the German language altogether. German place names were changed to patriotic—or at least, English— ones. A town in eastern Indiana changed its name from East Germantown to Pershing and today the sign reads "E. Germantown or Pershing." Parks and streets were renamed Liberty. While serving in Holland at this time, my grandfather became victim to some of the anti-German hysteria. On one occasion a nephew from New York dropped by to pay Grandpa and Grandma a visit. He had to stop and ask directions, so the story spread that an army officer was headed to Holland to take the German M. E. pastor into custody! In January of 1918, a government agent actually did pay Grandpa a call. He said rumors "had come to Washington concerning some of my sermons." Grandpa replied that he had done nothing against the government publicly or privately. He added that he had his Christian convictions on war in general, but didn't believe the government could prosecute him for that. The agent gave him a lecture on the cause and left without hauling him in as a traitor.[6]

In the 1920s a basement was excavated for the church. Electricity was connected to the pipe organ in 1924 and so ended the job of pumping the organ by hand. Some landscaping was done in 1925 and new church benches were purchased in 1928. The parsonage also underwent renovations. The basement was expanded and a new hot-air furnace, an automatic electric water pump, and complete bathroom on the second floor were installed. The kitchen received a new sink and a toilet was put in on the first floor. Parsonage renovations cost $1,570.

During the thirties and forties various repairs and upgrades were done on both the church and parsonage. Some of these included asbestos roofing for the church, repapering, replastering, and painting. Improvements were made on the cemetery which included new roads and landscaping. The parsonage received a sidewalk and a new furnace. In 1946 a new Wicks organ was purchased for the church. In 1947 a classroom addition, which also housed indoor toilets, was built onto the church. At the same time, old no-longer-used buildings such as horsesheds, woodshed, coal shed, barn, smokehouse, and summer kitchen were taken down. The church addition cost $4,750 and a new garage took another $585. In 1949 the pastor's salary was $2,936.

In 1956 the Holland church celebrated its one hundredth anniversary. On September 9 the evening service was held on the site of the old Central German M. E church. Former pastor Rev. Carl Allinger conducted the service in both

English and German. A Monday evening service was sponsored by the W.S.C.S. and Wesleyan Service Guild and featured a speaker on missionary work. Other services featured Revs. Ben Wibbeler and Alfred Wellemeyer who grew up in the Holland church. On Friday evening a pageant of the church history, written by Frank Hunefeld, was performed. After the Sunday service, featuring Holy Communion, everyone enjoyed a basket dinner and a time of fellowship which included sharing letters of congratulations from those who could not be present.

A new parsonage came on the scene in 1961. The old one was showing its age and so it was decided to build a new one on property across from the church. The modern home was a four bedroom tri-level made from Indiana limestone and aluminum siding and was erected for the sum of twenty-eight thousand dollars. Holland trustees purchased Zoar's share of the old parsonage and rented it out until it was torn down in 1974.

In 1974 the third Holland church, a red brick and limestone building was erected. Many furnishings of the old church were incorporated in it including the bell, minister's chairs, pulpit, and worship center. Some of the old benches and the altar were put in a small chapel in the new church. Church members did much of the work such as painting and carpeting. The total cost of the new building was $174,386.73. On January 19, 1975, everyone gathered in the old church and followed Rev. Max O'Dell who carried the cross from the worship center to the new church for the consecration. Former pastors spoke at an open house in May.

The old church was torn down, but the stained-glass windows were saved and then sold after the religious symbols were removed from them. A wooden cross was made from the old altar which was then hung on a wall in the new building.[7]

In April 1987 a building committee planned an addition to the church. Groundbreaking ceremonies held a year later featured a carry-in dinner and in January 1989 the new addition was consecrated.[8]

The Sunday school was organized in February 1856 at the old Central church. The twenty-two members had very few materials for their church education, as they met in homes and such materials had to be carried from place to place. The first Sunday school superintendent was Albert Rixse. When the new church in Holland was built, the Sunday school finally found a permanent home. All work was in German and children were encouraged to memorize Bible verses and then given a ticket with a Bible verse on it as a reward. These could later be exchanged for Bibles, songbooks, or Bible pictures. Mrs. Theodore Rudin [grandma] started the Cradle Roll in 1914 which comprised all the babies under two years of age.

The Sunday school was a big help through the years, purchasing furniture, literature and songbooks for the primary department and helping financially with building new classrooms. Some of the adult classes were active in keeping the grounds and cemeteries mowed. The Young at Heart class started the tradition of serving coffee, juice, and donuts before and after Sunday school.

The Sunday school picnic was always an anticipated function. In the early days, it was on the Monday after Pentecost, but was later moved to the third Saturday in June. It started as a basket dinner, but then became a moneymaker when the women of the church cooked the dinner. Other church groups sold sandwiches and ice cream and the school band played. In 1978 the picnics ceased and instead donations were given to make money.

Music was always an important part of any church and the Holland church had a choir since the beginning. The first pipe organ was purchased in 1904 and there have been many organists through the years. Wilber Hemmer served at that post for forty-eight years. In addition to a youth choir, a teen-age choir was started in 1981. The Epworth League organized a band in 1899 which performed at church functions, picnics, weddings, and at county fairs.

An organization for the young people of the church was the Epworth League, started in 1893. The group met once a month in peoples' homes and sometimes at the church. Dues were two and a half cents per month. Socials were a popular fundraiser and the public was invited to these. One of these functions brought in $3.35 over a period of two nights. In later years the group evolved into the Methodist Youth Fellowship and, in 1968, became the United Methodist Youth Fellowship. Throughout the years the youth were active in raising money for such causes as church repairs, the Lebanon Children's home, and for the church and parsonage building funds. Some of their projects were making homemade ice cream for an ice cream social, paper drives, bake sales, suppers, car washes, and selling homemade Christmas ornaments.

The women first organized as the Woman's Foreign Missionary Society in 1910. In 1913 the Ladies Aid Society was formed which helped with the maintenance of the church. Members met on a regular basis to quilt. (Grandpa's diaries mentions some quilts the group made which were bought by members of my family, so the quilting must have been a moneymaker for the Ladies Aid.) The Standard Bearers was founded in 1915 and composed of young ladies who studied a missionary book and supported the education of a Korean child. In 1940 the three groups united to form the Woman's Society of Christian Service. The Wesleyan Service Guild, composed of the younger women of the church, organized in 1949. Both groups were involved in many fundraisers including writing and selling cookbooks, cooking meals, and having soup and bake sales. The groups became United Methodist Women in 1968 and formed three circles—the Delilah Circle, the Hannah Circle, and the Ruth Circle. When the new church was built in 1974, the group bought new appliances for the kitchen and also paid for sinks, paint, pews, lights, and for repairs on the organ.[9]

In 1954 another group, called KIC (Kids in Christ) was started for children from ages two to confirmation age. The programs consisted of lunch, choir and a lesson and the average attendance was forty to forty-five children. This began about a year after Rev. Tom Stiles introduced the practice of "children's sermons" during the Sunday service. Another activity aimed at children (and busy parents) was the Hummingbird Daycare Center and Nursery School which was started in 1986 to serve the community.

I was unable to find anything in the Holland church history that tells when the United Methodist Men's group started or if another group preceded it. After the 1970s, however, they were involved in many church projects. In August 1989, they cleaned out the church garage, held an auction, and cleared the trees from the back of the church. In 1991 they planned a shelter house. In 1993 the Holland and Zoar men went to Florida to help with the rebuilding after Hurricane Andrew. A year later they headed to Florida again, this time to help Habitat for Humanity.[10]

The Holland church history (cited in footnotes) is one of the most thorough I've seen and covers the years from 1856 to 1981 with an update to 2000. The church is still thriving into the present and an elderly friend of my mother's, Miss Nora Schoppenhorst, kept me informed on things until her death in 2005. The ladies group still quilts and Nora reported it was one of her favorite activities, although she was close to one hundred years old. The address of the Holland church is Holland UMC, 205 North Second Avenue, Holland, IN 47541.

My grandfather pastored at Holland from September 1914 to September 1920. My mother and Uncle John spent the major part of their childhood years there and my mother always spoke of Holland with fondness. In her later years she visited there at least once a year. I'm going to skip around in my grandfather's diaries of that period to give a sampling of the Rudin family's life there.

Sunday September 19, 1914

Had very little sleep last night on account of a very bad cold. . . . We enjoyed a rather slim breakfast amid the boxes and barrels. We managed to get to Sunday School in good time. Bro. Will Fenneman asked me to address the school which I did in English and in German. By the way, I was under the impression that everything was German in this place, but I was mistaken. Some of the brethren have already told me that English preaching was needed here.

Monday September 21

A number of people brought peaches and quinces and some of he ladies came around to help Till at canning. Went to the mill to buy some feed for the chickens, of which I have some 30. Worked hard at unpacking and placing things, but made little progress. We had a fine chicken supper at Werremeyers.

Tuesday September 22

We like the parsonage here much better than the one in New Albany, and when we are once settled we will have a very attractive and cosy home, but we miss the water and gas accommodations. To have to get the water outside is quite an inconvenience. Some of the ladies again helped Till at canning. Also, received more peaches and quinces. Till has to be in the kitchen all day, but she is bearing up bravely.

Wednesday September 23

Till is still at canning, and I am making slow progress at unpacking and uncrating. By the way, our children are delighted with Holland, The other day John climbed one of the big trees on the place and called out one time after another: "This is the life!"

Saturday September 26

By the time we are through, we will have spent nearly $300 on account of this move. I will have to use all the children's money besides borrowing $150 to enable me to buy a horse and buggy. I intend to buy Bro. Johannes' horse and buggy which will cost me $145. That is the way it goes: The longer we are in the ministry the poorer we get. However, we will not despair: we will trust our Heavenly Father.

Friday October 3

The more we see of Holland, the better we are impressed. It is a prosperous and clean looking place. All the houses seem to be freshly painted and the grounds about them are well kept. German thrift and orderliness is evident everywhere. Also, the people impress us favorably: They are goodhearted and obliging. I like the looks of everything here, and it seems to me we ought to spend some useful and happy days in Holland.

Later, the thriftiness Grandpa found so admirable, came back to haunt him, witness this entry in 1917.

Thursday November 1, 1917

Impressed on the official board last night that something must be done in the matter of meeting the financial obligations of the church. I suggested that the treasurer be empowered to borrow the necessary money from the bank, if sufficient funds are not at hand to pay the preacher and the sexton regularly every month. The board passed a resolution to that effect. One worry less for me.

A year later, the financial end of being a pastor was apparently looking better.

Monday September 2, 1918

Dan Weitkamp paid up my salary last night, so I need have no worry on that score. Called on Adolph Hemmers this morning and paid another $10 on the horse note. [See Sept. 26.] That debt is now reduced to $25. This evening Till and I called on Frank Katterjohns. Frank and I looked over the church accounts. Enough money has come in to meet every obligation, and my salary is paid up. It is remarkable how well Holland and Zoar have done this year.

My grandparents left Holland for a position at Second Church in Cincinnati in 1920. The leaving was rather bittersweet—they hoped that the city would give their children some advantages that a small country town could not.

Taking leave of friends was difficult, but at the same time, there were some people they were not unhappy to see the last of.[11]

Sunday September 19, 1920

Preached my last sermons in Holland and Zoar today. Had big congregations in both places. Made the 103rd Psalm the basis for my remarks. In both churches the financial reports were given before the sermon. The Holland report showed a balance of over $100 in the treasury. The Zoar report showed a balance of over $27.

Monday September 20

Till accompanied me to Zoar yesterday. The people showed genuine feeling when we said goodby, as did many in Holland. Louis Hemmer gave me $2 as a remembrance and I gave him a book. Adolph Wibbeler and Frank Katterjohn helped to crate this evening and we expect to get our goods away by Wednesday.

Tuesday September 21

. . . a committee of ladies in Zoar presented Till with a set of fine table linen and $5, and they also said some nice things. We are certainly happy to have gained the hearts of the Zoar people: that adds sweetness to the bitterness we have experienced from some Holland people. This evening we had supper with Frank Katterjohns. Frank seems rather pessimistic concerning prospects in the Holland church. He thinks the church has reached its highest state of development and now it will slowly go downward.

Wednesday September 22

Well, our goods went off today and we are temporarily without a home. We had a fine chicken dinner at Adolph Hemmers and supper with the Will Katterjohns. The Standard Bearers gaveTill a surprise this evening and presented her with a beautiful writing outfit. They met at Hufnagels and ice cream was served and a regular program was gone through. Sold our chickens for $11.27.

Thursday September 23

Frank K. took us to Huntingburg, as he brought us to Holland when we came 6 years ago. We did not find it as easy to break away as we thought we would. Our 6 years stay here has now gone into the history of the Holland church. I can truthfully say, we never sought our own advantage but wished only that the Lord's work would prosper. I leave the appointment in fine working order and splendid financial condition. As to the spiritual life, that might be much better, but something has been accomplished in that direction.[12]

Huntingburg—Zoar Church

There has always been a link between the Holland and Zoar churches as preaching in the area went back to the Evansville and Boonville missions. In 1848 a log church was built on two acres of ground that the Herman Katterjohn family in Pike County donated. Today that land holds the grove area and part of the cemetery for Zoar. William Katterjohn built the log church but members and the pastor donated much of the materials and their labor, as well. Windows came from Evansville by ox cart. Furnishings consisted of log benches and a log pulpit. This first church, costing $27.50, was part of the Boonville Mission.

By 1856 the Huntingburg Mission had been organized and gone through several changes so that it included Huntingburg, Central (Holland), and Zoar until Huntingburg became a station in 1908. The log church became obsolete by 1869 and a new building was needed. The new church was built two hundred paces east of the log one which put it in Dubois County. An acre of land was purchased for thirty-five dollars and the building was completed in 1871. The bricks were made on the nearby Tellejohn farm. Each family provided labor and also hauled materials to the site. When finished, the church was forty-by-sixty feet, had an eighty-six-foot high tower and cost $4,158.20. This was around the time that the church came to be called Zoar. The name Zoar first shows up on a land deed in the 1890s.

In 1901 a fifty-year jubilee was celebrated for the Huntingburg Charge with special services held in Huntingburg, Holland, and Zoar. In that year also, the tradition of a Sunday school picnic which was held on May 18 began. Later, the date was changed to Memorial Day, due to the unpredictability of the weather earlier in May. The picnics featured baseball games, supper for fifteen cents and refreshments (peanuts, Cracker Jack, ice cream, bananas, and soft drinks). Amusements included a large two-seater swing where the young men would take their sweethearts. This was pulled high in the air by ropes and the energies of the remaining young people.

Epworth League also provided special events one of which was a combined program with Holland and Huntingburg. Activities at these gatherings included readings, talks, quartettes, etc. Protracted meetings or revivals were often held in the fall and would go on for several weeks. They usually featured communion on Sunday morning and a love feast of bread and water in the afternoon. The Christmas Eve program was probably the most loved of the special events. Decorations included two cedar trees strung with popcorn and adorned with candles. When the candles were lit, a man stood nearby with a damp sponge on a stick ready to squelch any fire that might break out. A Christmas pageant and recitations were presented and at the end of the evening each child received an orange and a sack of candy.

An organ, furnished by pastor J. F. Severinghaus (who had bought it so his daughter might play it), was used for the first time at the 1879 Christmas program. In May 1885 the church purchased an organ from William Blesch which was used until 1907. At that point, the organ was sold for $15.00 and a new one purchased for $101.02.

Unlike many church histories, the Zoar account describes funeral customs

Zoar UMC, near Holland, was often on the same circuit with the Holland church.

and the part the church played. The church bell was rung twenty-four hours before the funeral and then the bell was tolled one time for each year the deceased had lived. This let everyone in the community know about the death. On the day of the funeral, a short service was held at the home of the deceased and then the funeral procession began. An ornate hearse pulled by two horses led the way, followed by the mourners. When they were in sight of the church, someone tolled the bell until the cortege arrived. After the service, when the procession to the graveyard began, the bell would be tolled again. The grave was usually dug earlier by neighbors and the tolling continued until the party reached the grave.

In the 1920s one big change that occurred was the switching from German to the English language. By this time, most of the German families and their descendants were fully assimilated and the use of German was no longer needed. Also, World War I put a damper on the use of the language. Indiana passed legislation that made it against the law to teach German in schools. With the younger generation not knowing the German language, it became imperative to switch to English.

Although a few people had automobiles, their use was not practical at all times of the year due to the dirt roads. Pastors on the Huntingburg Charge usually traveled by horse and buggy until Reverend Ackerman arrived in 1929. (Grandpa Rudin told how some who had autos would take off the wheels and put the bodies on blocks for the duration of the winter.) In the 1930s the construction of the state highway caused a change in church routine. With better roads and the use of automobiles, the pastor could now have morning services in both the Holland and Zoar churches.

Another change was that of families sitting together instead of women sitting on one side of the church and men on the other. In 1934, the church gained its first electric lights when a power line was run from Huntingburg.

Some changes and repairs to the church building included colored windows, which were installed in 1907 for $125. In 1923 a storm did major damage requiring $650 worth of repairs. The altar rail and pulpit were also renovated at that time. In 1940 a basement was dug under the church and a furnace installed to replace the two heating stoves on the main floor. By 1947, major repairs to the tune of nine thousand dollars were necessary, so it was decided to build a new edifice.

In 1949 the trustees contracted with the Huntingburg Lumber Company to build their new church for $18,549.32. The conference gave advice and, after studying the financial situation and the church's membership, advised building a smaller sanctuary in the new church. The demolition of the old church began in April. The tower proved to be so solid that dynamite had to be used to topple it. The bell, which had been removed earlier, was stored to be reused in the new building. While the new church was being constructed, services were held in the school. When everything was completed, including furnishings, the cost came to $23,820.

The last major celebration to take place in the old building was the 1948 Zoar Church Centennial. This was held from August 15 to 22 and included plays, special music, and talks. Guest ministers and their wives joined Rev. Carl Allinger in participating. The church history, prepared by Elmo Langebrake, was read at one afternoon service. The old church celebrated its final service on April 24, 1949, and featured communion, baptisms of several children, and reminisces of past years. After the service, the church bell tolled seventy-eight times in recognition of the end of the old building.

Ten years later, the church experienced more growing pains: there was a need for an educational facility. In 1960 a vote was taken and those for an educational addition with a basement, won out. Work on the basement commenced on August 24, 1960, and a cornerstone was installed on October 16. Due to many helping hands and donations of materials, the work was done for a reasonable price and the building was dedicated on October 15, 1961.

Early in the church's history, the Women's Foreign Missionary Society was formed. The ladies of the church later organized a Willing Workers group in 1931. This evolved into the Ladies Aid in 1936 and became the Women's Society for Christian Service in 1940. When Zoar became United Methodist, the women's group changed its name to United Methodist Women. One of the major projects that the women undertook was purchasing the old Zoar School building and transforming it into a church parish hall. This was done when the group was the W.S.C.S. and the hall was used for the quilting sessions and the Sunday school picnic.

The Zoar church history ends at 1973, although the church is still active. I think it is fitting to end this writing with the final sentence from the history describing the Biblical Zoar: "Behold, now this city is near to flee unto and it is a little place: Oh let me escape thither and my soul shall live."[13]

Zoar UMC is at 8818 West Old State Road, Holland, IN 47541.

Following are some recollections and thoughts on Zoar from Grandpa Rudin's diaries. For more, see his comments on Holland.

Monday, October 5, 1914

By the way, the Zoar people have quite a fine church. It is of brick and kept in good order. I intend to hold protracted meetings at Zoar during the first half of November. I can then get around among the people and become acquainted with them. It will take some time before I will know all the people on this field.

Monday May 31, 1915

This afternoon we went to the Zoar picnic. The crowd was not as big as I expected, though towards evening it increased considerably. Several of our Holland people were present, also a number from Huntingburg. We had quite a nice time and were given our supper for nothing. At Holland we had to pay for it like the rest of the people. At Zoar the supper cost 15 cents and you could eat as much as you could hold.

Friday December 3

Yesterday concluded to discontinue the protracted meetings at Zoar as the people are too busy butchering and starting Christmas preparations. Louis Hemmer called to say he thought it best to have the meetings now. A number of people have phoned to him about it. Well, I was under the impression that the people out there did not care about the meetings at this time. If they really do, however, I am willing to accommodate them.[14]

Santa Claus, Indiana

The area around Santa Claus has been known by many different names. At first it was known as Harris Settlement—another source says Harrison Settlement. When Christian Wyttenbach moved into the area, the name was changed to Wyttenbach Settlement. It was also known as Santa Fe and the church itself was called Salem. The name Santa Claus came about when the settlers met in December 1848 and decided to choose a name for the settlement. Some wanted to name it after Reverend Wyttenbach; others opted for the German Settlement. Since it was December and a compromise was needed, the gathering unanimously chose the name "Santa Claus."[15]

Rev. Christian Wyttenbach came to the Santa Claus area in 1847 representing the Boonville Mission. He was so impressed with the community that he settled there and urged other friends to do so. He and two German families, the Hannings and the Ludwigs, founded the church in 1849.[16] The group built a small log church about 1853 but in 1859 a frame building replaced the earlier church.[17] Other sources don't mention a log church, but say that a frame church was erected in 1853 and dedicated in 1854. The new congregation used this building until 1872.

The land for the church amounted to four acres and four families donated one acre each—the Haas family gave the land where the cemetery is now located, the Basakas gave land which later became part of the campground, the Kruse family donated the acre on which the parsonage now stands, and the Schmucker family contributed the parcel that the church occupies.[18] Another source describes the land as "four acres and several frames" and goes on to explain that a frame was a section thirty-by-forty feet.[19]

In August 1857 the church claimed ninety pupils in the Sunday school, twenty-one officers and teachers, and 164 books in its library. The congregation had paid the pastor $224 in salary and the rest of the charge had given $200 making $424 in all. At the next quarterly conference it was agreed to divide the Huntingburg charge into two: Huntingburg and Santa Claus. A few years later, the Santa Claus circuit included Oil Creek and, in 1862, Cannelton, Rome, and Settlement were added, making it a rather strenuous assignment for the preacher. A year later, the other locations were reassigned and Santa Claus was again on its own.[20]

It is difficult to separate the church history from that of the adjacent campground which was part of the property purchased for the church. The first camp meeting was held in the summer of 1851 and yielded sixty converts. Evening services were held outside by the light of the moon or brush fires which were lit on platforms. The people stayed in "rough tents" until a tabernacle and cabins were built, while stalls were provided for the horses. Someone from each family usually went home at some point during the day to feed and water the livestock and bring back provisions for meals at the campgrounds. In 1884 a

The Santa Claus, Indiana, UMC was first called Salem. When the community took the name of Santa Claus, the German church followed suit.

tabernacle was built for the cost of fifty dollars. People would come from all the surrounding communities and farther away to attend.[21] My mother was a frequent visitor to the camp meetings, especially when her father was pastor at Holland. The excitement, crowds, and perhaps food, must have been too much for her, because she said about all she remembers is getting sick almost every time they went to a camp meeting. Then poor Grandma had to stay in the cabin with her and was unable to enjoy the proceedings.

In the early 1870s many congregation members wanted to build a new church but could not agree on the particulars. In 1872, Rev. J. F. Severinghaus was sent to pastor the congregation and he reported, "They demanded to build three instead of one church and if the preacher and the Presiding Elder did not agree, they wanted to separate from the congregation." Severinghaus eventually worked out a plan which brought everyone together for the building of one church. He related, "We began to build on November 15th [1873]. I had to be the leader of all work and I had to work hard without being paid additionally. The church is 40 x 60 feet, the tower 70 feet and the auditory 22 feet high." The old parsonage was torn down and a new one ready for use on October 15, 1873. The cost of both buildings was $5,184.73. After the completion of the new church, the previously warring factions seemed happy and united again.[22]

The history, written by F. A. Hoff, points out that the Santa Claus congregation was not always an easy one to get along with. When he was pastor there he was involved in the following incident:

On November 12th, Hoff held a meeting in which several probationers were dismissed. H. Hoffmeier, an administrator who was not present in the meeting began to quarrel and because he did this several times, Hoff, S. Wetzel, Fr. Kokomoor and G. Schreifer went to him to reprimand him. Hoff took these brothers with him so that he had some testimonies and also because he feared to be beaten. He did well, for as soon as Hoff began to talk to Hoffmeier, his son attacked Hoff and we don't know what would have happened to Hoff if he had not taken his brothers along. Hoffmeier called Hoff lier, son of a b——h and all bad names. Hoff was quiet. This happened on November 16th, 1880 to a Methodist preacher, in the house of a Methodist administrator and by a Methodist!

The two were eventually reconciled but the incident upset some of the congregation to the point that they no longer attended church while Hoff was pastor.[23]

During the first quarter of the twentieth century a number of changes took place to both the church and the campgrounds. During World War I, the name "German" was dropped and the official name of the complex became Santa Claus Methodist Church and Campground. Despite the war, attendance at the campgrounds was still good. In 1917 the Santa Claus Association was formed and the Evansville District relieved the local church of some of the work and expense. Later, the South Indiana Conference took over the running of the campground. A community hall was built at the suggestion of Reverend Ackerman for the cost of two thousand dollars. This was put to use for basketball and other athletics and, during the camping season, used as a dormitory. In 1913 English preaching was eased into the camp meeting programs.

When some of the young men in the congregation joined the service during the war, the women helped out by sending their soldiers boxes of knitted socks and gloves and other small items. The winter of 1918 was bitter with the country roads being almost impassable from the continuing snow which was hard on everyone.

Some improvements to the church included electric lights in 1919. The parsonage received a paint job in the 1920s. New furniture was proposed for the sanctuary including benches, choir seats, a pulpit table and a chair, which were paid for on a five-year installment plan.[24]

In 1933, the pastor's salary was set at twelve hundred dollars. There were about 177 members, but the church continued to have problems paying debts. At times, when the money was not at hand, the board borrowed from the conference, took a special collection, or borrowed from the bank. Often volunteers were used when it came to projects like painting, planting shrubs, and other small jobs. When money was needed for mission projects, some proposals were raising chickens, borrowing the money, initiating a fund, or having "the Lord's Acre." This latter venture involved providing land to the church members to plant a crop. The profit from the harvest was then donated to a mission project.

Some interesting board decisions during the second quarter of the century included paying the janitor a fixed rate of $75 per year (1932). In 1927, the janitor had earned $110. In 1934 the board forbade any card playing on church property. In June 1949 the annual report gave the value of the church building at five thousand dollars and the parsonage at three thousand. Everything was free and clear and no debts were outstanding. [25]

In 1949 the Santa Claus congregation celebrated one hundred years of working to spread God's word in the community. This was not just a recognition of the past but also an embracing of the future. For the first part of the 1950s, church business was fairly routine. Then in 1958, it was decided to add a basement to the church. Each member was notified and by the next meeting a sum of four thousand dollars was on hand for partial payment of the project. The remaining five thousand was borrowed from the bank. Several people donated money or items to enhance the undertaking. In 1959 accordion doors were purchased for dividers in the basement and restrooms were added. The finished basement had a worship center in the middle section and Sunday school classes also found a new home in the addition.[26]

In 1968 the church transferred forty acres to the Indiana Conference Corporation and, at the same time, sold the parsonage to them for $11,250. The church was allowed to continue to use the parsonage until June 1969. Jim and Mary Ellen Hanning donated an acre of land on Highway 245 as the site for the new parsonage. Plans were chosen and work started, much of which was donated labor. By 1969 the house was completed and paid for with money from the sale of the old parsonage, pledges, and donations. In 1974 a new thirty-foot garage was built onto the parsonage and the old one turned into a church office and pastor's study. The estimated cost for this work was $9,000.[27]

In 1978 it was time for improvements in the sanctuary again, and to add an educational wing, so in 1979 a bid of $236,247 was accepted. Various accouterments, such as carpeting and furniture, raised the total to $240,000. The money for this came from local funds amounting to $65,000, a $25,000 grant from the conference, a $25,000 conference loan, and a $125,000 loan from the bank. Upon the completion of the work, the congregation celebrated the consecration on December 2, 1979, with an open house in the afternoon.[28]

In the early part of the twentieth century, Sunday school was a family affair because of the mode of transportation. Families came for Sunday school and then remained for the church service. In 1924 there were 247 members on the roll. At that time Sunday school was organized as a separate body of the church with a board of officers and teachers. The offering was separate from the church offering. The Sunday school board held meetings just as the official board did but discussed only business pertaining to Sunday school.

There were several special programs throughout the year, one being Children's Day. This was a day the children were allowed to "shine" when they sang, gave recitations and performed in short plays. Another favorite time was the Sunday school picnic, usually held in July. Some features of that event were swings, ice cream, a fish pond, and snacks such as candy, gum, cracker jack, and soda pop. The people enjoyed picnic dinners and all kinds of games and contests kept the younger set occupied. Christmas was always celebrated, also, with a tree, a program, and treats. Everyone in the congregation received an orange.[29]

The young peoples group, the Epworth League, reported fifty-one members in 1931. This included junior high and high school students and even young married couples. Activities included Christmas caroling, visiting the sick, mission studies, and devotions. In 1950 an intermediate group was formed. A gratifying yearly event was the Epworth League Institute held on the campgrounds. On the program were Bible study, vesper services, campfire meetings, prayer circles, and recreation. Each year the campers traveled to some nearby place of educational interest such as Lincoln Park.[30]

Twenty-four of the men organized into the Methodist Men's Group in 1954. Meetings were monthly and consisted of devotions, business, a program, lunch, and social time. The men held many fundraisers which helped pay for some of the improvements at the church.[31]

In the early years of the century there were two women's groups—the Ladies Aid and the Foreign Missionary Society. As in most other churches, the Ladies Aid directed their talents to the local church and area; the Missionary Society focused on overseas missions. The groups combined into the Woman's Society of Christian Service in 1940 and, later, in 1972, became the United Methodist Women. Within the latter group were three circles: the Mary Martha Circle, the Rachel Circle, and the Rebekah Circle.[32]

Santa Claus UMC celebrated 150 years in 1999. The festivities commenced with a New Year's Eve Watch Service on December 31, 1998, with games, fellowship, snacks, and a worship service. A History Night, held on Sunday, February 7, began with a carry-in meal. The church was famous for its smorgasbord which was usually held in the spring. This was scheduled on May 8 and barbecued chicken was the star of the event. Tabernacle Sunday, also a tradition at Santa Claus, was planned for August 29 to be followed by a Pork Roast and carry-in dinner. The yearlong festivities climaxed with an "Old Fashioned Christmas Eve Worship Service" stressing the German heritage and providing gifts for each family.[33]

To learn about the present day Santa Claus church, go to the website at www.santaclausumc.org. The church's address is 351 North Holiday Boulevard, Santa Claus, IN 47579.

My grandparents and their family had many opportunities to attend the camp meetings at Santa Claus when grandpa was pastor at Holland. Here is grandpa's description of a camp meeting in in 1918.

Thursday August 1

Asked the Schoppenhorsts to take care of our horse and the chickens and we went to Santa Claus early this morning on Harvey Fenneman's truck. With us were about 20 of our people. heard part of W. J. G. Bockstahler's sermon. Dr. J. W. Oborn representing the Joint Centenary Committee followed him on Christian Service. On his invitation some 30 persons, including Till and myself, Ed Hemmer and his father signified their intention of becoming tithers. Dr. Stiefel of Baldwin Wallace followed with a Bible study on Paul. In the afternoon there was a WFMS meeting. Till was one of the speakers, representing the Extension Work and she did very well. Mrs. Herman Hemmer presided. Dr. Musser preached on the Holy Ghost this evening.

Friday August 2

The early morning prayer meeting was conducted by Charlie Miller. Bro. Claus preached the morning sermon on Isaiah 40:31. Dr. John Storms Pres. of Baldwin Wallace followed with a lecture on the "Challenge of the Future." Dr. Stiefel had a Bible study on Peter. This afternoon Miss Rexroth, a returned missionary, addressed the WFMS. She was followed by Dr. Storms on education. This evening Dr. Musser spoke.

Saturday August 3

Dr. M. was at his best last night. I had charge of the early morning prayer meeting. There was a very good attendance, and our musical director, Bro. Hal Weigle said to me at the close that it was a good prayer meeting. Other speakers were A. C. Baur, Bro. Kaletsch, Dr. Stiefel, Dr. Oborn and Bro. Weiler. Rosmarie [his daughter] was sick all day and Till had to take her home this evening. Henry Weitkamp was kind enough to take them in his car. Santa Claus does not seem to agree with Rosmarie. I did not feel well myself today, my stomach still not being in order.

Sunday August 4

Bishop W. S. Lewis was supposed to preach but had to cancel. Bro. Edelmaier led the early morning prayer meeting which was followed by the Love Feast in charge of Bro. J. F. Sevringhaus. Dr. Stiefel preached the Communion sermon and several hundred people partook of the Lord's Supper. Dr. Koch preached the afternoon sermon on Rom. 5:20. He was at his best. Went home after the afternoon service with Frank Overbeck.

Tuesday August 6

Dr. Koch was fortunate in having Hal Weigle as his singing leader. Bro. W. was refreshing and a good offset to Dr. Koch's severity. As it was, however, the camp meeting was a very good one in my estimation, though, of course, there are some people still who prefer the former days. There were no conversions, but there was much that was instructive along practical lines of church work. The tone of the camp meeting was educational, and that is needed in our day. The refreshment stand was closed all day on Sunday and this doubtless had a good effect on the camp meeting. Last year the stand was open the whole day to the scandal of right-minded people.[34]

Notes

1. Goodspeed Brothers, *History of Pike and Dubois Counties, Indiana* (Chicago: Goodspeed Bros. & Co., Publishers, 1885),577–78.
2. "The German Methodist Church," *History of the United Methodist Church of Huntingburg, Indiana*, 1984, 8.
3. F. A. Hoff, "Historical Record Santa Claus," (narrative translated by Mario Pelli, 1962) The Archives of Indiana Methodism, Depauw University, Greencastle, Ind.: 2.
4. "The German Methodist Church," 8–10.
5. *One Hundred Twenty-Fifth Anniversary*, Holland United Methodist Church history (Holland, Ind.: 1981), 2–9.
6. Rudin, Diaries, 1918.
7. *One Hundred Twenty-Fifth Anniversary*, 10–18.
8. "25th Anniversary of the Holland United Methodist Church January 19, 1975 to January 16, 2000," four-page appendix to the church history, 2000.
9. *One Hundred Twenty-Fifth Anniversary*, 18–33.
10. "25th Anniversary"
11. Rudin, Diaries, 1914–18.
12. Ibid., 1920.
13. William E. Bartelt, *It is a Little Place*, (Zoar, Ind.: 1973).
14. Rudin, Diaries, 1914–15.
15. Harold Claycamp, *History of Santa Claus Methodist Church and Camp Ground* church history, Depauw University United Methodist Archives, Greencastle, Indiana.
16. Ibid.
17. *Rockport–Spencer County Sesquicentennial* [Rockport? Ind.: Sesquicentennial Committee, 1968].
18. Claycamp, *History of Santa Claus Methodist Church*.
19. Hoff, "Historical Record Santa Claus," 5.
20. Ibid., 6–7.
21. Claycamp, *History of Santa Claus Methodist Church*.
22. Hoff, "Historical Record Santa Clause," 9.
23. Ibid., 10, 11.
24. Mabel Schaaf Roell, *The Santa Claus United Methodist Church Historical Record 1899–1999*, church history, (Santa Claus, Ind.: 1999), 9–11.
25. Ibid., 18.
26. Ibid., 28–29.
27. Ibid., 33–36.
28. Ibid., 50–51.
29. Ibid., 24–25.
30. Ibid., 23.
31. Ibid., 37.
32. Ibid., 39.
33. Ibid., 65.
34. Rudin, Diaries, 1918.

CHAPTER 12

Other Churches in the Louisville District

There were a number of other churches connected with the Louisville District, some for only a year or two; others for a longer period. In many cases, the information is sketchy, but I'll mention them, nevertheless.

Nashville, Tennessee

The William Cortes family visited Cincinnati in the 1850s and converted to the German M. E. Church. When they returned to Nashville, they joined the English-speaking Methodists but were not satisfied because of the language problem. They asked for a German-speaking pastor and the Rev. Philip Barth came to Nashville to serve as the German minister in 1854.[1]

A "fine brick church" was built in 1855 on the east side of North College Street between Locust and Whiteside streets.[2] The first floor of the new church was consecrated on Christmas Day, 1855. A group of sixteen probationers joined in 1858.[3] Rev. Philip Barth served the fledgeling congregation for five years and in 1859 his brother, Sebastian Barth, took over the position until 1861.[4]

During the Civil War the church was used as a hospital by both Union and Confederate troops. Rev. M. Cramer, who was brother-in-law to General Grant, served as chaplain to the Union troops for a year and was active in renovating the building. Another Union soldier, Andreas Graessle, also preached at the German church during this time.[5]

At the beginning, the church was part of the Methodist Episcopal Church, South, but was reorganized in 1865 and became a part of the Central German Conference of the Methodist Episcopal Church. Rev. John Barth (brother of the other two Barths) took over the pastorship in 1865 and retained that position for four years. When the church perished in a fire in March 1867,[6] Barth took charge of erecting a new building on North Cherry Street (between Jefferson and Madison streets).[7]

The new church measured about thirty-by sixty-five feet and could accommodate three hundred people. A parsonage was built on the same plot of land and all the property had a value of eight thousand dollars. Membership stood at about 120 in 1890.[8]

Knoxville, Tennessee

For a short period the Nashville preacher also served the German people in Knoxville. That must have been some commute! No wonder it is listed in conference records only in 1869 and then again in 1874 as "East Tennessee."[9] After that, it either joined another conference or was too small a charge to keep up.

Cullman, Alabama

Another church associated briefly with the The Central German Conference was the German-English Methodist Episcopal Church of Cullman. The church was organized in 1879 and English was preached on the first and third Sundays of the month—German on the second and fourth Sundays. The church became West Cullman M. E. Church in 1884 and apparently German services were dropped. A frame church building was constructed at the corner of Seventh Street and Main Avenue.

The church fell on hard times in the 1930s and was about to be disbanded when a revival service, held nearby, revitalized the congregation and it began to grow again. The reenergized congregation built a new sanctuary in 1960 and the growing continued. In 1971 the church chose a new name, becoming St. Andrew's United Methodist Church. An education addition was finished in 1992, a new steeple adorned the church in 1995, and a new chapel was added in 1998.[10]

Golconda, Illinois, Circuit

For a little more than twenty years the Central German Conference sent pastors to the southern Illinois area to minister to four churches there. The towns of Golconda and Metropolis are listed on a circuit from 1868 to 1892. In Pope County, where Golconda is the county seat, there were two churches.

Golconda Circuit—German Methodist Church

The church in Golconda, Illinois, was simply called the German Methodist Church. The trustees acquired the "west half of lot no. 68" in 1885 while the English church got lot no. 78. A one-story, brick church building was raised on the south part of lot no. 78 in 1886. This building was shaped like a cross with two wings on each side of the structure. The German church was consumed by a fire in 1887 and the English church damaged.[11] The Germans built a new frame church and used it until 1912 when the congregation disbanded and many members united with the English church. The trustees sold the building for $506 and the old German church was remodeled into a home.[12] The former German church is still standing and until recently was used as a home.[13]

Golconda Circuit—Waltersburg, Illinois

The other Pope County church was located in Waltersburg about five and a half miles west of Golconda. There were two churches built on the site and the newest one is "still in pretty good shape." The parishioners hold a homecoming there every year.[14]

Metropolis, Illinois

Metropolis, in Massac County, is a little further west than Golconda and also on the Ohio River. Its claim to fame now is as the "home to Superman," being the only town in the USA named Metropolis.

Metropolis—Zion Church

Zion Church had its beginning in 1895 when two acres of ground across from St. Stephens Cemetery were purchased. The first meeting house was a log structure, later replaced by a frame one which burned in 1918. The congregation built another frame church which they used until 1963 when it closed. At that time the Zion property, including the church bell, was turned over to the Powers Church. The empty building was sold and found a new life as a hay barn.

Zion was on a circuit with Brookport and Powers until 1955. At that time, it joined a circuit with Upper Salem and Independence where it remained until it closed.[15] The church was located at Midway but has since burned. You can still see the bell which was installed on a pedestal at Powers church to serve as a memorial to Zion.[16]

Metropolis—Upper Salem M. E. Church

There were only two brief mentions I could find concerning the Upper Salem

German M. E. church. One source says it was organized as a German church in 1860, when the building was also erected, but later changed to English. In 1954 there were forty-five members.[17] Another pictorial source shows a photograph and notes that it was built in 1862 on the road to Round Knob. In 1993 a Baptist congregation owned it.[18]

Henderson, Kentucky

Henderson, Kentucky, across the river from Evansville, also claimed a German M. E. church. It was first listed in the conference records in 1870. In 1873 it was paired with Salem (which was then known as *Schweiz* for Swiss). In 1875 the listing read "Henderson and Salem." After that, things get a little hazy as Henderson is no longer named but Evansville Mission is introduced in 1886 and it appears that Henderson might have been included with it.[19]

A historical atlas says the church was organized in 1872 and held services in the Cumberland Presbyterian Church. In 1874 the congregation built a twenty-four-by-thirty-six-foot church for the cost of twelve hundred dollars at the corner of Adams and Third streets. In 1880 the church claimed 118 members.[20]

Notes

1. Golder, Horst, and Schaal, *Geschichte*, 364.
2. W. W. Clayton, *History of Davidson County, Tennessee* (Philadelphia: J. W. Lewis & Co., 1880), 332–33.
3. Golder, Horst, and Schaal, *Geschichte*, 364.
4. Clayton, *History of Davidson County, Tennessee*, 332–33.
5. Golder, Horst, and Schaal, *Geschichte*, 365.
6. Clayton, *History of Davidson County, Tennessee*, 333.
7. John Woolridge, *History of Nashville, Tennessee* (Nashville: Publishing House of the Methodist Episcopal Church, South 1890), 465.
8. Woolridge, *History of Nashville*, 30.
9. *Minutes of the Annual Conferences*, 1869, 179 and 1874, 82.
10. St. Andrew's United Methodist Church, "Our History," www.standrewsumc.org/history, accessed 2009.
11. *Pope County, Illinois, 1986: History and Families, 1816–1986*, Pope County, Illinois (Golconda, Ill.: Pope County Historical Society; Paducah, Ky.: Turner Publishing, 1986).
12. Gerald R. Traupe, *The Goldconda Methodist Church*, church history, 1955, Linda Isbell, Southern Illinois Conference Archives collection, MacMurray College, Jacksonville, Ill., 2004.
13. Cheryl B. Cossey e-mail to Barbara Dixon, 2004.
14. Ibid.
15. Otis Riepe interview, article sent to B. Dixon by Leonard Copley.
16. *Massac County Historical Society, Massac County, Illinois* (Paducah, Ky.: Turner Publishing Co. 1987).
17. George W. May, *History of Massac County* (Galesburg, Ill.: Wagoner Printing Company, 1954), 117.
18. Massac County Historical Society, *Pictorial History of Massac County, Illinois* (Metropolis, Ill.: The Metropolis Planet, 1993), 122.
19. *Minutes of the Annual Conferences*, 1870, 210; 1874, 82 and 1886, 254.
20. B. N. Griffing and D. J. Lake & Co., *An Illustrated Historical Atlas of Henderson and Union Counties, Kentucky* (Philadelphia: D. J. Lake & Co. 1880), 16, 31.

PART III

The German Methodist Episcopal Churches in the Michigan District

The Michigan District of the Central German Conference covered not only the southcentral part of the Lower Peninsula, but also northwestern Ohio and northeastern Indiana. The most northerly point in the district was Petoskey, Michigan, and in the south, the district stopped just north of Spencerville, Ohio. From east to west the district ran from Goshen, Indiana, to Elmore, Ohio.

CHAPTER 13

Western Michigan
Grand Rapids

Grand Rapids, Michigan

A group of dissatisfied Lutherans founded the first German Methodist church in Grand Rapids. In 1858 they broke off from the Lutherans and started meeting in a hall at the corner of West Bridge and Scribner streets under the guidance of Rev. G. Laas. After a disastrous fire destroyed this building and others in 1875, the group built a frame church on the northwest corner of West Bridge and Turner streets. It was soon necessary to plan a new building due to the growth and financial strength of the congregation. In 1888 the congregation sold the frame building for eighty-three hundred dollars and purchased a new site at Scribner and Second streets. The new two-story church, completed in 1888, contained a ground floor with rooms for classes and meetings and an auditorium on the second floor large enough to hold four hundred people. The new church property was worth eighteen thousand dollars, including the church building and parsonage. The dedication was held on February 17, 1889, when one thousand dollars was collected leaving a debt of only five hundred dollars. At this time, the membership was 150 and the Sunday school claimed 125 members.[1]

Other sources don't mention the break with the Lutheran church by the German M. E. founders, but state that Rev. G. Laas was sent to Grand Rapids in 1858 and found "The field was white unto harvest." The first Sunday school made its appearance in May 1859 and the first quarterly conference was also held there in May of that year.

In 1866 Rev. H. Mantz was called to the circuit and began working with the people in Montague and White Hall (Muskegon), organizing a class, as well as preaching. In succeeding years the pastors on the Grand Rapids Circuit were given assistants to help out on the large circuit. In 1875, with the appointment of Rev. H. Pullman, Grand Rapids was separated from the rest of the circuit and

Former Valley Avenue German ME in Grand Rapids, Michigan, now home to Resurrection Fellowship.

had its own pastor. In 1881 Rev. H. Jend became pastor and organized the Ladies' Aid Society, the Epworth League, and also oversaw a renovation of the parsonage.

In 1884 a lot at Scribner and Second streets was purchased for $1,250 for the purpose of building a new church. Reverend Pullman returned in 1887 for a second time as pastor and supervised the building of a new house of worship as well as a new parsonage and sexton's house. In 1908, the church celebrated its fiftieth jubilee. The Central German Conference met at the Grand Rapids church in 1913.

In the early 1920s, growing pains again caused the congregation to build; this time on Valley Avenue. The German M. E. church moved into their new seventy thousand dollar facility on March 5, 1922. The week of March 5 to 12 was devoted to the dedication with former pastors speaking different days of the week and Bishop Theodore Henderson performing the dedicatory services. The new church was described as a building "of face-brick, intermingled shade from a chocolate brown to a light brown, trimmed with Bedford sandstone."[2] The education section of the facility included a manual training room, a sewing apartment, and a specially equipped room for babies. The ground floor area was composed of a gymnasium, lecture hall, and church auditorium which were separated by folding doors. The three rooms could be opened up as one large room seating up to twelve hundred people. A new pipe organ, costing five thousand dollars, was purchased for the auditorium. The only second floor rooms were the restroom and a reading room which was to be outfitted as a library for the community. The basement included the church office, pastor's study, kindergarten, nursery, locker room and showers, women's restroom, primary department and heating equipment.

The church's philosophy was summed up in the following quote:

Believing that Christianity makes happier homes, men and women more useful, and is the surest protection for boys and girls, we invite you to the fellowship of our church and community house.[3]

A brief, one-page history of Valley Avenue Methodist contributes a few additional facts. The Valley Avenue parsonage was on Flora Street. The total cost for church and parsonage was ninety thousand dollars. During the 1930s the church listed three hundred members. A Jewish congregation bought the old church at Second and Scribner streets. Some organizations of the church included the Home Department, Queen Esther, Kings Heralds, and Mother Jewels societies, Women's Home, and Foreign Mission societies, the Faithful Few Circle, and the Wide Awake Circle.

In 1977 another change took place when Valley Avenue Methodist and Second United Methodist Church united and became Faith United Methodist Church.[4] The new church relocated to 2600 Seventh Street Northwest. You can learn more about its present activities by going to its Web site at www.grfaithumc.org.

Hopkins, Michigan, Circuit

Rev. Gustav Bertram first visited the Hopkins area in 1856 and preached to a few families in Allegan and then started congregations at Salem and Monterey. The German work didn't come to the town of Hopkins until 1875, after which the circuit had four preaching stations.[5]

Hopkins Circuit—Allegan German M. E.

The congregation at Allegan met in private homes but eventually outgrew them and started meeting in the old jail. That was not too satisfactory as prisoners were upstairs and rats were frequent attendees. They then moved to the courthouse, but this was not a compatible meeting place either, so they built a small church.[6]

Land was purchased for the Allegan church in 1864, the church built in 1865, and the dedication held on December 1, 1865. By the 1880s, the German Methodist Church in Allegan County had a membership of 160 with a Sunday school of 145 members.[7]

Hopkins Circuit—Salem German M. E

The congregation of Salem met first in the private home of Casper Raab and later, at the house of Jacob and Adam Raab. A brick church was built on Section 8 of the township in 1868.[8]

Doris Plogsterd from Hopkins, Michigan, wrote a letter to me giving a little more recent history on Salem Church. It was known locally as "Market

Salem German ME in Hopkins, Michigan, now unoccupied.

Street Church" because the families in the area were farmers who took fruit and produce to sell at the Fulton Street Market in Grand Rapids. The membership decreased when some left to join the Pilgrim Holiness Church. A Sunday school was maintained for a while but later the church building was sold and is now privately owned.[9]

Mrs. Plogsterd put me in touch with her sister-in-law, Elnora Zischke, who also sent some information on Salem. She is a descendent of the Raab family and her uncle wrote a history of the family which gave some details of the church. She says meetings were first held in a schoolhouse and a church was built in 1868 on one acre of land donated by Jacob Raab. This first church was called Zion and always on a circuit with Hopkins and South Monterey. In 1906 the "new" church was built by Frank Buege and Charles Raab. In 1933 the circuit became Burnips, Salem, and Monterey Center. At one point the Salem Indian Mission was added to the circuit and they had services every other Sunday at the church. Eventually Salem (by this time called Market Street) became independent but this did not last long and the conference put it on a circuit with Byron Center. No one was happy about this and many left the church. Eventually, those remaining transferred to Burnips and, as of 2005, the old Salem building was being used by an apostolic group.[10]

There are pictures of the Salem church on pages 405 and 406 of the *Geschichte* showing the old church (probably the one built in 1868) and the newer one. When we visited the area in 1998 the latter church was still standing, although I'm not sure if it was being used.[11]

Hopkins Circuit—Monterey German M. E.

In 1856 Rev. Bertram also started the German church in Monterey Centre. Rev. Jacob Krehbiel, who followed, organized the first class. In 1868 the first church building was erected for the cost of fourteen hundred dollars with many of the members contributing their labors. At the time of the county history's publication (1880), the church claimed forty members and an active Sunday school.[12]

A church history says the first church was built on land deeded to the church trustees by Christian and Mary Sebright. Rev. Conrad Wauas was pastor at the time and the church was erected, following a great revival. Mrs. Lizzie Dendel started the first English Sunday school.during Rev. J. J. Link's tenure from 1896 to 1902. The Ladies Aid Society was organized under Rev. H. Ruekheim who served from 1905 to 1907.

In 1908 the German language was given up in Epworth League, Sunday school, and preaching services, and replaced by English. German services were held now and then for the benefit of the older members.

A rededication ceremony celebrated renovations to the Monterey German M. E. Church on October 13, 1912. The structure was elevated several feet and a basement installed under half of the building. A vestibule and spire were added on the southeast corner with memorial art glass windows and a fourteen-hundred-pound bell completing the work. The rededication was held in both German and English.

In 1933 the Monterey Church was transferred from the Central German Conference (which was dissolved) and united with the English-speaking church. The charge then included just two churches—South Monterey and Hopkins, the third church, Market Street (Salem) having been dropped.

South Monterey Methodist celebrated its one hundredth anniversary on December 2, 1956. Rev. Donald Cozadd was pastor at this time and several former pastors returned to join the festivities which included greetings from former pastors who were unable to attend, a reading of the church history, and a reception with an anniversary cake.

In 1961 the church underwent another remodeling. The entrance was relocated to the east side of the building and a twelve-by-eighteen-foot narthex added. In the sanctuary, the ceiling was lowered and tiled, the pulpit platform lengthened and a new altar rail installed. Pews were made uniform in length and the floor was tiled except where carpeting was put in the middle aisle, platform, and altar areas. The wainscoting was taken off and the walls plastered.

Renovations were again undertaken in 1972 with the enlargement of the parking area. A well was drilled so the church would have its own water supply and a new hot water heating system was also added. The church plant itself needed expansion, so a twenty-four-by-thirty-foot addition, including a basement, was joined to the north end of the church. These areas were used for Sunday school and a fellowship room.[13]

At present, South Monterey is in the Kalamazoo District of the West Michigan Conference and you may contact them via the conference website at www.westmichiganconference.org.

Hopkins Circuit—Hopkins German M. E.

The congregation at Hopkins was a comparative latecomer to the circuit, not being started until 1875. In 1880, the group built a church.

Mrs. Plogsterd related some of the history of the Hopkins Church in her letter. In 1933, when the German Conference was dissolved, the meeting was held at the high school. She relates, "It was a sad Sunday when we left our church. People were sober and some crying. Someone decided English [the church building] to be in better shape. We had the people and they the church." The German church building was sold to the Lutherans to be used as a parish house, later the Masons took it over and still later, the Mormons. At present it is a "bible church."

After the churches united, the English and German pastors shared the pulpit, one preaching one Sunday, and the other the next Sunday. Mrs. Plogsterd relates, "The English one would look down his English nose and don't think he liked what he saw! Our Schaenzlin [Rev. Fred Schaenzlin] had a heavy German accent. Our first minister as one church was Warren Brown."

According to Mrs. Plogsterd, the Hopkins Church was originally in the country and had a cemetery which is still there. The church moved into town and a new building erected. These were stories that her father (born in 1890) told her which actually took place before his time.[14]

Montague and Muskegon, Michigan, Circuit

The Montague and Muskegon churches were grouped under the title of White Hall Mission which also included the preaching points of White River, Flower Creek, and Duke Lake (Duck Lake?). There was very little information to be found on any of them. The history of Muskegon County devoted only one sentence to the Muskegon church: "The German Methodist Episcopalians have preaching in their own language."[15] I was able to find the location by checking city directories and in the 1891–92 book it was listed as "w s Hudson 1 s of Washington Ave."[16] Later it was listed as "s w cor 5th and Washington Ave."[17] Either the location of the church changed or a street name was changed. I looked up the latter site but the church was no longer there.

According to the *Geschichte* and its translation, the German Methodists began preaching at Montague in 1867. They first preached at the schoolhouse in White Hall and later at sites at White River and Flower Creek. The area was designated the White Hall Mission in 1869. In 1871–72, the name was changed to Muskegon and White Hall Mission. George Klett donated a schoolhouse to the congregation for their church in 1875. In 1887, Jacob Link started a Sunday school at Muskegon. From 1892 to 1894, preaching was done at "Duke Lake" [I could find no Duke Lake, but there were a couple of Duck Lakes in the area].

As the lumber industry declined, so did the population, thereby depleting the church membership, as well.[18]

Conference records show that both Montague and Muskegon were active churches until about 1920. After that, the circuit is listed as having only one church and being served from Grand Rapids. After 1921, the circuit is no longer listed.[19]

Freeport, Michigan, Circuit

There does not seem to have been a church at Freeport but, rather, it was the midpoint between the churches at Irving, Woodland, and the two near Lowell. The circuit was organized in 1874 when the churches at Irving, South Lowell and Woodland transferred from the Grand Rapids Circuit. Then in 1891 the North Lowell church joined to make it a four-point circuit.

Freeport Circuit—Zion German M. E., Irving, Michigan

About 1858 Conrad Beeler organized a Methodist class at a schoolhouse in section 14 of the township. Once every three weeks a minister from Grand Rapids came to preach. The congregation started building a church on section 2 in 1860 which was completed in 1869, although it was used while under construction. Rev. Gustav Bertram preached to the congregation of the new church and by 1880 the membership totaled forty-two.[20]

The *Geschichte* notes that the congregation disbanded in 1906.[21] In driving through the area, I could find very little of Irving left. There was a crossroads where Irving Road crossed route 43. We drove down Irving Road for a short distance but found nothing resembling a town or church.

Freeport Circuit—Woodland German Methodist

Two histories state the Woodland Church began in 1855 with a class which met at the Galloway schoolhouse. The meetings continued there until 1871 when the group started meeting in the English Methodist Episcopal Church. Originally, the church was served from Grand Rapids, but after 1874 was on the Irving Circuit. There must have bee an upswing in membership after that, as the congregation built its own church in 1876.[22]

A township history also states that the church began in 1855 at the Galloway School. The church that was eventually built in 1876 cost a total of $3,250.29.[23] The *Geschichte* says that the Woodland Church was started in 1856. Rev. Daniel Matthai was pastor in 1876 when the building was erected.[24]

When we visited Woodland, we found a nice, friendly town but no signs of the church. The postmistress, Mary Makley, was very accommodating and gave me directions to the library and the name and address of a gentleman with local history knowledge. The library was not open, but we stopped at the library at Hastings, the county seat, and found the Woodland Township history book there.

I wrote to the gentleman, Tom Niethamer, who Ms. Makley referred me to; and he replied that he walked by the church when he attended school. He was born in 1921 and could recall no church activity at all during his lifetime. In the 1940s the church was remodeled into a home and is still used as such. It is at 198 West Broadway in Woodland. He sent two photographs of the church as it is today.[25]

Freeport Circuit—Zion German M. E., Lowell, Michigan

This Zion Church was started six miles north of Lowell in a former Christian Church in 1891 with Christian Spaeth as the organizing pastor. After five years, the congregation decided to build their own church which was done at the corner of Lincoln Lake Road and Hunt Street.[26]

Another good source of information was a Vergennes Township history which gave personal accounts of the settling of the area. The Zion church was started by Swiss settlers to the area who spoke a Swiss dialect but had been educated in German. The author of the segment told of memories of her baptism and Christian education in the Zion Church. Saturday catechism classes were mandatory for the young people for two years. As people grew up and moved away, the church became too small to support a congregation and so it was eventually disbanded. The last pastor of the church bought the parsonage when he retired.[27]

Conference records show that the church was still active in 1933 when the conference was dissolved. It had had no regular preacher since 1931.[28] The building was eventually torn down.

Freeport Circuit—South Lowell German M. E

The *Geschichte* says that Rev. Gustav Bertram also started this church in 1860. It was served from Lansing and later, the Grand Rapids Circuit, until it was joined to the Freeport Circuit in 1874.[29]

I could find no mention of this church in any of the county histories or local histories. I happened to stop in the Lowell Chamber of Commerce office and told the woman there what I was looking for. I showed her the picture of the church from the *Geschichte* and she said, "That looks like our church!" Her church was in the town of Alto, south of Lowell. She said it had been German and had been moved to its present site in town. She gave me directions and we looked it up. Sure enough, it appeared to be the same church and later information (given below) confirmed this.

Janet Van Wyck of the Bowne Township Historical Society validated what the lady of the Chamber of Commerce told me. She sent me a one hundredth anniversary pamphlet giving the details. The first two paragraphs confirmed

The charming Alto UMC in Alto, Michigan, grew out of South Lowell German ME.

what the *Geschichte* said. In 1874 when the Freeport Circuit was formed, the people of South Lowell decided to build a church. This was patterned after the churches from the area of Germany the people came from. Some years later (about the turn of the century), an English-speaking Methodist church was started in Alto which met in the American Legion Hall. The German Methodists no longer used their church on a regular basis, so a deal was struck and the two congregations shared the German church building. By 1907, the churches had merged and the building was moved from its location at Merriman's Corner to Alto. It took two days to move the building, using rollers, to the lot in Alto which had been purchased in January 1907. The congregation later purchased a parsonage in July 1907.

In 1921, Alto, Whitneyville, Snow, and South Lowell (English) Methodist churches formed the Alto Parish Charge. This was served by two pastors—one in Alto and one in Whitneyville. Later, Whitneyville and Snow broke off from the circuit to form their own.

The church was well built. It still has the same floor that was installed by the German Methodists. The large timbers supporting the floor are the hand-hewn timbers put in when it was built. Some changes through the years have been paneling of walls and ceiling, carpeting, new furnishings, and new windows. The original windows were a frosted glass with a flower design. In 1955 stained-glass windows replaced the original ones. A kitchen, restrooms, and the "Upper Room" were added in 1956.

A women's organization has been a part of the church from the first and has gone through many name changes but has always had "Service, Compassion and Love" as its goal.[30]

The Alto church, which is in the Grand Rapids District, may be reached through the West Michigan Conference website at www.westmichiganconference.org.

Petoskey, Michigan, German Methodist Church

This church did not last long—at least there are statistics for it from only 1880 to 1895. The first pastor (other than supply) was Theodore Schumann in 1881, and the last regular pastor was William Rogatzky in 1893. The church started with twelve members in 1880, reached a peak with thirty-five and then declined to eighteen in 1895. There was no information about what circuit it was on, if any.

A volunteer from Little Traverse History Museum in Petoskey, Lowell Kosloskey, sent some additional information he was able to find. The Petoskey German M. E. was located at 502 Michigan Street and was started in 1880. Abner S. Lee sold two lots to the congregation for five hundred dollars.[31] The building was later used by the Baptists and, in 1910, moved by them to the northeast corner of Michigan and Waukazoo streets. In 1911 the Ben Israel Congregation purchased the building from the Baptists.[32] The German Methodists evidently sold the building about 1895, as the proceeds of $765 were given to Detroit Third Church in that year.[33]

Notes

1. Albert Baxter, *History of the City of Grand Rapids* (New York and Grand Rapids: Munsello Company, 1891), 316–317.

2. *The Evangelist*, Grand Rapids: Valley Ave. Methodist Episcopal Church, vol. 2, No. 7, 1922, folder 40, box 2–56, Nippert Collection, Cincinnati Historical Society Library Archives, Ohio (hereafter cited as *The Evangelist*, Nippert Collection).

3. *The Evangelist*, Nippert Collection.

4. J. Lindholm, one-page history, 1989.

5. Golder, Horst, and Schaal, *Geschichte*, 404.

6. Ibid., 404.

7. Crisfield Johnson and D. W. Ensign, *History of Allegan and Barry Counties, Michigan* (Philadelphia: D. W. Ensign & Co., 1880), 162.

8. Ibid., 322.

9. Doris Plogsterd to author, May 25, 2004.

10. Elnora Zischke to author, Feb. 8, 2005.

11. Golder, Horst, and Schaal, *Geschichte*, 405, 406.

12. Johnson, *History of Allegan*, 286.

13. *South Monterey United Methodist Church*, history and dedication program, (South Monterey, Mich., 1973), 1–5.

14. Plogsterd to Dixon, Nov. 25, 2004.

15. H. R. Page and Co., *History of Muskegon County, Michigan* (Chicago: H. R. Page & Co., 1882), 145.

16. *Muskegon City Directory* (Detroit: R. L. Polk & Co.'s, 1891–92), 31

17. *Muskegon City Directory* (Detroit: R. L. Polk & Co.'s, 1912), 39.

18. Golder, Horst, and Schaal, *Geschichte*, 393.

19. *Minutes of the Annual Conferences*, 1920, 994; 1922, 912.

20. Johnson, *History of Allegan*, 446.

21. Golder, Horst, and Schaal, *Geschichte*, 390.

22. Johnson, *History of Allegan*, 507.

23. Catherine Mary Arnott, comp., *The History of Woodland Township* [Ann Arbor, Mich.]: C. M. Arnott, [1987], 22.

24. Golder, Horst, and Schaal, *Geschichte*, 390.

25. Tom Niethamer to author, Nov. 17, 2004.

26. Lowell Board of Trade, *Lowell: 100 Years of History, 1831–1931* (Lowell, Mich.: The Lowell Ledger, 1931), 3.

27. Marion Roth Yates, "The Swiss in Vergennes," *Vergennes Township Living History*, ed. Eunice Vanderveen, 45–46, 1984, www.vergennestwp.org.

28. *Minutes of the Annual Conferences*, 1933, 36; 1931, 454.

29. Golder, Horst, and Schaal, *Geschichte*, 391.

30. *One Hundredth Anniversary of the Alto United Methodist Church*, history pamphlet (Alto, Mich.:, 1974).

31. Liber 1, page 601. Emmet County Deeds, Petoskey, Mich., 1880.

32. Little Traverse Historical Society, *Historical Glimpses—A History of Petoskey* (Petoskey, Mich.: Little Traverse Printing, 1986).

33. Golder, Horst, and Schaal, *Geschichte*, 381.

CHAPTER 14

Detroit Area German Methodist Churches

Detroit, Michigan

Detroit—First Church

First Church was organized in May 1847 and held meetings in a building on Brush Street. In 1848 the congregation built their own church building at the corner of Croghan and Beaubien streets for the total cost thirty-three hundred dollars, including a three-hundred-dollar lot. The parsonage was built behind the church in 1857 and cost eight hundred dollars. In 1873 the church, which seated three hundred, underwent a twenty-six-hundred-dollar remodeling especially to the front of the building. Some financial figures for 1880 show the value of the church as ten thousand dollars, an annual salary of six hundred dollars for the pastor, and the annual expenses were one thousand dollars. The average attendance was 110 and the number of members, 133.[1]

The *Geschichte* gives a slightly different version of the church's beginnings. Revs. Peter Schmucker and John Martin Hartmann began a Sunday school and held preaching services in a schoolhouse in Detroit in 1846. A country mission ten miles away was also founded at this time by Reverend Hartmann. The congregation of fifty-six and was organized in May 1847.[2]

For many years the church was just referred to as the "Beaubien Street Church." Then (probably when a new building was erected at Campau Avenue and Heidelberg Street), it became "First Church" in the records. Other nearby towns and preaching points were served from the Beaubien Street Church, including Roseville, Grosse Point, Redford, St. Clair, Newport, Pontiac, and Ann Arbor. By 1864 (when the Central German Conference was organized), Ann Arbor became independent and Roseville was on its own by the 1870s.

The church underwent a renovation in 1874 for the cost of $2,586 and was also elevated from mission status to an independent station. A few years later the Beaubien property was sold for nine thousand dollars and a new two-story brick church, along with parsonage and sexton's home, was built at Campau and Heidelberg streets. The outlay of twenty-three thousand dollars for this complex brought some financial hardships which were eventually overcome under the leadership of Rev. O. Rogatzky. In 1901, the church received a renovation and a pipe organ for a total of three thousand dollars.

By the beginning of the twentieth century, the church was flourishing with 225 full members and 14 probationary ones. The many activities sponsored included a Home Department, Cradle Roll, singing group, youth group, Junior Epworth League, women's mission group, genealogy group, Flowering Promise Group, men's group, and the Mutual Support in Death group which was not restricted to just the congregation.[3]

Around 1921, the church took a new name and became Immanuel instead of First Church. Later, in 1928, the name underwent a spelling change and became Emanuel. It is not listed in the German Conference records after 1931.

Detroit—Second Church

In 1857 Rev. Gustav Bertram came to the area known as "West Detroit" and began Second Church. The first preaching place was a schoolhouse on Fourth Street and the congregation was made up of people in that area and some from First Church. A member of the English Methodist Church donated a piece of land on Sixteenth Street where members of the new church built a meeting place and parsonage in 1858. After forty years and a period of growth, the congregation purchased a lot at the corner of Twenty-fourth and Butternut streets. Although a new building was erected there during the tenure of pastor Ernst Werner, Second Church still struggled with debt and lost members when Third Church was organized. At last, in September 1902, the mortgage was finally burned.[4]

Another source is more explicit about the site of the church, describing it as being on Sixteenth Street, which at that time was called Lasalle, between Michigan Avenue and Dalzelle Street. The source also states that J. W. Johnston gave the greater part of a donation of one hundred dollars for the church lot. The completed church cost fifteen hundred dollars and seated two hundred people. The parsonage, built a year later, cost three hundred dollars. In 1880, the membership totaled about one hundred people.[5]

The church was often referred to in records as the Lasalle Avenue Church until 1868 when the street name was changed to Sixteenth. It was on a circuit with Roseville until 1871. In 1921 the church evidently moved again and was given the name of Twenty-Fourth St. Church.[6]

Detroit—Third Church

Third German M. E. in Detroit was founded in August 1894 in the western area of the city and at the writing of the *Geschichte* there were 114 members.[7] In

Farmer's history of Detroit and Michigan a Thirty-second Street German Church is mentioned located on Thirty-second Street near Michigan Avenue. The lot and the building, dedicated in February 1882, cost sixteen hundred dollars and had a seating capacity of two hundred. The first pastor was R. Pluddemann.[8] It is not clear whether Third Church and Thirty-second are one and the same or different churches.

In the Central German Conference statistics, Thirty-second Street Church first appears in 1882 and then disappears in 1885.[9] The minutes also list R. Pluddemann as pastor that first year. In 1893 "City Mission" appears for the first time and in 1894 is listed as Third Church in the statistics. W. F. Hayn was named as the first pastor.[10] In 1895, a church was built costing $7,174 which was, apparently, a bit of a hardship as George Kalmbach of Grand Rapids donated $2,000 and the conference gave $765 from the sale of the Petoskey church, to help defray the cost. Except for $800, the rest of the amount was paid off during the tenure of pastors Hayn and Giesen. The succeeding pastor, Paul Wurfel, paid off the rest of the debt and was responsible for acquiring land and erecting a parsonage next to the church. During the early years of the twentieth century, Third Church was renovated with new heating and electric lights.[11] Third Church continued to be listed until 1928.*

The annual conference of the Central German Conference was held four times at Detroit: 1874, 1901, 1919, and 1924. Grandpa Rudin attended the latter three of these. He didn't say much about the churches per se but following are some of his comments on the city and the conference, itself, in 1919.

> Monday, September 1
>
> Set out at 2:30 this morning for Detroit, the seat of the Conference. The 3:35 train was on time. Arrived at Detroit more than an hour overdue at 10 this evening and found nobody at the station to meet me. After riding around and tramping around with my heavy suitcase until nearly midnight, trying to find the home of my hosts, I finally put up for the night in Hotel Cadillac to the tune of $2. I was about "all in" when I got to my room.
>
> Tuesday September 2
>
> Had a few hours sleep last night and felt refreshed this morning. Lunched in a restaurant. After some more asking and tramping, I finally got the right car and arrived at the church at 8:30. Most of the people I asked for information did not know anything themselves. Was through with the examinations at 10. Took a walk over town and dined in a restaurant. Went and got my grip and then set out to find my boarding place. Found it after some more asking and tramping from one corner to

---

*. I apologize for any misinformation I may have given here about the Detroit churches—sources were confusing with street names changing and churches moving several times.

another and was mighty glad to have at last found a "haven of rest."

Wednesday September 3

Last night Bishop Henderson conducted a "Quiet Hour." He talked on Christian Service and Obligations. This afternoon Br. Edelmaier preached the Conference sermon. His text was Psalm 90:17. Dr. Diehl followed with an address on "The Rural Work." He said the country will face disaster if the tendency to leave the farm is not checked.

Thursday September 4

The Bishop gave us a long talk before the regular session of the Conference. The afternoon and evening meetings were held in 24th St. Church. A meeting in the interest of the WFMS and the WHMS was held. Missionary Schaenzlin and a representative of the WHMS were the speakers. Bro. Gustave spoke for the Orphan Home.

Saturday September 6

This morning Dr. Rice, the "greatest preacher in Detroit" spoke to us for over an hour. What he said was good, and he stuck to his topic: "Loving your Task." This afternoon there was a short session after which the preachers were given a sight-seeing auto trip. I did not take in the trip, as I wanted to do some shopping. I also permitted a Detroit barber to cut my hair and shave me for which he charged me 60 cents. They fairly rob you in this town.

Sunday September 7

Br. Schruff got home after 12 last night having been out with friends. I got home quite early and had a pleasant chat with Mayers on their porch before we turned in. This morning Bro. Schruff and I were among the first to arrive at the 24th St. Church.

Friday September 12

Bro. Schruff and I had a good stopping place. Mayers tried to make it as pleasant for us as possible. Bro. M. is foreman in a railroad shop and apparently gets good pay. He was for years supt. of their Sunday School and Mrs. M. is very active in the Ladies Aid. Bro. M. is much like his famous brother John, the district superintendent, with the highest opinion of himself. But then, who is not like that.[12]

Roseville, Michigan—Roseville German Methodist Church

Jacob Rothweiler began preaching on a regular basis in the Roseville area in 1847 in a building on the Bronnemann farm. By 1848 more families were coming to services so in 1849, he was able to organize a congregation. During the pastorate of Jacob Krehbiel a church was erected and since the upbringing of the children was a concern, a Sunday school was started in October 1851.

The district served from Roseville was large—one hundred miles long containing eight appointments so was quite a chore to care for. As if that wasn't hardship enough, for a period of two years the pastor had to live in a cow barn. This latter trial was rectified in 1860 when, during the appointment of Jacob Braun, a proper parsonage was built. By the early 1870s, the congregation had grown so much that a new church building was needed. While J. W. Freyhofer was pastor, this need was satisfied and the new church was consecrated shortly before the conference in 1873. In 1894, Roseville church became independent and the preacher no longer had to travel long distances to serve the people.

In July 1894, lightening hit a stable near the parsonage and soon the pastor's home was destroyed by the resulting fire. The congregation buckled down to the task at hand and completed a new parsonage for the cost of eleven hundred dollars.[13]

In the early twentieth century many changes transpired in the area as it became more urbanized. The widening of Gratiot Avenue (where the church was located) necessitated the moving of the church and parsonage back from the road so the road widening could take place. At this time, basements were also added to the buildings. Church membership increased to 150 and the Sunday school claimed 190 members. In May 1923, all services switched to the English language. There was an Epworth League of fifty-six members and the Ladies' Aid had thirty-six. Other groups formed included Woman's Foreign Missionary Society, Light Bearers, and King's Heralds.[14]

Marine City, Michigan, Circuit

The Marine City Circuit consisted of a number of churches and preaching points, some temporary and others lasting long enough for churches to be established and built. The *Geschichte* pictures three on page 393—Immanuel (Swan Creek), Salem (Belle River), and Zion. Other preaching points mentioned are St. Clair, Mt. Clemens, Newport, Port Huron, Lexington, Quicksroad, Richard's Schoolhouse, Baltimore Station, New Haven (Omo Zion—see below), and Chesterfield. Some of these mentioned may be name changes. For instance, Newport church may be the same as Marine City.

Marine City Circuit—Zion German Methodist Church

The Zion Church was started by Rev. John Neir in 1897 [*sic*] when services were first held in homes and in the Dryer schoolhouse. In 1870, land was donated by Chester Dryer but to be sure everything was legal, the congregation paid him ten dollars. The pastor in 1891 served two German congregations.

When pastor T. A. Speckman was called to the church (1904–1907), the building was enlarged with the additions of a new wing on the northwest corner and a bell tower over the main entrance. In 1922 a basement was installed and the front steps enclosed.

In 1942 the Methodist churches at Armada, Berville, and Omo (Zion) were merged. Some other subsequent changes were the purchase of two and a half acres of adjacent land to give more space for parking and for future expansion. In 1992 a well was dug so plumbing could be installed. The twenty-first century brought a new audio system, new wiring and a new drop ceiling in the basement.[15]

Omo Zion has a nice website that gives additional history and information about the former German church. See www.omochurch.org.

Marine City Circuit—Salem German M. E. Church (Belle River)

German Methodism came to the Belle River area of St. Clair County around the year 1851. Two young German men from Detroit, Heinrich Balzer and John Altmann, sought out their countrymen, settled along Belle River, and began to preach the gospel. Soon they persuaded their Detroit pastor, J. A. Klein, to join them from time to time.[16]

On September 19, 1851, the Ohio Conference of the Methodist Episcopal Church created the St. Clair and Mt. Clemens Mission with Rev. Jacob Krehbiel as pastor. This was a rather large circuit which spanned the area from Roseville to Lexington north of Port Huron. On November 17 of the same year, the presiding elder, Rev. N. Nuhfer, held a meeting at the home of Gottfried Diem and organized the Belle River German Methodist Mission which later became Salem Methodist Church.

The church grew steadily during the 1850s and the pastor reported a Sunday school with twenty-six students and six officers and teachers. A church library was started containing two hundred books and in 1853 the first church was built. In 1855 the circuit was divided and became St. Clair and Newport Mission. The following were the preaching sites for the circuit: Belle River, St. Clair, Newport, Swan Creek, Port Huron, Quicks Road, Richard's Schoolhouse, and Lexington. A parsonage was secured at Newport (Marine City).

In 1892 a new parsonage was purchased closer to Salem Church on Meisner Road. The trustees purchased three acres of land (which included the parsonage) and in 1894 moved the church there after which it was enlarged and fixed up. In the late 1930s it underwent another renovation including a fresh coat of paint. The trustees also applied the paint brush to the parsonage in 1942. In November 1941 Salem celebrated ninety years serving the people of the area.[17]

Until about 1926 Salem was on a circuit with Zion (in Macomb County) and Emanuel (in Ira Township) which counted 205 full members and 10 probationary ones. Each had a Sunday school and there were Epworth Leagues at two of the churches, two Ladies Aid societies and two choirs.[18] After 1926, only two churches remained on the circuit, the dropped one probably being Emanuel on Swan Creek.

From the disbanding of the Central German Conference until 1941, Salem had its own pastor. Then it joined the St. Clair Charge until 1946 when it became part of the Marine City Charge. In 1951, Salem celebrated its one hundreth anniversary.[19]

Marine City Circuit—Immanuel (Emanuel) German Methodist (Swan Creek)

Emanuel shares much of its early history with Salem. Its first mention was as a preaching place on the St. Clair and Newport Mission which was organized in 1855. In 1860 a church building was erected. About 1906 it was renovated.[20] Until 1928 it was on a preaching circuit with Salem and Zion.[21] At that time the circuit was reduced to two churches and the best guess is that Emanuel was closed or combined with another church.

NOTES

1. Silas Farmer, *The History of Detroit and Michigan* (Detroit: Silas Farmer & Co, 1884), 575.
2. Golder, Horst, and Schaal, *Geschichte*, 377.
3. Ibid., 378.
4. Ibid., 379.
5. Farmer, *The History of Detroit and Michigan*, 575–76.
6. *Minutes of the Annual Conferences*, 1867 to 1921 editions.
7. Golder, Horst, and Schaal, *Geschichte*, 381.
8. Farmer, *The History of Detroit and Michigan*, 576.
9. *Minutes of the Annual Conferences*, 1882, 218; 1886, 253
10. Ibid., 1893–1895.
11. Golder, Horst, and Schaal, *Geschichte*, 381.
12. Rudin, Diaries, 1919.
13. Golder, Horst, and Schaal, *Geschichte*, 396–97.
14. *Souvenir and Program of the Diamond Jubilee of the Roseville Methodist Episcopal Church*, Roseville, Michigan, 1924, folder 41, box 2–56, Nippert Collection, Cincinnati Historical Society Library Archives, Ohio.
15. "Omo Zion United Methodist Church," www.omochurch.org, 2009.
16. Golder, Horst, and Schaal, *Geschichte*, 392.
17. *Salem Methodist Church 90th Anniversary,* program, (China Township, St. Clair County, Mich.,194) 1.
18. Golder, Horst, and Schaal, *Geschichte*, 393.
19. Floyd Boughner, *History of the First Methodist Church in Marine City, Michigan*, church history (Marine City, Mich., 1949), 14.
20. Golder, Horst, and Schaal, *Geschichte*, 392–92.
21. *Minutes of the Annual Conferences*, 1928, 820–21

CHAPTER 15

Central Michigan Churches

Ann Arbor, Michigan—First German M. E. Church

In 1846, the Ohio Conference (meeting at Piqua, Ohio) decided the time was right to start a German Methodist Church in Ann Arbor and a sum of three hundred dollars was earmarked for a missionary's salary. John Seddelmeyer and his family arrived at the city in October 1846 and he secured permission to preach in a schoolhouse. During the first year, twenty-two members gathered and the mission was officially founded in 1847. The amount of three hundred dollars was raised and a building site was purchased on Devison [*sic*] Street. After six hundred dollars was pledged, the church was built in two years with all but three hundred of the cost being paid off. Soon thereafter, Ypsilanti, Chelsea, Francisco, and Waterloo were added to the circuit. Francisco later became independent and the other places were given up or attached to different circuits.

At the first quarterly conference, participants in 1895 decided to sell the church property and buy another site. The congregation realized six thousand dollars from this sale and purchased a new site at the corner of Fourth Street and West Jefferson. A new parsonage was built at 514 West Jefferson, as well as a new church building. Rev. Louis Allinger consecrated the new debt-free property on July 12, 1896.[1]

After converting to the English language during World War I, the church took the name West Side Methodist Church and later moved to Seventh Street. The Reorganized Church of the Latter Day Saints has been using the building since 1950.[2] In 1948, under the pastorship of Rev. Edwin Weiss, the church began to grow rapidly and soon doubled the size of its congregation. In 1950 the congregation purchased a new site on South Seventh Street. By 1952, a new church was built and the church expanded further in 1955 by purchasing property north of its location. Two years after that, they campaigned for funds for an

Ann Arbor First German ME, now used by the Reorganized Church of the Latter Day Saints.

educational building. This was so successful that a pipe organ was also purchased and a small plot of land for a driveway was also added. During the ensuing years stained glass windows were purchased, improvements made to the organ, driveways and parking areas paved and more land acquired. In 1988 the educational building was the target of more renovation and a connecting arm between it and the church was constructed . The current address of West Side is 900 South Seventh Street, Ann Arbor, MI, 48103.[3] See the website www.westside-umc.org/.

Ypsilanti German Methodist Church

So far I have been unable to find any information on this church.

Chelsea German Methodist Church

I have not been able to find anything more than a mention of this church.

The Salem Grove UMC was part of the Francisco Circuit in Grass Lake, Michigan, during its German days.

Francisco, Michigan, Circuit

The Francisco Circuit, which includes the churches at Francisco and Waterloo, was originally part of the Ann Arbor Circuit. It separated from Ann Arbor to become an independent circuit about 1874.

Francisco Circuit—Francisco German Methodist Church aka Salem Grove

The first German Methodist pastor to come to the Salem Grove area was Rev. Jacob Rothweiler in 1852. A year later Rev. John Schweinfurth founded the church society. People offered their homes for services for several years until about 1858 when a frame church was built during the second term of Reverend Schweinfurth. William Riemenschneider donated the land for the church and parsonage, which was not built until 1870.[4]

In the early years of the church, it was a part of the Ann Arbor Circuit and so the pastors resided there. In 1874, Salem Grove and Zion in Waterloo formed a new circuit and were separated from Ann Arbor. The *Geschichte* entry also states that the church met in a log cabin for five years before building their church in 1858.[5]

Michael Schenk donated the funds in 1887 for a new church building which became a reality in 1888. Many local materials such as stone for the basement and beams hand hewn from nearby trees were used. Area sawmills furnished other lumber and the male church members donated much of the labor. The architecture was in the German style reflecting the heritage of the members. The original frame church was moved and used first as a stable and, after a remodeling, as a garage.

Through the years other renovations took place. The basement was enlarged during the tenure of Rev. George Nothdurft. Originally, heat was provided by a large wood stove with a central register which had the disadvantage of roasting the people nearby and not warming those any distance away. A gas-fueled furnace solved this problem and gas, also, provided lights before electricity came to the area. Front entrances were rebuilt in 1952 and the sanctuary renovated in 1962. A new kitchen was installed in the basement, siding added to the exterior, and the stained-glass window in front redone. Other improvements included a new organ, a ramp, and a unisex restroom. In 1986 the chimney was rebuilt and later air-conditioning was added. The floors of the sanctuary were refinished, new carpet installed and the front doors refurbished in 2000.

Since its beginning, the church was referred to as the Francisco German Methodist Episcopal Church but after 1929 became Salem Grove. In that same year, the old parsonage caught fire and many church records were destroyed. When it was rebuilt, Rev. Henry Lenz and his family were the first occupants. At present the parsonage is not used by the pastors but is rented out providing additional income for the church.

The Ladies Aide Society was founded by Mrs. Militzer, wife of the pastor, in 1890. Like most women's societies of the Methodist Church, it has gone through several name changes and is now United Methodist Women. Soon after its founding, the group funded the church belfry. Today the Christmas Bazaar is their fundraiser and attracts people from all over the area.

The Epworth League for the young people was begun in the early years and is now the United Methodist Youth Fellowship. This group was instrumental in purchasing an electric organ for the church.

In 1874 when the Francisco Circuit was organized, Zion in Waterloo joined Salem Grove on the circuit, but by the 1920s, the Waterloo church was no longer connected to the circuit. In 1951, Salem Grove became part of another circuit with North Lake Methodist which lasted until 1974.

The anniversary booklet for Salem Grove's 150th anniversary in 2003, contained some reminisces that various members contributed. Nadine Artz and Virginia Elkins spoke of the Ladies Aide chicken dinners where each of the members would supply two chickens and some pies. Mashed potatoes and gravy, homemade rolls, and slaw rounded out the menu. The women would prepare the chicken (home raised, no doubt) for cooking at home and then peel potatoes and make the pies. Other dishes were brought by other members of the church to complete the meal. The young people of the church acted as servers. Mrs. Artz also recalls that in 1945 the pastor, Lewis Green, had gotten hold of some bear meat and a church supper was then held featuring that unusual commodity. Others mentioned enjoying the ice cream socials where the ice cream was hand cranked and packed in ice and salt. Virginia Wahl Hinderer mentions the maple nut ice cream as her favorite.[6]

Salem Grove's address is 3320 Notton Road, Grass Lake, MI 49240.

Francisco Circuit—Waterloo Zion German Methodist Episcopal Church, aka "the Trist Church"

The following information on Zion is from Mr. Albert Schweinfurth who sent me the Salem Grove anniversary booklet. He states that Zion Church (which the locals referred to as Trist Church since it was on Trist Road) was formerly a Lutheran Church which was built in 1840. The Lutherans taught German and held Lutheran services there. About 1853, the Methodists established a two-point circuit which included Salem Grove and Zion and lasted until 1908 or 1909.[7]

Two churches are listed in conference records until 1921, so perhaps use of Zion church was infrequent until that point. Mr. Schweinfurth sent me a hand drawn map showing the location of Zion on Trist Road. When we were in the area, we drove by the place but could find no remains of the church.

Lansing, Michigan, German M.E. Church, aka Seymour Avenue German M.E. Church

As with many of the German Methodist societies in the area, Jacob Krehbiel was instrumental in getting the Lansing one started. He came to the area in late 1853 from Ann Arbor and began preaching to the Germans. By spring of the next year, he had organized a class of eleven. By the following year, he had overseen the building of a church; and the next year, a parsonage.[8] The land purchased for the new frame church is still the site of its successor, although the building is no longer an active church. The dedication of the church was held in July (no date given but it must have been in the late 1850s). Two dedication services were offered—one in German and the other in English.[9] Eventually, twenty preaching points sprang up in the countryside surrounding Lansing. Two of these, the Holt and Dewitt circuits, eventually became independent in the 1870s.

In 1893 the church that stands on the site today was built for the sum of sixty-three hundred dollars. The congregation celebrated their fiftieth anniversary on April 28 and 29, 1905. By 1906, 113 members belonged with 2 probationary ones. The Sunday school numbered 92; youth organization, 27; Junior

The former Seymour Avenue German ME near downtown Lansing, Michigan, is now home to an attorney's office.

League, 30.[10] Eventually, the church took the name of Seymour Avenue Methodist Church.

In 1968 the former German church joined with the First United Methodist Church which had just built a new facility at the corner of Delta River Drive and Waverly Road in 1967. The united church maintains some of the traditions of both churches including an annual sauerkraut supper started by the German contingent.[11] The old church belonging to the German congregation still stands at the corner of Seymour and Saginaw streets, not far from downtown Lansing. It is now the home of a law office.

DeWitt, Michigan, Circuit

When the DeWitt church was founded, it was originally served from Lansing. The *Geschichte* says that there were also services in St. John and Riley and that they formed a circuit with DeWitt. I can find no information on those two. In the conference records for DeWitt, starting in 1887, only one church is counted on the DeWitt Circuit.[12]

DeWitt Circuit—German M. E. Church aka Emanuel

The church, which is presently Redeemer UMC, has a very good history on their website and most other sources agree with it. Rev. Jacob Krehbiel was a busy person, as he founded this church, too. In 1853, he began preaching in the Allen Schoolhouse, whose site was at the corner of Clark and Airport roads. Later, the Hurd Schoolhouse on DeWitt Road was the site of preachings.[13]

The first church was a large, frame building costing $2,117.54 which was erected in 1874 on the northwest corner of Schavey and Clark roads.[14] The on-line history states that the dedication service was in August 1872. The first parsonage was built in 1881 west of the church, at which time more land was secured to accommodate the horses. Additions to the church were built in 1893 and 1897.

Tradition was strong during the early years as all services were in German and the sexes were segregated with women sitting on the left side of the church and men on the right. World War I broke down these traditions and more English was used in the services until 1928 when the switch to English was complete. Also, the young couples began sitting together instead of separating.[15] The church took the name of Emanuel Methodist Church about this time, as well.[16] Another change took place in 1933 when the Central German Conference was dissolved and Emanuel became part of the Michigan Conference of the Methodist Episcopal Church and joined a circuit with the DeWitt Methodist Church.

On Palm Sunday, 1944, tragedy struck and the old church was demolished in a fire that broke out about noon. It was rebuilt through the diligence of its members. Charlene Schaar relates in a letter:

> At the time of the fire in 1944, many of the DeWitt area men helped rebuild the Emanuel Church as they were employed at Oldsmobile and were layed off for a period of time so were able to help. Both my father and grandfather were there each day working on the church. My husband's father also was out there and he hadn't been an American citizen very long at that time; having immigrated from Germany.[17] [The new church was finished on July 20, 1947.]

From 1948 until 1967 Emanuel was on a circuit with Gunnisonville. It was then teamed with DeWitt Methodist once again and talks of a merger began. In 1970 the merger became reality and the united church became Redeemer UMC.

In 1977 Redeemer built a new church north of Emanuel on four acres which had been purchased in the 1960s. The Emanuel building served the Sunday school classes until 1994. Its stained glass windows were transferred to the new sanctuary and the old building was decommissioned and torn down in 1997.[18] The parsonage was sold and moved in 1988 to a location on Clark Road about five miles from the church where it was remodeled into a modern home.[19]

The website mentioned in the first paragraph is no longer working. To find out more about Redeemer go to www.dewittredeemer.org. The same history information is on this site now with some nice photographs.

DeWitt Circuit—St. John

Little remains of St. John's history but presumably, it was founded by Jacob Krehbiel, also. The only reference to it is in the *Geschichte* where it notes that it was given up in 1905.[20]

DeWitt Circuit—Riley

The only mention of Riley was that it was still meeting but weak (in 1905).[21]

Holt, Michigan, Circuit

In earlier years this was also called Delhi and was in Delhi Township. The circuit consisted of three stations: Holt, Alaiedon, and Okemos. The first two were founded as German Methodist while Okemos belonged to the English conference. Services in German were held there occasionally.

Holt Circuit—German M. E. Church

German preaching was first held in the Holt area in 1853 by Brother Bos, a local preacher from Ann Arbor. He preached in all three places on the circuit but it was exhausting work as he traveled from place to place by foot. The conference was impressed with his work and sent Jacob Krehbiel to take up the slack.[22] The congregation was established in 1854 and the church was unofficially known as the "Five Corners" Methodist Church. Initially, they met in the North School and the Lott School; then in 1868 built their first church building.[23]

Another source gives a slightly different description of the church's beginning. According to it, the Germans in the Delhi area attended church in Lansing until 1860. Then at that time, a circuit was formed apart from Lansing and the people in the Delhi area met in the two schools mentioned until 1868. At this time, there were twenty-three families involved in the church. The German Methodist Church was the first church building in the area and was located where the Delhi Township Library and the Methodist educational unit are now. The church was of frame construction and had a steeple with a bell. For a time, the English Methodists used the building on Sunday afternoons.[24]

The *Geschichte* states that Holt and its circuit-mates did not separate from Lansing until 1873. At this time a number of families from Elmore, Ohio, moved to the area, giving additional support to the church. Rev. J. C. Gommel built the parsonage and Rev. G. Wahl built the first brick church building. Sister Julia Uebele gave the church a new pipe organ.[25]

Holt, Michigan, UMC was part of the German Holt Circuit along with two other churches.

At the time of George Wahl's tenure in 1894, the congregation numbered 170. When Rev. Theophil Hey was pastor, from 1910 to 1919, he terminated services in German. The German Methodist Episcopal Church of Holt became North Holt Methodist Church. In 1930, the Center Church (English Methodist) was destroyed by fire a week before Christmas. Under the guidance of pastor Emil Runkel, the two churches decided to merge and held their first service together on Easter Sunday, April 5, 1931. The merger became official in September 1933.[26]

The congregation built an education building and social hall during the tenure of Rev. Wilson Tennant in 1948. In the early 1950s the church took the name of Brotherhood Temple Methodist Church, but, by 1961 that name was changed to Holt Methodist Church. In 1968 "United" was added to the name. In the same year, the congregation felt the need for a new sanctuary and broke ground for this purpose. A year later, Reverends Philip and Alma Glotfelty conducted the consecration service for the addition. In 1984 Rev. Dennis Buwalda oversaw another building project which housed a chapel, classrooms, offices, a kitchen, and fellowship hall.

In 1998 the West Michigan Conference invited Holt UMC to start a new congregation from her membership. Rev. Barb Flory was chosen to be Associate Pastor/New Church Pastor at Holt to expedite the new church startup. In June 2000 Reverend Flory and a group of missionaries from the church were sent to Alaiedon Township to "plant" Sycamore Creek United Methodist Church.

Some of the groups and activities at the Holt church included a bell choir started in the 1980s. In the late 1990s the church inaugurated a contemporary service which joined an early service and a traditional one on the Sunday morning schedule. Some of the many ministries and activities included the Praise Team, Preaching/Drama Team, adult and children's Dance Choir plus regular adult and children's choirs. A Child Enrichment Center was organized in 1983 and has made Christian daycare available to the area. Other groups include the United Methodist Women, youth groups, a men's group and a quilt club.

Early in the twenty-first century, more upgrades were added to the church building. The altar area was expanded, a new sound system, carpeting, and pew cushions were added. The pipe organ was rebuilt and a baby grand piano purchased.[27]

Holt UMC has survived the years and today stands at 2321 North Aurelius Road near the same "Five Corners" where it started. Go to their website at www.holtumc.org for more information about the present church.

Holt Circuit—Alaiedon German M. E. Church

The Alaiedon congregation was organized about the same time as the one in Holt. The Alaiedon people got their own church building when Gustav Fiedler was pastor in 1876.[28] After that, there is not much information available about the church. It is listed as being on the circuit with Holt until about 1914 during the tenure of Theophil Hey.

Isabelle Wells from the Ingham County Genealogical Society was able to locate the church on several old maps. It was in the northwest corner of Alaiedon Township on the border of sections 2 and 11 and is shown on maps in 1874, 1895, 1930, and 1952. She said township officials told her that it stood abandoned for a number of years until someone bought the property intending to build a house. The church was torn down but the house, due to restrictions, was never built.[29]

Holt Circuit—Okemos M. E. Church

Okemos was founded as an English Methodist church and hosted the German congregation in a separate service at which the German pastor at Holt ministered. The Okemos church has a very thorough history which states,

> there was a German language service at both the Okemos and Holt churches but no other details are known; though retired minister George Grettenberger recalls his father, Louis, talking about being taken to the services as a young boy, presumably in the afternoon.[30]

There is apparently no record as to how long these German services continued. In the conference minutes (1876), only two churches (Holt and Alaiedon) are listed on the circuit, so either Okemos was dropped as a preaching point before the 1870s or it was not counted as part of the circuit because the church was in the English Conference.[31]

Flint, Michigan, Bethlehem German Methodist Church

Bethlehem German Methodist Church was unique in that its founding did not take place until 1918 (some sources say 1919), so it was a member of the Central German Conference for only about fifteen years. Rev. Henry Bank who came to Flint from Lowell (or Pigeon as some sources say) founded the church. The retired pastor met a number of German Russians at Flint who, on finding out he could speak German, begged him to preach to them. He agreed and began preaching in their homes. He turned out to be quite popular and soon larger quarters were required for the Sunday gatherings. Reverend Bank reported his success to Dr. F. W. Mueller head of the Home Mission Board who secured the use of a small schoolhouse for the budding congregation. Mrs. Bank began helping her husband and soon the conference sent deaconess Miss Pauline Bartruff to aid. In 1920, Rev. August Klebaattel of Toledo joined the team and helped out every other Sunday. Miss Bartruff left, due to other obligations, and Miss Julia Schuermause took her place.

The schoolhouse was sold in 1920 and the congregation began meeting in the Oak Park Methodist Church in the afternoons. The new time and place were not convenient, so building their own church was the only option. Ground was broken on July 1, 1920, at the corner of Leith and McClellan streets for the new church. At this point, Rev. O. E. Haueter became the first regular pastor to the fledgling church. When he arrived, he found no parsonage, forcing him to rent a house for seventy-five dollars a month. As a result of this, a new parsonage was soon in the works. In the meantime, some of the congregation members became discouraged and went to the Reformed or Lutheran churches. Once the new church was completed and the first service held on December 4, 1920, attendance increased. The church building was dedicated on February 18–20, 1921, with twenty-eight members. The revived congregation now had a debt of thirty-two thousand dollars, the church costing twenty-five thousand and the parsonage, seven thousand.

The debt load was quickly reduced with donations from other churches and the Home Mission Board, so that at the end of 1921 it amounted to twelve thousand dollars. By the fifth anniversary of Bethlehem it had been reduced to five thousand. By 1926, his last year as pastor there, Reverend Haueter had increased the membership to eighty-one and completely eliminated the debt. The congregation also did very well in benevolences and was honored for their accomplishment at a special meeting at Central Church.[32]

Rev. J. J. Link succeeded Reverend Haueter as pastor in 1927 and he served six years until his retirement in 1933. At this point, the Central German Conference disbanded and the church joined the Detroit Conference. In 1933 Rev. Theodore Rudin, a superannuated pastor of the Central German Conference, came and caused some dissension when he preached in both English and German. Some people left the church because they wanted only German

Bethlehem German ME in Flint, Michigan, had several homes including this building which is now Charity UMC.

preaching. The depression was in full swing and, with many members out of work, the church suffered a decline in attendance and funds.

In 1934 Rev. Dwight Lawson came to Bethlehem and generated a "great revival." He was a young man and stirred great enthusiasm with his English sermons. Soon the suppers and bazaars to raise money for church support, were no longer needed as, tithes and love gifts were sufficient.

Several pastors later, in 1956, the congregation had grown enough to need new quarters. Land was purchased on Clio Road and the cornerstone laid in 1960. The "new" Bethlehem Methodist Church opened with an "Abundant Life Crusade" on Sunday, February 26, 1961. Festivities included a homecoming, an open house and a Consecration Service. The new building cost $152,000 and could seat three hundred people. On the forty-fifth anniversary, in 1964, Bethlehem claimed three hundred members and a Sunday school of 470. The attendance had doubled since the new building had opened in 1961.[33]

By the early 1980s Bethlehem suffered a decline in membership. Population shifts forced the church to merge with Hope United Methodist on Beecher Road. The former Bethlehem building became the home of Charity United Methodist, a merger of Flint Park and E. L. Gordon Methodist churches.[34]

My grandfather Theodore Rudin was the pastor at Bethlehem and Flint Park for a year from September 1933 to September 1934. Below are some excerpts from his diaries which illustrate some of the problems the church faced at that time.

Sunday, September 10

My first Sunday in Flint. Here they have the church service before the Sunday School. There was a good turnout and the people looked good to me. I found it easy to preach to them. I had no trouble expressing myself [in German].

Tuesday September 28

Last evening I had a meeting with the official board of Bethlehem church. It was decided to have English preaching every second and fourth Sunday and the evening services, which will begin in November are also to be in English. The meeting was harmonious and pleasant. Was glad when it was over, however, as I was uncertain as to how it would turn out.

Wednesday October 4

There's a strike on in some of the auto plants in this town, which has thrown some of our men who are not strikers out of work.

Monday November 27

Yesterday preached to good congregations and felt in fine form. In the evening I preached again in Flint Park. My Bethlehem orchestra played 2 pieces, which were evidently greatly enjoyed. I felt pretty good after a rather strenuous day. Bro. Schwarzkopf called. . . . He wants our Bethlehem orchestra to play in his church.

Thursday January 11

Yesterday Till and I attended the monthly meeting of the Crusaders. The club or society is composed of the young people of Bethlehem. I asked the cooperation of the young people in building up Bethlehem and suggested the organization of a choir. They all seemed to be enthusiastic about it.

Friday March 30

Went to Flint Park this morning. The walking out there was simply awful, not so much on the street crossings as on the side walks. I don't wonder now that there were so few in church last night. This evening I preached in Bethlehem to a congregation of about 40 which was rather a pleasant surprise.

Sunday April 1 [Easter]

Preached in German to the biggest congregation I have had yet in Bethlehem, between 70 and 80. Some 50 took communion. Br. Riechner took me to Flint Park where I also had a large congregation.

Tuesday May 3

Worked some on my German sermon. I would have an easy thing of it here if I did not have to compose German sermons.

Sunday May 20

Had a congregation of about 30 in Bethlehem this morning and 17 all told in Flint Park. In summer it is too warm to go to church and in winter, too cold. A small crowd in Bethlehem tonight, was anything but inspiring. This is the last evening service in either church until next Fall, and then it will be a question whether they will be resumed. The people simply don't come to church, no matter what you may do to get them interested.

Tuesday June 19

I am not at all sure about spending another year in Flint. I am willing to serve one more year here if need be, but that is up to the D. S. If we could make our home with John [his son], I would prefer to retire. I am beginning to tire of the work.

Thursday June 21

Finished my English sermon and started on a German one. Mrs. Patow says that her husband finds it very hard to preach in German. I should think so, it is hard enough for me. In today's *Michigan Christian Advocate* I find my name on "Our Final Honor Roll of Living Heroes" because I secured 6 subscriptions to the paper. Well, I have done something anyway! This evening the Bethlehem L.A.'s Ice Cream Social came off. We certainly have a fine basement in the Bethlehem church, large and commodious, and now clean. The Social was a success according to Bethlehem standards.

Saturday July 21

Br. Link came around and we had quite a visit. He does not think I ought to give up, but stay another year. I might change my mind if I saw I could accomplish something. It is Br. Link's and my opinion that Bethlehem can't go on half English or all German. If the stubborn Germans in this congregation would consent to having all the services in English, there might be some hope.

Friday September 7

Finished my German sermon. I suppose this is the last German sermon I will have to worry about. This week's *Michigan Advocate* is a Saginaw number. It contains a short history of each M. E church in that town and pictures of the preachers, including Br. Karl Patow and A. F. Runkel. Bro. Runkel's church is said to be one of the finest rural church properties in our American Methodism.[35]

NOTES

1. Golder, Horst, and Schaal, *Geschichte*, 371.
2. Hazel Proctor and Ann Arbor Federal Savings, eds, *Old Ann Arbor Town* (Ann Arbor: Ann Arbor Federal Savings, 1974), 41.
3. *West Side United Methodist Church* (Ann Arbor, Mich.: 2009), http://www.westside-umc.org/.
4. Rev. Carolyn Harris, *Salem Grove—A Brief History* (150th anniversary booklet), (Grass Lake, Mich.: 2003).
5. Golder, Horst, and Schaal, *Geschichte*, 384.
6. Harris, *Salem Grove.*
7. Albert Dean Schweinfurth to author, 2003.
8. Golder, Horst, and Schaal, *Geschichte*, 389.
9. Joseph L. Druse, *Pulpit and Prayer in Earliest Lansing* (Lansing, Mich.: The Historical Society of Great Lansing, 1959), 8
10. Golder, Horst, and Schaal, *Geschichte*, 389-390.
11. *First United Methodist Church of Ann Arbor,* history, Ann Arbor Mich., www.gbgm-umc.org/firstumc/History, accessed 2009.
12. *Minutes of the Annual Conferences*, 1887.
13. *Emanuel German Methodist Church*, Dewitt, Mich., my.voyager.net/redeemer/About/History , accessed 2000.
14. Charlene Schaar to author, November 4, 2004.
15. *Emanuel*
16. Clinton County Historical Society, *History of Clinton County, Michigan* (St. Johns, Mich.: Clinton County Historical Society, 1980), 575.
17. Schaar to author.
18. *Emanuel*
19. Schaar to author
20. Golder, Horst, and Schaal, *Geschichte*, 382.
21. Ibid., 82.
22. Ibid., 388.
23. The Michigan Sesquicentennial Agency for Delhi Township, *A Michigan Sesquicentennial History of Delhi Township,* (Delhi Twp., Ingham Co. Mich., 1957), 51.
24. Alida Chapman, *Looking Back* (Delhi Township, Mich.: The Delhi Township Bicentennial Commission, 1976), 261.
25. Golder, Horst, and Schaal, *Geschichte*, 388-389
26. Michigan Sesquicentennial Agency, *Michigan Sesquicentennial*, 51.
27. Inge Logenburg Kyler, *Holt United Methodist Church Celebrating 150 Years of Fellowship: A Brief History,* (Holt, Mich.: 2003), 2–4.
28. Golder, Horst, and Schaal, *Geschichte*, 389.
29. Isabelle Wells e-mail to author, 21 March 2005.
30. David S. Evans and Lyle Blackledge, *A History of Okemos Methodist/Community Church* (Okemos, Mich.: Okemos Community Church, 1997), 15.
31. *Minutes of the Annual Conferences*, 1876, 291 (Delhi Circuit).
32. Henry Lane, *Bethlehem Methodist Church*, church history (Flint, Mich.: 1960), 1–2.
33. Blanche Tillman, *Bethlehem Methodist Church to Celebrate 45th Anniversary Sunday*, church history (Flint, Mich.: 1964,) 1-3.

34. Elaine Condon to author, 2000.
35. Rudin, Diaries, 1933–34.

CHAPTER 16

Michigan's "Thumb" and Adjacent Area

Ora Labora

Ora Labora, whose name means "work and pray," was a very interesting place—a utopian society founded by the German Methodists. The complete name of the organization was "The Christian German Agricultural and Benevolent Society of Ora Labora." The colony was formed on three thousand acres of land along Wild Fowl Bay near Bay Port on Michigan's thumb in 1862. Emil Baur brought a group of people from Pennsylvania which formed the nucleus of the society. The settlers brought with them most of the supplies needed including oxen, cattle, tools, tanning supplies, lumbering equipment, rhubarb, asparagus, horseradish roots, vegetable seeds, medicines, and powders. Each family received two cows and two and a half acres of land.

The work ethic was strongly encouraged. The members were summoned awake each day at five by the blowing of a horn. A lengthy devotion service was first on the agenda, followed by breakfast at six. Work was then begun and the day ended with another holy service at nine in the evening.

In its heyday, Ora Labora had about seventy-five buildings including a church, school, sawmill, tannery, store, gristmill, post office and a community bake oven. Two things contributed to the demise of the colony: the swampy, unhealthy location and the Civil War. The young men, having no money to pay for substitutes, were conscripted into the military, leaving only the women and elderly men to do the heavy work of clearing the land, farming, and lumbering.[1]

The dates of Ora Labora's existence are somewhat cloudy. Most of the above information is from a newspaper article which states that the colony was started in 1847 and given up in 1871. However, someone penciled in the date 1862 for its beginning and 1868 for its demise. Whichever dates are correct, it is clear that the Civil War had a role in the colony's demise having called to arms the most able members. It was only a matter of time before the remaining colonists became overworked and discouraged.

Rev. Emil Baur's son returned to the abandoned settlement when he was eighteen years old and farmed the land. The Baur family prospered as farmers and today the former Ora Labora lands are home to dairy cattle, chickens and a corn drying facility.[2]

Some of the German settlers of Ora Labora stayed in the area and for a few years were served by circuit riders—Gustav Bertram, Jacob Braun and Heinrich Pullman. A short time later, the Ebenezer Mission was founded and churches sprang up along the Pigeon River, at Caseville and on State Road.[3]

Pigeon, Michigan, German M. E. Church

The Ebenezer Mission was founded on November 18, 1871, at Caseville with twenty-three members, eleven probationary members, six teachers and a Sunday school of thirty. A building which served as both church and parsonage was built. In 1872, two other churches were built south of Caseville to serve the families there. One was located on State Road (now called South Bay Port Road) and the other on the east bank of the Pigeon River. The latter was simply a building with no pews or organ and was pastored by the Rev. George H. Maentz, the first full-time minister for the Ebenezer Mission.[4] A letter from Mr. Richard Gwinn of Caseville gives an interesting story about the old church. The building was always filled with mosquitos but it was noted that the insects "sang" in the key of "C." Since there were no musical instruments at this church, the mosquitoes provided the key for the singing of all the hymns.[5]

A more traditional-style church building was erected in 1874 in the town of Berne at the corner of Caseville and Town-line roads. This church featured a bell tower, pews, chancel platform and furniture, and space for a cemetery outside. A bell and organ were installed during the pastorate of Rev. Oscar Rogatzky. These amenities attracted more people to the congregation and the church experienced a time of growth. Also, during this period, the old church/parsonage in Caseville was sold and a modern parsonage built in Berne.

By the late nineteenth century, the town of Pigeon had grown into a thriving community, so the congregation decided to set up shop there. They built a new brick church at the corner of East Michigan Avenue and Frank Street. In November of 1899, Rev. Henry Bank dedicated both the church and an adjoining brick parsonage. The church served the congregation well until they decided in 1946 to do some remodeling for the seventy-fifth anniversary. After two years, Rev. Herbert Duttweiler performed the rededication services in the spring of 1948. Construction on on a new educational unit and social hall began in the spring of 1963 and Rev. Marvin McCallum consecrated the additions in October 1963. In the 1980s Rev. Gordon W. Nusz oversaw the repairing of the stained glass windows, the restoration of the Steinway piano, installation of seat padding, and the hanging of a new dossal curtain. Rev. James P. Schwandt saw that the church was made barrier free (allowing disabled people free access) and that the pipe organ was restored and enlarged .

With the 125th anniversary coming up, the church did more redecorating, painting, refinishing of furniture, and installation of new carpets. The UMW lounge received a new floor incorporating a Star of David pattern which reflected the theme in the stained glass windows. Roof repair and bell tower restoration were also undertaken.

The church celebrated its 125th year with several events. The first was an annual Lawn Service on Sunday July 21, 1996, at the Ebenezer Berne Memorial Cemetery. On September 8, a musical homecoming service was held. On September 15, Bishop Donald A. Ott preached at the Anniversary Worship service. A family dinner in the Fellowship Hall followed with a historical program and displays after the meal.

The United Methodist Women's group was an early church society which began in 1895. At that time, it was called the Ladies Aid and went through the usual name changes until it became the UMW. Among the functions they supported were a prayer chain, funeral lunches, Bay Shore Camp and Thumb Leisure Ministries and Global Concerns and Social Involvement. Two circles, the Rebekah Circle and the Martha Priscilla Circle, represented the group.[6]

The *Geschichte* takes the Pigeon church's history only up to its date of publication about 1907. At that time, the church property was worth seven thousand dollars and the membership stood at 160. There were two Sunday schools with a total of 150 attendees and, also, a youth society with sixty members.[7]

The Pigeon German M. E. is now Pigeon First UMC located at 7102 Michigan Avenue, Pigeon, Michigan, 48755. The church has an interesting presentation on You Tube instead of a regular website. Go to www.youtube.com/watch?v=L_3N3szgWkg [accessed 2009].

Bay City, Michigan, German M. E. Church, aka Adams Street aka Van Buren Street

Rev. Jacob Krehbiel first brought Methodist preaching to the Bay City area in 1857 with Rev. John Horst and Rev. John Braun continuing the tradition in 1858.[8] The Union schoolhouse was the meeting place until a church was built on Adams Street. The new church building, constructed of wood, was thirty-three-by-forty-five feet inside and cost about two thousand dollars. By 1869, the church claimed twenty-nine members and a library of 117 books.[9] The first pastor of the new church, the Rev. Henry Pullmann began his tenure in 1869. Elisabeth Lindner was the first member to join the fledgling church.[10]

Bay City, Michigan's German M.E. building is now Infant of Prague Church.

In 1883, the congregation had outgrown the church building so constructed a new church and parsonage at the corner of Van Buren and Thirteenth streets.[11] Pastor Karl Treuschel oversaw the completion of the buildings at a cost of $7,300. A kitchen was added to the parsonage in 1891 for $400. In 1897, the church received a new foundation and a furnace for the cost of $750. The parsonage was the focus of remodeling in 1906 at the cost of $1,100 bringing the total church property value to $7,000.

In the early twentieth century, the church claimed 125 members with a Sunday school of 100, a *Jungendbund* (youth organization) of 40 and a junior league of 40. The Ladies Aid had a membership of 36.[12]

Although I could not find a great deal of history on the church, I was able to find the Van Buren Street Church, itself. It still stands today as the Infant of Prague Catholic Church at 112 South Van Buren Street.

Tuscola Street German M.E. in Saginaw, Michigan, now serves the congregation of St. Luke's AME.

Saginaw, Michigan, German Methodist Church, aka Tuscola Street M.E. Church

A history of Saginaw County gave only a brief paragraph on the German M. E. Church, so most of the history is from the *Geschichte* (which had a fairly detailed two-page entry) and from newspaper articles published at the time. The *Geschichte* begins its story 1855 when some Methodist families from the Cleveland, Ohio, area moved to the city, known for its sawmills. A short time later the German Methodist preacher Gustav Laas was sent to minister to them. However, it is reported that he was "timid and shy" and only preached in the outlying settlement of Hermannsaue. This did not please the powers that be, so they sent Rev. J. Schweinfurth. This pastor secured the use of a schoolhouse in the city and before long had a flock of two dozen. He only stayed for eleven months because the area was rife with malaria and other fevers due to the swampy environment. His parting words were that "he would not die in Saginaw."[13]

Rev. Jacob Krehbiel came to the area in the fall of 1856 and liked what he saw visioning a lot of promise and future growth to the area. His family joined him and his ministry began, although accommodations were a bit cramped because his house also served as the church building. He quickly made arrangements to build a church and was able to get most of the wood free of charge. The resulting edifice was a "stately building with beautiful perfect wood tower." One of the first members was Herman Goeschel who joined in 1857 and wrote the entry for the *Geschichte*. The wood structure burned down and was replaced by a brick building in 1867.[14]

The first brick church was erected on Warren Street between Lapeer and Tuscola and had two stories—the lower one consisting of two rooms for Sunday school and the upper one for church. The church measured sixty-six-by-thirty-six feet. Money was raised by subscription after the old church burned and the construction was soon started by Gustavus Koepke. When completed, only one thousand dollars was still owed, the bulk of the amount (fifty-five hundred dollars) having been already pledged. At this point the church had 138 members.[15]

By 1912 the congregation saw the need for a new church building and the Warren Street church was sold to the Italians to become Our Lady of St. Carmel. The German Methodists then built a new church at the corner of Tuscola and Fifth Avenue. The architecture of the church was in the Roman style and the building costs amounted to a little more than $11,500. The parsonage had been built in 1886 but received a basement in 1914.

During World War I the church received its gas and water bills with the word "German" marked out. The church took the hint and made a name change to Tuscola Street M. E. Church on November 11, 1918. In the early 1930s one service was still given in German with the remaining in English. A thirty-two-hundred-dollar pipe organ was given to the church as a memorial gift in the 1920s and the Ladies Aid helped purchase some of the pipes that went with it.[16]

In 1957 the former German church celebrated its centennial with three centennial services, a potluck lunch and many musical performances and speeches. The following organizations were associated with the church: Ladies Aid founded in 1878, Junior League in 1893, choir in 1893, Epworth League in 1895, and Adult Bible class in 1895.[17]

At present the Tuscola Street church no longer ministers to its former congregation but is still in the Methodist fold, serving as St. Luke's A.M.E.

Kochville, Michigan, German M.E. Church

In the year 1857 Jacob Marti, a Kochville area resident, invited Rev. Jacob Krehbiel to come and speak. Most of the people living in that area had come from Switzerland and had been served occasionally by Lutheran pastors. When it came time to christen a baby born into one of the families, however, the Lutheran pastor refused when the settlers said they had been members of the Reformed Church in Switzerland. This refusal led the people into the arms of the German Methodists.

After meeting in various homes for a while, it was soon apparent that a

Kochville UMC began as a German M.E. in the country near Saginaw.

church building was needed. Gerhardt Krapohl contributed an acre of land and a building was moved to the spot. Adam Marti donated one hundred dollars for its remodeling into a church. This primitive building, with plank floors and unfinished walls, served well until 1873 when a larger church became necessary. After much effort fifteen hundred dollars was collected and the construction began under the direction of carpenter Jacob Stengel. In 1875 Rev. George Reuter dedicated the church which featured a high tower and a spire. Rev. F. A. Hamp became the first resident pastor in 1879. Until 1881, when the church gained its independence of Saginaw and took the name Kochville German Methodist Episcopal Church, it was referred to as the *Schweiz* (Swiss) Church.

A number of single, student ministers served the flock until 1891 when Reverend and Mrs. Baumann arrived. In 1899 Reverend Ruckheim and his wife came to the church and the problem of the lack of a parsonage became critical. The old church of 1864 was called into service again—this time as the parsonage, after a little rebuilding and remodeling.

During the World War I years the church suffered a decline due to the shortage of ministers—some Sundays no services were held and the German language became irrelevant. By the early 1920s, the parsonage needed attention again and in 1923, it was moved again and remodeled into a modern home.

Building fever took hold and the congregation decided it was time for a new church building, too. In 1924, the foundation was laid and in 1925 the cornerstone put into place. By December 1925, the building designed by William Mueller and erected by Carl Schoberth, was completed. Rev. A. Runkel performed the dedication on December 13. The kitchen furnishings and church carpet were provided by the Ladies Aid while some of the sanctuary fittings were given as memorials for the thirty-two-thousand-dollar building. In 1932, a mortgage burning was held for the last ten thousand dollars owed on the church.[18]

The church continued to grow and serve the community until the sad day in 1955 when the church caught fire and burned to the ground. The congregation immediately made plans to rebuild. The sum of forty-three thousand dollars was gained from insurance, another twenty thousand was collected in donations and thirty-thousand pledged. By May 20, 1956, the new ninety-five-thousand-dollar church was completed and consecrated. During the rebuilding, services took place in the Kochville Township Hall and Sunday school met at the Jewett School.[19]

By its 125th year, the country surrounding the church had changed from woods to prosperous farms to an urban setting of businesses, shopping malls, and homes. In 1966 plans for an addition to the church were in the works. This project, finished by September 1967, included three classrooms, a new covered entry, pastor's study and office, storage area and furnace room. A new parsonage was in order by the 1970s and a home was purchased for forty-five thousand dollars in 1976 for that purpose. Other changes in the seventies included tearing down the old parsonage and garage and erecting a new garage for equipment; while the church received a covering of aluminum siding.[20]

During its more than 150 years, the Kochville United Methodist Church has sponsored many organizations and activities. One of the first to be formed was the Ladies Aid started in 1893 by the pastor at that time, the Reverend Baumann. His wife was the first president of the group. Four circles have been active in the group at one time or another, including the Mary Martha, Priscilla, Ruth, and Dorcas circles. The group has supported the Salvation Army, Veteran's Hospital, Christian Children's Fund and others to help make this a better world.

The youth group or Epworth League was founded in 1897 when Rev. Carl Buerkle was pastor. In 1939, the name was changed to Youth Fellowship. Later the group suffered a decline and was discontinued for awhile although many of its former members took an active part in the choir. The group was reorganized when Rev. Joseph Ablett became pastor.

The Methodist Men began with twenty-seven men on October 22, 1947, under the pastorship of Rev. Alfred Hunter, later receiving their charter in 1953. Some of the activities sponsored by them have been softball and basketball teams, Father-Son and Father-Daughter banquets, pancake suppers and Christmas tree sales. They also helped with church repairs and upkeep such as finishing work on the new church including painting, sidewalks, landscaping, electrical work and the church parking lot.

Other activities include choirs, both adult and youth. There have been a number of organists and choir directors through the years including Marilyn Ennis who wrote and directed Christmas pageants. In the 1970s Julie Boettcher organized a Girls' Teen Choir and accompanied them on piano and guitar. A children's choir called the Singing Disciples was created by Jane Levi and Barbara Hoffman in the 1980s.

Sunday school has been an important part of Kochville church since the early years. Among the activities the Sunday school has supported include the Hanging of the Greens, vacation Bible school, Christmas and Easter programs, children's choir, Third Grade Bible presentation, Little Learners preschool, Mothers Day flowers, missionary Easter project, Thanksgiving and Christmas dinner for the needy, and "white" gifts for Detroit Childrens Village.

The Kochville Senior Citizen Group was established in 1981 by seventy interested people. A Shepherding Program (which kept people who missed a worship service informed) began around this time.

In the early twenty-first century I found the following information about Kochville (at 6030 Bay Road, Saginaw, MI 48604) on their website. Regular activities include a Bible study at a retirement home, youth groups, the UMW, and an adult Bible class meeting on Wednesdays and Sunday mornings. The youth group, called BIG (Believing In God) Youth Group, is made up of both junior high and high school members. Outreach projects the church is involved in are a Haiti Hot Lunch program, Hispanic Ministry Shalom (in Saginaw), God's Country Co-Op (in the Upper Peninsula), SVSU campus ministry, Unity Club, and Love by the Pound (potatoes for the hungry).[20] A revisit to the website in 2009 listed only the worship time—10:30 a.m.

Toward the end of his time in Flint, Michigan, my grandfather made a reference to the Kochville church in his diary.

Friday September 7

This week's Michigan Advocate is a Saginaw number. It contains a short history of each M. E. church in that town and pictures of the preachers, including Bro. Karl Patow and A. F. Runkel. Bro. Runkel's church is said to be one of the finest rural church properties in our American Methodism.[22]

Notes

1. *Bay City Times*, June 27, 1971 (copy sent to me by Richard Gwinn who got copy from Bentley Historical Library, University of Michigan, Ann Arbor, Michigan).
2. Ibid.
3. Al Robinson and Brent Woodward, *First United Methodist Church Pigeon, Michigan, 1871–1996*, church history, (Pigeon, Mich.: 1996).
4. Robinson & Wodward, *First United Methodist Church.*
5. Richard Gwinn to author, 2001.
6. Robinson & Wodward, *First United Methodist Church.*
7. Golder, Horst, and Schaal, *Geschichte*, 396.
8. Augustus H. Gansser, *History of Bay County, Michigan* (Chicago: Richmond & Arnold, 1905), 272.
9. "German Methodist Episcopal Church," *Bay City Directory*, 1868–1869, 54.
10. Golder, Horst, and Schaal, *Geschichte*, 376.
11. Ibid., 273.
12. Ibid., 376.
13. Ibid., 398.
14. Ibid., 398–99.
15. *Saginaw* (Mich.) *Weekly Enterprise*, "German M. E. Church," 1867.
16. *Saginaw* (Mich.) *News*, "Tuscola Street M. E. Dates to Saginaw Early Days," 1934.
17. Ibid., "Tuscola Street Methodists Marking their Centennial," May 18, 1957.
18. Mrs. Fred Balesky, *The History of the Kochville Methodist Church,* church history (Kochville, Mich.: 1932), 7–10.
19. Henry Bueker, *Our One Hundredth Year at Kochville Methodist*, church history (Kochville, Mich.: 1957), 12–13.
20. Anonymous, *One Hundred Twenty-five Years with Kochville United Methodist* church history (Kochville, Mich.: 1982), 14–17.
21. *Kochville United Methodist Church*, Program page, www.gbgm-umc.org/kochville/programs, accessed January 1, 2004.
22. Rudin, Diaries, 1934.

CHAPTER 17

Churches in Other States

Defiance, Ohio

The Defiance, Ohio, area consisted of two circuits—the Stryker Circuit and the Defiance Circuit. Some of the churches reported to have been on this circuit, I have not been able to locate or get any information on.

Stryker, Ohio, Circuit

According to the *Geschichte*, northwestern Ohio was organized as the Brunersburg Circuit in 1842. This circuit split in 1874 to form the Stryker and Defiance circuits. The Stryker Circuit included churches at Stryker, West Unity, and Evansport. The Defiance Circuit claimed the church in Defiance and one at New Bavaria.[1]

Stryker Circuit—Stryker German M. E.

Goodspeed's county history says, "There are a few Presbyterians and German Methodists at Stryker. They have preaching occasionally."[2] Apparently, the German Methodists used the English-speaking Methodists' church in the afternoon for their services. This arrangement went on from 1874 to 1906. At that point, the members were transferred to Emanuel Church which was near West Unity, in Floral Grove Cemetery. They remodeled and rededicated the new church for the occasion.[3]

Another source does not mention the Stryker German Methodists coming to the old Emanuel Church. It mentioned the Emanuel congregation going to West Unity and, later, refers to the old church being reroofed and "made safe in every way, and repapered and nicely repaired." It was then rededicated, as the Stryker source said. After that, it was apparently only used for special services and funerals.4 The assumption is that both the Stryker and Emanuel congregations joined with the West Unity Methodist Church.

Stryker Circuit—West Unity Emanuel German M. E.

The West Unity Church aka Emanuel M. E. is still standing and open to those who would like to see what a nineteenth century German M. E. church looked like. It is located on the grounds of the Floral Grove Cemetery east of West Unity on County Road K.

The first German M. E. missionary to the northwestern Ohio area was E. Riemenschneider who preached in the log home of John and Sarah Gares in 1842. Rev. John Bier followed him in 1843 but was hindered in his work because he had to come from Perrysburg and serve ten appointments. Christov Hoefner organized a class in 1846 which met in the homes of the faithful. In 1851, $330 was pledged to build a small, frame church so the members did not have to trek seven miles to the prayer meeting location. Joseph Wagstaff and John Blair built the church on land owned by Bonaparte Nichter. On a three-to-four-week cycle, the pastor arrived on Wednesday for midweek prayer meeting and would stay through Sunday for the preaching service and the afternoon Sunday school. The congregation would quit whatever work they were engaged in early, to prepare for the church service. The minister tried to stay with a different family each visit and called on as many families as he could and always read from the Bible and prayed with them.[5]

In 1869 the frame church was replaced by a brick building which is the one still standing today. Not much history survives on the brick church's active years. In 1899 the need for German services had diminished so the congregation joined the English speaking M. E. church, along with the Stryker Germans and eventually, in 1906 merged with West Unity M. E. The old Emanuel Church was not forgotten, however, as it was reroofed and rededicated (as mentioned earlier) in a community service with West Unity pastors taking part.[6]

Although, the members of Emanuel transferred to West Unity, the Sunday school still met in the building until 1914. In the 1930s and '40s, some church services were held once again at Emanuel while the West Unity Church was painted. In the 1960s the roof was replaced and a brick walk constructed. The altar holds a German Bible which was rebound at that time. A new altar table runner and organ stool cover were made and donated, also.[7]

If you are ever in northwest Ohio, look up the church (location given in first paragraph). It is usually open and it is a real treat to "go back in time" and see how our ancestors worshiped. There is a mention and brief description of Emanuel German M. E. at the following website: www.holidaycityohio.org/west_unity_attractions.

Churches in Other States / 221

The people of West Unity, Ohio, have preserved Emmanuel German ME in Floral Grove Cemetery, just as it was when it served a German-speaking congregation.

222 / A Forgotten Heritage: The German Methodist Church

Interior of Emmanuel from front to back.

Front of the German church including the German pulpit Bible.

German pulpit Bible.

Epworth pump organ with song books.

Heating stove in Emmanuel.

A Bailey Kerosene Reflector provided light in the West Unity Emanuel German M.E..

Stryker Circuit—Evansport St. John German M. E.

St. John German M. E. church, near Evansport, Ohio, was founded about 1840 near the intersection of Gruber and Gares roads. Then, about 1890, an English-speaking Sunday school class was organized there which held services on alternate Sundays with the German group. The English built their own church across the road and dedicated it in 1896. A story is told about how Reverend Sehnert, the German pastor, one Sunday opened services in the old German church, picked up the Bible and walked to the new English church on the other side of the road. The congregation followed and services resumed in the new building. The German contingent continued alternating Sundays with the English group awhile and later held services once a month. German services were given up altogether about 1900 and all were incorporated into the English church.[8]

St. John's celebrated their sixtieth anniversary in 1954, but by 1966 the congregation had grown too small to support the church; therefore, conference approved a merger with Evansport. Memberships and property were transferred while a small amount of money from the German church made up a scholarship fund. The land where the church stood reverted to the donor and the building was abandoned.[9]

The only remainder of the old church, besides the cemetery, is the bell which for seventy-one years occupied the belfry at St. John's. The bell weighs sixteen hundred pounds and is forty inches high and forty-three wide at the base. Today it sits proudly on the front lawn of the Evansport Church, located at 1560 West Street in Evansport.[10]

Defiance, Ohio, Circuit

Defiance Circuit—Defiance German M. E.

The Defiance congregation formed in 1850 and was part of the Brunersburg Circuit or the West Unity Circuit.[11] When Frederick Ruff was pastor, land on Wayne Street was purchased for three hundred dollars and the church was built there for the sum of seven hundred dollars. The Presbyterian church generously presented a bell for the new church building. A parsonage was built in 1860 and also cost three hundred dollars. When the county history was written, the German church was on a circuit with one other church at South Ridge. At that time, the value of church property was assessed as two thousand dollars for the frame building and one thousand for the parsonage.[12]

The former Defiance German ME was moved to its new site and is now a Christian church.

By 1928 the congregation had declined and the church finally disbanded most of the members joining St. Paul's Methodist Church. The church building then became the Gospel Temple.[13] In 1935 the church building was moved from its site at the corner of Wayne and Juliet streets to the north side of town at the corner of Broadway and Pearl. At this time, it was the second oldest Defiance church building in existence. In the late 1990s the building was still being used as the Gospel Temple.[14]

A recent trip to Defiance revealed that the building is now La Iglesia de Dios, Inc. So once again, the old church has as its mission to bring those from a foreign land closer to God.

Defiance Circuit—New Bavaria, Ohio, South Ridge

There was a second church paired with the one in Defiance which was frequently listed as "South Ridge." Unfortunately, no one seemed to know where South Ridge was and it was not in any atlas nor most of the county histories. I finally narrowed it down to either Ayersville or New Bavaria. When my husband and I checked out the area of New Bavaria, we stopped at the post office and I asked the postmistress there. She informed me that the main road through the town was called "Ridge Road" by the locals. Later, I confirmed that by discovering that St. Stephen's Lutheran Church, even today, is listed as being on "South Ridge, New Bavaria."

I only found a brief mention of the South Ridge church in Aldrich's county history: "The German Methodist, a fine, roomy frame building, situated a short distance north of Pleasant Bend and northwest of New Bavaria, near to both places and well attended."[15] We drove to Pleasant Bend to see if we could find the church. Pleasant Bend does have a Methodist church and on a visit to the UMC Archives at Ohio Wesleyan, I found a brief history of the Pleasant Bend United Methodist Church. It notes that St. Paul's South Ridge Methodist united with them in 1950. It also mentions that St. Paul's was founded in the 1840s when Engelhardt Riemenschneider came to preach to German families in the area.[16] I could not find the former St. Paul's building on South Ridge, but we did not cover all the side roads.

Pleasant Bend UMC is located on County Highway 17, New Bavaria, OH 43548.

Edgerton, Ohio, Circuit

The Edgerton Circuit went through many name changes. It was originally called the Angola, Indiana, Mission of the Ohio Conference until 1853. After that it was referred to as the Auburn, Indiana, Mission, then Auburn and Bryan Mission followed by the Auburn and Kendallville Mission. From 1866 the circuit was Edgerton, Ohio, Mission which became just Edgerton Circuit. After 1895, it was known as the Edon, Ohio, Circuit and then the Edgerton, Ohio, Circuit.[17] The *Geschichte* shows photos of four churches—Immanuel Church, Zion Church, Freemont Church, and Salem Church. Immanuel was spelled "Emanuel" in the text and is not to be confused with Emanuel near West Unity in Floral Grove Cemetery. Zion Church seems to be the one north of Edon. The "Freemont" Church was located in Fremont, Indiana. Salem Church was east of Edon in Center Township. An entry by the Steuben County, Indiana, county recorder in 1873 refers to the German Methodist parsonage in Edgerton and lists the trustees for the parsonage property.[18]

Edgerton Circuit—Emanuel German M. E.

This church, like most in the area, started with a visit by Rev. Engelhardt Riemenschneider in the 1840s. The German churches of the area were under the auspices of the Angola, Indiana, Mission of the Ohio Conference, at this time, and churches included Emanuel, Salem, Edon, and West Unity in Ohio and Kendallville and Auburn, Indiana. As explained earlier, the circuit underwent a number of changes and shifting of churches from one circuit to another, but by the early twentieth century, the name Edgerton Circuit had stuck.

Emanuel Church was organized in its present form about 1872. In 1873 Mr. and Mrs. George Weber donated a quarter of an acre to the congregation and Peter Strausberger erected a frame building there measuring twenty-five- by thirty-six-feet for $616. Local pastors and circuit riders conducted most of the early services. When Reverend Werner came in 1889, he encouraged the formation of the first Youth Group. A few years later, during the pastorate of Reverend Dangel, Mary and George Maier donated another quarter acre of land. When Reverend Nagler served, he organized a choir and invited anyone in the area to join. Music became very important at Emanuel and many special programs and cantatas were part of the worship. Rev. Emil Runkel oversaw the transfer of the church from the Central German Conference to the Ohio Conference about 1928, five years before the dissolution of the German Conference.

A new $4,184 brick church was built in 1904 on the site of the frame church which had been moved across the road. In 1941, the basement was given a makeover. In 1961 the sanctuary underwent remodeling and was praised as one of the most beautiful rural churches in Ohio. Another makeover took place in 1968 with the addition of four classrooms and, later, a kitchen in 1973.

The Youth Group met on alternate Sunday evenings. Another youth group called the Echo Club was formed by Reverend Smith and later became an Epworth League which disbanded in the 1960s.

A township Sunday school convention was organized in 1889 in which four Sunday schools participated. Meetings were held annually on the third Sunday in June until 1973. These began with Sunday school classes in the morning taught by teachers from the various churches. Everyone enjoyed the potluck dinner at noon. In the afternoon group singing began the session and was followed by special music and speakers.

The Ladies Aid became the Women's Society of Christian Service in 1940 and in 1968 changed names again to United Methodist Women. One of their projects included a family night when everyone was invited to a special program followed by ice cream and cake. Another was a reception for newlyweds which included a potluck meal, special program, and the presentation of a wedding gift to the couple. Others were a mother-daughter potluck and a Christmas party. Partying wasn't the only function of the group, which also worked out a schedule for its members to clean the church each week in addition to seeing that altar flowers were in place each Sunday.

Edgerton, Ohio's Emanuel UMC.

Keystone of the Emanuel Church.

The Edgerton and Emanuel churches organized a men's group in 1960 which became the United Methodist Men in 1968. They held monthly meetings and sponsored a Father-Son Banquet and a pancake supper. One of their service projects was packing used clothing for Henderson Settlement in Kentucky.[19]

An update to the 1975 history tells about a tape ministry for the benefit of shut-ins that was begun in 1980. After 2000 the church invested in an advanced sound system. Also, in 2000, the church celebrated the commemoration of 160 years of Methodism in northwest Ohio with an all-day service where former pastors and their wives visited.

A dream of the women of the church was to have a "Free Store" to minister to the needy. Clothing, toys, furniture and other items were given to those in need, free of charge. This was so successful that it quickly outgrew the available space and evolved into The Edgerton Community Outreach Ministry and Free Store. All the churches in the Edgerton and Melburn area became involved.

In 2004 a special service and potluck was held to celebrate the one-hundredth year of the building of the church. A special gift earmarked for the handicapped, along with donations from the congregation, purchased an elevator which church members installed. This was dedicated during the 2004 centennial celebration.[20]

The following excerpts are from a taped interview with Paul D. and Rosa Krill and Hulda Valet. Leona Krill Betts (daughter of Paul and Rosa) kindly shared this with me.

> The first settlers walked to services at Hard Corners which was located at what is now the corner of Scott and Rosedale roads. They also walked to services at Gypsy Hill carrying the babies on their backs. Later they met in the local one-room schools. When two families, namely, George Weber Sr. and Gotlieb Koerner, built their new homes, they built large parlors so they could be used for church services. They alternated between the two homes. In 1873 the first church was built where the present church now stands. It was a wooden structure twenty-five-by-thirty-six feet with straight back benches on each side and a stove in the middle. The men sat on one side and the women on the other. This seemed to be more of a habit than a rule. When the congregation needed a larger church, the frame church was moved across the road and the people worshiped there while the new church was being constructed in 1904. After completion of the brick church, the frame church was purchased by the Schott family. . . . Paul said he rode on the ridge of the church when it was first moved across the road.

> A special time was the Fourth of July when the church sponsored a day of celebration for everyone in the area. It was held at Little Lake just south of the church. A patriotic program was given in the morning. After a potluck at noon there were games and contests such as sack races, pole vault, high jump, carrying an egg on a spoon, and others. Small prizes were given to the winners. . . . Peanuts, candy, ice cream, real lemonade, homemade bread, pies and cakes were sold to pay for the prizes. The young men created something like a merry-go-round. To a sixteen-foot pole they fastened four ropes with a type of chair on the end of each rope. It was powered by a gasoline motor. When the motor started, the chairs and the person on them would swing out straight. They also had a cable strung across the lake and a pulley with a hand

hold on it was on the cable. They climbed the tree to where the cable was fastened and tried to swing to the other side. Usually they dropped in the lake.

The frame church had kerosene lamps. The brick church had four pitner gas lights with mantels. They were first pumped to generate pressure. Then a wand was dipped in wood alcohol, lit with a match, and held up in the air to light the lamp.[21]

As of this writing, the Emanuel United Methodist Church is still meeting. It is located at 4763 Kramer Road, two miles south and a half mile east of Edgerton in Defiance County. Visit their Web site at www.archives.umc.org/Directory/ChurchDetails.

Edgerton Circuit—Salem Church

In 1868 Salem started as a log church which was pastored by Henry Krill and was then called Central German Church. In 1887 Samuel and Angeline Lint sold a parcel of land where a new church was eventually built. Although the date of the deed was August 9, 1887, the cornerstone was not laid until 1892, after Ernst Werner became pastor. The new church was frame and had a bell weighing five hundred pounds plus a new organ costing $1,600.57.[22]

A handwritten history of Salem included in Steven Bloir's compilation, states that the church records dated before 1910 were lost but Mr. Bloir gleaned some information by talking to older members. The pulpit of the Salem Church dated back to 1887. Two white benches and two tin collection plates were used in the old log building. Three rostrum chairs came from the Garret, Indiana, church and were donated to Salem in 1922. Gas lighting came to the church in 1915 for a cost of fifty-three dollars. In 1916 a furnace was put in, which involved excavating a basement, raising the church building, refinishing and installing the furnace a total of seven hundred dollars. In 1922 the church was wired for electricity and electric lights installed for a cost of eighty-seven dollars.

In 1930 the old parsonage in Edgerton was sold for $1,900.00 and the money gained was split between Salem and Emanuel. Salem received $732.14.[23]

In 1929 the church hosted a homecoming which many visitors attended, including some former pastors. "A rare treat was a song 'There's a Land That is Fairer Than Day' by Dale Thomas of Bryan (in German) and all repeated in English."[24]

Jack and Helen Bloir bought the church and one acre of ground in March 1967. On April 3, 1967, the couple opened the church for a last service at two thirty and at that time presented the pulpit and three chairs to the Williams County Historical Society.[25] Salem German M. E. in Williams County was on County Road 7 between roads D and F. It was remodeled and is now a private home.[26]

Edgerton Circuit—Edon

There were two German Methodist churches in the Edon area but facts are sketchy about their history and location. In the 1840s services were held in an old log cabin and then a few years later another log building was erected strictly for church services and events. Since there were both English and German Methodists in the area, they went together to build the church and both used it for worship (It is not clear whether they had services together or separate services in the same building). Later a frame church served the growing congregation and then in 1878, the congregation built a brick building.[27]

Another source says that the first meeting place was a log cabin owned by David Singer, Sr., in Florence Township. Then in 1848 or 1850 a group of men from the German and the English factions built a church from logs. A severe hail storm hit one day when the men were working and they had to take shelter in a nearby schoolhouse. It is told that one of the pastors of this church (probably a local pastor), George Donutt, made a name for himself for his gesticulations while preaching. He would gesture with one hand and clasp his ear with the other, then switch hands, and when he got really worked up, would grab an ear in each hand and blast away at the sinners. A frame church about one mile north of Edon replaced the hewn-log church after 1865. In the late 1870s, a Dunkard Society purchased the building.[28]

The so-called Donutt Church was at the corner of State Route 49 and County Road K and was evidently a forerunner of the Edon Methodist Church. A history of that church presented on the one hundredth anniversary, November 14, 1943, says, "So today we commemorate the founding 100 years ago of what is the Edon Methodist Church, the 95th anniversary of the building of the log church (Donutt Church)."[29]

Edgerton Circuit—Zion Church

The *Geschichte* refers to the 1848 log church as one mile north and one mile west of Edon. Then another was built about nine miles east of the original by the Germans and the English Methodists. Another church, Zion, was built in 1860 by pastor G. Trefz. In 1885, this latter church added a tower and bell.[30] Unfortunately, neither the *Geschichte* nor the English sources make clear where the Zion Church was located or whether it was one of the ones already described.

Edgerton Circuit—Weitz Chapel

Another church in St. Joseph Township was described briefly in Shinn's county history. The information is given that two German M. E. ministers named Baker and Deemer preached for a while in the "Weitz neighborhood" which was in the northwest area of the township.[31] I have looked in the *Geschichte* but have been unable to find the names of the preachers or anything similar. However, Knepper's history of the Edon Methodist Church mentions a Weitz

Chapel, "five miles southwest of Edon" as being on a circuit with Edon in 1901. Later, Weitz Chapel was dropped from the Edon charge sometime before 1924.[32]

A resident of Edon, Ohio, Marilyn Toner, was kind enough to do some research on Weitz Chapel for me. She sent information to me from the county histories, including maps and a biography of Adam Weitz. She also gave her best guess as to what happened to the church building. After it closed, the building was moved. Eventually the land it was on was sold to the R. C. Cornell family whose son married Mrs. Toner's older sister. When visiting at the Cornell farm, Mrs. Toner noticed the church-like building. She relates in her letter

> the building size was around 20' by 24'. . . . The front at the church had a raised platform (for the preacher), two church windows (each came to a point at the top) on either side, (4 windows in all). The lower part of the wall was wainscoting, while the upper portion and ceiling were plastered.[33]

According to a 1918 map of Florence Township in Williams County, Weitz Chapel was located in the northwest corner of section 8.

Edgerton Circuit—Fremont, Indiana, German M. E.

The Fremont German Methodists shared a building with the English congregation which was the joint property of both. The church was consecrated in 1873 and both groups used the building until 1880 at which time the English congregation built its own church.[34] Apparently, the Germans continued using the old building until 1906 when the group disbanded and sold it.[35]

Fremont, Indiana's German M.E. was remodeled into a home.

A newspaper article reports that the cornerstone for the church was laid on July 7, 1872, and the building dedicated in the spring of 1880. Its location was the corner of Bell and West North streets. There is now a house at that location built from the bricks of the church "which was torn down."[36] On a recent visit to the Fremont area, we had no trouble locating the church site. You can see the church origin of the house very clearly, even down to the shape of the windows, so I would question whether it was actually torn down or simply remodeled.

Kendallville, Indiana, Circuit

The Kendallville Circuit consisted of churches in Kendallville, Auburn, Garrett, and Fort Wayne. In 1909 Kendallville and Goshen were paired for a year and after that, associated with the Edgerton, Ohio, Circuit briefly.

Kendallville Circuit—German Methodist Church

The Kendallville church began in a private home east of the town and then moved to a schoolhouse nearby. In 1861 a wealthy individual gave the fledgeling church land for a building and parsonage. Five years later, the building project began under the direction of Rev. George Schwinn and the dedication took place in 1866. The church was remodeled around the turn of the century. Services were in German until the arrival of Rev. William Weiler who instituted Sunday evening services in English.[37]

By 1898, the Kendallville church was the only one left on the circuit and was reunited briefly with Auburn and Garrett in 1906. In 1909 Auburn and Garret joined the Edgerton Circuit and Goshen and Kendallville were paired. By 1910 it was no longer listed in the conference minutes as a separate charge.[38] According to a letter from John C. Koch detailing the church's history, the congregation became too small to support the church and the building was sold to the Christian Science Church.[39]

Kendallville Circuit—Auburn German Methodist Episcopal Church

German Methodist preaching was first held in the area in 1845, but it was not until 1858 that Rev. Friedrich Ruff organized the Auburn German Methodists into the Kendallville Circuit. By 1874 the group was viable enough to consider building a church. Five men, who were chosen by the quarterly conference at Kendallville as trustees of the Emanuel Methodist Episcopal Church, promptly found a lot on which to build their church. On August 24, 1874, the trustees purchased land from Andrew Mayer for $250. Church construction was completed with the additional cost of $2,740. All but $200 was paid by donations and subscriptions and the Central German Conference took care of this debt. In 1892, a parsonage was built for $1,400.[40]

Former Auburn, Indiana, German M.E. now serves another denomination.

The German Methodists disbanded in 1927 and sold their building to the Brethren Church. It still stands at the northeast corner of South Jackson and Seventeenth streets in Auburn.[41]

Kendallville Circuit—Garrett German M. E.

At the same time the Auburn church was started, the German Methodists in Garrett conducted services in homes. When they raised enough money, they constructed a one-room, frame church about the turn of the century, on South Cowen Street in the two hundred block. Eventually, the church was sold and members went elsewhere. At present the Garrett Post Office stands on the site.[42]

Kendallville Circuit—Sedan German M. E.

Another church was located on the circuit north of Sedan but there is very little information on this church. In 1875, trustees were elected at a meeting in Auburn under the auspices of Elder G. Trefz, presumably, to build a church building.[43] The *Geschichte* states that the Sedan church disbanded in the early twentieth century.[44] The building was located at the crossroads of CR 19 and CR 20 but there was no sign of a building having ever been there, when I visited the area.

Kendallville Circuit—Wawaka German M. E.

The English- and German-speaking Methodists of Wawaka worked together to

Wawaka, Indiana, UMC, formerly German ME.

organize a church before 1869. The two groups were fortunate in acquiring the first schoolhouse built in the town, where they subsequently held services. In 1881 the congregations purchased lot no. 12 of the Tibbott addition in Wawaka for two hundred dollars. A short time later, they spent three hundred dollars for an adjoining lot to use for a parsonage.

Each group had services in its own language with the Germans worshiping in the afternoon when their pastor came over from Kendallville. When their numbers began decreasing in the early twentieth century, the Germans decided to merge with their English-speaking brethren in 1907.

The first church building was constructed from bricks kilned at Rochester and transported in horse-drawn wagons by the church members. The church featured beautiful multicolored stain glass windows which were much admired. In 1929 a lightening strike severely damaged the church, including the treasured windows, resulting in considerable repairs.

In the 1960s the church began a three-phase building project. All of the extensive remodeling and building projects were completed by 1973 and the church was debt free. The parsonage, dating back to 1881, also needed an upgrade and this was accomplished in 1981.

In 1986 the church, located at 7238 North Albion, Wawaka, Ind. 46794, was on a charge with Kimmell. Fifty-two pastors have served the church since its inception in 1869.[45]

Goshen, Indiana, German M. E.

Goshen first entertained a Methodist preacher in 1859 when Roman Straub opened his home for the preaching. Mr. Straub soon helped organize the first Sunday school class. The fledgeling church first met in the downstairs of the English Methodist church, but, as more families were converted, was able to build a small, brick church at Pearl and Fifth streets in 1862. The church cost $2,570 and soon after, a parsonage was also built.

The congregation continued to grow and in 1875 purchased more land at Madison and Fifth streets for $1,100 where a new church, costing $1,400, was built and consecrated in 1876. The English Lutherans purchased the old building at Pearl and Fifth streets, but, by 1894 the German congregation had dwindled and no longer needed the commodious building on the corner of Madison and Fifth. An agreement was made with the Lutherans to again exchange buildings, so the German Methodists moved back into their earlier church building. The congregation also received $3,250 in the exchange which they used to build a house and buy two others which provided extra money from rent.

The church had a Sunday school since 1861 which claimed seventy-five members, but in the early 1900s, membership had decreased to forty-six. Around the turn of the century, the church also had a youth group and Ladies Aid, each with more than thirty members, which had been founded ten years earlier.[46]

The German church continued services until World War I when decreased membership and anti-German sentiment prevailed and the congregation disbanded. In 1924 the Church of God took over the church building and used it until they built a new church. Though the old church stood empty for a number of years, it was opened as a disaster center after a Palm Sunday tornado in 1964. It once more became a house of worship when Our Saviour Lutheran Church organized. In 1967 the venerable church met the wrecking ball because it was necessary to widen Purl[*] Street and provide parking for a new library.[47]

Elmore, Ohio, Circuit—St. Paul's German Methodist

When Englehard Reimenscheider began preaching in northern Ohio, his circuit was bounded by Delaware in the south, Ashland in the east, Lima in the west and Toledo to the north. One of the preaching points in this area was at Elmore. The area around Elmore was reorganized in 1865 as the Portage River Circuit with five preaching points.

The first building for Elmore's St. Paul's congregation became a reality in 1867. The congregation purchased Lot no. 7 on Fremont Street from Daniel and Matilda Ulmer and built a frame church building. In 1890 the trustees purchased Lot no. 181 on Rice Street from August Seefeldt and, a year later, more

---

[*]. I know Purl Street has two different spellings in this entry, but that is the way the sources spelled it.

land from George Luckey. In October 1891 the new St. Paul's German Methodist Episcopal church was dedicated. This new building was thirty-by-forty-five feet, had a twenty-eight-by-twenty-eight-foot annex and a steeple that was sixty-eight feet high. The two six-light gas chandeliers which were installed in 1898, were the first of their kind in Elmore. In 1924, a basement, to be used for Sunday school rooms, was constructed under the building.

Parsonages had been on Fremont and Toledo streets, but in 1912 a new one was built on Rice Street on land had formerly used for horse sheds.

In 1954 St. Paul's merged with Trinity and the St. Paul's property was sold. The first St. Paul's building was converted into a house; the second building was purchased by St. John's UCC and is still used as a parish hall.[48]

Elmore Circuit—Woodville German M. E.

The previously mentioned Englehard Riemenschneider also preached in Woodville, Ohio, in the early 1840s and in 1843 helped found the first German M. E. church there. The congregation had about twenty members at this time and Riemenschneider was their first pastor. A frame church was immediately built but used only until 1844 when it was sold to the United Brethren so the M. E. group could move into a new frame building. The church was located on a section of land bordered by Bridge, Water, and First streets.[49]

A member of the Woodville Historical Society reported in a letter that the church was gone when he was a boy in the 1920s with only the basement remaining. There was no swimming pool in town, so after a hard rain, he and his friends went swimming there. In the 1950s a motel was built on the site.[50]

A Sandusky County history says that services were still held in the church up to 1909 (date of publication of the history), although there was no resident pastor.[51]

Elmore Circuit—Perrysburg German M. E.

In 1861 the Perrysburg German Methodist Episcopal church was founded and a building erected on the "south side of West Indiana Avenue, just east of the first alley."[52] Although listed on the Elmore Circuit at its founding, by 1866 it was on the Toledo Circuit where it stayed until 1917, according to conference records. By 1918 it no longer appears in the Central German Conference listing, so the congregation probably joined the English Methodists.[53] The sources disagree on the date of this union.

A timeline of the First United Methodist Church claims that the German M. E. was united with them in 1898 which contradicts the Central German Conference records.[54] Danford states that the uniting took place in the early twentieth century.[55] At present, the old church serves as a very attractive bed and breakfast called The Guesthouse and is located at 122 West Indiana Avenue.[56]

This guest house in Perrysburg, Ohio, was once the German ME church.

Elmore Circuit—Fishing Creek (Zoar)

The mission field to which Fishing Creek belonged was the Lower Sandusky Mission and included Woodville, Perrysburg, and Mud Creek, as well. A class was organized in 1865 by C. G. Herzer and in 1873 a small church was erected.[57]

Another source says that the Zoar German M. E. was organized in 1844 and located in the central part of Rice Township. The church building was constructed in 1873.[58]

I looked up the building and found one which is now labeled "Rice Twp Tool Shed" at the corner of CR 119 and 170. Comparing the present-day building (even with its alterations) to photos of Zoar Church show that it was most likely the old Fishing Creek or Zoar Church.

Elmore Circuit—Mud Creek Church

The Mud Creek Church is first mentioned in the *Geschichte* as being a member of the Lower Sandusky Mission, but later, the entry says, "Mud Creek has entirely ceased to exist."[59] It was not mentioned whether a church building was ever erected. Mud Creek is a stream that is to the northwest of Fishing Creek and probably the two congregations united and used the Fishing Creek facility.

This old Rice Township tool shed in Sandusky County, Ohio, once housed a German M.E. congregation.

Toledo, Ohio

Toledo—Emanuel German M. E.

In 1849 Rev. Peter F. Schneider came to the Toledo area to preach at the home of Johann von Gunden. and Emanuel, the father of all the Toledo German M. E. churches, was born. Not long after, a small church building and house on Huron Street were purchased for the sum of one thousand dollars. At the 1850 Ohio Conference, the Reverend Schneider extolled the virtues of the Toledo undertaking. He made an impression and was given three hundred dollars (a grand sum in those days) for the betterment of the new church enterprise.[60]

According to one source, the church on Huron was moved to Ontario Street near Walnut and used in that location until 1880 when a new building was constructed for twenty thousand dollars.[61] Another source mentions that the building on Huron Street, previously owned by the English Methodists, was located at 479 Huron. It also states that the church was moved to Ontario Street and was used until a "fine edifice . . . on the Northwest corner of Walnut and Ontario Streets" was erected.[62]

The *Emanuel-Centarian* declares that the plot on Ontario Street was purchased in 1862 and a new church building and parsonage were erected for $6,127.17. Then in 1880 another building lot at 802 Walnut Street was bought and the "present" church erected.[63] A newspaper article gives additional information on the early church buildings. In 1862 the property at Walnut and Ontario streets was purchased. In 1880 property on the opposite corner was purchased and a church built for $20,000.00 during the tenure of Rev. Henry Jend.[64]

During the late nineteenth century, two more German M. E. churches were started by the Emanuel congregation. In 1858 a mission was opened in the southern part of the city which became the Zion congregation in 1872. In 1887 the eastern area of Toledo became the home of Salem church. The Galena Street Mission followed in 1891.[65]

There is not much information available about Emanuel from the 1880s until the mid-twentieth century. The church had its Ladies Aid (no date is given for its founding) which eventually became the Women's Society for Christian Service. This group engaged in supporting missionary work, promoting financial aid for the church and in spiritual support.

Rev. Daniel Matthai began the men's Brotherhood in 1907 which served as a fellowship vehicle but also sponsored church projects. Eventually, athletic groups fell under its jurisdiction.

The Girl's Missionary Circle was organized as a Sunday school class early in the twentieth century. The group started with a specific missionary purpose but as the years went by became more focused on friendship and fellowship. The original girls were twelve to fourteen years old, but in time the group consisted of the younger women of the church, some of whom also belonged to the WSCS.

By the mid-twentieth century, several other groups functioned at Emanuel. There were both a senior and a junior choir which, combined, had a membership of 50. Also, at this time, an MYF claiming a membership of 30 existed. Church school or Sunday school had been a part of the church from the beginning. During this time, the membership totaled about 180.

Some highlights through the years included the building of a new parsonage in the late nineteenth century. At the same time a pipe organ was installed in the church. The fiftieth anniversary was celebrated in 1899. A church fire struck in 1918 which precipitated a renovation and a rededication. A Diamond Jubilee was held in 1924 and at this time a rebuilding program spanning six years and totaling fifteen thousand dollars, took place. New windows, showers, updating of the old kitchen and a basement dining room were some of the improvements.[66]

In 1949 another fire struck on Sunday morning, March 13, 1949, with damage amounting to fifty thousand dollars, but covered by only eighteen thousand dollars of insurance. Nevertheless, a rebuilding plan was put forth: the pews and other church furniture were restored, debris was cleared out and three large meeting rooms constructed. So instead of celebrating their centennial in "an atmosphere of antiquity," the 350-member congregation marked the occasion in a brand new sanctuary. The centennial festivities took place over a three-day period from October 25 to the 27, 1950.[67]

The church seems to have disbanded after 1969. Records are listed up to and including that year.[68]

Toledo—Zion German M. E.

Zion M. E. (now Zion UMC) was organized in 1858 as a mission from Emanuel. The church was located in the "bloody fifth ward" which was famous for its strong drink and riotous living. People in that area had no respect for the sabbath and built houses, repaired property, and slaughtered hogs and cattle on Sundays. The first meeting was held in a woods known as City Park. In spite of the disturbances, the congregation grew and in 1859 was able to purchase a lot on Harrison Street. One of the founders, Frederick Schweizer, dug the foundation for the church by hand. The owner of a tile factory donated building material. The structure was completed and dedicated in the same year and organized as the Toledo Mission with twenty-eight members. The first membership list still in existence (dated September 1868) enumerates twenty-three members. Rev. G. A. Reuter was the first regular pastor appointed to the Toledo Mission in 1868. In 1873 the church on Harrison Street was sold and a lot on Segur Avenue purchased for $2,250 for a new church and parsonage.[69]

The new Segur Avenue building and parsonage cost twelve thousand dollars to erect. At first only the lower section of the building, where church and Sunday school both met, was completed due to lack of funds. In 1879 the upper floor was finished and, fortuitously, some church property in Ft. Wayne was sold and the conference gave the proceeds to Zion. In 1881 a Thanksgiving service was held celebrating the completion of the building.[70]

There is an interesting side note on Alfred E. Baur, the first sexton of the church, who had the duties of filling and trimming the oil lamps, sawing four-foot logs for the two heating stoves, dismantling the stove pipes once a year for cleaning, and ringing the church bell for services. It was customary to ring the bell forty strokes at that time, and he had to climb a ladder through a hole in the unfinished upper floor to reach the rope. At times he let willing young men do the chore for him. The overeager youths would often turn the bell completely over winding the bell rope up an extra turn. Mr. Baur would then have to climb up anyway, to unwind the rope.[71]

Subsequent improvements took place in 1905 when an annex was built which was constructed at the rear of the building and contained a sexton's apartment. Also, a pipe organ was added in the main auditorium. In 1910 there

*Old Zion German ME on Segur Avenue, Toledo, Ohio,
now home to another denomination.*

was a three-thousand-dollar renovation which was paid for by a freewill offering. In 1913 new heating equipment was purchased and other improvements made for a total of fifty-seven hundred dollars—four thousand of which was paid off by the end of the year.

During the World War I years, the use of the German language was questioned as English became the dominant language among those with a German background. Children were no longer reared speaking German so they got little out of the Sunday school and church services in that language. In 1925 Rev. Elias Roser began an evening service in English. In 1933 when the Central German Conference was dissolved, Zion was taken into the English-speaking conference. This presented a problem as Zion, competing with the nearby

Present Zion UMC on Copland Boulevard, Toledo, Ohio.

Broadway Church, found it difficult to grow. A move to a new location was initiated by 1947.[72]

An untitled church history states the criterion for locating to the new site: "In relocation here we picked what we thought the best location—no church." in the community.[73] First to be built was a parsonage on Beverly Drive which cost $26,000 and was completed in April 1948. The construction of the new church began in the fall of 1948 with a ground breaking. The cornerstone was laid in October 1949 and the building ready for occupation in June 1950. The new church cost $107,977. Selling the old church and parsonage on Segur Avenue realized $23,700 so that still left a debt of $111,000 for the new church and parsonage. The new location, however, proved advantageous for attracting new members and soon the congregation of 200 had increased to 733.

The increased growth was a mixed blessing, for the building was soon too small for the larger congregation. In 1956, the church fathers decided it was time to build an educational annex. A pledge drive generated $124,134 which opened the door for a $130,000 loan from Toledo Trust Co. These monies were used to pay off the debt and finance the new building project. Ground was broken in August 1956 and a little more than a year later, in September 1957, the educational unit was consecrated. The church now had eighteen classrooms, a large social hall with new kitchen, a stage, and a parlor with a Pullman kitchen. The parking lot was also expanded and finished with blacktop. The sum for the completed project came to $162,000. A larger sanctuary, with a removable partition between it and the social hall, was also constructed. In 1975 Zion celebrated the burning of the mortgage and an end to the debt generated by the building projects of the 1950s. In 1978 some renovating was done including a new roof and a resurfacing of the parking lot.[74]

Zion's current address is 2600 Copland Boulevard, Toledo, Ohio 43614.

Toledo—Salem German Methodist Episcopal Church

In 1874 the Ohio Conference of the Evangelical Congregation sent a missionary to preach in the eastern part of Toledo. Rev. R. C. Militzer eventually organized the group as the East Toledo German Methodist Mission. Trustees of the new church held their first meeting at the pastor's home on Walnut Street in October 1888. Soon they purchased a building lot at the corner of Federal and Nevada streets for four hundred dollars. They subsequently constructed a brick church twenty-eight-by-forty feet which included a small tower. The cost was broken down as follows:

> They paid $49.40 for bricks, $10.45 for sheet metal for the tower, $216.13 for carpentry, $109.85 for plaster and plastering, $17 for a bookcase, and $2 for an extra table.[75]

The adjacent lot was purchased for $125 in 1889 to build a parsonage. The pastor's salary in the 1880s was $550 annually.

The administration meetings, which started in October 1889. always opened with certain questions being posed:

> Is anyone ill? Is anyone in need of aid? Are there any notable changes in behavior? Is anyone being neglected? Are there or should there be any changes in the classes?[76]

In 1895 Rev. J. J. Link organized a youth group which met Tuesday nights in members' homes. In addition to fellowship, the group was involved in stewardship and outreach to the needy. In December of 1895 they collected twenty-two cents, two loaves of bread, and some clothes for a family in need.

The Ladies Aid Society, dating back to October 1900, met in the afternoon between two and four o'clock and devoted their meetings to making quilts, bedspreads, aprons, and other things to sell. The proceeds from these went to purchase items for the church and parsonage such as carpeting. The constitution of the organization had some intriguing rules:

> During dinners when guests are present, the members shall take special care and preventions in all their discussions. . . . Each person shall speak only once the first time around until it is their turn again. . . . All personal problems are to be avoided in discussions. . . . No one should speak longer than five minutes without permission.[77]

In 1908 a new church was built on the lot for three thousand dollars. The fate of the old church is uncertain but some senior members maintain that it was

Salem UMC, formerly German ME, on Federal Avenue in Toledo.

moved to the southeast corner of the intersection and remodeled into apartments. Others state this is incorrect but don't seem to have an alternative suggestion.

In 1921 conference documents show that the church property was valued at forty-five hundred dollars with the parsonage being worth eighteen hundred. In 1926, the pastor's annual salary was twelve hundred dollars (which included rent). In that year the church land was worth ten thousand and the parsonage thirty-five hundred. Salem Church claimed ninety-four members.

During the 1920s, the men's Brotherhood became an active force. It was actually organized in 1919 and usually opened with devotions followed by a business meeting and refreshments. The group helped take care of the physical plant of the church by doing such chores as roof repair, installing cupboards, painting, wallpapering, repairing windows, etc. In the summer, lighter activities took place at the farms of some of the members where they enjoyed baseball, horseshoes and other pastimes.

In May 1925 the board approved of services in both German and English. and in 1928, all services became English except for a Sunday school class.[78]

During the 1930s Salem underwent some changes. The Central German Conference was not able to find a pastor for the church and there was also financial need. As a result a local pastor took over some of the ministerial duties and the Epworth League was also dissolved. When it became known that the Central German Conference was going to merge with the English Conferences, Salem's congregation decided to take action. They contacted the Ohio

Conference of the Evangelical Church and asked to be taken in. On May 1, 1932, fifty of Salem's members transferred to the Evangelical denomination, thus going back to their roots in 1874 and leaving Methodism behind.

Salem began to prosper once again. The Sunday school had 60 members at the time of transfer but by the end of that year had increased to 75. In 1936, 40 members of the Collingwood Evangelical Church transferred to Salem when their church was sold. By 1938 the membership had grown to 164. In 1933 the Evangelical League of Christian Endeavor organized the youth.[79]

In the 1940s the church acquired a new parsonage at 840 Main Street. In 1942 Salem celebrated ten years as an Evangelical Church. The war years took many of the young men of the church off to combat causing the music ministry to suffer until seven ladies, led by Opal Wendell, organized a choir. In 1945 the congregation celebrated both the end of the war and the burning of the parsonage mortgage. Other highlights were starting of the first vacation Bible school in 1946 and, a year later, the Salem softball team winning the Class AA Church League championship.

Shortly after the war ended, part of the church basement and the parsonage were painted and new carpeting was installed in the church aisles. In the late 1940s, the basement floor was tiled and a new furnace put in the parsonage. A movie projector and typewriter with a wide carriage were purchased for church use.[80]

The 1950s saw more growth with membership of 230 people on the roll at one point. Salem had a good sports program and sponsored a basketball team, a dartball team and a softball team. The softball team again proved themselves with championships in 1955, 1957, and 1958. The Ladies Aid sponsored delicious sauerkraut suppers during this time period.

More remodeling was done with the redecoration of the main floor including new furniture. A new organ was purchased and faithful members donated a pulpit, reading stand, communion altar, altar cross and candelabras. The congregation saw the need for adding an educational unit and architects were engaged to draft the plans.[81]

On April 23, 1968, Salem E.U.B. once more became Methodist when E.U.B. churches merged with the Methodist church creating the United Methodist Church.

In the early 1960s both the church and parsonage underwent a facelift, with plumbing, siding, painting, and stained glass window repair taking place at the church; and roof repair, aluminum siding, and screens were installed at the parsonage. The church also received a new Wurlitzer piano and Wurlitzer organ which were dedicated in 1963. Sunday school classes donated new hymnals and tables. In 1968, while more renovation took place to the tune of thirty-four thousand dollars, church services moved to the Glass Workers Union Hall for eight weeks.[82]

In the 1970s Salem started some events that were enjoyed for many years which included the Great Day of Singing begun in 1972, and the outdoor morning worship and picnic, and the Golden Age Dinner (both started in 1973). The following year, KIT letters (Keep in Touch) were introduced and in 1975, the Ash Wednesday Soup Supper/Communion was launched, as well as the Feed Your Neighbor program. Children's Storytime became a regular feature in Sunday morning worship at this time, and a Christmas tree-decorating ceremony also originated in the 1970s. Several older traditions such as the Mother/Daughter Banquet and an annual spaghetti dinner continued to be popular.

The building committee, organized several decades earlier, disbanded when priorities shifted. Plans for building an addition were dropped and instead funds were used to remodel the Fellowship House and sheath the steeple in aluminum siding.[83]

The new pastor in 1983, Rev. Brian Staub, promoted the Membership Care Committee whose focus was on the worship service; the Outreach Committee, which oversaw missions; the Age Level Committee, which directed Sunday school activities; and the Pastor-Parish Relations Committee, whose job was to determine goals. Members volunteered weekly at the Helping Hands Food Kitchen, as well as Festival of Sharing, the Friendly Center, a food pantry, and a Christmas food basket project.

The biggest event of the 1980s, however, was the celebration of the one hundreth anniversary of Salem. Former pastors spoke, special music enjoyed, a tea and open house held, and memorabilia showcased. On various Sundays members recounted stories from the church's past and a subcommittee researched and prepared a history.[84]

When I visited Salem in 2001 it was still active and located at 602 Federal Street in Toledo.

Toledo—Galena Street German Methodist Church

In 1892 Emanuel started a mission at the corner of Galena and Ontario streets in the northern part of the city which became the fourth German Methodist church.[85] Apparently, Galena never grew to be as strong a church as her three sisters. In 1904 it was put on a circuit with Perrysburg; then was an independent charge again for a few years before it was again linked to Perrysburg. In 1916, its mother church, Emanuel, took Galena under its wing again until 1918 when it was once more independent. After 1920 Galena is no longer listed in the records.[86]

Notes

1. Golder, Horst, and Schaal, *Geschichte*, 376.
2. Weston Arthur Goodspeed, *County of Williams, Ohio, Historical and Biographical* (Chicago: F. A. Battey, 1882), 115.
3. Anonymous, *60th Anniversary of The Stryker Methodist Church Structure*, church history (Stryker, Ohio: 1962).
4. B. M. Beach, *History of the Emanuel M. E. Church near West Unity, Ohio* (Stryker, Ohio: Stryker Advance Print, 1908), 5.
5. Beach, *History of Emanuel M. E. Church*, 1–3.
6. Anonymous, *Historical Note*, church history, Emanuel M.E. Church, County Road K, Floral Grove Cemetery, Brady Township, Williams County, Ohio.
7. Kevin Maynard, "Emanuel M. E. Church the Pride of German Emigrants," *A Guide to Williams County's History* (Montpelier, Ohio: Williams County History Society, 1995), 102.
8. *From Hand to Hand and Heart to Heart for 125 Years,* church history (Evansport, Ohio: Evansport UMC, 1999), 18.
9. *Evansport United Methodist Church, 1874–1974*, centennial history and program (Evansport, Ohio, October 13, 1974).
10. *From Hand to Hand*, 19.
11. Warner, Beers, & Co., *History of Defiance County, Ohio* (Chicago: Warner, Beers & Co. 1883), 192.
12. Ibid., 193.
13. Anonymous, *History of St. Paul's United Methodist Church*, church history, Defiance, Ohio.
14. J. A. D., "Moving Old German M. E. Edifice Recalls Notable History of Parish" church history, newspaper article on file at Defiance Public Library, Defiance, Ohio.
15. Lewis Cass Aldrich, *History of Henry and Fulton Counties, Ohio* (Syracuse, NY: D. Mason & Co., 1888), 267.
16. Anonymous, *Pleasant Bend, Ohio: Pleasant Bend UMC, 1994*, on file at Archives of Ohio United Methodism, Ohio Wesleyan University, Delaware, Ohio.
17. Golder, Horst, and Schaal, *Geschichte*, 371.
18. R. D. Dale, recorder, book 1, (Edgerton mission parsonage handwritten deed filed in Steuben County, Indiana) August 5, 1873, 161.
19. *Emanuel United Methodist Church*, church history, prepared under the pastorate of Rev. Harley Martin (Edgerton, Ohio: 1975).
20. Historical update (to *Emanuel United Methodist Church*) 2004.
21. Transcribed interview with Paul D. and Rosa Krill and Hulda Valet, taped by Thelma Riehle, 1976.
22. Steven C. Bloir, comp., *History of West Buffalo*, (n.p.: self published, 53).
23. Bloir, handwritten copy "The Salem Church" by Alice Kinzer, 57–67.
24. Ibid., 54.
25. Ibid., 50.
26. Leona Krill Betts to author, August 29, 2004.
27. William H. Shinn, *The County of Williams* (Madison, Wis.: Northwestern Historical Association, 1905), 221–22.
28. Goodspeed, *County of Williams, Ohio*, 466–67.

29. Mrs. W. H. Knepper, *History of the Methodist Church, Edon, Ohio*, church history (Edon, Ohio: 1943).
30. Golder, Horst, and Schaal, *Geschichte*, 373.
31. Shinn, *The County of Williams*, 187.
32. Knepper, *Methodist Church, Edon.*
33. Marilyn Toner to author, April 2005.
34. *History of Northeast Indiana* (Lewis Publishing Co., 1920), 238.
35. Golder, Horst, and Schaal, *Geschichte*, 373.
36. *Fremont* (Indiana) *News*, "Fremont Church Celebrates Anniversary," August 1991, 1.
37. John C. Koch to Mrs. H. G. Misselborn, 1946.
38. *Minutes of the Annual Conferences*, 1906, 494; 1909, 565; 1910, 466.
39. Koch to Misselborn, 1946.
40. B. F. Bowen and Co., *History of DeKalb County, Indiana* (Indianapolis: B. F. Bowen, 1914), 203–204.
41. John Martin Smith and DeKalb Sesquicentennial, Inc., *DeKalb County 1837–1987* (Auburn, Ind.: DeKalb Sesquicentennial, Inc., 1990), 790.
42. Ibid., 790–91.
43. Ibid., 791.
44. Golder, Horst, and Schaal, *Geschichte*, 375.
45. Noble County History Book Committee, *The History of Noble County, Indiana* (Tex.: Taylor Publishing Co., 1986), 47.
46. Golder, Horst, and Schaal, *Geschichte*, 384–386.
47. *Goshen* (Indiana) *News*, "Old Church of God, Fifth and Purl, Is Razed," 1967.
48. Charles W. Dibert, *St. Paul-Trinity United Methodist Church: A History within a History*, church history (Elmore, Ohio: 1984).
49. Woodville Historical Society, *A Sketch Book of Woodville, Ohio, Past—Present: To Commemorate the Woodville Village Sesquicentennial 1836–1986* (Woodville, Ohio: Woodville Historical Society, 1986), 35.
50. Kermit Hoesman to author, 1997.
51. Basil Meek, *Twentieth Century History of Sandusky Co.* (Chicago: Richmond-Arnold Publishing Co., 1909), 350.
52. Ardath Danford, *Perrysburg Revisited* (Perrysburg, Ohio: Way Public Library Foundation, 1992), 97.
53. *Minutes of the Annual Conferences*, 1918.
54. Judith P. Justus, *Friendly First Church*, church history, (Perrysburg, Ohio: 1995).
55. Danford, *Perrysburg Revisited*, 97.
56. Annie Ciesiukowski, "Nearby Getaways," Toledo online, toledoblade.com, 2004.
57. Golder, Horst, and Schaal, *Geschichte*, 382–84.
58. *Twentieth Century History of Sandusky Co.*, 333.
59. Golder, Horst, and Schaal, *Geschichte*, 382–84.
60. Henry J. Werner, Jr., *Emanuel–Centenarian,* church centennial publication, (Toledo, Ohio: ca.1949).
61. John M. Killits, *Toledo and Lucas County, Ohio* (Toledo, Ohio: The S. J. Clarke Publishing Company, 1923), 341.
62. Clark Waggoner, *History of the City of Toledo and Lucas County, Ohio* (New York: Munsell & Co., 1888), 586.
63. Werner, *Emanuel-Centenarian.*

64. *Toledo* (Ohio) *Times*, "Church Has New Dress for Centennial," October 23, 1950.

65. Werner, *Emanuel-Centenarian.*

66. Anonymous, *Emanuel and the Next Century,* church history,(Toledo, Ohio: ca. 1950).

67. *Toledo Times*, "Church has New Dress."

68. Lucas County Chapter of the Ohio Genealogy Society, *Lucas County Church Records Inventory* (Lucas Co., Ohio:1990), 65.

69. *Diamond Jubilee and Home Coming*, anniversary program and church history, Zion, M.E. Church, (Toledo, Ohio, 1933).

70. Anonymous, *Zion United Methodist Church, 125th Anniversary Celebration*, historical pamphlet, church history (Toledo, Ohio: 1979).

71. *Diamond Jubilee,*

72. *Zion United Methodist*

73. F. Haus, untitled church history, Zion M. E. (Toledo, Ohio: 1957).

74. *Zion United Methodist*

75. Pat Christy, "Salem Before 1900," *Salem United Methodist Church, A History*, ed. Larry Morgan (Toledo, Ohio, 1989), 2.

76. Ibid., 2.

77. Ibid., 3.

78. Larry Morgan, "Salem the 1920s," in *Salem...*, 5.

79. Linda DeNeve, "Salem in the 30s," in *Salem...*, 7.

80. Robert Souders, "Salem in the 1940s," in *Salem...*, 9.

81. Margaret Welker, "Salem in the 1950s," in *Salem...*, 10.

82. Robert Newton, "Salem in the 1960s," in *Salem...*, 12.

83. Mauvareen Klingbeil, "Salem in the 1970s," in *Salem...*, 13.

84. Theresa Schneider, "Salem in the 1980s," in *Salem...*, 13.

85. Elias D. Whitlock, et al., *History of the Central Ohio Conference of the Methodist Episcopal Church* (Cincinnati: The Methodist Book Concern, 1913), 321.

86. *Minutes of the Annual Conferences*, 1904–1911 and 1912–1920.

PART IV

The German Methodist Episcopal Churches in the North Ohio District

The Central German Conferences, North Ohio District extended from Lake Erie to the Ohio River, from north to south. To the west, the boundary was Spencerville and New Knoxville, Ohio. The eastern border went into Pennsylvania taking in the German churches in the Pittsburgh area and also Wheeling, West Virginia, to the southeast. Along Lake Erie, the lake towns of Cleveland, Rockport, Vermillion, Sandusky, and La Carne were served.

CHAPTER 18

Lake Erie Area

Cleveland, Ohio

There were eight German Methodist churches and missions in Cleveland, starting in 1845 with First Church. Two years later, a church was started in nearby Rockport. In 1850 St. Paul's made its appearance and Quincy Street Mission followed two years later. After Immanuel's founding in 1855, there was a long interval until 1893 when Bethany came on the scene. Zion arrived in 1897 and Salem was started in 1909 as the last German Methodist church to find a home in Cleveland.[1]

Cleveland—First Church

The "grandfather" of all the Cleveland German M. E. churches has had a long, distinguished career and several name changes from the time of its founding in 1845 to the present. On September 3, 1845, the Ohio Conference met in Cincinnati and sent the first German pastor, Ernst H. Buhren, to Cleveland. He preached in the English Methodist Church located at the corner of St. Clair and Wood streets. Soon after he had started a Sunday School with fifty children, eight people banded together to found First Church on January 2, 1846.[2]

The new church began meeting in a building on South Water Street (Columbus Road) but soon acquired a building lot on Prospect Street between Huron and Miami. During the tenure of pastor J. A. Klein (1848–50) the congregation built a brick church but soon outgrew this building also, and in 1860 erected a two-story building on Erie Street (East Ninth Street).[3] The *Geschichte* alludes to some problems, including money difficulties, which then forced the congregation to move once again.[4] Emma Herwig, a member of the Erie Street church reported some of her memories.

Our church home was located on old Erie Street [East Ninth Street] on the site where the present Good Will Industry now has its home. We worshiped there many years and I was always taken to Sunday School regularly. Then came the time when the complexion of the neighborhood changed materially and our church board thought it wise to look around for another location.[5]

An English Baptist church which was also looking for a new site, stood at the corner of Scovil and Sterling avenues (East Thirtieth Street). An exchange was effected and First Church moved to this location in 1878. A parsonage was built nearby two years later. Mrs. Herwig continued her description.

How well I remember being taken to that new church. We thought it was beautiful because it was nicely decorated and carpeted. The building, however, was very old and it did not take us long to outgrow its capacity.

Because most of our members still lived in the vicinity of our church, we planned and built a new building on that same location. When the new church was finished and dedicated on September 17, 1893, we had what we believed was the most beautiful church in Cleveland. What a pipe organ and what beautiful church furnishings. Best of all, we finally had a roomy, wonderful Sunday School room, something we did not have in the old building.[6]

Only a year after the new Scovil and Sterling avenues building had been completed, a fire gutted the interior. Nevertheless, the people set themselves to the task—performing the necessary repairs and renovations and the building served the congregation until 1903. At this time, the Immanuel Mission (founded in the mid-1880s and described later in the text) was discontinued and the congregation joined First Church. Once more, First Church began the search for a new home.

The new pastor, Dr. F. W. Mueller, and his committee found a plot of land at the corner of Cedar and East Seventy-first streets and the building on Scovil and Sterling was sold to a Jewish congregation. A. Klotzbach, an architect and member of the church, drafted plans for both the church building and parsonage. Work proceeded rapidly after the groundbreaking on March 28, 1904, with the laying of the cornerstone on May 22, 1904, and the completion and dedication on December 11, 1904. The congregation met at Woodland Dance Hall while the construction took place. The people of First Church worshiped at their new building until 1926 when once again a move seemed warranted.

The fifth building for the church, now called Church of the Cross, was erected in Cleveland Heights at the corner of Caledonia and Winsford roads after the old church was sold to Seventh Day Adventists. The congregation met in space provided by Nela Park and Caledonia School until the dedication of the new facility on September 26, 1926.[7]

Through the years First Church and its successors have had many organizations including a women's group. Before 1940 there were three women's groups—the Ladies Aid, the Foreign Missionary Society, and the Home Missionary Society. In 1940 these combined to become the Women's Society of Christian Service which which was broken down into seven Circles. These smaller groups were organized by streets and met in the homes of members on the fourth Wednesday of each month. The WSCS, itself, which met on the second Wednesday of the month at the church, was a big help to the church giving fifteen hundred dollars a year to the church budget and five hundred to missions.

Other groups included the Ushers Club (1942) with its goal to help Sunday morning services run more smoothly; the Hilltop Service Club, a support group for servicemen's wives and fiancees; and the Ministry of Music (1944), which promoted a program of religious music and music education. The altar of the sanctuary was cared for by the Altar Guild which sought to keep it attractive and conducive to worship each Sunday.

The young people of the church have had their own organization, first the Epworth League and later Youth Fellowship, for one hundred years. The group met Sunday evenings from 7:00 a.m. to 9:00 p.m. and engaged in devotions and fellowship. Throughout the year activities included mission speakers, picnics, holiday parties, and pot luck suppers. The highlight of the year was always a trip to Lakeside for a week of spiritual instruction and recreation.

In the 1950s thirteen hundred members were on the roll at Church of the Cross, but by the 1970s this number had shrunk by half. The neighborhood character had changed and many of the members of German ancestry transferred to other churches. Rev. Douglas B. Denton sought to diversify the church service and reach out to those coming into the neighborhood. In 1982 the first African-American pastor, Rev. Joseph Primes, became pastor with Rev. Charles Frost following in 1983. A five-year plan was put into effect to stabilize finances and attract new members. Soon the membership was growing again and reached two hundred. A Gospel choir started by Reverend Denton made two trips to Georgia to perform which encouraged the congregation. In 1999 it was decided to change the name of the church to Community of Living Hope United Methodist Church. In 2002 Rev. Sade Davis-Reynolds became the first female pastor continuing the church's ministry of 160 years.[8]

Cleveland—Rockport German M. E.

The second German Methodist church founded in the Cleveland area, in 1847, was in South Rockport. Valentine Gleb and his wife were the "guiding lights" of the church, which first met in a schoolhouse until a church building was erected in 1851.[9]

Another source gives the year of 1848 as the year the first church was built. The church seemed to have had a difficult time attracting and keeping members, perhaps because Immanuel Evangelical Church nearby competed for the German worshipers. In 1893 the church on West 130th Street was given up and and many of the members chose to unite with Bethany which was in the western section of Cleveland. The old Rockport church building found a new use as a wagon shop for a while. Today a cemetery, featuring the names of many of the early German settlers of Cleveland, marks the neighborhood where the church once stood.[10]

Cleveland—Second German M. E. (later, St. Paul's)

In 1851 Rev. C. Gahn started a German Methodist mission in a house at the corner of Lorain and McLean streets in an area known as Ohio City. By 1853 there was enough support to make the mission an independent society with John Balduff as pastor.[11] Soon a second church building was erected at the corner of Lorain and North streets and became known as Cleveland West Side Church. By 1880 the congregation had increased enough in size to make a third church building a necessity. With God's blessing and many sacrifices by the members, a beautiful church and parsonage were built for twenty thousand dollars and the name was changed to St. Paul's. In the late nineteenth century St. Paul's claimed a congregation numbering 175 and also had an enthusiastic youth organization.[12]

The beautiful St. Paul's eventually fell into disrepair and in 1905 the congregation opted to rebuild the church with more modern facilities on the same site (Bridge and Harbor—now West Forty-fourth Street). This did not become a reality until 1911 due to the death of the pastor, John Gommel. The new facility was dedicated on December 8, 1912, and the next spring a new parsonage completed the building project. In 1947, St. Paul's invited the congregation of Franklin Boulevard Methodist to merge with them when that church's building was destroyed by fire. On May 11, 1947, the two became one taking the name Wesley Methodist Church.[13]

The former St. Paul's German M. E. saw many changes as it proceeded to the end of the twentieth century. In the early part of the century, English became the dominant language, replacing the German of its founders and early members. In the late twentieth century, Spanish became the prevailing language of the area and the church rose to the challenge by reinventing itself once again, as Primera Iglesia Metodista Unida Hispana en Cleveland. One of the early ministers of the Hispanic church, Rev. Modesto Espinoza, recalled that there were 78 members when he arrived in the 1980s. Ten years later the congregation had grown to 126, with a quarter of the membership being young people. One of Reverend Espinoza's priorities was to erect a prominent sign identifying the church, so others would not have the problem he had trying to find the church for the first time. Most of the congregants understand English so the service is in that language. Music and singing is supported by guitars, bass fiddle, key board, piano, and tambourines. A children's choir and a vigorous outreach ministry are planned for the future.[14]

Cleveland—Quincy Street Mission/Immanuel

The Immanuel German M. E. was first started in 1852 in a hall at the corner of Burwell and Arch (now East Thirty-fifth Street) streets. Meetings continued at that location until 1860 when the mission moved to Quincy Street near Southern Avenue and then, subsequently, to a property at Luffenden Avenue (now East Seventy-seventh Street) and Quincy Street. A chapel was built and at the consecration in 1886 the name was changed to Immanuel German Methodist Episcopal Church.[15] Immanuel was active until 1903 when the conference sold the property and the congregation joined First Church. First Church was having some growing pains and searching for a new location, so in 1904 the united congregation settled into a new church at Cedar Avenue and East Seventy-first Street.[16] As already mentioned, church went through two more name changes to become Church of the Cross and then in 1999, Community of Living Hope. The Immanuel building on Quincy Street is now the Allen Temple African Methodist Episcopal Church.

Cleveland—Bethany German M. E.

Members of the Rockport church started a Sunday school in the spring of 1893 which later became Bethany. The week following this effort the organizers made house-to-house visits in the neighborhood inviting the people to Sunday school and preaching. The invitations brought two children to the Sunday school and three adults to the church service. The founders persevered and soon were meeting in an old house nearby whose cramped quarters did not suit the fledgeling church for long. A church building constructed on the corner of Ursula and Willard streets was consecrated in December 1893. However, this left the church with a large debt which caused much worry until 1905 when all was paid off and the note was burned in a celebration.[17]

Bethany continued prospering and in 1915 Sunday school facilities were enlarged, a new pipe organ was donated by a member of the congregation, and new church windows were installed. About this time the church received new members from a United Brethren congregation in the area.

In 1936 a church committee was chosen to search for a new location. The Immanuel Pentecostal Church bought the Bethany building (which later became Trinity Freewill Baptist) for ten thousand dollars. In the meantime, Bethany found West Park Methodist, which had been having some problems, and proposed a merger.[18]

On June 19, 1938, the Bethany congregation met at their old church, formed a motorcade and proceeded to the West Park church where the two met at the new church, Christ Church, for the first time. Two months after the first combined service, groundbreaking took place and in October work on the sanctuary was started. Cornerstones from Bethany and West Park were placed on opposite sides of the new building and one for Christ Church placed in the center. Bethany's bell was installed in the steeple. Consecration services were held in November and December 1939 and the new Christ Church now had 632 members and a Sunday school of 369.

The church continued to grow and by the 1950s, expansion of the facilities became a necessity. A building program was initiated which provided a larger sanctuary, a lounge, chapel, fellowship hall, and more Sunday school rooms. The work was completed in early 1956 for the amount of $2,500,000 and the consecration was held on February 12, 1956. In 1964 Christ Church held a week-long silver anniversary celebration. In 1975 the church joined the rest of the country in helping to celebrate America's bicentennial. Due to its size and age, the ancient oak tree on the east side of the church was proclaimed a historic site by the City of Cleveland.[19]

Christ Church was always home to many small groups. United Methodist Women and United Methodist Youth have been fixtures for many years throughout various changes. Some organizations that are no longer active include the Opportunity Class, the Inspiration Class, Doublets, Singlets, and the Men's Club. The Kumduble Class formed in 1946 and was instrumental in raising money for various projects while also promoting various social activities. In 1967 the R. F. M. class, whose name was chosen by a contest and means "Room For More," organized. Their first projects were to donate a set amount each month to a woman who ministered to needy families and to make a pledge to the church. Other activities soon followed such as pancake breakfasts, spaghetti suppers, sales of pies and chocolate chip cookies and a Craft and Fun Fair. The Reflections Class, a young adult group, organized in 1985, and has studied personal and social concerns and engaged in service activities. A quilters' group, meeting once a week, began in 1973 and has the impressive record of making 240 quilts and raising $19,000 for church projects. The Heavenly Bargains Thrift Shop, although now now longer operating, raised $10,850 in its heyday. A "Sharing Our Losses" group was devoted to helping those with grief issues and became an ecumenical organization serving the community. This group, which met on the first Wednesday of the month, is also no longer functioning.[20]

A check of the website in 2009 showed the following activities at Christ: UMW, UMYF, adult fellowship groups, adult and children's choir, and adult and children's bell choir. Worship times are Wednesday at 7:00 p.m., Sunday at 10:30 a.m. with Sunday school at 9:00 a.m. The church address is 3625 West Eighteenth Street, Cleveland, OH 44111.[21] Their website is www.christumc.com.

Cleveland—Zion German M. E.

Immanuel German M. E. started Zion as a mission in 1897 by sending two ministers door to door in the area of East Ninety-third Street to see if there was interest among the people in having a German language church. An empty store room was found and services held here until the church building at Bessemer and Woodland Hills (now East Ninety-third Street) was completed. Church services took place on Sunday mornings and the afternoons were devoted to Sunday school, at which the children also received German lessons.

The Ladies Aid was founded before the church was erected and was a big help financially for this project.[22] In 1926 the Ladies Aid reported a membership of twenty-seven. Some fundraising projects they sponsored included sponsoring a Chop Suey Supper, a bazaar, a Sauerkraut Supper, and a Strawberry Festival which earned them $188.55.[23] Another report stated, "We always visit the sick, those in need and the indifferent." There was evidently a Sewing Club connected with the group because it helped them with fundraisers.[24]

A Sunday School report from the 1920s states that attendance varied from forty-five to fifty-five individuals. A "red letter" day was July 11, 1926, when the children from the Berea Orphanage visited the Sunday school. It was reported that

> They were called for in machines. A joint program was rendered by the school and the orphan family. Then a dinner was provided for all the guests. And then the machines were again put to use giving all an afternoon of sightseeing and returning the entire family by 5:30 P.M. This is the seventh time that the orphan family have been our guests in this way and the event has become a fixed arrangement of good will and pleasure.[25]

Zion United Methodist Church dissolved in June 1974 and Greater Whitestone Baptist Church took over the Zion building.[26]

Cleveland—Salem German M. E.

Salem was the last of the eight German Methodist churches to be founded in Cleveland. Reverend Beyer, a pastor of Bethany, wanted to start a mission where the theological students at German Wallace College could have practical experience in the preaching field. He surveyed the people in the Pearl and State roads area and determined this might be feasible. A site at 4004–06 Cypress Avenue was chosen for the location of the small church which was dedicated in October 1909.

Salem only lasted for twenty years and in 1929 the church was sold. Several groups have used the building and, at present, it is Westside Independent Baptist Church.[27]

Berea, Ohio—Emmanuel German M. E.

As early as 1845 missionaries from Cleveland visited the Berea area and preached to the Germans there. In 1854 a circuit of six preaching places was created which included Vermillion, Brownhelm, Rockport, Olmsted Falls, Lake Abram, and Berea.[28] In 1859 Vermillion and Brownhelm were switched to the

Norwalk Circuit and in 1893 Rockport united with Cleveland's Bethany. Emmanuel in Berea received its first members in 1856 and by 1863 the young church had accepted twenty-eight new members on probation. In those days, membership in a church was a privilege not taken lightly. Fifteen of these new members were dismissed in disgrace due to "immoral conduct," "dancing," and spreading rumors about other members. In spite of such strictness, membership climbed to seventy-seven by 1875, not counting the college students and contingent from the orphan home. When these two latter organizations were founded, (German Wallace College in 1864 and the orphan home in 1863) the Berea church was invigorated with new energy and direction due to their attendance and involvement.[29]

Church services were first held in the homes of members; then switched to Baldwin Hall. After that, the church met in a brick building on the college campus.[30] The *Geschichte* gives slightly different information saying that meetings were first held in an old church, then Baldwin Hall and, finally, in the old Wallace Hall.[31] The trustees of German Wallace College and those of Emmanuel joined together to build a church building. Emmanuel provided five thousand dollars of the amount needed and the church was consecrated in 1872. In 1899 the interior of the building was renovated.[32]

Until 1926 Emmanuel Church was always ministered by professors from the college. One of the professors took on the role of head pastor and assigned each of the other professors a Sunday to preach. The pastor in charge, who received a small allowance for his duties, also took care of other pastoral work. The head pastors usually served in that capacity at least for one year and later for three or more. After 1926 Emmanuel was served by a full-time pastor.[33]

After World War I the use of the German language fell out of favor and English became the language of choice in the church services and business. Then in 1933, when the Central German Conference was dissolved, the Berea church became a member of the East Ohio Conference. Berea had few commercial and industrial operations which meant the young people often left home for greener pastures where there were more job opportunities. Another obstacle was that many of the townspeople felt they couldn't compete with the college professors and divinity students so they were hesitant to take on church leadership positions. In spite of these problems, the many factions of the congregation got on well and the day to day running of the church was harmonious and the spiritual life of its members full.[34]

Mary Marting Pendell (her father was German M. E. pastor Albert L. Marting) gave a little of her personal experience at Emmanuel Church when she was a young girl.

> I was 10 years old when we moved to Berea. The College Chapel was then known as Emannuel German Methodist Church. German was spoken in the church service. It soon changed to an early service in German and the second service in English. When I joined the church in 1923 there were 14 in our class. The Catechism books from which we were

*Berea, Ohio, former Emmanuel German M.E.,
now chapel for Baldwin-Wallace College and Berea Orphan Home.*

instructed were in German on one page and English on the other. There were 100 questions and answers each with a Bible verse for each answer.[35]

In 1953 Emmanuel and First Methodist Church in Berea, known as Old Stone, united and became the Methodist Church of Berea. This uniting was advertised as "the Big Wedding" and was "performed" when Bishop H. Lester Smith announced on June 28, 1948, at the closing of the Northeast Ohio Conference that Rev. William Phillips would be the new pastor of the Methodist Church of Berea. The new sanctuary of the united church was dedicated in 1952 and an education wing and chapel added in 1961.

Of the many mission projects sponsored by the church, a recent one stands out. The church "adopted" a family from Sierra Leone in West Africa. Getting to know the family of Melrose and Edward Kargbo-Davis and their children was an enriching experience for all connected with the church.[36] A recent check of the church website (which is www.umcb.org) showed that the church supports the following activities: adult and children's education, college and youth councils, music groups, Stephen ministry, UMW, and a number of worship services.[37]

The beautiful Emmanuel church, now United Methodist Church of Berea, is located at 170 Seminary Street in Berea.

Henrietta, Ohio—Henrietta German Methodist Church

In 1867 Rev. George Berg and John Haueisen moved from Cleveland to the area of Henrietta with their families. Reverend Berg belonged to the Central German Conference but had to quit preaching due to a throat ailment. Nevertheless, preaching was where his heart was, so he and Mr. Haueisen started looking for German families to preach to. In 1869 and 1870 a number of Swiss families moved into the area so that meetings that had once been held in homes were now large enough to be moved to the schoolhouse of district one.

On April 24, 1872, the German Methodist Church was officially organized. Members congregated in the old schoolhouse and elected to buy land for a church building and cemetery.[38] The church was built on a three-quarter-acre tract for the amount of twenty-five hundred dollars, and consecrated on September 5, 1875. Two dedication services were held—one in the morning in German, and another in English in the afternoon.[39] The church furnishings included a bell for $186.00, a clock for $5.75, two heating stoves and equipment, $38.84, and a pulpit Bible for $3.50.

When the congregation built their church, the Central German Conference assigned them a regular pastor, Rev. Wesley Freyhofer, who had a circuit of three churches: Lake Shore, Vermillion, and Henrietta. Lake Shore was soon given up and its building moved to Vermillion where the parsonage was which was owned and supported by both remaining churches. The pastor preached mornings and evenings alternating between churches. Travel was by horse and buggy and if the weather turned bad he spent the night with a member of the congregation and returned to Vermillion the next day.

In 1901 some renovations were undertaken including removing the old heating stoves and installing a modern furnace. Seating was rearranged—no more did the women sit on one side of the church and the men on the other; now the families could sit together. When the church was built, it featured an attractive steeple capped by a weather vane. In 1912 a storm destroyed the steeple and despite repairs it fell victim to a second storm two years later. At this

Henrietta UMC, formerly German ME in Lorain County, Ohio.

point it was taken down.

In 1922 more updating was done and a basement was installed under the church. After the area was dug out by hand, the building was raised two feet and the basement was completed. The basement area was used for a Sunday school room, kitchen, and furnace room. The new basement cost approximately two thousand dollars and was dedicated in July 1922.

By 1914 the Vermillion church had closed because of a decline in members and the Henrietta church became independent. This meant it was necessary to build a parsonage which was done on a lot opposite the church and cost four thousand dollars. The church remained independent until the Central German Conference disbanded at which time the Henrietta church became a member of the local English-speaking conference. Then it was once more on a circuit—this time with Birmingham.

A well-digging project was necessary in 1934 when it became apparent that the parsonage needed a better water supply. Two "water witchers" were engaged and they indicated a spot which they thought had a strong stream about twenty feet underground. The diggers got busy and were soon past the twenty foot mark. Still no water came in so they kept digging on past fifty feet. At this point the water gushed in and soon the parsonage had a good supply of drinking water. This was later piped under the road for the church, as well.

In 1950 it was building time again and an addition in the back provided three Sunday school rooms and a basement for a new oil furnace.[40] The addition also had space downstairs for a new kitchen, nursery, restrooms, and gas furnace (this source says) which totaled eight thousand dollars. In 1954 the parsonage underwent major repairs when a gasoline truck jackknifed on the road and caught fire igniting the house and fatally injuring the driver. The parsonage repairs amounted to eight thousand dollars. More renovation, costing about nine thousand, was done on the church in 1969–70. Carpeting was put in the sanctuary and downstairs; the church entrance remodeled with new doors installed and the church interior painted.

The former "Swiss Church" (as it was often called) always had a missionary-minded congregation. It supported missionaries in South America, Singapore, Cuba, and, in 1962, Lebanon. The Buchs family went to that Mideast country to teach modern methods of breeding dairy cattle and were sponsored by CROP and Church World Service. The Sunday school, Youth Fellowship and United Methodist Women have always been active and ready to serve the church.[41]

Grandpa Rudin spent a few days in Henrietta while attending the yearly district meeting of the North Ohio District in May 1910. He mostly wrote about the papers and speeches given, including his own.

Wednesday, May 4, 1910

Was Bro. Nicholaus Baumann's guest at supper yesterday, and after church I went home with Bro. Godfrey Reusser, a son-in-law of his. It was a cold drive of three miles, but I found a warm welcome at his house. Bro. Boch is also to be his guest at night, while both Bro. Boch and I are the guests of N. Baumann at dinner and supper. The District Meeting was opened this morning by the District Superintendent.

Thursday, May 5

Read my paper this morning: "The Biblical Conception of God in the Light of Modern Science." It was very favorably received, especially as a literary production.[42]

Henrietta United Methodist Church is still active and located at 52148 State Route 113 in Lorain County, Ohio.

Sandusky, Ohio, Circuit

Engelhart Riemenschneider and J. A. Klein first visited the Sandusky area in 1847 and preached at the courthouse whenever they traveled that way.[43] In

1850 the Ohio Conference of the Methodist Church, held in Chillicothe that year, organized the Sandusky City Mission[44] as well as the Lake Shore Mission. Rev. G. A. Reuter was sent by the conference to form a class and build a church. Before the first church was built the circuit consisted of preaching places in Thomson, Vermillion, Republic, Braunhelm, Amherst, Flat Rock, Fisher Settlement, Venice, Tiffin, Norwalk, Peninsula, Schulland (La Carne), and Fremont.[45] Most of these places were eventually dropped until the only viable churches left were in Vermillion, Sandusky, La Carne, and Venice.

In the early twentieth century, La Carne and Venice were on a circuit with Sandusky. Grandpa Rudin served the Sandusky area from 1900 to 1904. He had to take the train across Sandusky Bay to reach his church in La Carne. Venice was somewhat closer and he either walked the approximately ten miles or rode a bicycle.

Sandusky Circuit—St. Paul's German Methodist Church

A plot of land at the corner of Central Avenue and Adams Street was obtained, but that was sold and a church on Jefferson Street acquired. This, according to the *Geschichte*, did not seem like a fitting place, so it, too. was sold and the property at Shelby and Tyler streets purchased.[46] Peeke (*The Centennial History of Erie County*) tells it a little differently. The congregation bought "the little brown church" located on the West Public Square and used it at this site until 1880 when they moved the building to the south side of Jefferson Street. In 1896 they sold the little brown church on Jefferson Street to the Zion German Lutheran Church and then made the move to Shelby and Tyler streets.[47]

St. Paul's was not in good shape memberwise when Grandpa took over in 1900. I suspect he didn't help matters either with his strict ways. This was his first appointment and he was going to be sure his parishioners walked the straight and narrow and toed the line! In 1908 Sandusky was put on the Berea Circuit, became independent again in 1911, and was paired with Vermillion in 1913, after which it is no longer listed.[48] Peeke says church property was sold in 1913 and most of the congregation joined Trinity M. E. Church.[49]

Here are a few of my grandfather's comments on his experiences at the Sandusky church.

Saturday, September 23, 1899

> I had to take the 7:30 train for Elyria and wait in the dimly lighted station for nearly four hours for the Sandusky train. It was great fun. I felt anything but good, being uncertain as to whether I could get any accommodation in Sandusky or not. Arrived at Sandusky in the neighborhood of one A. M. A nice time to arrive a stranger in a strange place. I was lucky, however, in finding a hotel across the way where I put up for the night. Had a sandwich and coffee. Was given a nice room and bed for fifty cents.

Sunday, September 24

*Sandusky, Ohio, house at Tyler and Shelby streets
remodeled from St. Paul's German M.E.*

Got up a few minutes after seven. Breakfasted on a cup of coffee and a sandwich. Consulted a city directory to find the location of St. Paul's German M. E. Church. As the church is not far from the station it did not take me long to find it. There were about twenty in the morning service and thirty in the evening. The people are plain and seem to be nice.[50]

My grandparent's first child was born shortly after they moved to Sandusky. As the little boy was stillborn, it was not a happy experience.

Sunday, November 12

This afternoon a few minutes after one, Till gave birth to a 10 pound, well formed boy, but he was dead when he was born. Till had to suffer very much, but tonight is feeling as well as can be expected. How I managed to preach I do not know.

Monday, November 13

Till had another ordeal of intense torture to go through this afternoon, the doctor being obliged to put a few stitches into her. I don't see how she could stand it all. It was all that Mrs. Rau and I could do to stand it. Why must women suffer so much? I was wishing myself a thousand miles away. I have learned much in the past two days. This evening I felt quite depressed, the sufferings of Till being constantly before me.

Friday, December 22

Frank F., Mr. S. and myself went out to buy Christmas supplies for the Sunday School. We bought about 60 lbs. of candy, several pounds of nuts, oranges, cakes, etc. I thought we were entirely too extravagant, but Mr. S. would have spent more had he been alone. We have only 50 all told in our Sunday School. When I was on the car I could not help but think of my own present poverty. My companions were ignorant of the fact that I had not five cents to spend for Christmas presents. I have never been so poor at any Christmas. When I got home I found a letter from Mr. Schaal on my desk. Till asked me to open it right away. I did so and found a check for $31.25. Here is a transition from "abject poverty" to "untold wealth."

Saturday, December 23

Having come into a fortune last night, I went over town this morning to buy Christmas presents. You feel much different in a store when you have money. Bought three sterling silver pencils for Pa, George and Charlie, two Dewey balls for Corinne and Charlie's adopted little girl and a picture for Rose. The whole pleasure cost me $2.25. Also sent off some presents which Till had prepared for my folks.

Thursday, July 26, 1900

Mrs. R. and for that matter others, seem to think that the minister's wife ought to make regular calls as well as the minister. I do not think so. If the church members expect their minister's wife to make regular calls they ought to pay her a salary. I consider the minister's wife a private person.

Wednesday, November 7

In the meeting of the trustees it was decided to put gas in the church. We need better light very much. The whole improvement will cost us about sixty dollars.

Friday, November 9

Picked the last bouquet of Nasturtiums this morning. It is gradually getting colder. The gas connection from the street into the church were made today. We hope to have gaslight by Thanksgiving.

Friday, November 30

The gas fitters finished their job by this evening. Tonight our new light did duty for the first time. It is a decided improvement over the old system. Frank F. was in ecstasy over it. There will be much less work for him now.

Friday, June 14, 1901

I feel like ignoring the Frauenverein for a time, as the members seem to be inclined to get too fresh. They are seemingly getting the big head and think we can not get along without them. I am becoming thoroughly disgusted with this charge, at least the Sandusky part of it. Opposition confronts one at every turn. Former pastors of this Sandusky crowd must have come to the same conclusion judging by old quarterly reports.

Monday December 2

Our church cellar is causing me some worry, as there is over a foot of water in it. Some men from the water works were around this afternoon to flush the sewer. Digging will be necessary. There is always something to cause additional expense.

Tuesday December 3

I wish that church cellar were all right again. It's in an awful condition. Joe R. was around to dig up. Thus far the drain pipe is not yet in sight.

Wednesday December 4

There must be a colony of rats in our cellar. In one night they got away with a peck of apples that Br. K. gave us last week. I never thought such a thing could be possible. Bought a big trap and hope to catch the whole batch of those expensive visitors.

Thursday December 26

Mr. V. pumped nearly all day. As a result our cellar is now dry, though anything but clean. This nuisance is going to cost us not a little.

Tuesday February 10, 1903

Mr. S. was around this afternoon and staid quite awhile. He said that he met Mr. K. last week and that he had spoken to him again about the painting of the church. Mr. K. said he would do his share if we would go ahead. I'm beginning to think that the thing is possible.

Wednesday February 11

Our trustee meeting was held tonight. The regular business was transacted the painting of the church was discussed. It was thought feasible. We hope to launch this undertaking in the spring.

Thursday April 23

We decided last night to have the church painted. The contract will be given to J. H. A., who will do the job for $65. It was also decided to have the roof gutters repaired.

Thursday May 14

Received a season ticket for Cedar Point. This is the first one I ever received and I intend to make use of it. When I first came here I was led to believe that Cedar Point was an awful place and that one could not possibly go there without losing respectability. I have changed my opinion somewhat. Cedar Point is simply a popular pleasure resort: you can be bad there if you want to, but you don't need to if you don't want to.

Wednesday June 17

The painter finished his job yesterday and our church looks very nice. The neighborhood and well-meaning (?) friends can now see that our little congregation is still about to accomplish things.[51]

At the 1904 conference Grandpa was transferred to Baresville, Ohio, where he was to have a new experience with a country charge and a circuit of four churches. Here are his parting thoughts on his post at Sandusky.

Wednesday, September 28, 1904

Well, good-bye Sandusky! It is not a place I wish to return to. Sandusky with all its discouragements is now behind me, thank God for it! They were hard years, but they were profitable to me. It is true: discouragements, opposition and the machinations of evil-minded persons are beneficial to me. May God bless the good people of Sandusky and may he have mercy on the benighted.[52]

The church at Shelby and Tyler streets is still there, but now it is a duplex housing two families. If you look carefully you can see the lines of the old church in spite of its different use and appearance.

Sandusky Circuit—La Carne German M. E.

La Carne was a country church attached to the Sandusky circuit and was on the other side of Sandusky Bay. I don't know how former pastors reached it, but in the early twentieth century grandfather took the train. The church was built in 1878 and in grandpa's time had about thirty members. According to the *Geschichte*, the church once had a thriving congregation but "while the dear old Brothers and Sisters go to heaven, the next generation is not German enough and the German immigration does not come here."[53]

A history of the La Carne Methodist Episcopal Church (English) states that two other churches—Erie and La Carpe—decided to unite (no date given) and met in the German M. E. church at one thirty in the afternoon. In 1919 the German church joined the other two churches and "brought to us many steadfast and valuable members."

Eventually, in 1971, the La Carne Methodist Church united with La Point UMC which still exists.[54] In 1920 the old German church was put to use as a Grange Hall. Esther Sinclair, a resident of La Carne, bought the property in 1968 and later had it torn down because it was being vandalized.[55] The La Carne Post Office now sits on the site.

Grandpa Rudin got along fairly well with his La Carne congregation. Many of them were very good about sharing their farm produce with the minister and his family. Here is Grandpa's first impression of La Carne and its people.

Saturday September 29, 1899

Took an evening train to Lacarne. Was met by Fred S. Weather was unusually cold.

Sunday September 30

It was pretty cold in my bedroom last night. What will it be when its twenty below zero! I hope they'll have stoves in the bedrooms up there when its as cold as that. Went to Sunday School with Mrs. S. The whole congregation is the Sunday School. There are three churches in Lacarne, two Methodist and one United Brethren. Had good congregations both morning and evening.

Monday October 1

Fred S. took me to the station. Was met at the station by Br. H. who presented me with two large baskets of beautiful peaches. Was really agreeably surprised. It was not so agreeable, however, to carry them home. I had besides these two baskets, my valise and another small basket which Mrs. S. gave me.[56]

Grandpa's last visit to Lacarne was the weekend of September 24–25, 1904.

Saturday September 24

Did not like the idea of going to Lacarne this evening, as I would rather have worked to get the goods out of the way. [he was packing in order to move to his next appointment] I had to go, however, having promised. Stopped for the last time at "Hotel H." Br. H. gave me another $2 for salary.

Sunday September 25

Preached to the usual audience. Was affected some. Did not have any service tonight, as I did not want to preach two farewell sermons. Mr. Ed Z. came around for a little while. He said he was sorry to see me go.

Monday September 26

Left Lacarne on the 10:56 train, having first called on Haus. and Mrs. S. Mrs. S. was pleasant but I do not think she's sorry I'm going. Mr. and Mrs. H. seemed to feel bad when I took leave. I spent many a pleasant hour with them and enjoyed stopping at their house. Mr. H. is a rather queer chap though, and I was never absolutely sure of him. I wonder that he and I got along so well.[57]

Sandusky Circuit—Venice German M. E.

It takes some doing to find the location of Venice nowadays. If you look at an Ohio state atlas it will be on the map west of Sandusky near State Route 2. The German M. E. church was built at Venice in 1885 but then twenty years later was sold due to a decrease in membership.[58] The church was in Margaretta Township and had a membership of about thirty-five in 1889. The property was worth twenty-five hundred dollars.[59] During my grandfather's tenure the church was sold to the Lutherans for about five hundred dollars. The remaining members of the congregation then came to the Sandusky church.

Here are a few snippets from Grandpa's diaries concerning his Venice charge. They evidently did not have regular Sunday services when he came in 1899.

Sunday October 9, 1899

Br. K. from Venice was in church [St. Paul's]. I asked him if a meeting had been given out for this afternoon and he said no. He thought the meetings up there might be dispensed with for the present, as so few attend them. Well, I shall have to see about it.

Monday October 10

A Br. J. from Venice called on me shortly after noon. He wanted to find out why no meeting was held in Venice yesterday. I told him the reason. He thinks they ought not be given up. There does not seem to be a unanimity of opinion up there.

Sunday October 22

Br. J. had dinner with us and then took me out to Venice. Visited two of his son-in-laws. One is a hard drinker and the other broke his leg some weeks back. This home [that of the hard drinker] was anything but inviting. Neither was the other home, which was in a barn, but they are having their house renovated. The church was not yet open when we got there, so we visited Mr. K. He lives in a fine house and is apparently well off. Preached to about 17 including children. Mr. H. took me as far as the RR from where I walked home.

Sunday October 6, 1901

Went to Venice with Mr. K. Took my wheel [his bicycle] with me. Had as usual a good dinner. Preached to about 25 in the afternoon, including a lot of Lutherans who came in after their Sunday School was dismissed. Collected $.59 in Venice.

Sunday April 19, 1903

Mr. K. took me out to Venice. Preached in English in the afternoon. The preaching of that sermon was not satisfactory to myself. Mr. W. was in church, and it seemed out of place to preach English, knowing that he does not understand the language very well. I excused myself to him after the meeting.

Thursday January 28, 1904

Mr. Seher called this evening. He is to go to Venice with Mr. K. He said that Rev. Dornbirer is willing to give $500 for the Venice church property, but he thinks we can get more.

Tuesday February 9

Mr. Seher told me yesterday that he had seen Mr. Dornbirer and that he said that some of the farmers at Venice are not willing to give us our price but would give us $500.[60]

Other churches connected with Sandusky

One German M. E. church was located on the Marblehead Peninsula and was referred to in the records as "Peninsula" or "Danbury." It was built about 1861 but only survived for about ten years.[61] Another source gives a little more information saying that the church was built about 1860 on Lot 11, Section 4, Danbury Township. C. Ahrens donated the land and the completed church was dedicated by Reverend Krehbiel. The English-speaking Methodist church eventually absorbed the German church.[62] The church had a cemetery and was seven and a half miles east of Port Clinton on Von Glahn Road. Neither the church nor the cemetery are at that site any longer, having been removed.[63]

Another German M. E. church or meeting house may have been located closer to Lakeside off of Route 269 on property owned by the Hartshorn family in 1874.[64]

Vermillion, Ohio—German Methodist Church

Around 1850 Brothers Klein and Jung first came to the Vermillion area bringing German Methodist preaching. They preached in homes and schoolhouses but most of their meetings were in the home of Joseph Delker who was also their first convert. Soon the pastors organized a class and built a church three miles east of Vermillion on the shore of Lake Erie. Meetings also took place in the city of Vermillion and at other outlying communities. The German Methodist worshippers were not always welcomed and frequently met with hostility from their neighbors. The church on the lake shore was eventually given up and the land sold to a nearby farmer. Meanwhile, a church in town was thriving and was known for its attractive property and modern parsonage. Eventually, the founding families died off and their sons and daughters moved away due to the scarcity of jobs in the area.[65]

The only other source I could find that discusses the Vermillion church is a history of the Henrietta church. When the Henrietta church was founded it was put on a circuit with Vermillion and Lake Shore churches. In the 1870s the Lake Shore church was given up, the building moved to Vermillion and the circuit became Vermillion and Henrietta. The parsonage at Vermillion was supported by both churches and the pastor preached in the morning at one church and the afternoon at the other; then reversed the process the next Sunday.

By 1914 the Vermillion church was in decline due to the deaths and removals of many of its members. The Vermillion parsonage was given up and a new one built at Henrietta.[66] The Vermillion church was paired with Henrietta in 1924 and then no longer listed in 1930.[67]

One interesting piece of trivia about the Vermillion German M. E. church is that it had "an elaborate wooden fish that graced the steeple of the little South Street building" and the children of the town dubbed it the "Fish Church."[68]

Notes

1. Gracelouise Sims Moore, ed., *Tapestry of Faith, Cleveland, Ohio* (Cleveland, Ohio: The Methodist Union of The Cleveland District of the United Methodist Church, Inc., 2003), 172.
2. Golder, Horst, and Schaal, *Geschichte*, 421.
3. "The History of the Church," *1845–1945 Centennial Program* (church history) Cleveland, Ohio 1945, 1–2.
4. Golder, Horst, and Schaal, *Geschichte*, 422.
5. "History of the Church," 2.
6. Ibid., 2–3.
7. Albert F. Weiss, *History of the Church of the Cross*, anniversary pamphlet and church history (Cleveland, Ohio: 1965).
8. *History of Community of Living Hope United Methodist Church*, church history (Cleveland: Community of Living Hope, 2002).
9. Crisfield Johnson, ed., *History of Cuyahoga County, Ohio* (Cleveland: D. W. Ensign & Co., 1879), 507.
10. Moore, *Tapestry of Faith*, 168.
11. Johnson, *Cuyahoga County*, 25.
12. Golder, Horst and Schaal, *Geschichte*, 423
13. Moore, *Tapestry of Faith,* 169.
14. Wyllene B. Wall, "Primera Iglesia UMC," in *Cleveland Together*, Cleveland, Ohio (Summer 1998), 3.
15. Golder, Horst, and Schaal, *Geschichte*, 422.
16. *Church of the Cross Centennial Program* church history (Cleveland, Ohio, ca. 1945), 3–11.
17. Golder, Horst, and Schaal, *Geschichte*, 420.
18. *The History of the Christ United Methodist Church–Bethany Church*, anniversary program and history (Cleveland, Ohio: 1988), 1–2.
19. Ibid., "Christ United Methodist Church," 4–6.
20. Ibid., "Organizations," 8–9.
21. *Christ United Methodist Church*, Cleveland, Ohio, www.christumc.com, 2009.
22. Moore, *Tapestry of Faith*, 143
23. Report of the Ladies Aid, Zion M.E. August 1926–27, box #97, United Methodist Archives, Ohio Wesleyan University, Delaware, Ohio.
24. Report of the Ladies Aid, n.d.
25. "Report of the Sunday School Superintendent," Zion M. E., August 1926, box #97.
26. Moore, *Tapestry of Faith*, 143.
27. Ibid., 172
28. C. W. Hertzler, "When Emmanuel Church Accepted the Immigrant 85 Years Ago" (speech, Berea, Ohio, 1939), 3.
29. Golder, Horst, and Schaal, *Geschichte*, 415.
30. Hertzler, "When Emmanuel Church," 5.
31. Golder, Horst, and Schaal, *Geschichte*, 415.
32. Hertzler, "When Emmanuel Church," 5.
33. Ibid., 6.
34. Ibid., 7–8.

35. Mary M. Pendel to author, 1998.
36. Moore, *Tapestry of Faith*, 25–27.
37. The United Methodist Church of Berea, Berea, Ohio, www.umcb.org, 2009.
38. Lena Geissendoerfer and John Baumann, *The History of the Henrietta Methodist Church,* church history (Amherst, Ohio: 1951).
39. Anonymous, "Church History," Henrietta UMC, Amherst, Ohio 1962.
40. Geissendorfer and Baumann.
41. John Baumann, *Then and Now: a Family and Community History* (Amherst, Ohio: 1964), 45–46.
42. Rudin, Diaries, 1910.
43. Golder, Horst, and Schaal, *Geschichte*, 434.
44. Hewson Peeke, *The Centennial History of Erie County* (Cleveland, Ohio: The Penton Press Co., 1925), 175.
45. Golder, Horst, and Schaal, *Geschichte*, 434.
46. Peeke, *Centennial History*, 176.
47. Golder, Horst, and Schaal, *Geschichte*, 435.
48. *Minutes of the Annual Conferences*, 1908, 427; 1911, 564; 1913, 471.
49. Peeke, *Centennial History*, 176.
50. Rudin, Diaries, 1899.
51. Ibid., 1899, 1900, 1901, 1903.
52. Ibid., 1904.
53. Golder, Horst, and Schaal, *Geschichte*, 435.
54. Mamie Rymers Brunkhorst, *History of Methodism in Erie Township*, church history (1952).
55. Esther Sinclair to author, 1997.
56. Rudin, Diaries, 1899.
57. Ibid., 1904.
58. Golder, Horst, and Schaal, *Geschichte*, 435.
59. Lewis C. Aldrich, ed., *History of Erie County* (Syracuse, NY: D. Mason & Co., Publishers, 1889), 364.
60. Rudin, Diaries, 1899, 1903, 1904.
61. Golder, Horst, and Schaal, *Geschichte*, 435.
62. O. L. Shepard, *The Story of Lakeside* (written for the Golden Jubilee of Lakeside, Lakeside, Ohio, 1923), 6.
63. "Cemetery Inscriptions of Ottawa County, Ohio," (preface), Ottawa County Chapter of the Ohio Genealogical Society, Port Clinton, Ohio 1970–76.
64. *Combined Historical Atlas of Ottawa County, Ohio* (Chicago: H. H. Hardesty 1874) Danbury map.
65. Golder, Horst, and Schaal, *Geschichte*, 437.
66. Geissendoerfer and Baumann, *Henrietta Methodist Church*.
67. *Minutes of the Annual Conferences*, 1924–1930.
68. Betty Trinter, *The Way it Was* (Norwalk, Ohio: Ebert's Inc., 1976), 57.

CHAPTER 19

Central Ohio

Columbus, Ohio

Columbus—First Church

John Barth first brought the word of God in German to the Methodists in Columbus in November 1843. The first meetings were held in a schoolhouse at the corner of Third and Mound streets, but later moved to a firehouse on Mound Street. The first quarterly conference was soon held in December 1843, and by the third quarterly conference in June 1844 they decided to acquire land and build a church.[1]

One source says that the group obtained a "good-sized brick building" where they worshiped until there was need for a larger building.[2] However, most sources say land was purchased for $450 and a brick church erected for $1,700. This building was consecrated in February 1845 and the final costs paid off in March 1851. In the early years the church was called "Zion" but was officially known as the First German Methodist Episcopal Church by 1886. During these early years a number of other churches and Sunday schools sprang from the Columbus church, including ones at Circleville, Hocking, Liberty, Dumontsville, Chillicothe, Delaware, Dresden, Etna, and Newark.[3] Some of these developed viable congregations and will be described later; others have been buried with the memories of their founders.

The church at the corner of Livingston Avenue and Third Street served well for twenty-six years, but then in the early 1870s the need for a larger meeting place became apparent.[4] Some renovations had taken place in 1855 and in 1860 more work had been necessary to repair walls and the roof. In December 1870 the church fathers resolved to erect a new building and the cornerstone was laid in May 1871. By December of that year the first Sunday school met in the new building and by September 1872 the church was consecrated. The

*Livingston UMC, successor to Zion German M.E. (also called
First Church) in Columbus, Ohio.*

church paid off its building debt of $16,088 in September 1880.[5] Some improvements followed later with the installation of a pipe organ in 1894 and the addition of stained glass windows in 1897.[6]

There was a church parsonage built in 1867, but a new one was proposed in 1882 and 1884. In 1886 the congregation acquired land near the church for $1,625. The new parsonage cost $2,790 and the remaining debt was discharged in 1896.[7]

First Church membership increased from 84 in 1859 to 308 by 1894. After that date, the membership fell off temporarily when Second Church, which started as a mission in 1892, became firmly established. Both Sunday school and church membership at First Church expanded in the early twentieth century to 301 for the Sunday school and 248 for church membership. Other mission efforts were made and a Sunday school on the "north side" was held from 1881 to 1885 as well as the one on the south side from which Second Church grew.

Organizations at First Church included the Ladies Aid which was founded as the Frauenverein in 1871. The group had seventy-three members in the early twentieth century and was a big help to the church financially. Other groups were the youth organization, the Junior League, and a singing group which was said to be "the most excellent, if not the best group in our conference."[8]

The church underwent another name change in 1917 becoming Livingston Methodist Episcopal Church while dropping the use of the German language in preaching services. In 1923 some changes to the outside of the church were made when the steeple was removed. The church celebrated its one hundredth anniversary on November 7, 1943.

In the 1960s Columbus made plans to build an expressway just south of downtown and the land needed, included the church parcel. In 1963, the city purchased the church property and the final service took place on August 25, 1963. After that, Livingston Church met with First Methodist at their Bryden Road facility from September 1963 through early November 1966. During this period plans went forward to build a new church for the Livingston congregation. Land was purchased at Fourth and Livingston streets and the groundbreaking took place on December 12, 1965, with the laying of the cornerstone on Palm Sunday in April 1966. The consecration of the new facilities was celebrated on November 13, 1966. One unique feature of the new church was a ninety-foot cross constructed from an I-beam which was placed outside of the front entrance to the church. In 1973 a "shadow image" became a feature on the west side of the building. This shadow is a figure of Christ with outstretched arms which is projected most of the year giving rise to the church nickname—"The Church of the Shadow."

The old church owned a bronze bell, cast in Cincinnati, which had been a prominent feature of the belfry. After the church had been torn down, the bell was installed in a new bell tower constructed in 1980. Also, in 1981 a permanent structure was created to house the shadow.[9]

The Livingston United Methodist Church still stands at Fourth and Livingston streets and can be seen from the expressway I-71, the cause of the demise of the old church building. Livingston sponsors youth, men and women's groups plus a prayer group, book club, and Weight Watchers. The church is home to a food pantry and supports other community projects including the Faith Mission meal for homeless men, "Bag of Blessings" and a community garden.[10] Visit their website at www.livingstonumc.com.

Columbus—Second German M. E. Church

The lore of the founding of second church was related in a letter from the pastor, Rev. Ellen Phillips. "The story is that Livingston, which was at that time First German Methodist Episcopal Church, had decided to begin to worship in

Gates Fourth UMC, formerly Second German M.E. in Columbus, Ohio.

English. A certain group of folks were against this idea, and so, decided to build a new church. This group of people marched down from the North of German Village to this present location, singing hymns of the faith. Here they set the cornerstone. Reverend Phillips added, "I'm sure there must have been much more to the story!"[11]

As Reverend Phillips said, there was more to the story than just a group of people being in a snit about a language change. Many of the members of First Church lived south of Schiller Park so in the 1890s a mission was started at Fourth and Mozart streets to serve these people.[12] The Newark church was sold at this time so the proceeds went toward building a German church on this corner. A Sunday school had been started in 1891 and with prayer, revivals, the Newark church profit, a donation of $1,000 from the youth group and $3,990 from First Church, land was purchased and the Second Church became a reality.[13] The new brick church was consecrated on May 3, 1896, and had a flock of 45 members. Within ten years, the church had grown had grown to 152 members. Soon a parsonage was needed so, in 1901, the congregation built a modern home for $3,000. In 1905 they acquired another lot so that the total worth of the Second Church property was $15,000.

Second Church had an active and flourishing Sunday school which, at the beginning of the twentieth century, had 160 students and 21 teachers. An Epworth League and a Junior League had from the start 38 and 20 members, respectively. The Ladies Aid, also, existed from the beginning and its 35 members were especially supportive to the church financially.[14]

During the World War I hysteria many streets in areas settled by Germans went through name changes. Mozart was considered too German and was replaced with the name "Gates." The church was renamed Gates Fourth Methodist Church and it is still serving the community at 1234 South Fourth Street in Columbus.

The Central German Conference's annual meeting was held in Columbus in 1931 and my grandfather attended it, as required. His nephew Charles and his wife lived in Columbus, so Grandpa had a ready-made hotel awaiting him.

Tuesday September 1

Took the 2:50 train to Columbus and arrived there a little before 6. Otto M. was at the station to direct the incoming brethren. Lunched in a restaurant and then had a taxi take me out to Charles.

Wednesday September 2

It started to rain last night and it rained all day today. Charles took me to the Gates-Fourth Church last night. He had a time to find it. The 68th session of the Central German Conference was opened this morning by Bishop Ernest G. Richardson. After the Lord's Supper. . . . Bro. Severinghaus presided and Dr. John C. Marting made the memorial address which was simple and not overdone. This afternoon the annual meeting of the Preachers' Mutual Aid Society was held. $14.00 will again be paid to the superannuates for each year of active service. The District Superintendent read their reports which indicated that some of the churches suffered greatly on account of the financial depression.

Friday September 4

Yesterday Charlie Miller told me that I had been elected secretary of the Committee on Publications and a little later John Mayer told me the same thing. That means that I have to write the report. John M. also said there was no need of a meeting: that they would trust me to write a good report. Yesterday I attended the anniversary of the WFMS and WHMS in the Livingston Church. In the evening the anniversary of the Board of Foreign Missions was held in the same church.

Sunday September 6

The Conference adjourned yesterday afternoon. A number of the preachers including the Bishop went to see a ball game. This morning "Chuck" took Gertrude and me out for a ride before church. He drove through the grounds of the Ohio State University which is immense.

Monday September 7

Last night the Bishop read the appointments. They were very few in number. After all the talk of disgruntled churches and preachers, this was a great surprise. I suppose the Bishop and cabinet thought it best under the circumstances to make as few changes as possible. So now churches and preachers that were tired of one another will have to try to get along with each other for at least another year.

Thursday, September 10

Only two more years and the men of the Central German Conference will be scattered to the 4 winds, so to say. Our next Conference will be held in Berea and the last in Race St. Cincinnati where the first session was held in 1864.

Friday September 11

Bishop Richardson is quite democratic and plain. He put on no airs whatever and stuck strictly to business. The Gates-Fourth Church, by the way, is situated in a very nice and quiet neighborhood which cannot be said of the Livingston Church. That neighborhood is worse than that of the Market St. Church in Louisville. Bro. Schreiber evidently has a fine working church [Gates-Fourth] and he seems to be well liked. I was not so impressed by Bro. Mayer's church [Livingston]. It is an old building, though kept in good condition.[15]

Columbus—Delaware German M. E.

Shortly after the founding of the Columbus First Church, missionaries went to surrounding communities, including Delaware, to start Sunday schools and classes. Delaware was served from First Church until 1853 when Columbus was separated from most of its mission starts.[16] Another source dates the church back to 1836 when William Nast was traveling from the Ohio River to Lake Erie. In 1844 Rev. John Barth returned to the area and held revivals in the Delaware area. Converts first met in private homes but soon moved to a stone schoolhouse at the corner of Franklin and Winter streets. The next meeting place was an old Methodist church south of the schoolhouse and then an old academy building on Hill Street. In 1847 "Father" Albright donated a lot on Henry Street and a frame church was erected.[17]

The *Geschichte* has conflicting accounts on the early days of the Delaware church. As mentioned earlier, it states that Delaware was connected to Columbus until 1853, but in another account Delaware is named as the headquarters of a mission that included Galion, Mansfield, Shelby, Bucyrus, and other communities. Until 1849 the Delaware circuit embraced six counties and twenty-two preaching posts which covered four hundred miles.[18] Galion and a few smaller churches remained with Delaware until 1854 at which time Delaware became a station.

In 1854 the Henry Street Church became too small for the growing congregation which purchased a lot on Hill Street . There they built a brick church and then dedicated it in 1855. The church declined with the coming of the twentieth century and for a few years was attached to Second Church in Columbus. In 1907 the church was sold to William Nye although the auditorium was still used for religious meetings.[19]

Hill Street was later changed to University and in 1900 the church address was Washington and University streets. When we tried to find it, we could locate no such intersection. It had evidently been gobbled up by Ohio Wesleyan University expansion.

Columbus—Newark German M. E.

The Newark church was also one of those founded from the Columbus First Church Mission and, until its demise in 1893, it was connected with the Columbus church off and on. Other times it was paired with Zanesville or Dresden.[20] The Newark German Methodist Church got its start in 1847 with meetings which took place in a schoolhouse. In 1856, the group was large enough to support their own facility and erected a frame church building on Fourth Street which cost them $1,408. A Sunday school, started in 1850, was still meeting in 1881 and had twenty members. In 1874 a parsonage costing $900 was built.[21] The church property was sold in 1893 and the proceeds used to help pay for the construction of Second Church in Columbus.[22]

The Newark church building is no longer standing.

Columbus—Dresden German Methodist

Columbus First Church also founded the Dresden German M. E. in the 1850s. For most of its life, the Dresden church was on a circuit with Columbus, Newark or Dover.[23] In 1852 the twenty-four member congregation met in the Market House until a frame church was erected in 1858.[24] The church was built to seat 125 people and cost six hundred dollars. Like its sometime circuit partner, Newark, the Dresden congregation was small and by the early 1880s claimed only twenty members with no Sunday school.[25] The congregation eventually broke up and the church, located on West Fifth Street, was sold and converted into a home used by Francis Williams in 1967.[26]

Columbus—Other German M. E. Churches

The *Geschichte* mentions other congregations and Sunday schools started in the 1850s including ones at Circleville, Hocking, Liberty, Dumontsville, and Etna. Some of these places are so small today that they have very few resources where I could check the history of the churches. Others, such as Hocking and Liberty, appear to be townships and pinpointing the churches (if there were actual church buildings) is even more difficult. Although Circleville is a sizable town, I drew a blank in searching for information on the church there.

Galion, Ohio, Circuit

The Galion circuit began when William Nast arrived in the area about 1836 and grew to be quite extensive. In Germany Nast had known Johannes Schneider who was the father of John Schneider who lived west of Galion. When Nast was in the area he looked up the son of his old friend and was invited to preach and start a class. A few years later, in 1846, when Nast was the editor of the *Christlich Apologete*, he was instrumental in sending John Bier to continue the work he had started. Soon there were seventeen members and in 1847 Galion became part of the Delaware Mission.[27]

Another source states that the Rev. Nicholas Nuhfer was the pastor who followed Dr. Nast and organized the class into a church. By 1849 there were fourteen preaching stations in the Galion Circuit: Zoar, Galion, Seif's Baker School House, The Plains, Bucyrus, Brokensword, Oceola, Mansfield, Shelby, Ashland, New Winchester, Williams Schoolhouse, and English Sixteen Church.[28]

There is a discrepancy in the above listing of churches—its says fourteen but only thirteen are listed! I believe that may be due to a typing or proofing error. Other sources seem to indicate that Seifs (also called Salem) and Baker's Schoolhouse are two different places. The *Geschichte* gives rough directions for some of those preaching places.

> Seif or Salem church, six miles south of Galion. . . . Williams Schoolhouse [7 miles southwest from Galion], Winchester west of Galion, Baker Schoolhouse [6 miles north of Galion] . . . a church on Brother Neff's land . . . . Immanuel.[29]

Some of the preaching places flourished and grew into viable churches; others disappeared after a few years, others lasted a number of years but finally were given up in the twentieth century. I could find no information on the Oceola, Shelby, Ashland, New Winchester and Williams Schoolhouse appointments. Others like Baker Schoolhouse I was able at least to verify the location (it is now a private home). The following are histories of the churches on which I could find details. Bucyrus and Brokensword separated from the Galion Circuit in the 1880s forming the Bucyrus Circuit (along with Plains), so they will be dealt with later.

Galion Circuit—Zoar

Zoar was the first church to be organized on the Galion Circuit and is marked today by the old cemetery at Iberia Road and Route 19 in Polk Township. The *1873 Crawford County Atlas* shows the church on John Snider's (sometimes found as Schneider) land[30]

The Zoar Church was the result of William Nast's visit in 1836 to John Schneider. When John Bier came in 1846, he soon organized the class into a church and held the first quarterly conference in July of the same year. John Schneider donated land and in 1848, Zoar Church was built. Not long after, a parsonage was also built which was sold in 1864. By 1874 Zoar Church was no longer viable and services there were given up.[31] Zoar was located only about two miles from Galion so presumably its members left to join the newer German M. E. in town.

Galion, Ohio, St. Mark's UMC, formerly Market Street German M.E. It has recently been replaced by a shopping center and school.

Galion Circuit—German M. E. (in town)

The Galion congregation organized about 1849 and held their meetings in a log schoolhouse and in other churches until they purchased the English Methodist Church building in 1859. This was an old frame building which cost seven hundred dollars and stood on the south side of West Main Street west of Union Street. This land was originally owned by the first settler of Galion, Benjamin Leveridge. The German congregation used this building until 1873 when they sold it for eighteen hundred dollars and bought a lot at South Market and West Atwood streets.[32] The total cost of the new church property was five thousand dollars. A new parsonage was built in Galion in 1887.[33] A grocery store had been on the site of the new church and it was moved south of the church and used as a home. In the 1920s the church found many uses for the former grocery. It was remodeled into a social hall in 1924 and served as a meeting place for Sunday school classes, the church board, rummage sales, voting and parties. A private kindergarten class was also held there as well as choir practice and church suppers.

In 1915 the steeple of the church was judged to be unsafe and was removed leaving the belfry in its place. New carpet was installed and art glass windows put in at a cost of nine hundred dollars, after which a rededication was held. A few years later, the church underwent a name change and became Market Street

Methodist Episcopal Church. Strangely, this change did not become official in the court records until 1957. During the 1920s the use of German in church services was suspended since by this time very few still spoke the language.

The church building suffered some fire damage in 1925 when a piece of brick in the chimney worked loose. Consequently, repairs were required on the northeast corner of the church and a few years later, lightening struck the northwest corner where more work became necessary.

In the late 1920s the handwriting was on the wall—the Central German Conference was no longer needed, there not being a language problem any longer in most churches. The 1930 conference was held in Bucyrus and most representatives from the German churches voted to dissolve the German Conference and let the churches become part of the English conferences. In fact, this did not take place until 1933, but the wheels were set in motion. Rev. H. C. Heinlein who became Market Street's pastor in 1930, was the last appointee to the church by the Central German Conference. He served through 1934 seeing the changeover of the church into the English Conference.

Changes to the church facility in the second half of the twentieth century included painting and sandblasting the exterior in 1953. The interior was also given a facelift with a new furnace, carpeting in the aisles, and ceiling and wall refurbishing. Donations of a painting of Christ, candlesticks, a cross, collection plates, and vases rounded out the decorating efforts. The next year a Consonnata Electric organ was given by Clara Manzer in memory of her mother. A dedication ceremony and organ concert were held to display the gift.

A couple of years later a new education building almost became a reality when a bequest of ten thousand dollars was given from the estate of Mrs. W. J. Dennig. The present social hall (the former grocery) was taken down and excavation for the new building begun. Progress was cut short when the southwest corner of the church collapsed. The damage to the eighty-three-year-old building was extensive and was estimated to be forty thousand dollars. All the furnishings and equipment were removed and stored and demolition began on July 25, 1956. The Seventh Day Adventists offered the Methodists the use of their church for the time being, and the Market Street congregation held their first service there on July 29, 1956. Oddly enough, the previous Sunday's sermon had been "How Firm a Foundation."

Donations for a new church building arrived, including $550 from Peace Lutheran Church and gifts in other amounts from other local churches. By August 16, $4,086 had been contributed toward a new church building. A crusade raised the rest of the money needed and by November 12, a total of $26,640 had been promised.

Since the new church would no longer be on Market Street but North State Road, it needed a new name. At a specially called quarterly meeting in July, L. D. Stover suggested "St. Mark." A site was purchased for twenty thousand dollars and on January 11, 1958, and the mortgage for the land was burned in a ceremony, having been paid in full. The first phase of the building project was for a 104-by-38-foot building which would house a sanctuary, seven classrooms and kitchen and dining area. On July 13, 1958, the congregation took part in the groundbreaking and on May 3, 1959, were able to attended the first service in the new church.

Soon after the new church was completed, a new parsonage also became a reality. The parsonage, which had been on Atwood Street next to the church, was sold for eighteen hundred dollars. The proceeds from this sale funded the new parsonage built at 950 North Market Street and ready by December 1959 for the pastor and his family.

Groundbreaking for a new sixty thousand dollar education facility was April 25, 1964, and by August, the first classes met in the building. Some additional work was done on the south end in the church in 1970 because of weather damage. A wood and glass section was removed and replaced by brick. In 1972 a pavilion (dedicated to the memory of the Thomas family which had been killed in an auto accident) was constructed on the back acreage to be used for outside activities. Other improvements included a new Allen computer organ and a new roof on the church, both in 1976.[34]

Through the years many social and service groups were connected to the church. One group called the Church Aid evolved into the Ladies Aid Society in 1921 when the men bowed out. One project they are remembered for was making robes for the choir. In September 1940 the Ladies Aid became the Women's Society of Christian Service whose duties were to make calls and raise missionary funds to send overseas. One long-lived Sunday school class was the "Queen Esther" class (organized in 1938) whose goal was to buy music for the choir. Twenty years from its founding, the class members changed the name to Queen Esther Bible Study. Other groups were the Methodist Men's Organization, Methodist Youth Fellowship, World Fellowship for Girls, and Friendship Sunday school class. The groups engaged in many service and moneymaking projects including collecting sales tax stamps (which could be redeemed for money), making rag rugs to sell, sponsoring booths at festivals, serving sauerkraut suppers, and holding bazaars and bake sales.[35]

The church gained the nickname of the "Little Church with the Big Welcome" and the present St. Mark building still served its congregation at Portland Way North until recently. One more story of interest is that of the "Bachelor Preacher," Raymond Butler. He came to the church in July 1951 and moved into the parsonage at the end of July, after commuting from Youngstown for a few weeks. It was said that he lived mainly on dill pickles and milk until he went to Atlanta, Georgia, in September and returned to Galion with his bride, the former Peggy Jean Brown. They were the first pastoral couple to marry and set up housekeeping while serving the church.[36]

A recent trip to Galion showed that there is now a shopping center on the St. Mark's site. A little investigation indicated that St. Marks sold their property and merged with Christ UMC.

Grandfather Rudin was pastor at on the Galion Circuit in 1910 but only remained there one year. That was the one year he did not keep a diary—perhaps this charge kept him too busy as his circuit would have included Plains and Sixteen, as well as Market Street Church in Galion. He did attend a district meeting there in 1906 and, though he doesn't mention the church itself, he discusses the proceedings .

Tuesday May 1

Took the B & O at Wheeling for Mansfield, going from thence by trolley to Galion. Met Bros. Herzer and Oetgen on the train. Told Bro. O. that he was my choice for P. E., but he said that he did not desire the job. Bro. Boch awaited us at Galion where we arrived about half past five.

Wednesday May 2

Bro. Burkle and I are stopping with Mrs. G. who is a widow with five daughters. They are a lively set: one is a school teacher, two work and the others go to high school. Bro. Kaletsch preached an earnest sermon on 2 Cor. 12:1–9. The District Meeting was opened by Bro. Pullmann. Fred Muller was elected secretary. Beyer and I were made the traveling expenses committee. Bro. Kern read the first paper: "How Can the Divine and the Spiritual be Distinguished from the Human and Natural in the Experience of Man?" It received nothing but praise. My paper followed. It was well received, though some slight criticisms were made.

Thursday May 3

Yesterday two papers were read, one by Bro. Oetgen on "The Evangelization Methods of our Time: Are they Timely and do they Insure Success?" The other by Bro. Baumann was on "The Preacher and his Bible." Bro. O. believes in revivals but not the circus kind. A purse of $28 was presented to Bro. Pullman [retiring P. E.]. The P. E. seemed quite surprised. He said he would buy something that would always remind him of his brethren. Bro. Allinger read his paper.

Friday May 4

Dr. Nuelsen lectured last night on "The Queen of Methodism." According to him the countess of Huntington is the queen of Methodism. Other papers were read by Bro. Schanzlin (on Moses and Hammurabi), Bro. O. Rogatzky and Bro. J. Bockstahler. Left Galion early this morning and arrived at home [Hannibal, Ohio] at nine tonight.[37]

Galion Circuit—Sixteen German M. E.

In 1857 the "Neff Class" was started in Tully Township and not long after, Gottlob Neff donated land for a church. In 1859 the church, called Immanuel, was completed and consecrated by the presiding elder, Jacob Rothweiler.[38] The church was popularly known as Sixteen Church as that was the number of the section of land it was built on. There was also an English Sixteen church and the German church was comprised of members from it and the Williams

Schoolhouse congregation. A history sketch of the church noted that "Disturbance frequent. John Horst with the help of Abe Guinther and a Strickler put out a man who during Horst's prayer snapped corn grains at people."

The Immanuel building was thirty-by-forty feet and cost three hundred dollars to erect, some of which was paid in farm produce. An organ was purchased in 1870 and later a piano was bequeathed to the church.[39] The building had no basement or classrooms and was erected with a raised platform in the front for the pastor, organist and choir. The church windows were narrow and embellished with red and blue glass in the top portion. A potbellied stove, which was later replaced with an oil stove, provided warmth. More recently, two propane gas furnaces supplied the heat. Seating was plain oak benches which were still being used in 1996. Some upgrades were added in 1921 with the addition of a vestibule and bell. A sound system was donated but its use proved to be impractical when squirrels found enjoyment from chewing on the speakers.[40] Other changes and additions cited by Tropf include remodeling done "during the pastorate of Nachtrieb" which must have been 1865 to 1867 as that was the last time a Nachtrieb was the pastor. These included a new roof, new windows, benches, lights, and pulpit chairs for a total cost between seven and eight hundred dollars. In 1913 a woodshed was added.[41]

The German language was in use for services until World War I when the

Sixteen UMC belonged to the Galion Circuit and is located in Tully Township, Marion County, Ohio. When German, it was Emanuel.

switch was made to English. The church never had many organizations due to its small size but those it did have include a women's group (now United Methodist Women), a youth group and a Bible study group. One important social function has been the annual Sunday school picnic which featured a cable swing merry-go-round, teeter-totter, and horse shoes.[42]

Sixteen Church was still standing on its donated plot on Morral-Kirkpatrick Road in Tully Township in the early twenty-first century. A check in 2009 showed that it is on a circuit with Iberia UMC.

Galion Circuit—Mansfield German M. E.

The Mansfield German M. E. Church was founded in 1861 as part of the Mansfield Mission which also included the preaching places in Ashland, Shelby, and Troy.[43] "One Hundred Fifty Years of Methodism" names the founding date as 1859. In 1861 it claimed twenty-two members with three probationary ones. The frame church built in 1863 on Diamond Street cost $1,100 to raise and the parsonage expenditure was $750. The congregation struggled until 1866 when it broke up; although later attempts were made to revive the church but were not successful.[44] The Mansfield church property was sold in 1880.[45]

Galion Circuit—The Plains

The Plains Church belonged to both the Bucyrus Circuit and Galion Circuit at various times during its existence. Its history is somewhat shadowy and the information available, scanty. It appears to have originated on the Galion Circuit and then switched to the Bucyrus Circuit about 1855. The one solid piece of information is that, at the 1856 Third Quarterly Conference, The Plains paid $13.50 toward the Bucyrus Circuit's pastor's salary.[46] Copies of the Minutes of the Annual Conferences from 1875 to 1922 indicate that by 1875 The Plains was no longer a part of the Bucyrus Circuit. Figures show only two churches on the circuit and the second church was probably Brokensword since it did not leave the Bucyrus Circuit until 1923.[47]

One other source, a 1982 Local Church History Survey from the East Ohio Conference and History Commission, adds a few more details. The Plains Church stands on Old New Winchester Road in Crawford County. The building, which was still there in 2002, was built in 1881 and used until 1925 when the congregation united with the Bucyrus church, at that time called Lincolnway Methodist.[48] Confusion, however, still reigns. The Bucyrus church history begs to differ with that date and lists the merger as 1928.[49] The church and a one-room schoolhouse, which shared the plot of land, reverted to the landowners who used the former church for storage.[50]

Bucyrus, Ohio, Circuit

In 1849 Brokensword was the first church founded on the Bucyrus circuit, followed by the one in Bucyrus in 1852. The Plains Church was a sometimes member of the Bucyrus Circuit and has been dealt with under the Galion Circuit. There were two other small congregations in Cranberry Township and Osceola. They apparently lasted into the 1870s as by 1875 only two churches were listed on the Bucyrus Circuit until 1933 when the conference dissolved.[51]

Bucyrus Circuit—Brokensword German M. E.

Nicholaus Nuhfer began preaching in the Brokensword neighborhood at a schoolhouse near Ridgeton in 1849. By 1852 the congregation, under G. A. Reuter, built the first church north of Brokensword Creek for the cost of $277.35.[52] Another source states that a Mr. Plummer donated land where the church was built in 1854. During the Civil War, things were not always peaceful at the Brokensword German M. E. as the pastor, Rev. Phillip Weber, preached that the people should obey the laws and those drafted should serve willingly. Those who didn't agree tore down the altar, broke windows, and vandalized the church. Pastor Weber was not discouraged by these actions and kept persevering until a mob set fire to the church on May 20, 1863. Within a year a new building was erected at a new site one-half mile south of the original one.

Part of the Galion Circuit, the old Plains German M.E. closed in 1925 and lives another life as a farm storage building.

At this time Rev. John Haas was pastor to the congregation which numbered about ninety.[53] A different source says the new church building was put up in 1865. Although this building was not attacked, things were far from peaceful as the preacher was the target of some gunfire during one of the services.

In 1892 the current building was erected and the older one moved north to a farm. Brokensword and the Bucyrus German M. E. Church were on the same circuit from 1855 to 1936, after which retired pastors served the church for twenty-three years. Major renovations were done in 1956 and consisted of enlarging the basement to provide a spacious fellowship hall, Sunday school classrooms, a new furnace area, restrooms, and a kitchen. Shortly after this, in 1959, Brokensword and New Washington were paired on the same circuit for the next twenty-one years.

A name change took effect in March 1969 when two Brokensword United Methodist churches materialized after the merger of the Methodist Church with the E.U.B. Church. The former E.U.B. near the village of Brokensword kept the name while the former German Methodist congregation chose the name Scioto U.M.C.[54]

In the same year as the name change, a building fund was initiated to update the sanctuary and Sunday school rooms. The ceiling was lowered and paneling installed in the vestibules and front of the church while the Sunday school room was converted into three rooms including a choir room and secretary's office. All the rooms received a paint job, new lights and new carpeting. Soon after, in 1973, a new organ was purchased for thirty-five hundred dollars, including treble and bass pipes for six hundred dollars. The previous organ was twenty-two years old and the same piano which had been used for seventy-five years, was replaced by a new one for eight hundred dollars. The following year the Faithful Workers class spruced up the fellowship hall, restrooms, and kitchen with a paint job.

Brokensword Methodist celebrated one hundred years of existence in 1949. After a celebratory worship service, the congregation enjoyed a basket dinner at Holmes-Liberty High School and an afternoon service preached by the district superintendent.[55]

In 1980 the New Washington–Scioto Charge was terminated and Scioto was paired with Harmony U.M.C. The address of the former Brokensword church is 3203 Lemert Road., Bucyrus, OH 44820.

In 1904 Grandfather Rudin went to a North Ohio District meeting that was hosted by the Brokensword people.

Wednesday April 27

Went to the North Ohio Dist. meeting this morning. Bro. Schieber, my host awaited me at Brandywine Station. His "hand" drove me to the church. Bro. Nocka who is my partner at Schieber's read an exegesis on Col. 1:9–16. F. W. Mueller read a paper on: "The First and Second Resurrection—How are they to be Regarded?" The opinions in regard to

Scioto UMC was formerly on the Bucyrus Circuit and known as Brokensword German ME.

this subject were conflicting, but most of those who spoke sided with Bro. M. H. Rogatzky read his paper: "What Hopes does the Present Tendency of the Church Justify."

Thursday April 28

Read my paper yesterday afternoon: "The Importance of the Sermon for the Religious Life." Bro. Kern and several others complimented me after the close of the session. Mine and two or three others were recommended for publication. Bro. Schaal read his paper on: "The Scriptural Teaching Concerning the Kingdom of God."

Friday April 29

The Dist. meeting was enjoyable. If only the weather had been better! Still considering all things, the people turned out encouragingly. Bro. Schieber told me that the church could not have held the people had the weather been favorable. Left my kind hosts this morning. The farmers out here seem to be all well-to-do. Many have pianos and are otherwise "up to date." The Brokensword church is a large brick structure and the congregation a good one.[56]

Bucyrus Circuit—German M. E., Emannuel, and others

The Bucyrus German Methodist Episcopal Church went through several name changes through the years, starting out as the German Methodist Church until

World War I when it became Emannuel. That name had been carved on a stone to be put above the main entrance when it was decided to change the name to the Lincoln Way Methodist Church after the church's address. The stone was returned to the carver and the new name engraved on the other side. Then in 1932, the street name was changed from Lincoln Way to Hopley Avenue so another name for the church was sought. The new church name chosen was Epworth and it has remained that to the present.[57]

When William Nast first started preaching in the area in 1835, he had a grueling circuit that would have driven lesser men to an early grave. The circuit took five weeks to complete and started in Columbus where he preached the first Sunday. After that came stops in "Basel, on the canal," and Thornville where he spent the second Sunday. Next he traveled to Newark, Mount Vernon, and Danville where he preached the third Sunday. The next week took in five stops at London, Loudonville, Mansfield, Galion, and Bucyrus (the fourth Sunday). The fourth week of travel took him to Marion and a German settlement near Delaware in time for services on the fifth Sunday and then to Worthington and back to Columbus to start all over again. Often he preached at other places along his route, as well.[58]

In 1849 Nicholaus Nuhfer was the first to found a church in the Bucyrus area. In 1852 a Sunday school was organized in Bucyrus and two years later a church erected on Warren Street under the administration of Bro. C. Gahn. This

Epworth UMC in Bucyrus, Ohio, began as the German Methodist Episcopal Church, then became the Lincoln Way Methodist Episcopal Church and, finally, settled on its present name.

property was sold in 1883 and a new church built for fifty-five hundred dollars when J. Haas was pastor.[59]

Baskin and Battey's history seems to differ from some other sources on the beginnings of the church. Their history states that the English Methodist Church allowed the Germans to meet in their building until 1855 because the "congregation was very weak." At this time, a number of German families moved to Bucyrus and joined the congregation strengthening it enough for a church to be built in 1854. At the dedicatory service a Dr. Warner preached in the morning in English and Dr. Nast preached a German message in the afternoon. A collection netted $143 to help with the expenses of the church construction.[60]

At the second quarterly conference on December 29, 1855, a report stated that there were thirty-four members of the Sunday school class, eight teachers, four reading classes and two spelling classes. The library contained 150 books. At a later quarterly conference, a breakdown of the preachers salary read: $28.05 from Bucyrus, $29.34 from Brokensword, and $13.50 from Plains. However, the pastor had received only $29.03 of what he was due out of the total of $83.03.

The church built in 1854 served the congregation for twenty-nine years until 1883. At that time it was sold and the site on Lincoln Way (now Hopley) was purchased. The building erected at this site served the people for thirty-four years until 1917. While a new church was being built on the same site, the congregation met in the Union School building. The first order of business was to tear down the old church which Rev. C. F. Buerkle proceeded to do even before the schedule was official. After the pastor got the ball rolling, many of the members helped in pulling down walls, digging the basement, cleaning the bricks and hauling away the dirt. The building finally became a reality and a dedication was held on June 30, 1918, where eighteen thousand dollars was raised in pledges to help offset the total cost of fifty-five thousand. The new church was described at the Festival of Dedication in this way:

> The Church is a dignified example of Tudor Gothic, built of rough face brick in mingled shades of brown, green and tan and trimmed with Bedford stone trimming and a green slate roof. All wood work, pulpit, pews, organ case and all fixtures are individually treated and designed by the architect. The windows are of the beautiful imported antique art glass. The building is heated and ventilated by mechanical system, and the lighting of auditorium and sabbath school is indirect.[61]

The last of the debt for the 1918 building was settled by 1923 when pastor Oscar Rogatzky left for his next appointment. In 1928 the Plains Church disbanded and, as a result, the Bucyrus church gained some more members. In 1930 the Central German Conference held its annual meeting at the German Church. In 1933 when the Central German Conference dissolved, Epworth joined the English Conference and was unhitched from Brokensword to become a station with its own pastor.

Through the years more improvements and repairs were made; in 1947 new floors were installed in the basement and a radiant heating system was added to heat the basement area. In 1952 a financial campaign was launched with a church dinner and eventually brought in about sixteen thousand of the twenty-thousand-dollar goal. Work was started which included a new hot water heating system, electrifying the organ and installing a new console. Other sprucing up involved pointing and waterproofing, new lights and decoration of the church for the centennial program on May 2, 1954. Many special music numbers were offered for the program, as well as speakers including the Bishop, district superintendent, and former pastors.

In 1962 more repairs and work were in order which included redecoration of the sanctuary, remodeling the kitchen, soundproofing and making other improvements on the basement classrooms, and adding carpeting and a folding door upstairs. Three families of the church footed the bill for a parking lot expansion. At this time parsonage improvements were also made. A new home on Spring Street was purchased for the pastor and his family and the old parsonage which was used for classrooms, was redecorated and christened the Epworth Parish House. In 1980 pastor E. Parker West expressed a desire to purchase his own home rather than live in the parsonage, so that building was sold for the sum of $32,000. Meanwhile the pastor and family bought a home on Sitler Ave. In 1992 the church was in the market for another parsonage and found the house at 1265 Southland Avenue to meet their needs. The cost of $78,000 was taken care of by the seed money left from the sale of the former parsonage, $11,500 in donations and a mortgage for the remainder.

At a cost of $10,559 in 1974, new carpeting was installed in the sanctuary and cushioned pews improved the comfort of the congregation. A speaker system and amplifier were additional improvements. Also, in 1974 pastor West and his family traveled to Ipswich, England, to exchange pulpits with Rev. Bernard Marks and his family. The purpose was to learn about churches where Methodism was founded and to extend the hand of friendship to the English family who now lived in the parsonage. When the West family returned, they shared their experiences in an evening service with the Epworth church family.

In 1976 the Epworthians enjoyed hearing a new Holloway organ (purchased for thirty-six thousand dollars) for the first time on Christmas Eve. In 1979 a major addition to the church was completed for $65,000 which included a pastor's study, secretary's office, foyer, storage room, and restrooms. This addition caused changes in other parts of the church as well, and included painting and enclosing classrooms. When the refinishing and reinstalling of the cabinets was completed, the church property was valued at $375,000. A consecration and 125th anniversary celebration was held on October 20–21, 1979, which featured a chicken barbecue, a historical musical drama "Our Church Through the Pages of Time" and a consecration service on Sunday.

In 1984 Epworth celebrated the founding of Methodism with a special service at the Old Mission Church near Upper Sandusky. It was there that the first

American missionary, John Stewart, founded a Christian community and school during the settling of the Ohio lands. Another celebration was on May 15, 1988, to recognize Aldersgate Sunday. This was held in the First United Methodist Church of Bucyrus and involved all the Methodist congregations in the area.

In the latter half of the twentieth century a number of projects were undertaken including recycling by the Mary-Martha and Epworth Men's Sunday school classes. A capital funds campaign was started in 1992 to add to pension programs for the clergy in the East Ohio Conference. New equipment was purchased or donated including air conditioners, office equipment, a new Christmas tree, new paraments, a carpet sweeper, microwave, storm windows, and altar cloths. A new grand piano was dedicated on March 3, 1991, followed by a recital and reception in the afternoon. The church library had grown from 150 volumes in 1855 to more than one thousand, covering a wide range of topics. In the 1990s Epworth sponsored a coed softball team and and two basketball teams.

Music has always been important at Epworth since the early days when the choir was volunteer and sang to the strains of an old-fashioned organ. In 1939 Mrs. Margaret Kuehnle started a Carol Choir of seventeen teenage girls and, in 1942 they were joined by a junior choir of boys and girls which later formed the Chancelette Choir in 1954. The Wesley Choir was founded in 1955 of high school age people and later expanded to include any who wanted to sing on a part-time schedule. In 1963 the church made a recording of the three choirs called "Epworth Sings" and in 1973 produced another called "Joyfully Unto God." The Bucyrus Ministerial Association sponsored a Children's Choir Festival involving the whole county on Palm Sunday evening 1983.. Another favorite choir presentation was the "Festival of Carols" presented each December. In December 1983 Epworth honored Mrs. Kuehnle for her forty-five years of service to the music program of the church with a reception and a gift to the church of a Vigil Lamp in her honor.

Mission projects Epworth has been involved with include One Great Hour of Sharing, UMCOR, Flat Rock Children's Home, Berea Children's Home, Red Bird Mission School, and a selected mission family. The church also sponsored a Blanket Sunday to give relief to people in time of disaster. The congregation also collected nonperishable food items and other supplies as well for the Friendly Pantry and Salvation Army.

The first women's organization was the Women's Foreign Missionary Society founded in 1884. It had 26 active members and 31 extension members in 1940 when it evolved into the Women's Society of Christian Service. In 1915 the Ladies Aid Society was organized by the members of the disbanded Dorcas Bible Class. This new group helped raise funds for the new church building with bake sales, a chicken supper, bazaar and handkerchief booth, and many others. By the time the Ladies Aid merged with the WSCS, they had raised many thousands of dollars for the building of the church and also for supplies such as a stove, coffee urn, dishes, and table linen. When organized the WSCS had 107 women on the roll and soon decided to divide the larger group into four circles. This group continued some of the church improvements started by the Ladies Aid and paid for tiling in the basement, redecorating the parsonage and remodeling its kitchen. Missionary work was continued, also, with support of Wesley Foundation, sponsoring two girls to the Lakeside Girls' School each summer and others. In 1970 the organization became United Methodist Women which continued many of the old projects while introducing some new ones. A Spring Luncheon was a feature which included a quilt show one year, and later, antique shows and wedding gown displays. The UMW ladies liked to bake and from 1990 have held cookie sales for such special occasions as Valentines Day, Halloween, and their Spring Luncheon. The cookie sales brought in ten thousand dollars in a period of two years.

The United Methodist Men, chartered in 1968, meet monthly for breakfast and an educational and inspirational program. Once a year they combine with other Methodist churches in the Bucyrus area for a meeting. Activities they are involved in include a father-son banquet, serving at the mother-daughter banquet, and the Harvest Home collection of items for the Salvation Army and Friendly Pantry.

The Epworth League began in 1889 for young people up to the age of twenty-five and in the early twentieth century had one hundred members. In 1939 the group became Methodist Youth Fellowship and, later, United MYF. The youth traditionally conduct an Easter Sunrise Service which is followed by a breakfast. Fellowship activities have been bowling, hay rides, and ski outings, among other activities, along with many service projects, which included car washes, lawn socials, adopting a family at Christmas, caroling, and remembering those in nursing homes.

Younger children are listed on the Cradle Roll at Baptism and are encouraged to be involved in church activities such as the Children's Day Program in June and a Christmas program in December. In 1943 Vacation Bible School was started in conjunction with a citywide ten-day event sponsored by the Bucyrus Area Ministerial Association. In the 1970s VBS classes were held for all grades and rotated to a different church each year. In 1989 classes were moved from morning to evening so adults could also participate in classes.

The first Sunday school in 1855 reported 34 members which, more than one hundred years later, had grown to 459. Some of the later classes included the Mary-Martha class, the Loving Hearts, Loyal Sons, Young Men's, and Epworth Men's. The Anti-Can't class formed in 1953, as well as, the Co-Workers. In the 1960s came the Come-Join-Us Class and in the 1980s, the Builders Class.[62]

The Epworth United Methodist Church still stands "on the Point" at 216 Hopley Avenue in Bucyrus. The website bucyrusepworthumc.com[63] has current information about services times and other activities.

Grandpa Rudin, who was stationed at Hannibal, Ohio, at the time, visited

Bucyrus in 1909 for a district meeting.

Monday May 31

Took the 8:42 train to Wheeling, where I arrived at about 10. The train for Mansfield left at 11:15 and I arrived there at about 4. Walked about town until the electric car started for Bucyrus. Tried to get into several barbershops but they were all closed on account of Memorial Day. How dirty one gets on the steam cars! Arrived at Bucyrus a little after 6, the trolley ride having been the pleasantest part of the whole trip. The English preachers do not have to make such long trips to get to their district meetings. An Epworth League convention was in session when I arrived at the church.

Tuesday June 1

Professor Hertzler gave a lecture on "The Twentieth Century Crusader" yesterday. I think his lecture would have been better in English. German does not seem to come easy to the professor. Bro. G. Yaussey took me to his home, where I had a good night's rest. He brought me to church in the morning. To my surprise I was made secretary of the District Meeting and also correspondent to the Apologete. After some business was transacted, Bro. Boch read his paper on "The Future of our German Churches." A spirited discussion followed.

Wednesday June 2

Bro. Mueller followed Bro. B. yesterday with his essay on "The Administration of our Benevolent Collections." It was quite humorous. Other papers were "The Conversion of Children" by Bro. Roesner and "The Preservation of Children for the Church" written by Bro. Baechtold but read by Bro. Pullmann. This morning Bro. Harrer on "How can the Preacher Secure Mental Vigor and Maintain it?" Bro. Marting said we should take frequent baths, work the dumb bells, etc. Bro. Paul Pluddemann said he found pitching hay very helpful. Bro. F. J. Baumann followed with "Shall our Conference be Reduced to Three Districts?" The brethren were not in favor of it.

Thursday June 3

Other papers from yesterday were "The Unity, Truth and Glory of the Church of Christ" by Bro. Beyer and read by Bro. Burkle and "The Scriptural Teaching Concerning the Angels" by Bro. J. Bochstahler. This morning Bro. C. Baumann read an essay on "The Healing Miracles of Jesus and Psychotherapeutic" followed by Bro. J. C. Guenther on "The Emmanuel Movement." Bro. A. L. Marting read an "Exegesis on the Passion of Jesus in Gethsemane" which was excellent; followed by "The Eschatology of the Gospel of St. Luke" by Bro. H. Bau. The discussion of some of the papers brought out the fact that a number of our brethren have had wonderful spiritual experiences.

Friday June 4

Left Bucyrus early this morning. Stopped in a little while at the parsonage. Bros. Blume and Pluddemann accompanied me as far as Mansfield, where I left the car to take the train to Wheeling. Had a wait of nearly two hours at Mansfield. Took a walk about town and bought some things for the children. Arrived at New Martinsville at about 8:00 and had to tramp it from Texas.

Saturday June 5

Got home dirty and sweaty last night. The children were delighted with their paint boxes and pencils. It was the general opinion that our dist. meeting was one of the best held in years. There was a marked brotherly spirit and everybody took part. The Bucyrus people made it as pleasant for us ministers as they could and we had an enjoyable time all around. I am glad I did not miss it.[64]

Marion, Ohio—Station and Circuit

Dr. Nast came into the Marion County area about 1843 to preach the Gospel and a short time later organized classes and congregations. Peter Schmucker was the presiding elder and John Barth was his assistant at the time of the founding of Bethlehem and Zion congregations in 1843.[65] In 1849 the congregation in the city of Marion (which would eventually become Prospect Street UMC) was founded. The last to join the circuit was Salem in Bloomington which Rev. John Schweinfurth founded in 1865.

The Marion Circuit was first formed in 1854 and consisted of Zion, Bethlehem, and Marion.[66] Before that, Zion and Bethlehem were on a circuit with Delaware. The Marion Church became a station in 1891 and the Marion Circuit then consisted of only Zion, Bethlehem, and Salem.[67] Eventually, in the 1940s the circuit churches, which had decreased in membership, were given up and most of their congregations joined with their city sister.[68]

Marion Circuit—Zion German Methodist Church

Dr. Nast was the first to preach to the future Zion congregation, at a meeting held in the home of "Father" Sailer. Not long after this a revival was held at the home of Daniel Seiter and the congregation of Zion was organized.[69] In 1846 a log church with rough seats was erected on the Seiter property. The building was thirty-by-thirty-four feet and located in section 7 of Richland Township[70] on Richland Road.[71] A new church replaced the log one in 1879 for the cost sixteen hundred dollars. This church continued serving the people until 1942 by which time German was no longer spoken. Advances in transportation allowed the people to travel further, so the Zion Church congregation united with Prospect Street Church in Marion and the old church building was sold.[72]

Prospect Street UMC began as First German M.E. in Marion, Ohio.

At the dawn of the twenty-first century, the old Zion Church was still standing surrounded by the graves of its former members.

Marion Circuit—Bethlehem German Methodist Church

The Bethlehem congregation built a log church south of Marion in 1847.[73] The church stood not far from Waldo in Pleasant Township on what is now Bethlehem Road. By the 1860s the congregation had outgrown the log church and needed larger accommodations so the Trustees purchased a half acre site from the Snyder family for the sum of five dollars. A new church was built for a cost of $2,360 which served the congregation well until 1941 when, following Zion's lead, Bethlehem merged with Prospect Street Church . The building was sold but it is no longer there nor is there even a cemetery to mark the spot on Bethlehem Road.

Marion Circuit—Salem German Methodist Church

In the beginning, the First German Methodist Church in the town of Marion was on the circuit with Zion and Bethlehem but it soon became a station and was replaced on the circuit by Salem—a relative late comer to the area. In 1866 Rev. John Schweinfurth organized a congregation in the Bloomington area which became known as Salem.[74] They first met in a schoolhouse until, in 1872, the trustees built a one-story, frame church. A Mr. Schertzer provided land and $2,118 was raised for building expenses. Ferdinand Kraus built the

The Marion Circuit, at one time, included Prospect Street Church as well as the country church Zion (now closed).

church for $1,850 and shaped the beams with his own hand. This church building was used until 1930 when a congregation of another denomination purchased it. Many of its former members had drifted away, joining other Methodist churches in the area or uniting with Prospect Street Church.[75] The Salem church building is still standing with its cemetery nearby, but does not appear to be in use at present. It is located in Big Island Township in section 17 not far from New Bloomington.

In June 1892 it was decided to build a parsonage for the Marion Circuit. The former Holverstot property was acquired on South Prospect Street and the parsonage finished by September 1892 for the sum of $1,665. This was the home of the circuit preachers until student ministers began serving the circuit. In 1933 it was deeded over to the Marion church and when the country churches merged with Prospect Street Church, the parsonage was sold.[76]

Marion Circuit—First German Methodist Church, Prospect Street Church

First German M. E. Church was founded in 1845 with services held in the courthouse at first, but eventually moved to the basement Sunday School room of Wesley Chapel.[77] A different source says that several families met in the home of Mr. and Mrs. J. H. Sauer in 1849 and organized the Methodist society. By 1868, 123 people had joined the church and wanted their own meeting place. Land was purchased at the corner of South and West streets (now Pros-

Salem, near Bloomington, Ohio, was another member of the German Marion Circuit.

pect and Church streets) and the First German Methodist Episcopal Church was erected by the end of 1869. The 38-by-58-foot brick building was two stories with a 120-foot tower containing a keystone which was later moved to the south entrance of the educational wing.[78]

The land for the church, bought from Frank Gutting and Miss Robins for $1,369, was originally the site of Duncan's Brewery and, after that, a private residence. Reverend Fleiner, the pastor at the time, did a great deal of the brickwork, having formerly been a brick and stone mason. At that time pastors customarily stayed only one year at a church so Christian Nachtrieb took over the post before the church was finished. Reverend Nachtrieb engaged his brother-in-law, Mr. Messiner of Bucyrus, to complete the building. Dr. Nast dedicated the church which was paid for in full and had 165 members.

The Sunday School rooms of the new church were on the first floor while the auditorium was on the second. Heat was provided by two coal stoves. A new pump organ costing three hundred dollars was purchased in 1879 and used until 1923 when it was stored until it was motorized and rebuilt in 1961. The church building, itself, was used until 1913 when it was torn down. Services were held in Marion High School (later Central Junior High) while a new church was erected on the site of the old. The sum of thirty-five thousand dollars was raised for payment at the dedication on May 10, 1914, which left a debt of nine thousand dollars. At the evening service that same Sunday, seventy-five hundred was pledged and the district superintendent promised that the Church Extension Board would supply the rest.

More property was purchased in 1952 providing a parish house which was used for classrooms. By 1961 the need for an education unit was apparent and more adjacent property was purchased while building plans were hammered out. Groundbreaking was on Sunday morning June 20, 1965, for the 13,500-square-foot addition. The $160,000 structure furnished eleven more classrooms and activity areas including basement with three classrooms, a large fellowship area, a kitchen, serving room, and janitor's rooms. The ground floor contributed pastor's and secretary's offices, a nursery, and kindergarten and primary classrooms. The top floor was devoted to four classrooms for the young people of the church. Although all parts were air-conditioned, the congregation was especially happy with the brick facade of this new section which perfectly matched the fifty-year-old original building. In 1954 the church sanctuary was the first one in Marion to have air-conditioning.

When the main part of the church was built in 1913, the cornerstone proclaimed "First German M. E. Church A. D. 1869–1913." At some point the name was changed to Prospect Street Methodist Episcopal Church (Prospect Street United Methodist Church). The best guess is that this name change took place in the 1930s when the Central German Conference was dissolved. Later, in 1969, changing the name was again discussed but the majority still favored the present name so no change was made.

A church history reports that a new parsonage was built in March 1877 to replace the old one which was moved to the northwest corner of the church lot. It was not reported when the "old" parsonage was built. Most likely both of these served the First German M. E. as well as the country churches since they were all on the same circuit until the early 1890s. The "new" parsonage, completed in 1879, served the pastors and their families for eighty years. In 1956 a modern parsonage was purchased at 528 Summit Street in a residential area of Marion for sixteen thousand dollars. The old parsonage provided rental income for a while.

Prospect Street Methodist Church was involved in many programs throughout its long history. Support was always given to the Berea Orphanage and the Worthington Children's Home and other institutions sponsored by the conference. In 1956 the church supported a refugee family from Holland. Numerous church suppers, car washes, rummage sales, bake sales, ice cream socials, and other projects fostered fellowship as well as raising funds. Music has always been important to the Prospect Street Church as demonstrated by their Junior Choir, Senior Choir, soloists, duets, and quartets throughout the years. One group of note was the Grandmothers' Quartet, organized in 1925, which sang in German as well as English.

Some important dates in the history of Prospect Street Church are the dedication in 1869 by Dr. Nast, and a camp meeting at the fairgrounds on June 15 and 16, 1895, where breakfast was served for $0.15 and dinner for $0.25. A collection was received of $99.28 covering expenses of $81.28 with the remainder going to the missions. On April 12, 1913, ground was broken for a new building which was dedicated in May 1914. On October 28 and 29, 1939, a triple anniversary was held celebrating the ninetieth anniversary of German Methodism in Marion, the seventieth anniversary of the old church, and the twenty-fifth anniversary of the present one. October 9, 1949, was observed as the one hundredth anniversary of the congregation and included the singing of German hymns. A centennial celebration was held on October 19, 1969, in observance of "100 Years on this Corner"—a Methodist church being on that site for that period of time.

Sunday school was always an important element in the life of Prospect Street Church from the time of the old style class meeting to the present structure. Through the years the classes have been the Sunshine Class, Faithful Workers, Loyal Daughters, Willing Workers, Loyal Sons, King's Messengers, Anchor, Busy Bees, and William Gracely Class. The various classes have contributed much to the care and renovation of the church.

The youth groups started with the Epworth League and eventually became Methodist Youth Fellowship and then United MYF. Some activities they supported were providing a pipe organ to the church in 1914, purchasing stockings for the Berea Orphanage, and Harvest Home Festivals. Trips to Lakeside and Camp Wesley were also high points for the groups.

The men of Prospect have not always had an organized group but have still served the church as trustees, ushers, and in making many repairs on the building. Through the years there have been many women's groups including the Ladies Aid, the Missionary Society, and the Women's Society of Christian Service. Others have been the Light Bearers, King's Heralds, Standard Bearers, Go Ye, the Service Society, and the Wesleyan Service Guild.[79]

Currently, Prospect UMC has two Sunday morning services—a Praise Service at 8:45 a.m. and a Traditional Service at 10:30 a.m. and many special interest groups. Check their Web site for additional information.[80]

Prospect Street United Methodist Church still stands on the same corner, now close to 140 years. The address is 185 South Prospect Street, Marion, Ohio 43302-3986.

In 1915 the general conference of the Central German Conference was held in Marion from August 24 to August 30. Grandpa Rudin who was stationed in Holland, Indiana, at the time, made the trip to Marion by train to attend the activities.

Tuesday August 24

Took the 2:55 train [from Cincinnati] for Marion. Met Bros. Phillip and Becker on the train. Arrived at Marion at about 6:30 and a Bro. Rousch took us to our boarding places in his auto. Received a cordial welcome at Lagemann's. Dr. Morlock preached the Conference sermon this evening. His text was Rom. 8:16–17: "The Spirit itself beareth witness with our spirit that we are the Children of God, etc." Dr. M. did not appear at his best. Br. Guenther made a short and good speech of welcome and Fred Mueller answered.

Wednesday August 25

The Conference opened this morning with Bishop Anderson in the chair. After the opening exercises, which included Holy Communion, a memorial service was held. Bro. J. G. Schall preached the sermon and he did fine. He gave character sketches of the 7 brethren who died during the year. Took a walk with Bro. Phillip this afternoon.

Thursday August 26

I preached the missionary sermon last night and Dr. C. M. Boswell of the Board of Home Missions followed me. When I sat down, Dr. Nast asked me for the manuscript, wishing to print it in the Apologete. Also, many of the Brethren told me how much they enjoyed my sermon, even Dr. Boswell and Dr. Mavsety of the Freedmen's Aid, complimented me. I can say for myself that I never felt in better form in the pulpit than last night. The reports of the District Superintendents were read this morning. Bro. Treuschel could not refrain from giving his preachers a parting shot.

Friday August 27

The meeting last night was in the interest of education. Dr. Nicholson, Sec. of the Board of Education was the speaker. He is a forceful speaker and at home with the subject. The meeting this evening was in the interest of Sunday School and evangelization. Dr. Edgar Blake was the speaker and claimed rather much for the Board of Sunday School.

Saturday August 28

The election of the delegates to the General Conference took place this morning. Dr. Nast and Bro. Oetjen were elected. Bro. F. W. Mueller was a candidate, but he was badly defeated. The laymen elected C. A. J. Walker and Louis Fritsche as their representatives at the General Conference. After dinner today members of the Board of Trade took us on an auto trip around Marion. Bro. Wuerfel, who was my partner at Lagemann's, left for home this afternoon. He had had himself placed on the retired list. Bro. Schweitzer has also gone home, his poor health being the cause.

Sunday August 29

Last night there was an open air service at the court house. The Conference male chorus sang and two of the preachers spoke. There was a lot of noise around, so I don't see what good could have been accomplished. I preached in the United Brethren church this morning and enjoyed myself. Quite a number expressed their appreciation. One man said to me that it was a "glorious sermon." Well, if I did some good I am satisfied. This afternoon the ordination service was held. This evening Bishop Warne spoke on Missions in India.

Monday August 30

Conference closed a little before I expected. The Conference has been reduced to three districts and John Mayer is our District Superintendent. J. M. is a "live wire" at any rate. Took the 10:30 train for Cincinnati.

Friday September 3

I never enjoyed a Conference more. Lagemanns live in a modern parsonage kept in the best of condition by Bro. L.'s people. Bro. L. I consider a very good man, devoted to his work and not in the least conceited. He had been returned to his charge for the fifth time. My stay with him and his good wife will always be a pleasant remembrance.[81]

New Knoxville, Ohio, Circuit

New Knoxville Circuit—New Knoxville German M. E. Church

The New Knoxville German M. E. began in an unusual way. A recent arrival in the community, William Dering [Doering], made a trip to Sidney where he attended a preaching service. On returning to New Knoxville, he was a changed man which did not altogether please his New Knoxville friends and relatives. When they expressed skepticism he told them to "Come and see." A group accepted his challenge and went to Sidney with him to hear Rev. John Kisling. They were so impressed that they insisted Kisling come to New Knoxville to preach. A class was organized as a result of his visit and included the Bragsick (Brocksick), Redwill (Rethwelm), and Kruse families. A short time later, the Meckstroth family and others joined, making the congregation healthy enough to build a log church.[82]

Rev. John Zwahlen followed Reverend Kisling in 1843 and formally received the first members in the new Salem Methodist Episcopal Church. The ten charter members of the New Knoxville church were received on May 18 and 19, 1843. About this time, also, the New Knoxville Circuit was designated with the St. John's, Kossuth, and Spencerville Methodist Churches as additional members.[83]

Soon after the building of the log church at the corner of St. Mary's and Bremen streets, Mr. and Mrs. E. Brown donated lot no. 27 to the church which was used for a cemetery for twenty years. In 1864 a new frame church was built on the site of the log church where the German Methodists had worshiped for twenty-five years.[84] In 1890 the congregation had the opportunity to purchase the Reformed Church building which was used for twenty-five more years. In 1916 growing pains caused the congregation to build the church that is still their house of worship today. Many of the members gave of their talent and hard work to complete the structure.[85]

The first parsonage, a frame building, was built in 1861 on twenty acres of land on Spring Street. The congregation wanted to make sure their pastor had a

New Knoxville, Ohio, German ME still lives as New Knoxville UMC.

sufficient amount of land so he could plant crops and, no doubt, contribute to his support. A new brick parsonage replaced the thirty-eight-year-old home in 1899 and the old frame building was torn down. Over the years, most of the twenty acres was sold off when there was less need for the pastor to grow his own food. A third parsonage, at 106 East Spring Street, was purchased in 1978.[86]

The New Knoxville church acknowledges a number of "unique standards of loyalty to Christian ideals" in their 1943 history:

> In the almost regular attendance at the Sunday morning worship service of ninety-five percent of all resident members. In the highest per-capita giving to budget expenses in the Lima District . . .
>
> in the three years course in catechetical training of the classes for confirmation.
>
> In the high moral and spiritual living. . . .
>
> Reasons for this loyalty come from
>
> In the traditional patterns of devotion, derived from their German ancestors in the Fatherland.
>
> In the standards observed in the whole New Knoxville community.
>
> In the former tendency of our people to live their own lives in this community, rather than to mingle with unworthy elements too often found in the outer world.

And in the inheritance from that Godly line of ministers....[87]

Various church organizations include the administrative council which oversees the programs of the church, business activities, and the administrative board. The New Knoxville Administrative Council meets on the second Sunday of the month. The Board of Trustees takes care of church property and keeps the church and parsonage in good repair. Some of the projects they have undertaken include replacing roofs on the parsonage and church, remodeling the sanctuary and kitchen, restoring and waterproofing the bell tower, putting in a new heating system, and repairing the organ. They also purchased new equipment such as chairs for the Sunday school and storm windows for the stained-glass windows. Trustees meet the second Monday of the month and serve three-year terms.[88]

Pastor John Zwahlen first organized the Sunday school in February 1846 with 9 pupils, 2 teachers, and a superintendent. In the 1940s the classes were known as "Church School" and had an enrollment of 110 with an average attendance of 83.[89] By the early 1990s the classes were again referred to as "Sunday school" and had an average attendance of 70. The Sunday school has sponsored an out-of-doors worship service, an annual picnic including a hog roast, decorating the church for Advent, and paying part of the church's World Service Mission apportionments.[90]

The women's organizations date back to 1913 when the New Knoxville chapter of the Woman's Foreign Missionary Society was founded. Around that time a chapter of the Woman's Home Missionary Society which dealt with missions closer to home was also established. There was also a Ladies Aid society whose purpose was the "edification through Christian fellowship and deeds of kindness confirming the Christian life."[91] These groups were replaced by the Woman's Society of Christian Service in 1939 which became the United Methodist Women in 1972.

The youth of the church participated in Epworth League which was organized at New Knoxville in 1916. This organization followed the path of the women's groups becoming Methodist Youth Fellowship in 1939 and United Methodist Youth Fellowship in 1969. At present the group is composed of a senior youth group for young people from ninth grade to twelfth and a junior group for those in grades seven and eight. The junior group has sold fruit baskets to raise money for the poor and sponsored church dinners. The senior youth conducts the Easter Sunrise Service every year. Both groups have enjoyed activities such as hay rides, retreats, and "lock-ins."[92] In December 1927 there was also a group organized called Fellowship League for those who had graduated from the Methodist Youth Fellowship. Its purpose was to provide fellowship and activities for those young people and meetings were held quarterly at church or in the homes of members.[93]

In the 1990s New Knoxville had three church choirs including two children's choirs: The Cherub Choir for children age three to kindergarten, and the Rainbow Singers for elementary age children. The Chancel Choir was composed of teens and adults and performed from September through May. They also sang for special services through out the years and presented a cantata during the Advent season.[94]

The 1993 history of the church has a section devoted to church memories which give a valuable insight into history and some of the activities of the church in the past. I'll quote some of them here.

> When midweek services were held, the German language prayers of the older women were especially meaningful. While I was unable to understand them, their sincerity was never in doubt.—Irene Howe.

> While the new church was being built, we had a Christmas program on the second story of the old Town Hall. After the basement of the new church was finished, we had Sunday School and church in the basement while the rest of the church was being built.—Norman Katterheinrich

> My recollections go back to approximately the very late "20s" I can remember every pastor from Rev. Worthman to the present. Most all of them brought something positive to the Church. . . . I remember when we had a coal fund taken every last Sunday of the month in Sunday School to help heat the church in the cold months. I think that after we quit that, we then took an offering for World Service. . . . I remember when a vote was taken in the "30s" to decide if we should close the Church because of lack of money. But a resounding "no" vote seemed to encourage us and we did survive.—Curtis Kruse

Alice remembers back before the efficient heating system was installed.

> . . . There was a stove in the sanctuary. People sitting near the stove came away from the service red faced from the heat, while people sitting away from the stove came away from the service very cold. She also remembers the barns that were located behind the church. People used to ride to the church in their horse-pulled buggies. The horses were hitched outside or taken to the barns while the families attended worship.—Alice Kuck.[95]

Former pastors and pastor's wives also contributed their memories. Below is one of the many published.

> Our first impression was arriving out in flat farm land where no weed was permitted to grow. Hearing the German language spoken among the older citizens was distinctive. We loved the big brick parsonage on the East side of town. One whole acre to now keep our boys, Jeff, Dan and Mark busy in the summertime. There was a tree in the southeast corner where they laboriously built a tree house. The hammering of pounds of nails let me know where they were. The organ was a major component of our worship. Elmer Katterheinrich showed me the door in the organ console and the long handle which he operated when he was a lad to pump up the air to make music in the pipes. With the help of the Lima Organ Company and the talented trustees, the organ continues to give its

lovely tones. Bill Siegrist made a shaft for the blower. Elmer made a maple bearing to steady the end of the shaft. The trustees replaced the blades on the blower. This is just one example of the dedicated ingenuity of those trustees.—Ray and Marian Thompson.[96]

And lastly is my grandfather's experiences in New Knoxville when he attended the 1926 meeting of the Central German Conference held there.

Tuesday August 31

Took the 8:00 B & O train for the seat of our Conference, New Knoxville. Arrived at Wapakoneta at 3:15. Dr. Nast got on the train at Cincinnati. At Wapakoneta, Bro. Noah Katterheinrich, who is treasurer of Auglaize Co., took us in charge. He brought us (Schaenzlin, Zarwell, Link and myself) to his brother's place in the country where we were served a good farmer's supper. This evening Dr. John Marting preached his jubilee sermon: he entered the ministry 50 years ago. After the service a reception was tendered the ministers by the Epworth League.

Wednesday September 1

At the reception last night no less than 7 celebrities were given the chance to shine in oratory, and they all made the most of the opportunity. It was past eleven when we got home. Did not sleep well. There are 4 of us in one small room with two beds and two chairs. The beds are too small for two sleepers. Bro. Link is my bedfellow and he lay in the middle all the time and I on the outer edge. The Conference was opened by Bishop Nicholson and the usual communion service was held, followed by the Memorial service. This afternoon Beuscher, Weiler, Beyer and I made a trip to St. Mary's in Beuscher's auto. Bro. W. treated us to ice cream soda in honor of the 25th anniversary of his entrance into the Conference.

Thursday September 2

Slept hardly at all last night. Bishop George A. Miller, resident Bishop of the M. E. church in Mexico was the speaker last night and he explained the origin of the present trouble in Mexico. This afternoon the Preachers Aid Society held its annual meeting. We now have an endowment fund of $239,399. Tried to get my committee together this afternoon but did not succeed. The annual meeting of the WFMS and WHMS was also held.

Friday September 3

Link and Zarwell moved to another "hotel," so Schaenzlin and I had our beds to ourselves. Consequently, I had a fairly good night's rest. This evening, however, Bros. Grob and Ellinger became our bedfellows, so there you are! The irrepressible John Mayer made a monkey of himself as he usually does when he gets a chance. The speakers apparently did not enjoy his antics. Bro. Hausser gave a program with some of the children on the Berea Orphan Home. Later Charlie Allinger gave a moving picture show consisting of pictures he took in the Holy Land. They were not very good and flickered a great deal, so that I became quite dizzy. The same thing happened to Bro. Beuscher, so he and I left and took a nice walk into the country.

Saturday September 4

Dr. Carl Stiefel gave us a fine address last night. The Conference business session came to a close this afternoon. A baseball game was to be played this afternoon between the ministers and the laymen, but rain put an end to it at the end of the 4th inning. The score was 7 to 2 in favor of the laymen. The ministers played well after the first disastrous inning. This evening we were guests at a banquet of the laymen. It was a splendid success.

Sunday September 5

We have had rain every day since the beginning of Conference. Attended the Laymen's Bible Class in the town hall this morning. Heard Bishop Nicholson in a great sermon on Faith. He does not indulge in flowery language, but he does say weighty and impressive things. We had a fine chicken dinner at our host's today. Tonight's service was held in the beautiful Reformed Church. Bro. John C. Kluesner preached the sermon in German.

Monday September 6

Wesley Katterheinrich, our host, took me to Wapakoneta last night right after the service. Cannot say that I enjoyed Bro. Kluesner's sermon. He was slow of speech and evidently conscious of the fact that he was a Conference preacher. The appointments were read at the close of the service. I go back to Louisville as pastor of Second and Third churches. Took the 2:48 train this morning for Louisville and arrived at the parsonage at about noon. Took it easy after the strenuous days at New Knoxville.

Tuesday September 7

Had a fine night's rest, the first in a week. It was the unanimous opinion of the brethren that the Conference in New Knoxville was one of the best we ever had. The meals were fine, the service fine and all the arrangements and accommodations in the church were fine. Bro. Klotz and his people deserve great credit, and it was freely given them by the Bishop and others. That a country church could do so well was a revelation to all.[97]

The New Knoxville United Methodist Church continues to serve the people of the area at the corner of Main and German streets in New Knoxville, Ohio. The Sunday schedule is Sunday school at 9:00 a.m. with worship at 10:15 a.m. The church's Web site is www.newknoxvilleumc.com.[98]

New Knoxville Circuit—St. John's German M. E. Church

The town of St. John's in Auglaize County was also the site of a German Methodist church on the circuit with New Knoxville. After 1882, there were only two churches listed on this circuit so the second one was presumably the one in St. John's. The *Geschichte* says that this church was "given up" in 1900.[99] Conference records record the actual demise as being in 1904.[100]

In pursuing the St. John's Church at the Auglaize County Library, I discovered that it was not *in* St. John's but south of it in a little village called Geyer. A county history noted that there was a German Methodist cemetery there, also called George Geyer Cemetery. It is located on the east edge of Geyer on Township Road 108-A, Geyer Drive.[101] Another source on township cemeteries says that it is one-half acre with only a few stones which are piled in the middle. Unfortunately, there was no information on the church that probably stood on that same half acre. We followed the directions and found it. Although it was no doubt neglected in the past (the stones now being all piled together), someone is taking care of the site now as the half acre was mowed and there were flags decorating the stones.

Spencerville, Ohio, Circuit

Spencerville Circuit—Kossuth German M. E.

Bernhard Graessle brought German Methodism to Auglaize County and the vicinity when he moved there from Marion in 1854. He had been a licensed exhorter in his previous home area and when he discovered there were no German services in his new surroundings, he determined to change that. He invited his German neighbors over for Holy Services and "little by little they filled the house good." His services and revivals resulted in a number of conversions and eventually the people in Spencerville heard about him and implored him to come there. Bro. Graessle then traveled to Sidney, the seat of the Sidney Mission, and asked Reverend Schimmelpfennig, the pastor in charge, to come and organize the Kossuth and Spencerville groups into official congregations. They were then attached to the Sidney Circuit.

In 1864 Spencerville and New Knoxville were dropped from the Sidney Circuit and became a circuit of their own sharing the same preacher until 1883 when each got its own pastor.[102] The Zion German M. E. church building was dedicated in 1870 and was used by both the German congregation and the English-speaking congregation. In 1877 a new church was built and then used exclusively by the German congregation. This building was used for fifty years at which time considerable repairs were needed on both it and the English M. E. church. The leaders of both churches held discussions about uniting and this

Kossuth-Zion UMC near Spencerville, Ohio, is a merger of the English-speaking (Kossuth) and German-speaking (Zion) branches of the Methodist church.

plan was approved in 1927 by both churches.

Zion held a farewell service on June 5, 1927, which included an address by Rev. F. W. Mueller whose father had dedicated the church fifty years earlier. The Lima District Board chose the site where the new united church was to stand and the old Zion building was taken down.[103] Parts of the old Zion building were used in the construction of the new Kossuth-Zion including the curved ceiling in the sanctuary of the new church. The dedication on Armistice Day in 1928 was followed by a week of special services.

Glenna Meckstroth gives a good history of the church in her book *Tales from Great-Grandpa's Trunk* in the chapter "The Little Country Church." She described how the Sunday school collection was handled.

> As the money was collected from each class, it was counted into a little wicker basket. The classes came together at the close of the service and the secretary's report was read: how many had attended and how much had been in the offering that day. The secretary then took that little basket down the side aisle to Mr. Hoverman. He always sat in the same pew, and as she approached, he stood up and pulled open the side pocket on his suit coat as she dumped in the money. He took it home and as the preacher's salary needed to be paid or more coal bought, or whatever the need, he paid the bill.[104]

Ms. Meckstroth also described how the church ladies earned money for the church by managing the dining room at the Auglaize County Fair during the

1930s. In the morning one shift prepared bacon, sausage, and eggs for the farmers and fair workers. After the dishes were done another shift arrived bearing homemade pies, cakes, vegetables fresh from the garden, and meats. At noon fairgoers and workers alike arrived to enjoy such home-cooked fare as vegetable or chicken noodle soup, fried chicken, meat loaf, mashed potatoes and gravy, fresh green beans, slaw, and the homemade desserts. The evening meal provided more of the same delicious fare. This project was no easy task and required the cooperation of everyone as everything was made from scratch. Ms. Meckstroth mentions how her grandfather and other retired men came throughout the day to lend a hand at washing up or whatever needed doing. Throughout the years the ladies earned enough money with this venture to pay off the cost of the church basement and, eventually, the church mortgage. The Ladies Aid also participated in other projects which included quilting, making clothing for an Indian Mission in New Mexico and giving clothing and gifts to the Worthington Children's Home.[105]

Other church organizations of note were the Gleaners Sunday School class which continued to meet for fifty years and was lead by Ms. Meckstroth's Grandpa Frank, and later by her father. Every month the class met at the home of one of the members for a dinner and party. The Youth Fellowship included all the church youth on the circuit and alternated between the circuit churches. Since the circuit covered a lot of ground (literally), the youth group members had the opportunity to meet contemporaries from many different surrounding towns and school districts.[106]

In the 1940s Kossuth Zion was on a four-point circuit which included Walnut Grove, Olive Chapel, and Christie Chapel churches. This meant the pastor had to do some fancy juggling to meet the needs of all four churches. Ms. Meckstroth related that when Kossuth had the early service Walnut Grove held Sunday school. After church, the Kossuth Sunday school convened and the pastor headed to Walnut Grove to hold their church service. The next Sunday the two churches offered only Sunday school and Olive Chapel and Christie Chapel took their turn splitting the morning between Sunday School and church service. To make sure each church was treated equally, those that had the early service, switched at midyear and held their service second so the other churches could have a turn at the early service. After the circuit was reorganized, the preaching service was held every Sunday.[107]

Sometimes there were problems getting all four churches to agree on church matters. Each church owed a certain amount for the preacher's salary, the district superintendent, missionary support, and other district supported projects. When a church owed money for a mortgage or repairs, it was sometimes difficult to make all the payments. Some churches on the circuit had wealthier members than others and the Great Depression didn't help the finances of either the church or its members. Those who had money were sometimes critical of those who didn't and sanctimoniously advised the "have nots" to "pray more" in order to "pay more."[108]

The Kossuth Zion United Methodist Church is still active and is located at 05431 State Route 197 near Spencerville, Ohio.

Spencerville Circuit—Spencerville German Methodist

The history of the Spencerville German M. E. Church is sketchy at best. It was founded at the same time as Kossuth Zion and New Knoxville German M. E. according to the *Geschichte*. In 1883 when the Sidney District was split, the Kossuth and Spencerville churches, as well as another church—Salem—remained together. The Spencerville church was still viable in 1907 when the *Geschichte* was written and it states,

> We occupy here 2 good frame churches and a parsonage. Their worth is estimated for Zion Church $2000, the Spencerville Church $2000 and the parsonage $2000.

It was also noted that since the fall of 1905, the Sunday evening service had been in English due to the lack of understanding of the German language.[109]

A newspaper article written in 1929 declared that the Spencerville G. M. E. suffered a decrease in membership and the church was not being used any more.[110] Conference records support this as the Spencerville church is listed with Piqua in 1928 and then dropped altogether in 1930.[111]

Spencerville Circuit—Salem German Methodist

I almost overlooked this one, as I thought it was the same as the Spencerville church. However, the *Geschichte* states that Salem and Zion remained with Spencerville when the split took place in 1883. Then it goes on to say that Salem was abandoned in 1894.[112] The conference records also show a third church on the Spencerville Circuit from 1888 to 1896.[113]

The 1880 Allen County map of Auglaize Township shows an M. E. church and cemetery in section 20 at the intersection of what is now route 117 and Bowdle Road. A cemetery Web site for Allen County lists a Salem cemetery at this location. Could this also be the location of the Salem Church that was on the Spencerville Circuit?

Notes

1. Golder, Horst, and Schaal, *Geschichte*, 423.
2. *History of Franklin and Pickaway Counties, Ohio* (Evansville, Ind.: Unigraphic, Inc., 1974), 518.
3. Golder, Horst, and Schaal, *Geschichte*, 423.
4. Sue Porter, *Livingston United Methodist Church* (church history, Columbus, Ohio, 1981).
5. Golder, Horst, and Schaal, *Geschichte*, 424.
6. Porter, *Livingston.*
7. Golder, Horst, and Schaal, *Geschichte*, 424.
8. Ibid., 424–25.
9. Porter, *Livingston.*
10. "Welcome to Livingston UMC," Columbus, Ohio, www.livingstonumc.com, 2009.
11. Reverend Ellen Phillips, letter to Barbara Dixon, 1997.
12. Porter, *Livingston.*
13. Golder, Horst, and Schaal, *Geschichte*, 424.
14. Ibid., 425–26.
15. Rudin, 1931.
16. Golder, Horst, and Schaal, *Geschichte*, 423.
17. James R. Lytle, *History of Delaware County* (Chicago: Biographical Publishing Co., 1908), 250–51.
18. Golder, Horst, and Schaal, *Geschichte*, 430.
19. Lytle, *Delaware County*, 251.
20. Golder, Horst, and Schaal, *Geschichte*, 423.
21. N. N. Hill, Jr., *The History of Licking County* (Newark, Ohio: A. A. Graham & Publishers, 1881), 575.
22. Golder, Horst, and Schaal, *Geschichte*, 424.
23. Ibid., 423.
24. Glenn Longaberger, *Dresden, 1817–1967 "Pioneer Days to Modern Ways"* (Dresden, Ohio: Lindsey Printing, 1967), 37.
25. *History of Muskingum County, Ohio* (Columbus, Ohio: F. J.. Everhart & Co. 1882), 358.
26. Longaberger, *Dresden*, 37.
27. Golder, Horst, and Schaal, *Geschichte*, 426.
28. Anonymous, "A Summary of the History of St. Mark U. M. C." (church history, Galion, Ohio, St. Mark's UMC).
29. Golder, Horst, and Schaal, *Geschichte*, 427.
30. H. T. Gould and J. W. Starr, *An Illustrated Atlas of Crawford County, Ohio* (Bucyrus, Ohio: Gould & Starr, 1873).
31. Golder, Horst, and Schaal, *Geschichte*, 427.
32. William Dennig, Mrs. Ira Rizor, Mrs. T. A. Johnston, Miss Laura Koppe, and Mrs. C. A. Koppe, "Time Turns the Pages of Church History" (church history, Galion, Ohio, St. Mark's church, c. 1978), 4.
33. Golder, Horst, and Schaal, *Geschichte*, 427.
34. Dennig, et al., "Time," 4–11.
35. Ibid., 6.
36. Ibid., 7.

37. Rudin, 1906.

38. Golder, Horst, and Schaal, *Geschichte*, 27.

39. Clarence Tropft, "A Sketch of a History of Immanuel (German Sixteen) Church" (church history, c. 1960), 1–2.

40. "Sixteen United Methodist Church," *Mansfield District Local Church Directory* (Mansfield, Ohio, 1996), 60

41. Tropf, "Immanuel (German Sixteen) Church," 2.

42. "Sixteen U. M. C.," 60.

43. Golder, Horst, and Schaal, *Geschichte*, 427.

44. "One Hundred Fifty Years of Methodism in Mansfield and Richland County" (church history, Richland County, Ohio, n.d.), 27.

45. Golder, Horst, and Schaal, *Geschichte*, 427.

46. *Honoring the Past . . . Celebrating the Present . . . Embracing the Future*, (church history, Epworth United Methodist Church, Bucyrus, Ohio, 2004), 1.

47. *Minutes of the Annual Conferences* (various publishers, 1875–1922).

48. East Ohio Conference and History Commission, "Local Church History Survey," 1982, United Methodist Archives, Ohio Wesleyan University, Delaware, Ohio.

49. *Honoring the Past*, 2.

50. Local Church History Survey (The Plains).

51. Golder, Horst, and Schaal, *Geschichte*, 427., 416.

52. Ibid., 416.

53. *History of Crawford County* (Chicago: Baskin & Battey, History Publishers, 1881), 574–75.

54. "Scioto United Methodist Church," Mansfield District Local Church Directory, Mansfield Ohio 1996, 56.

55. Elmer Lutz, "125th Anniversary Scioto United Methodist Church" in Tracking in Crawford County Ohio (Galion, Ohio: Crawford County Chapter Ohio Genealogical Society, October 2000), 105–106.

56. Rudin, 1904.

57. Caroline McGrew, ed., *75 Years of Celebrating Past Commitments & Future Dedication at Epworth Church* (church history, Bucyrus, Ohio, 1993).

58. *History of Crawford County*, 390.

59. Golder, Horst, and Schaal, *Geschichte*, 416–17.

60. *History of Crawford County*, 391.

61. McGrew, *75 Years*.

62. Ibid.

63. Bucyrus Epworth UMC!, Bucyrus, Ohio, www.bucyrusepworthumc.com

64. Rudin, 1909.

65. Golder, Horst, and Schaal, *Geschichte*, 29.

66. Ruth E. Schott, *One Hundred Years on this Corner*, church history (Marion, Ohio: 1969).

67. Golder, Horst, and Schaal, *Geschichte*, 430–31.

68. Schott, *One Hundred Years on this Corner*.

69. Golder, Horst, and Schaal, *Geschichte*, 429

70. *History of Marion County, Ohio* (Chicago: Leggett, Conaway & Co., 1883), 952.

71. Trella H. Romine, ed., *Marion County 1979 History* (Dallas, Tex.: The Taylor Publishing Co., 1979), 166.

72. Schott, *One Hundred Years on this Corner*.

73. Ibid.
74. Golder, Horst, and Schaal, *Geschichte*, 431.
75. Schott, *One Hundred Years on this Corner*.
76. Ibid.
77. *Marion County*, 519.
78. Ibid., 60.
79. Schott, *One Hundred Years on this Corner*.
80. Prospect Street Church, http://www.gbgm-umc.org/prospectst)(accessed 7/10/2009).
81. Rudin, 1915.
82. Golder, Horst, and Schaal, *Geschichte*, 433.
83. George, H. Smith, *One Hundredth Anniversary*, church history (New Knoxville, Ohio: 1943), 8.
84. Sesquicentennial Committee, *The New Knoxville United Methodist Church*, church history (New Knoxville, Ohio: 1993), 12.
85. Smith, *One Hundredth Anniversary*, 10.
86. Sesquicentennial Committee, *New Knoxville United Methodist Church,* 12
87. Smith, *One Hundredth Anniversary*, 15.
88. Sesquicentennial Committee, *New Knoxville United Methodist Church,* 13–14.
89. Smith, *One Hundredth Anniversary*, 18–19.
90. Sesquicentennial Committee, *New Knoxville United Methodist Church,* 15.
91. Ibid., 16.
92. Ibid., 16–17.
93. Smith, *One Hundredth Anniversary*, 21.
94. Sesquicentennial Committee, *New Knoxville United Methodist Church,* 18.
95. Ibid., 20–23.
96. Ibid., 30–31.
97. Rudin, Diaries, 1926.
98. New Knoxville United Methodist Church, New Knoxville, Ohio, www.newknoxvilleumc.com
99. Golder, Horst, and Schaal, *Geschichte*, 434.
100. *Minutes of the Annual Conference*, 1905, 612. (circuit reduced to one church)
101. The Auglaize County Historical Society, *A History of Auglaize County, Ohio* (Defiance, Ohio: The Hubbard Company 1979), 50.
102. Golder, Horst, and Schaal, *Geschichte*, 435–36.
103. "History," Centennial Worship Service, church history, Kossuth-Zion United Methodist Church, November 8, 1970).
104. Glenna Meckstroth, *Tales from Great-Grand-pa's Trunk* (Wooster, Ohio: Wooster Book Co.), 350.
105. Meckstroth, *Tales*, 352–55.
106. Ibid., 355–56.
107. Ibid., 356–57.
108. Ibid., 357.
109. Golder, Horst, and Schaal, *Geschichte*, 436.
110. *Journal-News*, "Scrapbook History of Spencerville, Ohio," 1929.
111. *Minutes of the Annual Conferences,* 1928, 622, and 1930, 623.
112. Golder, Horst, and Schaal, *Geschichte*, 436.
113. *Minutes of the Annual Conferences*, 1888: 414.

CHAPTER 20

Northeastern Ohio

Akron, Ohio

Akron—Trinity German Methodist

It was not until 1885 that German Methodist services were held in Akron. A German member of the English Methodist church continued to hold periodic prayer services after initial preachings by several visiting German M. E. ministers. Then a theological student from Berea held services in the undercroft of the English Methodist Church for several months. In the fall of 1885, A. J. Bucher took over the work and organized twelve members into a congregation. Meeting at the English Methodist church was not entirely satisfactory as services had to be held Sunday between 3:00 p.m. and 4:00 p.m. Other meetings had to convene in private homes. The congregation longed for its own church building but funds were lacking. The presiding elder at that time, F. L. Nagler, gave an impassioned sermon on the necessity of supporting the German work which was then seconded by Dr. Young, pastor of the English church. A. J. Bucher and his wife sang two German duets which convinced those holding tight to their purse strings to open them.

    A trustee board was organized which proposed building a church for thirty-five hundred dollars if the pastor first succeeded in getting twenty-five hundred pledged. After much work and many prayers this was accomplished and construction was started in the summer of 1886 with the consecration taking place on December 12 of that year.[1] In 1892 the membership stood at fifty-five with a Sunday school of sixty having twelve teachers.[2] Later when a parsonage was built under the administration of Rev. W. Andree, the property at the corner of Pearl and Exchange streets was valued at six thousand dollars. After twenty years the German church had eighty members and a Sunday school of seventy plus a Ladies Aid, Epworth League, and Junior League.[3]

In the 1950s the German Church, now called Trinity, suffered a decrease in membership and funds. At its strongest point, German-speaking people came from as far away as Cleveland, Youngstown, and Medina to attend its services. For many years supply ministers served the church but the congregation became dissatisfied with this system and were determined to disband. In 1952, when the church no longer wanted to continue the supply arrangement, Rev. P. Raymond Powers was appointed. After services one Sunday he met with the official board, hoping to encourage the church to stay afloat. The board agreed to give him a year's trial during which time First Methodist Church, Trinity's mother church, proposed a merger. Some of the other area Methodist churches opposed this as they did not want First Church to have Trinity's membership and property. Trinity eventually agreed to the merger with the stipulation that a Trinity educational building be built. First Church accepted those terms and the condition that 20 percent of the proceeds of the sale go to the district for distribution. The last service at Trinity was on Easter Sunday 1955 when many of the old German members from the surrounding area attended.

A bronze plaque was installed in the entry of the Trinity Educational Building which says, "Trinity Educational Building of First Methodist Church commemorating the merger of Trinity Methodist Church with First Methodist Church Easter, 1955. Ministers at the time of Merger—Rev. P. Raymond Powers, D.D. Trinity Church, Rev. M. S. Harvey, D.D.D.H. First Church."[4]

On April 29, 1994, tragedy struck as fire from an electrical source destroyed First Church. The Trinity Education Building,, however, survived the fire but was torn down in order to rebuild the entire church. Church services were held in the Central Hower High School until May 18, 1997, when the congregation moved into the new building. The complete project cost $7,168,895 which was paid off by April 16, 2006.[5]

Akron—South Akron Mission

In the conference records another church is listed as being on a circuit with Trinity from 1924 to 1933 when the German Conference disbanded. This was known as the South Akron Mission. At times, two churches in addition to Trinity were enumerated making a circuit of three.[6]

Canal Dover, Ohio, Circuit

Canal Dover Circuit—Canal Dover German Methodist

Today Canal Dover is known as just plain Dover, having dropped the "canal" from its name when that form of transport was no longer relevant. Brother Wunderlich started the church in this location in 1853. It apparently never had a large congregation as the *Geschichte* reported thirty-nine members in its entry.[7] According to a county history, the congregation met in the town hall until a small church was built in 1880. The Canal Dover church was on a three-point circuit which also included Chili and Berlin. In the 1880s the membership was thirty people.[8]

A history of the First Methodist Church of Dover mentions the German Methodist Church. Apparently, the church decided to disband about 1918 and most of its members went to First. The German M. E. church property on Singluff Avenue was sold and later used by the Four Square Gospel Church.[9]

Canal Dover Circuit—Chili German Methodist

The Chili church was a fairly latecomer to the German Methodist fold and was started in 1875 after Rev. Karl Koch had come from Canal Dover to preach a number of times. The local preacher of Canal Dover, Philipp Geib, assisted him on this hazardous undertaking—hazardous, because they had to travel a distance of twenty-two miles to reach Chili, mostly on horseback or on foot.[10] The second pastor, Rev. O. C. Klocksiem, held a successful revival bringing the membership up to about sixty.

The group met first in private homes and a schoolhouse, but when the membership increased, plans were made for a church building. Gottlieb Fellers provided a lot located close to the Crawford Township line and a frame church was erected for the cost of twelve hundred dollars. By 1881 the church sponsored a Sunday School of sixty members which met only during the summer.[11]

The history after the 1880s is sketchy at best. Some church record forms note that it was reorganized in 1932 and became the M. E. Church at Pearl, Ohio.[12] On a second form it is noted that the church was in Pearl, formerly Chili Station, and that the building was frame with no bell and a seating capacity of 150.[13] A paper from the Fresno Charge file lists Chili on a circuit with Fresno, Orange, and Baltic churches from 1929 to 1954.[14]

A few years ago, we looked up the Chili church and after traveling and zigzagging over multiple country roads, we found Chili. The church is no longer standing, but there is a cemetery and a wall (which can be seen in a photograph of the *Geschichte*) which marks the site.

Canal Dover Circuit—Berlin German Methodist

This church is not listed in the *Geschichte* and was probably short-lived. The only mention I could find was in a county history: "His [Rev. William Andree] circuit embraces this congregation [Dover], a church at Chili, Coshocton County, and one at Berlin, Holmes County."[15]

Notes

1. Golder, Horst, and Schaal, *Geschichte*, 408–409.
2. Ex-Sheriff Samuel A. Lane, *Fifty Years and Over of Akron and Summit County* (Akron, Ohio: Beacon Job Department 1892), 206.
3. Golder, Horst, and Schaal, *Geschichte*, 409.
4. "Why it was named Trinity Educational Building," *Fifty Years in First Church*, history of First M. E. Church in Akron, Rev. P. Raymond Powers, Akron, Ohio, 13.
5. First United Methodist Church, "Church History," Akron, Ohio, www.acorn.net/fumcakron/ 2006.
6. *Minutes of the Annual Conferences*, 1925, 863 and 1928, 821.
7. Golder, Horst, and Schaal, *Geschichte*, 418.
8. John Brainard Mansfield, *History of Tuscarawas County* (Chicago: Warner, Beers & Co. 1884), 540.
9. Anonymous, "The History of the First Methodist Church," (of Dover Ohio) East Ohio Archives, Delaware, 5.
10. Golder, Horst, and Schaal, *Geschichte*, 418.
11. N. N. Hill, *History of Coshocton County* (Newark, Ohio: A. A. Graham & Co., Publishers, 1881), 621–22.
12. Works Progress Administration Survey of State and Local Historical Records: 1936, Ohio Historical Records Survey, Church Records Form, no. 1.
13. Ibid., no. 2.
14. Fresno Charge file, North-East Ohio Conference, Methodist Church, East Ohio Archives, Delaware, Ohio.
15. Mansfield, *Tuscarawas County*, 540.

CHAPTER 21

Southeastern Ohio

Baresville, Ohio, Circuit

The hilly and picturesque Baresville Circuit along the Ohio River included the Hannibal, Buckhill Bottom, Mt. Vernon, and St. John's churches. When Grandpa Rudin first went there for a district meeting in 1900, the landscape reminded him of his native Switzerland and he referred to it as "Beautiful Baresville." After he was assigned there from 1905 to 1910, I'm not sure he was so enchanted with the area. Being the pastor there meant arduous trips by horseback or horse and buggy in all kinds of weather in all kinds of terrain.

Baresville Circuit—Buckhill Bottom German M.E.

G. Danker and Engelhart Riemenschneider first came to Buckhill Bottom to preach in the late 1840s and the first quarterly conference was held there in September 1847. The church was built in 1853, at which time it was on a circuit with a church at Malaga. The circuit claimed 107 full members, 28 probationary ones, 15 Sunday school teachers and 93 students. The circuit name was changed in 1859 to Baresville Circuit.[1]

The Buckhill church building was constructed from bricks of clay made on a nearby farm. The windows were placed high on the walls to prevent unbelievers from disturbing the services until the church was remodeled in 1883 when the windows were lowered. In 1933, when the Central German Conference disbanded, the Buckhill Bottom church closed and its congregation merged with another. The building stood until 1956 when it was razed so the land could be used by the Olin Mathieson Chemical Corporation for its new aluminum plant. The graves in the cemetery were exhumed and moved to new locations.

Baresville Circuit—Hannibal German M.E.

The date for the beginning of the Hannibal church is unclear: one historical source says there was no regular preacher there until 1833 when Wilhelm Nast became the pastor. Then in 1871 the German Methodists erected a brick church on Main Street.[2] The *Geschichte* does not give a date for the first preaching but says the work there was begun in the "50th year" [1850s?][3]

Another history states that the German Methodists organized a congregation first, but that the first Methodist church was built by the English-speaking congregation about 1842. This church was called Mary's Chapel in honor of Jacob Bare's wife, donor of the land. It was a frame building on Main Street where both congregations worshiped for almost thirty years. In 1870/71 the Germans built their brick church a few blocks further up on Main. In 1954 the members of the former German M. E. church voted to build an educational wing and to remodel and update the sanctuary.[4]

The Hannibal UMC is still an active church and still at the same site on Main Street (527342 State Route 536, Hannibal, OH 43931)

The only surviving church of the old Baresville Circuit in eastern Ohio, Hannibal UMC.

Baresville Circuit—St. John's German M. E.

St. John's got its start before 1845, that being the year the first church building was erected. In 1870 a new building was built on the site at the junction of Township Road 438 and County Road 43 (Locust Stump Road).[5] About 1910 the church was renovated under the pastorate of Rev. Theodore Rudin with the inside and outside receiving a paint job.[6] On May 11, 1960, it was rededicated but closed about a dozen years later. The building is still standing and has a

The third church of the Baresville Circuit, St. John's, is no longer in use. The fourth, Buckhill Bottom, was torn down.

Bible on the altar dedicated in May 1932 by Miss Nina Haueter in memory of her parents, Mr. and Mrs. Felix Haueter. There is a cemetery adjacent to the church.[7] St. John's records are with the Hannibal-Sardis Charge of the United Methodist Church.[8]

Baresville Circuit—Mt. Vernon German M. E.

Mt. Vernon church was the last of the four churches on the Baresville (later, Hannibal) Charge to be built. Many of the members formerly belonged to the Buckhill Bottom Church but wanted a church in the Mt. Vernon community near the school. The contractor for the building was Charles Ingold but many of the members helped in the construction including the families of Christian Gehring, David Spring, Randolph Marty, Gottlieb Thonen, Lewis Singwald, Charles Brenzikofer, and Yaussey.[9] Mt. Vernon is now closed although the building is still standing. Two-day camp meetings were often held at the "park," a large oak grove adjacent to the church.[10] This area is still used for reunions and other gatherings.

Grandpa Rudin was pastor of the circuit from October 1904 until September 1910. I will devote a few pages to his memories of serving this four-point charge.

Mt. Vernon German Methodist, from the Baresville Circuit, is now closed.

Friday September 30, 1904

Arrived at Wheeling we had barely time to catch the train for Hannibal, so that getting something to eat was out of the question. In fact, the train was already in motion when we stepped on the cars. To make matters worse, the expressman had not brought our trunks to the Wheeling station, so that I was unable to check them to Hannibal. That made our cup of unpleasantness full. We arrived at Hannibal at about 5, having had nothing to eat since about nine in the morning. Miss Minnie M. met us as we were coming up from the landing and took us to the home of her brother, Captain M.

Saturday, October 1

We had a good supper last night and did full justice to it. I worried mostly about John yesterday, but he stood the trip well. He made friends with the M's at once. The captain has not much to say, especially to babies with whom he does not feel at home. His sister keeps house for him and is a very active member of our church.

Sunday, October 2

Today was my first Sunday in my new charge and I can say I am well pleased. Julius H. took me around in Bro. Bockstahler's buggy. It was a pretty rough and steep road that took us up the hill. I did the driving and managed to do it well. Preached to the St. John's congregation in the morning. There must have been from 150 to 175 people in my audience, including a large number of young people. I had rapt attention and my sermon seemed to be blessed of God. It is indeed a pleasure and an inspiration to preach to such an audience.

Monday October 3

Preached in English in the "Bottom" church yesterday. Had pretty much freedom despite my unpreparedness. Preached at Baresville in the evening to a good audience. Was pretty well tired out last night, but it was a pleasant kind of tiredness.

Thursday October 6

The people here are mostly Switzers or of Swiss descent and most talk Swiss as if they had but landed yesterday. The German spoken here is to a great extent Swiss and it quite amuses me to hear the people speak my mother tongue. There are many things that one has to dispense with here. There is one butcher shop which is open only part of the time. The bread you have to get in a private family and the goods you buy you have to carry home yourself. We miss some home conveniences here which we had at Sandusky: We have no bathroom, range and hot water boiler. But we have natural gas for lighting and heating which is a great boon. The people here are friendly and sociable without being intrusive.

Sunday October 9

Preached at Mt. Vernon this afternoon for the first time. It is quite a distance from St. John's. The people here have a pretty little church which was built a little over a year ago.

Wednesday October 12

Have ordered buggy from Bauer Bros. It will cost me $40, as I have ordered it wide track.

Thursday October 13

We are still at "fixing up." The horse worries me more or less. I don't mind the driving so much, but I do hate to harness him. My fingers are yet too tender for the hard leather and buckles. John likes papa's and mama's and baby's Prince, as he calls him. He is always ready to go to the stable to see him.

Monday February 26, 1906

L. M. congratulated me on my sermon last night and said it was the best one he had heard me preach yet. How differently people judge sermons. A sermon that appeals and is interesting to one may seem common place and uninteresting to another. Some people can grasp and understand what you mean while others cannot understand no matter how plain and simple your language may be. Some people think a loud sermon is a good sermon; others think "hollering" is a proof of its being poor. Some people want to be built up in the faith, some thrilled, some edified, some amused, some entertained, some taught and some "tickled." Is the sermon that caters to all the different tastes and desires the great sermon?

Tuesday May 22

The drive up to St. John's last evening was very enjoyable. The roads were in fine condition and there was a starlit sky. Another thing: The trustees up there did something which cannot be said of them often. It was decided to clean the cemetery and surroundings of the church and to build a closet. I am glad those trustees have at last waked up. The cemetery is in a shocking condition and has been so for years. The next thing in order is the renovation of the church.

Saturday July 15

Wrote up a Memorial of Buckhill Bottom church to be read tomorrow, and also prepared the program. Called on Minnie M. for a final talk on the celebration. The renovation cost $250 which has all been raised.

Sunday July 16

Fair weather today and a great day for Buckhill Bottom. The reopening program went off without a hitch. Rev. Wm. M. preached an impressive and appropriate sermon to a full house. The afternoon service was interesting. Bro. H. M. on "The Church in Community" and Prof. G. M. on "The Sunday School in the Community." I read an historical sketch of the church and Till recited "The Model Church." A collection for the Missions was taken amounting to $14.

Monday July 23

Called on the B's to get some information concerning the history of the Baresville church. Bro. B. told me that the church was built in 1871, the congregation having worshiped in the English M. E. church since the beginning of the German work in the early fifties. It took these people a long time to decide to build and they built because the English tried to get the advantage of them, Bro. B. told me.

Monday July 4, 1907

Had a good day for our Frauenverein social, though at times it looked like rain. Capt. M's grove is an ideal place for a small picnic. Bought John some harmless fireworks and put a new stick on his flag, and he celebrated this glorious Fourth all day. Rosmarie also had a good time. She is a cute little prattler. Prince broke his bit and bridle, a boy having set off a big firecracker near him and frightening him. I shall have to buy a new bridle now, which means an outlay of two or three dollars.

Tuesday December 3

Went to Mt. Vernon this afternoon and called on Jacob S. Had the privilege of preaching to seven persons this evening. Pig killing prevents some good people from coming to church at the present time. In summer some good people can't come to church because they have to make cheese. If it isn't cheese or pigs, it is either too cold and stormy or too sultry and hot. Serving the Lord and performing your churchly duties is regulated by personal inclination, not by love or a sense of duty.

Sunday August 8, 1909

F. H. is telling everybody that St. John's is taxed too high for preacher's salary and that Hannibal ought to pay more. It was the first thing he told Br. L. this morning, but Br. L. cut him short. Otto H. also told me the same thing after church, but I told him that he was mistaken.

Thursday August 12

Otto Haueter made the motion last night that the Jugenbund give $10 to the stewards for the salary of the preacher. As nobody seconded it, I did and it passed. The J. B. could and ought to give $20 but the young ones are like the old: all right as long as you do not touch them for money. St. John's still owes me over $100 on my salary. Looking over the books I find that St. John's pays much less salary per member than the rest of the charge. Mt. Vernon and Buckhill Bottom stand highest. I shall make a public statement at St. John's next Sunday.

Wednesday April 5, 1910

I made the beginning last night towards the renovation of St. John's church. I told the brethren we must begin with ourselves and set the good example and then said I would give $10. Having set the good example I asked Br. Haueter if he would give $25. He answered unhesitatingly that he would, and the rest followed. I was empowered to get the subscriptions of the people. May much success attend this enterprise!

Wednesday May 18

The Henrietta [near Lorain, Ohio] people have a nice church and I told our St. John's people about it on Sunday. Br. Bockstahler told me that he did the papering himself as there was no one else to do it. We will have a regular paper hanger and painter. Some people are in great fear and trembling today as tonight the earth is to pass through the tail of Halley's comet.

Wednesday May 25

There was to be a Bible class parade the other day in connection with the World's Sunday School Convention at Washington, from which the Negroes were to be barred. The English delegates objected to any such proceeding. It is a rather sad commentary on the Christianity of the leaders. They will invite an unbelieving President [Taft, who apparently didn't believe in the divinity of Christ] to address and open their convention, while they ostracize orthodox Christians because they are Negroes.

Tuesday July 6

Took Mr. Bare to St. John's to take measurements for an estimate. He said he would do the whole work for $197, painting the church inside and out and using the best material. The trustee meeting was a great success. I got all I asked for. The interior will be done entirely in paint, no paper being used. The altar platform will be enlarged and ornamented with an up-to-date railing.[11]

Clarington, Ohio, Circuit, aka Captina Circuit

The Clarington Circuit was formerly called Captina Circuit and included Baresville, Miltonsburg, and Switzerland Township in Monroe County. Bethel, one of the first German Methodist churches in the United States, was founded in "The Dark Hills of Monroe," as the rugged ridges and hills in Switzerland Township were called.[12] When each of the previously mentioned areas received their own pastors, the circuit was reduced to two churches—Bethel and Zion and became known as the Clarington Circuit.[13]

The town of Clarington was originally called Clarinda (named after Clarinda Pierson, daughter of one of the first settlers). Clarington is in Switzerland Township about thirty miles south of Wheeling, West Virginia, at the junction of Sunfish Creek and the Ohio River.

Clarington/Captina Circuit—Bethel German M. E. Church

The first preacher to the area was Reverend Daescher from Buckhill Bottom who came in 1835 and held services in the homes of the people. William Nast and John Zwahlen also often visited the area to share the gospel. In 1837 Brother Best came to minister to the people although still no church building had been erected. (The *Geschichte* states about Brother Best, "I suppose an American who had command of the German language.") "Father" Danker was the next pastor of the Bethel flock which, at this time, endured much persecution, the *Geschichte* claims.[14]

It was during Danker's pastorate that the first church or meeting house was built. Members of the church, Freudiger and Blattler donated land where a log church was erected. A parsonage soon followed during the tenure of Reverend Bahrenburg in 1845. In the early 1860s, when Rev. A. Graessle was pastor, the parsonage burned down resulting in great hardship for both pastor and congregation. Rev. J. Rise, who served from 1861 to 1862, led the efforts to rebuild the parsonage. By the mid sixties the old log church was in need of repairs, so a new one was built on the same site. In the 1880s a tower was added to the building and a bell installed. During Rev. C. W. Bockstaler's (other sources say C. W. Bockstahler) term of office, from 1896 to 1900, there was a thorough renovation of the church which cost $925. A few years later, Reverend Roesner oversaw the construction of a new parsonage and the sprucing up of the church.

More renovations in both Bethel and Zion were carried out during Reverend Plueddemann's term plus a basement added at Bethel and new lighting at both churches, during his successor, Reverend Kaetzel's pastorate. In 1917 Monroefield joined the circuit. In the 1930s, during Rev. John Herion's time, more updating and improvements were made at both Bethel and Zion, as well as at the parsonage.[15]

The Ladies Aid at Bethel organized during Reverend Wahl's pastorate, while the one at Zion began in 1917. A third Ladies Aid group, called Grandview Ladies' Aid, was founded in 1933. The churches began sponsoring camp meetings in 1916. When Reverend Heinlein took the reins in 1927, he established Epworth leagues at both Bethel and Zion.[16] In the early years of the twentieth century, the circuit claimed 169 members.[17] In 1935 the Bethel congregation celebrated one hundred years as a church.

Little information on Bethel from the years 1935 to the 1960s has survived. I could find nothing on when the church actually disbanded, but the building was sold in 1962 to Donald and Shirley Baldwin for forty-five hundred dollars.[18] By 2002 the church was no longer standing although there is a cemetery to indicate the location which is on the right side of State Route 556 about six miles from Clarington.[19]

Clarington/Captina Circuit—Zion German M. E. Church

The congregation of Zion organized some years after Bethel and first met in a thirty-by-forty-foot log building.[20] This structure used to stand across the road from the present frame church.[21] In 1887 members made plans for a new church building and raised money by donations, "frolics," and volunteer work. Jacob Ebert sold an acre of his land to the church trustees for seventy-five dollars to be used for the site of the new church. Much of the construction work was done by local workmen and members of the congregation, although Joseph Ward was the actual contractor. On the day of the cornerstone placement, services were held in the old log church and then the congregation went to the site of the new. The cornerstone which contained the names of the trustees, coins that were currently in circulation, a hymn book, and a Bible, was then put in place in the partially finished foundation.

The new Zion building was dedicated in the fall of 1888 with a service starting in the log church and culminating in the new one. The congregation carried the pews with them as they moved from the old church to the new. The new church was almost debt free on completion, lacking only a small amount which had not yet been received.

In the 1880s services were held in both German and English with the English pastor from Clarington preaching in the morning and the German pastor holding afternoon services. Joint revival meetings were held where each sang the hymns in his own language. These revivals were often held at the Bethel Church in Sailer's Grove. Then the Zion people would trek across the "hills and hollows" to the campground where they would stay all day for services.

Zion UMC, the only survivor of the Clarington Circuit, looks much the same as it did as Zion German ME Church.

Some improvements made to the church included a Delco lighting system which was installed prior to 1920. A furnace was first installed during the tenure of Reverend Worthman who, himself, made the concrete blocks and built the chimney. In 1935 a community hall was erected during the term of Rev. John Herion. The Epworth League played a large part in providing funds for the structure putting on socials and plays to raise money. One play was so popular they took it "on the road" to various nearby communities. The community hall served the area people until the 1950s when it was ravaged by fire. Redecorations of the actual church building took place in 1912, 1932, and 1953. In 1962 major work was done by the congregation when the ceiling was lowered, the interior redecorated, and a new heating system installed. The years 1971 and 1973 saw more improvements in the form of more interior work and a new roof. New carpeting was added and a fence surrounding the cemetery and church installed in 1980. A campaign for new siding for the church was started in 1983.

Several groups associated with the church were formed, including a Ladies Aid in 1917 and an Epworth league during the Reverend Heinlein's pastorate (1927–30). The men's group was a comparative latecomer being organized by Reverend Lehman in 1963.[22]

Since early times, Zion and Bethel had been on the same circuit and the Bethel history notes that after 1917 the Monroefield church was added.[23] The conference records don't seem to support this statement as the Monroefield church is listed as a separate charge, although Reverend Worthman is listed as pastor of all three churches in 1922, 1925, and 1926. Other years, the pastor is listed as "to be supplied" until 1927 when Monroefield is no longer listed on its own.[24] When the Central German Conference disbanded in 1933, the Clarington Circuit joined the Cambridge-Barnesville District of the Northeast Ohio Conference.[25] More changes took place in 1971 and Zion became a part of a new circuit which included Sardis, Hannibal, Clarington, St. John's, and Valley. St. John's and Valley closed not too long after this. In the 1980s, attendance at church services averaged twenty-five to thirty. There were three Sunday school classes: a primary class, junior and senior high, and adult classes.[26] The former German church celebrated its one hundredth year in August 1988. The Rev. Donald Shank conducted special services and many of the previous ministers joined the celebration. Music was provided by the Riverfront Choir.

You can still find Zion Church and cemetery on County Road 64 and Eberts Lane, Cain Ridge, Salem Township.[27] We traveled to the area in the fall of 2009 and found Zion in a very picturesque setting on a gravel road. It is in the Southern Hills District and the address is 48806 Cain Ridge Road.[28]

Clarington/Captina Circuit—Monroefield German M.E.

The Monroefield church originally was part of the Monroefield Circuit which also included churches at Bonn, Leith Run (also known as Lees Run), and Trail Run. It became part of the Clarington Circuit in 1927.

Not much of its history has survived to the present but what little is known and what I can glean from church records will be noted under the Monroefield Circuit following this section.

In the early twentieth century Grandpa Rudin pastored at Hannibal, Ohio, a few miles down river from Clarington. In 1907 he visited the circuit to hold the quarterly conference in January at Bethel Church. Following are his comments and experiences there.

> Friday January 25
>
> Left for Switzer [Switzerland Township] early this morning. Roesner did not get to Clarington until after eleven and we did not start for Switzer until after twelve. When R. and I left for his home it began to snow and it continued all afternoon and evening. Bro. Roesner's "Dolly" is anything but good looking, but she makes good time, better than Prince is inclined to make unless I urge him. We arrived at the parsonage between two and three and Mrs. R. soon had a good dinner ready for us. The new parsonage is a great improvement.
>
> Saturday January 26
>
> A heavy snow fell last night and today there is sleighing. It is also very cold. Roesners have not the convenience of natural gas, so Bro. R. has to waste much time on account of the fires. Their water is also outside of the home. Altogether, we are much more conveniently settled at Hanni-

bal. Preached to a fairly good congregation this afternoon and presided over the Quarterly Conference.

Sunday January 27

Zero weather this morning. Was glad I did not have to make the trip to St. John's and Mt. Vernon. Preached to a pretty good house. My text was from Rev. 1:8. Bro. and Sister Roesner told me that they greatly enjoyed my sermon. This afternoon we had a good lovefeast though the attendance was rather small. There was no service tonight on account of the weather.

Monday January 28

It was quite a trip across the river, there being much ice. My train was nearly an hour overdue and I arrived at New Martinsville at about two o'clock. Then again a battle with the ice in the river and a tramp in the snow from Texas to the parsonage. Enjoyed my visit with Roesners. Mrs. R., I think, will make a good preacher's wife. She is friendly, gifted and unassuming. As a preacher's daughter, she must know something of the joys and cares of a preacher's wife.[29]

Monroefield, Ohio, Circuit

The Monroefield Circuit was founded as the Malaga and Matamoras Mission in 1845 when it was served by John H. Koch.[30] This was one of the most rugged circuits in southeastern Ohio covering Bonn in Washington County about ten miles north of Marietta, to Trail Run and Lees Run (see later comments on this name) about twenty to twenty-five miles due east of Bonn and then northwest about twenty-five more miles to Monroefield, Miltonsburg, and Malaga. My grandfather who once did a quarterly conference there, referred to it as one of the most difficult circuits in the conference.

Monroefield Circuit—Monroefield German M.E.

There is not much information on the church itself. As noted previously, it became part of the Clarington Circuit about 1927. A log church was built when Reverend Koch was pastor, in the 1840s. In the 1880s a frame church was constructed and completed during the administration of Rev. B. C. Fischbach in 1889. The *Geschichte* notes that "it stands on a high hill with a magnificent view."[31]

At the time of the dissolution of the Central German Conference, the Monroefield church was still active and part of the Clarington Circuit. Information on its later state is gleaned mostly from letters discussing the sale of the church property. In a letter dated July 1960, the writer mentions the church having been vacant for twenty-five to thirty years. Also, with this letter was a copy of an advertisement stating that the trustees of the Monroefield Methodist Church were accepting sealed bids for the building.[32] Unfortunately the date of the notice was not legible.

When I was researching the history of the Monroefield church, I was put in touch with Mrs. Cleo Carpenter who wrote an interesting and informative letter to me describing the fate of the church building. She and her family had been members there when the church was still active and many of her ancestors are buried in the adjoining cemetery. She wrote that the building had been sold to her brother, Lee Christman, in 1961. He dismantled the church and used the stone foundation to build a retaining wall on his property and removed the bell which he displayed on his lawn. Mrs. Carpenter mentioned that the congregation paid five hundred dollars for the bell when it was purchased about 1895. She commented that the cemetery was owned by a man from northern Ohio who takes good care of it, keeping it mowed, the flags flying and having installed benches for visitors to use.[33]

Monroefield Circuit—Lees Run German M.E.

When researching this church, I could find no place named Lees Run on any map of the area. Both the *Geschichte* and my grandfather always called it Lees Run but apparently this was either a mistake or the name was misunderstood or changed to "Leith Run." The *Geschichte* gives the following information: "Elizabeth Rollman, a widow who felt the call to serve God, started the congregation and hosted services in her home. In 1857, the group built a log church which was later covered with clapboard and "thus it still stands in the valley around which thick woods encircle it."[34]

The next information came from the Cambridge district superintendent concerning a visit he made in June 1958 to the Leith Run Methodist Church. He stated in a written description that the church stood in a wooded area surrounded by a cemetery. Both were in a deplorable condition. He noted that they are located in Grandview Township in Washington County and are "just off a county road back in the hills, north, northwest of New Matamoras."[35]

The above information states that the Leith Run church was in Grandview Township. This rang a bell and in looking over the Bethel Church history (Clarington Circuit), I note that the Grandview Ladies Aid was organized by the Rev. John Herion in 1933. This seems to point to the fact that the Leith Run church, as well as the Monroefield Church, was put on the Clarington Circuit.[36] The person who filled out the Zion Local Church History Survey in 1982 noted that Grandview (closed at that time) had once been on the same circuit as Zion, so this seems to confirm a connection between the Leith Run church and the Clarington Circuit.[37]

Monroefield Circuit—Trail Run German M.E.

The Trail Run church is often referred to as the "Frobisch Church" since it was built by a settler in the area, John George Froebisch. When Mr. Froebisch moved to this area he felt the need of a church and in 1856 built a log structure which was later covered with clapboard.[38] The church bore the inscription *Die Klein Kappelle im Tal* (The little chapel in the dale).

Not much of its history survives, but there is one interesting story told that the German Methodist pastor during World War I, Reverend Wenckebach, was a German spy. This had an unfavorable affect on the church and it consequently closed about 1918.[39] This was apparently the straw that broke the camel's back, as all the Monroefield Circuit churches were having problems at this time.

The site of the church is on Joe Frobisch Road (County Road 11) about three miles from State Route 800. We tried to find it in 2005 but my husband balked when the road turned into not much more than a cow path. The building is approximately thirty-four-by-thirty-four feet with a stone foundation and metal roof.[40] A cemetery sits on the hill behind the church.

The most recent news of the church that I could find is a copy of a letter from the Board of Trustees of the East Ohio Conference expressing plans to transfer the property to the Little Dutch Church Association.[41]

Monroefield Circuit—Bonn German M E.

The Bonn church was established at the same time as the church in Marietta when the congregation built the first meeting house in 1840. In 1869 they purchased an already existing church building and moved it to the site of the first church.[42]

Another source states that the first church was replaced by a newer one in 1871. A parsonage had been built in 1852 and that, too, was replaced with a new one in the 1870s.[43]

Even when the *Geschichte* was written, the Bonn church was struggling. The entry comments that the congregation was successful for many years but at the present was suffering due to the "home-going" of the older brothers and sisters and the moving away of the younger members. However, the entry states, that the remaining members hold firm and refuse to separate from their beloved church.[44]

A history of the Marietta German M E. church gives a little more information on the one at Bonn which was also known as Duck Creek. When Rev. Henry Koeneke was appointed to Marietta in 1840, he was able to win twelve more members to the Bonn church. He also was responsible for the first church building at Bonn. Later, the history states that in 1912 Bonn was taken from the Marietta Circuit and joined with Monroefield. This, however, does not agree with the *Geschichte* which puts it on the Monroefield Circuit at least as early as 1905.[45]

Grandpa Rudin officiated at a quarterly conference at the Leith Run church when he was pastor at Baresville. The following are his comments:

Saturday April 7, 1906

Yesterday took an early train to Matamoras. Bro. Fred Lantz took me and Bro. Herzer to his home. Preached to a fairly good crowd last night. The congregation at Lees Run [sic] is a rather peculiar one, being composed of Methodists, Presbyterians, Christian Unions, United Brethren, Baptists, Germans and Americans. The membership consists of only four families, who have to bear the financial burden, while the others simply come because there is church and get out of paying by saying that they are not members.

Sunday April 8

Went to Sunday School, a Baptist, Bro. Adamson, is the superintendent. Preached to a crowded house and the Lord helped me wonderfully. The sermon seemed to produce a deep impression: I had rapt attention and a number were in tears, while Bro. Herzer once broke out into an exclamation of praise. I was surprised at myself.

Monday April 9

I am glad Bro. Herzer thinks well of my preaching, as he is a competent critic. He is a man of education and an active experience of fifty years, enjoying also a great reputation as a scientist. He seems to bear up well, though Monroefield Circuit is one of the hardest in the Conference. He is simply supply, however, so he takes it rather easy.[46]

Marietta, Ohio—Marietta German M E.

The Marietta German M. E. church was organized in 1839 by Carl Best of the Monroe Mission. Twelve families composed the charter membership. Other Germans who came to the region from northern Germany remained loyal to the Lutheran Church of their homeland. George Danker became the leader of this Lutheran group and preached both to them and, once in a while, to the Methodists. The Lutheran congregation were opposed to him preaching to the Methodists which caused a split. Danker then joined the German Methodists, bringing forty-two former Lutherans with him. The presiding elder bestowed on him a local preacher's license and he became assistant to Carl Best. In 1840 Danker was sent to Captina (Clarington) and Henry Koeneke became the Marietta pastor. He added forty-seven new members to the Marietta church and twelve to Duck Creek (see Bonn).

The group first held services in the Helwig home at the corner of Second and Scammel streets (400 Second Street) A former English Methodist Church (situated at 411 and 413 Second Street) became available and the German M. E. trustees purchased the building for eight hundred dollars.[47] The congregation moved into their new church in July 1841 and continued to meet there until

Trinity German ME in Marietta, Ohio, now is used by the Evangelical Lutherans. The German Methodists merged with Christ Methodist across the street from their originial church.

1877.[48] The next few years were rocky ones for the Marietta congregation as dissension caused a loss in membership. By 1843 things had turned around and new converts joined the church at Marietta and the circuit at large. In fact the circuit grew to include Chester in Meigs County and other preaching places.[49]

Growing pains increased until, in 1876, the congregation felt the need for a larger church building. They purchased property at the corner of Third and Wooster streets from the estate of William Ward. The site cost the trustees fifteen hundred dollars and work on a building began immediately. The dedication was held during the pastorate of Rev. J. W. Fischbach and total cost amounted to seventy-four hundred dollars[50] or seventy-three hundred,[51] depending on which source is correct. On dedication day the amount still owed was two thousand dollars but thirteen hundred was raised that day. A church bell weighing approximately eighteen hundred pounds was donated by Martin Seemann and P. C. Fischer. The ministers of the conference donated money for purchasing a communion service. In 1880 a new parsonage was also built for the sum of fifteen hundred dollars. In 1906 continued growth required the building of a Sunday school room which was joined to the main church building with a hall. Other upgrades in the basement area were also made and the total cost was ten thousand dollars.[52]

When Rev. John Oetgen became pastor in 1905, he introduced an English language service on Sunday evening. Also, during his tenure, the Marietta Circuit (which included Bonn aka Duck Creek and Hill Grove) was disbanded. Bonn joined the Monroefield Circuit and Hill Grove had closed some years earlier. A seventy-fifth anniversary celebration was held in 1914, a year after the disastrous 1913 flood. At that time many church records had been lost, but Reverend Oetgen was able to preserve some of the historical material. In 1918 there was a move to change the name of the church from the German Methodist Episcopal Church to the Trinity Methodist Church. Votes were cast at the Wednesday evening prayer meeting on February 27, 1918, and forty-two of the fifty-two attendees approved the name change.[53]

The Sunday school was created soon after the church itself became a reality. Originally, the classes met on Sunday afternoons, but in 1884 they switched to Sunday mornings. In 1939 the Sunday school claimed 233 participants. There is no clear date of the beginning of the church choir, but it seems to have originated back in the 1870s. A junior choir was later organized about 1930.

The Ladies Aid Society began as the *Nea Verein* (sewing circle). This group met in the members' homes to sew and socialize and charged a ten cent monthly fee. The group was responsible for earning most of the money for the church building site. A later organization of younger women was called the *Damen Verein* which was then changed to Ladies Aid sometime during the war years. The Ladies Aid was broken down into smaller units among which were the Gleaner's Division, Friendly Division, Happy Hustlers' Division, and Loyal Workers' Division. In the 1890s the Woman's Foreign Missionary Society organized at the encouragement of Mrs. George H. Jones, wife of a missionary to Korea. Miss Anna L. Bowers spearheaded the founding of a Woman's Home Missionary Society in 1926. These two groups combined in 1936 and took the name of Woman's Missionary Auxiliary of the Trinity Methodist Episcopal Church.

The young people of the church formed the "Yugend [*sic*] Bund" in the 1880s. This society held meetings Sunday evenings before the church service as well as social activities. Later, this group became the Epworth League. In 1929 Reverend Dickhaut encouraged the the formation of a brotherhood of the men which held ten meetings a year each with a program and a social hour. The group supervised the Boy Scout troop and also was involved in other church activities. The Boy Scout troop formed in the 1920s under Reverend Schruff's pastorate.[54]

In 1969 Trinity Methodist united with First Methodist and the new church took the name of Christ United Methodist Church.[55] The old German Methodist building found new life as another church of German heritage—the Crown of Life Evangelical Lutheran Church at 300 Wooster Street. Christ United Methodist is directly across the street at 301 Wooster Street.

In 1907 Grandpa Rudin visited Marietta for a district conference. His diary describes his experiences there and his opinion of the town of Marietta.

Tuesday May 6, 1907

Bro. Bockstahler and I went to Marietta this evening. It was quite dark when we arrived and we had a long walk to the church. At the church I met Bro. Otto, my host. Bro. Baechtold preached the sermon on "Am I my Brother's Keeper?"

Wednesday May 7

A reception was tendered the ministers last evening after the service, ice cream and cake was served. The District meeting was opened this morning with Bro. Kern presiding and Bro. Bockstahler acting as secretary. After some business the first paper was read by Bro. Jend on "The Attitude of the Preacher toward False Doctrines and False Teachers in his Congregation." Bro. J. told us a great deal about false teachers but very little about how to meet them. Bro. Harrer read the next paper: "The Importance of the Enlightened Conscience In the Church and World." In my opinion Bro. H. understood his subject. Bro. Weiler's topic was "The Expiatory Death of Christ." It was handled in a masterful manner.

Thursday May 9

Bro. Roesner spoke on "Evangelism of the Local Church in Sunday School, Epworth League and Congregation" and Bro. Schruff on "Evangelism of the Local Church among the Unsaved and Unchurched." Bro. R. did remarkably well; Bro. S. was rather theatrical and spoilt it. The title of Bro. Boch's paper was, "In How Far do the Signs of the Times Assure us the Certainty of Victory?" It was declared by all an able paper. This morning Prof. Schneider gave us a lecture on Unitarianism. It seems to be impossible to give a reasonable orthodox explanation of the Holy Trinity. I do not think God will hold us accountable for not comprehending it.

Friday May 10

The District Meeting came to a close last night. Prof. Schneider gave us a lecture on Christian service. It was helpful and earnest. Bro. Beal and I got to bed late last night. Mrs. Otto, who is a daughter of Bro. Andre, seems to have been quite a singer in her younger days. She sang for us last night and Beal and I also sang. Bro. Otto is much more reticent than his wife. He is a member of Otto Bros., the largest dry goods firm in

Marietta. They are also wholesalers. Bro. O. took us through their building yesterday morning and I found it a very interesting trip. Had to get up at three this morning to make the early train for home. I had a very long walk to the station and arrived within five minutes of train time.

Wednesday May 15

By the way, Marietta is a fine and interesting town. It has many points and buildings of historic interest. In the Mound Cemetery are the graves of many revolutionary heroes, besides the great mound which gives it its name. The mound has never been opened. Stood on the Campus Martius where the first settlers of Marietta camped to protect themselves against the Indians. Also saw the oldest house in Ohio and another one of the time of the Indians.[56]

Notes

1. Golder, Horst, and Schaal, *Geschichte*, 414–15.
2. Monroe County Historical Society, *Nine Communities of Monroe County*, (Woodsfield, Ohio: 1984), 73.
3. Golder, Horst, and Schaal, *Geschichte*, 415.
4. Theresa and Stanley Maienknecht, *Monroe County, Ohio: A History* (Mt. Vernon, Ind.: Windmill Publications, Inc., 1989), 1990, 315.
5. Monroe County Chapter of the Ohio Genealogical Society, *Monroe County, Ohio Families* (Dallas, Tex.: Taylor Publishing Co., 1992), 24.
6. Rudin, Diaries, 1910.
7. Maienknecht, *Monroe County, Ohio*, 323.
8. Monroe County OGS, *Monroe County, Ohio Families*, 24.
9. Ibid., 23.
10. Maienknecht, *Monroe County, Ohio*, 323.
11. Rudin, Diaries, 1904, 1906, 1907, 1909, 1910.
12. *One Hundredth Anniversary,* Bethel Methodist church history (Clarington, Ohio: 1935), 4.
13. Golder, Horst, and Schaal, *Geschichte*, 419.
14. Ibid.
15. *One Hundredth Anniversary*, 5–6.
16. Ibid., 6–7.
17. Golder, Horst, and Schaal, *Geschichte*, 420.
18. Bill of sale no. 16,185 Switzerland Township, (photo copy of) Monroe County, Ohio, July 11, 1962.
19. Shirley Neiswonger, e-mail to author, 15 August 2002.
20. Anonymous, *History of Zion Church*, church history (Clarington, Ohio, June 27, 1984), 1.
21. "Local Church History Survey," (Zion UMC, Clarington, Ohio)The Archives and History Commission,1982, #10, United Methodist Archives, Ohio Wesleyan University, Delaware.
22. Anonymous,*History of Zion Church*, 1–5.
23. *One Hundredth Anniversary*, 6.
24. *Minutes of the Annual Conferences*, 1917, p. 494; 1927, p. 587.
25. Anonymous, *History of Zion Church*, 3.
26. Ibid., 5.
27. Monroe County OGS, 32
28. UMC.org Regional Offices, Find-A-Church at http://archives.umc.org/Directory/Church.Details, October 2009.
29. Rudin, Diaries, 1907.
30. Golder, Horst, and Schaal, *Geschichte*, 431
31. Ibid.
32. Franklin S. Neuhardt to Rev. Richard Drake, July, 1960.
33. Cleo Carpenter to author, September 2002.
34. Golder, Horst, and Schaal, *Geschichte*, 431–32.
35. Thurman F. Alexander, (superintendent, Cambridge District of the Methodist Church) description of Leith Run Methodist Church, June 11, 1958.
36. *One Hundredth Anniversary*, 7.

37. The Archives and History Commission, Local Church History Survey, 1982, #25, United Methodist Archives, Ohio Wesleyan University, Delaware, Ohio.

38. Golder, Horst, and Schaal, *Geschichte*, 432.

39. Monroe County OGS, 20.

40. Abandoned Church Listing, Frobisch Church, January 1971, Ohio United Methodist Archives, Ohio Wesleyan University, Delaware, Ohio.

41. Richard Buzza (letter concerning disposition of Frobish Methodist Church, June, 1995) to attorney Rex W. Miller, copy to Jean Ritchie who sent me a copy.

42. Golder, Horst, and Schaal, *Geschichte*, 432.

43. *Williams History of Washington County, Ohio* (Cleveland, Ohio: H. Z. Williams & Bro. Publishers, 1881), 588.

44. Golder, Horst, and Schaal, *Geschichte*, 433.

45. Bernice Graham, *Early Methodism in the Northwest Territory* (N.Y.: Carlton Press Corp., A Hearthstone Book, 1996), 86, 90–91.

46. Rudin, Diaries, 1906.

47. Graham, *Early Methodism*, 84–86.

48. Golder, Horst, and Schaal, *Geschichte*, 428.

49. Graham, *Early Methodism*, 86–87.

50. Golder, Horst, and Schaal, *Geschichte*, 428.

51. Graham, *Early Methodism*, 88.

52. Golder, Horst, and Schaal, *Geschichte*, 428.

53. Graham, *Early Methodism*, 89–91.

54. Ibid., 95–99.

55. Christ United Methodist Church anniversary plate, Marietta, Ohio, 1974.

56. Rudin, Diaries, 1907.

CHAPTER 22

Churches East of Ohio

Pittsburgh, Pennsylvania

William Nast brought German Methodist preaching to Pittsburgh in 1838 when he arrived there at the request of some English Methodists. He preached frequently to his fellow Germans and also handed out copies of the church discipline and other religious literature. Two Sunday school classes containing thirty-five members were formed as the result of a revival and by the end of the year this had grown to one hundred converts. There was so much opposition to the German congregation that, at times, the police had to be called out to quell the disruptions.

Pittsburgh—First Church

Soon a Dr. Doering was sent to minister to the people and he procured a chapel on Smithfield Street. The group flourished and soon erected a two-story brick church on Strawberry Alley. This location did not prove to be propitious as "people would not go to a church in an alley."[1] Another source pinpoints the location of the church as "on Strawberry Alley behind Seventh St." The next move was to Ross Street on the South Side and after that to the Allentown District.[2]

All sources I have found are a bit hazy on events from the founding until the 1880s. In 1884 pastor John R. Bodmer, guided the building of a church and parsonage on Sixteenth Street near Carson Street. Through great sacrifices by the congregation, the church, which featured stained glass windows and a pipe organ, was soon debt free. At that time the congregation numbered 150 members with a Sunday school of 90 attendees.[3]

The Warner history gives a few more details on the years when the church was located on Ross Street. Evidently, this was not a smart move as the area was predominantly Irish Catholic. The relocation was in 1870 when the congregation acquired a building formerly used by the English Methodists. When this change did not work out, the congregation united with a South Side church from Bingham Street. The merged congregation used the proceeds from the sale of both church properties to help fund the building of the Sixteenth Street church.[4] It was around this time that the church took the name of First Church.[5]

I could not find much history on the church up to the present, but the building is still standing. When we visited Pittsburgh in the early twenty-first century, it appeared to be undergoing a renovation. According to a newspaper article, Philip Pelusi, owner of a chain of hair salons, restored First Church and now lives in the building.[6]

Pittsburgh—Second Church

In the 1860s many members of First Church moved into the Lawrenceville area, a suburb of Pittsburgh to the northeast of the city center. Rev. Ehrhard Wunderlich started a congregation there in 1867 which purchased a wood church from an English congregation for thirty-five hundred dollars. The church stood on Fortieth Street near Butler Street across from the arsenal of the federal government.[7] A current map of Pittsburgh shows a park on Fortieth called Arsenal Park. Another source states that the congregation was organized in 1868 and purchased the English church then.[8] Until 1869 the church was on a circuit with First Church and the same pastor served both. At that time there were fifty members. By the year 1869 the church became self-supporting and Rev. John Ficken served as its first pastor. The congregation then built its own parsonage in 1883 for the sum of three thousand dollars. Pastor Richard Plueddemann oversaw the construction of a new church which was completed under his successor, F. F. Bauman. The church was consecrated on October 29, 1899, and cost nine thousand dollars. Even as the new church was taking shape, however, the German neighborhood was changing with the migration continuing toward the eastern reaches of the city.[9] Currently, the former Lawrenceville German M. E. church building is the Refuge Church of God in Christ at 167 Fortieth Street.[10]

Pittsburgh—Park Avenue Mission

Second Church started a mission church in the East Liberty area of Pittsburgh in 1885 when its pastor, Rev. Christian Golder, went there to preach on Easter Sunday. He first preached in Hall & Nelson's hall[11] at the corner of Penn and Collins Avenue. That same year Rev. P. F. Magly continued the preaching in a rented store at the corner of Park Avenue and Polk Alley.[12] Reverend Magly received so much support from the English church pastored by Rev. A. L. Petty[13] that the German congregation was able to purchase a building site on the corner of Carver Street and Park Avenue. A frame church was soon erected there measuring fifty feet long by thirty feet wide. The lot cost fifteen hundred dollars and the building with furnishings came to thirty-nine hundred. The new church was consecrated by Bishop J. J. Hurst on July 19, 1886. Twenty members from the mother church (Second Church) joined the mission and helped swell its ranks.

By 1890 the new church was stable enough to become independent and separate from Second Church. The church had an active *Frauenverein*, founded in 1888, and by 1890 there were fifty-six full members and two probationary ones on the church membership roll. Mr. Ch. L. Flaccus presented the church with a bell in 1891. The Frauenverein helped finance a parsonage, completed in 1895 for $1,975, by purchasing shares in a building society. In 1899 the church underwent a makeover which cost $860. At the time the *Geschichte* was published, membership stood at about seventy-two.[14]

Pittsburgh—Allegheny German M. E.

In the 1840s Allegheny City (located north of the Allegheny River not far from where it joins the Monongehela to form the Ohio) was a separate municipality but has since been swallowed up by Pittsburgh. Warner's history reports that the German work began there in the 1840s and Rev. J. Smith was sent to serve the rapidly growing congregation.[15]

The *Geschichte* is less specific saying that the beginnings of the church are shadowy, at best. According to that source, a William Engel and Emil Baur (Emil Baur later founded a German Methodist utopian society near the town of Pigeon, Michigan. See entry on Ora Labora) probably served in the early 1850s although they are not mentioned in the record books. Baptism records showed that from 1853 to 1855 C. Wyttenbach officiated and the presiding elder was John A. Klein. The records seem to have had insertions and deletions executed by Hermann zur Jacobsmuehler. At this time, the church had about fifty-four members who were meeting in a small church, "probably rented," on Chestnut Street.

In 1856 Karl Bozenhard came to serve the congregation and accomplished much in the year he was there, including the building of a church which was still being used in the early twentieth century.[16] This church stood at the corner of Ohio Street and Union Avenue and its congregation was reported to have been one of the most influential in the conference. In the 1870s the wealth and membership of the Ohio Street church suffered a setback due to the panic of 1873.[17] The *Geschichte* confirms this and also states there was another crisis when some of the members fell under the influence of "Russelism."

At the time of the writing of the *Geschichte* more than 900 people had been members of the Allegheny church with the average for the last forty years being 186. At the present year [about 1907] the membership was 200. Also, at that time the congregation had 5 members who had been affiliated for fifty years.[18]

Pittsburgh—McKeesport German M. E.

The McKeesport church was one of the youngest in the conference at the time the *Geschichte* was published. In 1886 Hartmann Bau came from Baldwin-Wallace College in Berea, Ohio, to start a mission at McKeesport. He was followed by D. A. Stoll in 1887. The fledgling group purchased the old Second Methodist Church on Fifth Street for their home but it was quickly sold and a church built on Hazel Street. Later, another church building was erected on Bridge Street. A weekly German service was also held in Duquesne.[19]

Pittsburgh—Birmingham (or Bingham) Mission

There was another German Methodist congregation that was started on the South Side in the 1840s. Its first church was "upon the hill" and after about ten years, the group bought the English church on Bingham Street near Thirteenth.[20] This seems to be the same church mentioned in the *Geschichte* which was started by First Church in 1849 and called the Birmingham Mission. It was on Manor Street between Eleventh and Twelfth streets. This property was sold and a church with a parsonage and schoolhouse was bought on Birmingham near Thirteenth Street in 1855. This church suffered a decline in membership and once again was served from First Church in 1876. It rejoined First Church in 1882 and soon after, in 1884, the merged church built a new home on Sixteenth near Carson.[21]

I think it is probably safe to say that Bingham and Birmingham are the same church. I was able to find a Bingham Street on a current Pittsburgh map but no Birmingham.

Pittsburgh—Muhleman Memorial German M.E.

This was a fairly latecomer to the fold of Pittsburgh German Methodist churches. In 1914 Rev. Dietrich Worthman and some Baldwin-Wallace students started a Sunday school in Braddock for some German-speaking Methodists. They met in the Brinton Avenue Presbyterian Church but quickly outgrew these accommodations. The group was able to purchase a building site and then Miss Minnie Muhlemann promised to finance the construction of a church in memory of her brother, Capt. Charles Muhlemann.* It was an independent church until the 1980s but since then has been on a circuit with Braddock Fourth Street The church is located at the corner of Grandview Avenue and Willow Street in Braddock. In 2002 the membership numbered ninety.[22]

In 1902 the annual conference of the Central German Conference was held

---

*. During the time my grandfather served on the Baresville Circuit (1904 to 1910), he got to know Miss Minnie and the Captain quite well as they were living in Hannibal at the time. During that period his diaries are full of references to both of them. He considered Minnie a pillar of womanhood as she was a staunch supporter of the church both in actions and finances.

*The last German Methodist church founded in Pittsburgh is
Muhlmann Memorial UMC, organized in 1914.*

in Pittsburgh which my grandfather attended as a neophyte minister. He was pastor at Sandusky, Ohio, and not having an easy time of it.

Tuesday September 10, 1902

Took the noon train of the Pittsburgh and Lake Erie RR for Pittsburgh, the seat of the Central German Conference. Was very glad that I met no one on the train as it gave me a chance to brush up on my studies. By tomorrow the agony will be over. Then I can enjoy life again. Got to Pittsburgh between 5 and 6, a stranger in a strange town. Boarded a Carson St. car intending to call on Bro. Mueller, but was fortunate enough to meet someone who knew Mr. Bayer, who directed me so that I found my "hotel" without any trouble.

Wednesday September 10

Bayers live in a fine house. Mr. B. is a retired butcher but is at present running his brother's establishment, as he is sick. Started for the seat of the Inquisition at about half past eight, determined not to be worried. By two o'clock I was through with my examinations and they did not seem as hard as I expected. Schruff gave me only eighty on my sermon. He said I wasn't methodistic enough. Well, I have my ideas about that.

Thursday September 11

The Conference began this morning with the Lord's Supper. Bishop Fitzgerald is evidently a hustler. He did not give us a long opening speech, but got right down to business. I have been put on that Reiskosten Comite again—just my luck.

Friday September 12

Lamy, Magdanz and I were taken into full connection this morning. At last, in my fortieth year, I have reached the goal. The Bishop gave us a splendid talk. Our committee worked all afternoon, so there was no chance for any of us to go and see the sights.

Saturday September 13

We got home quite late last night, having had to wait at the barber's. Sousa gives concerts at the Exposition afternoons and evenings. He remembered the German ministers by rendering "Die Wacht am Rhein." Had dinner with Bayers. In the afternoon Beyer and I went to Smithfield English M. E. Church, where the ordination of deacons and elders took place.

Monday September 15

Conference adjourned today and I have been sent back to Sandusky. Very few changes were made. I shall work this year as if I expected it to be my best. Bro. Rogatzky told me that the Conference trustees have given Sandusky $125. That takes a deal of worry off my mind.

Tuesday September 16

Till does not mind it much that we have to stay in Sandusky for another year. I would not care to live in Pittsburgh, by the way. It may be nice on the hills, but below it is a regular inferno. It's up and down and around curves all the time. You are jerked and bumped on the cars that it is enough to make one sick. Pittsburgh is a hustling town alright. I have not seen as many people on the streets anywhere since I left New York.[23]

Wheeling, West Virginia—German M. E. Church

The Wheeling German Methodist congregation was one of the earliest formed in this country. In 1835 there was a German Wesleyan group already organized, however, their pastor moved to Pittsburgh and the members united with Fourth Street Methodist.[24] By 1838 Dr. Nast had sent John Zwahlen to Wheeling and, on Christmas Day 1838, Zwahlen held three services there for interested Germans. He held two weeks of meetings after that resulting in ten converts and, not long after, a congregation of twenty-four members was formed. During the next year, membership increased to seventy and a subscription of one thousand dollars had been raised toward the building of a church. William Chapline sold a lot on Chapline Street to the congregation for four hundred dollars and a brick

The former Fidelity building in Wheeling, West Virginia, became home to the Fourth Street Methodist in 1950. A year later Central Methodist (the former German ME) joined the fold.

church, measuring forty-by-forty feet, was constructed on the site. The building cost two thousand dollars and was one and a half stories high with the top floor housing an apartment. On March 22, 1840, Dr. William Nast dedicated the church.[25] During these early years, the pastor received a salary of one hundred dollars a year and the janitor one dollar per month for his custodial duties.[26]

The congregation built a parsonage behind the church in 1846. The first church building was torn down in 1860 as it had become too small for the burgeoning congregation and was replaced by a two-story building. The new brick building measured sixty-four-by-forty feet. In 1871 a new parsonage was purchased a few blocks from the church. More construction and improvements to the church followed with an addition to the back of the church built in 1897. At the same time, a porch with entry room and new stairs were added. In 1903 semicircular benches and a new pipe organ were installed. Another addition and modern furnishings were included in the renovation of 1904.

By 1907 the church could claim 264 full members, 19 probationary ones, and a flourishing Sunday school. Other organizations included the *Jugenbund*, Junior Epworth League, and a *Frauenverein* of close to 100 members. For a while the church had two small satellite churches—one in South Wheeling, which built a small chapel, and another, a mission which closed after a few years.[27] Worship was conducted in the German language until 1918 when the switch was made to English. There was also, at this time, a name change and the official name became Central Methodist.[28]

In 1951 Central church's mother church, Fourth Street Methodist, had moved into a new facility (the former Fidelity Building). This new building afforded much more room and up-to-date facilities making the time ripe for Central to return to its mother. On June 17, 1951, Central returned to the fold at the first service of the united church.[29] The old Central Methodist has been torn down, but the Fourth Street Methodist is a prominent building in downtown Wheeling. There is a photograph and history of Fourth Street Methodist on the following website www.wheeling.weirton.lib.wv.us/landmark/churches/FourthStreetMethodist2 or google Ohio County Public Library and put Fourth Street Methodist Church in the search box.

W. H. Schulz, a member of Central Church, wrote the following hymn on the occasion of Central's centennial in 1938:

> Twas on Sunday, day fore Christmas,
> Eighteen hundred thirty-eight,
> When a circle of God's children
> Met his blessing to await.
> German Methodists, devoted,
> Zealous and with love aglow,
> Founded here a congregation
> Just one hundred years ago.
> Came John Zwahlen, the exhorter,
> Preaching Christ and His great love;
> Converts to the group were added,
> Striving for the home above.
> With much sacrifice and labor,
> In accord and of one mind,
> A church building was erected—
> The first German of it's kind.
> In the spring of eighteen forty,
> William Nast, the pioneer,
> Dedicated it for service,
> God to worship and revere.
> Fostered by his care and blessing,
> Obstacles though did appear,
> Central M. E. church rejoices
> To observe Centennial Year.[30]

NOTES

1. *History of Allegheny County Pennsylvania* (Chicago: A. Warner & Co., 1889), 360-361.

2. *Holy Pittsburgh Records: A Partial List of Early Churches and Synagogues* (Pittsburgh, Pa.: The Western Pennsylvania Genealogical Society, 1990), 26.

3. Golder, Horst, and Schaal, *Geschichte*, 410.

4. *History of Allegheny County*, 361

5. Golder, Horst, and Schaal, *Geschichte*, 410.

6. Marc Luksiak, "Converting churches, mindful of their past," *Pittsburgh Tribune-Review*, July 29, 2000.

7. Golder, Horst, and Schaal, *Geschichte*, 412.

8. *History of Allegheny County*, 361.

9. Golder, Horst, and Schaal, *Geschichte*, 412.

10. James Wudarczyk, *Historical Sites and Lost Landmarks of Lawrenceville's Historical Ninth and Tenth Wards*, ed. Cynthia A. Wudarczyk, (Pittsburgh, Pa.: Lawrenceville Historical Society, 1998).

11. *History of Allegheny County*, 361.

12. Golder, Horst, and Schaal, *Geschichte*, 410.

13. *History of Allegheny County*, 361.

14. Golder, Horst, and Schaal, *Geschichte*, 411–12.

15. *History of Allegheny County*, 361.

16. Golder, Horst, and Schaal, *Geschichte*, 413.

17. *History of Allegheny County*, 361

18. Golder, Horst, and Schaal, *Geschichte*, 413.

19. Ibid., 414.

20. *History of Allegheny County*, 361.

21. Golder, Horst, and Schaal, *Geschichte*, 409–410.

22. "Church Records," Western Pennsylvania Conference of The United Methodist Church comp. and ed. Rev. Norman Carlysle Young, M.Div.; M.Ed., umchurchrecords.org (accessed 2009).

23. Rudin, Diaries, 1902.

24. Golder, Horst, and Schaal, *Geschichte*, 438.

25. Ottis Rymer Snodgrass, "One Hundred Years of Change," sermon on Central Methodist Church (Wheeling, W.Va.: December 25, 1938), 9–10.

26. Albert E. Klebe, *History of Central Methodist Church*, church history (Wheeling W.Va.: 1951), 2.

27. Golder, Horst, and Schaal, *Geschichte*, 439.

28. Klebe, *Central Methodist Church*, 2.

29. Anonymous, *Bicentennial Anniversary, Fourth Street United Methodist Church* church history (Wheeling, W.Va.: 1985).

30. W. H. Schulz, unnamed hymn, (Wheeling, W.Va.: 1938).

Acknowledgments

GRANDPARENTS REV. THEODORE AND OTILLIA WEIDMANN RUDIN, Great-grandparents Rev. John C. and Katherine Ribbe Weidmann, Great Aunts Anne Weidmann and Rose Collier all inspired me to learn about my ancestors and thus also learn about German Methodism.

Roy, my husband, read, advised, and critiqued various drafts. Our daughters, Tara and Gini also critiqued and encouraged.

Carol Holliger, archivist at the United Methodist Archives at Ohio Wesleyan in Delaware, Ohio, and the archivists at the United Methodist Archives at DePauw University in Greencastle, Indiana; The Cincinnati Museum Center and Archives; and the Hamilton County Public Library of Cincinnati also gave me help in finding materials and in operating the various machines. Without my German teacher, Herta Moore, at Partners in Prime Senior Center in Hamilton, Ohio, I'd never have been able to read the *Geschichte* and other sources in German.

Others who sent me materials, letters, E-mails, and pictures, among other things, often made the difference between a church's history being described or the church merely mentioned. These include

The Cincinnati District: C. O. Langebrake, Virginia S. Bryant, Judy Tonges, (Batesville Memorial Public Library), Jackie Hildebrand.

The Louisville District: Sue Goff, Mary Miller, Sharon O'Bryan, Rev. Bill Reid, Vivian Taylor, Phyllis Allen, Marjorie Hedegard, Evelyn Lasley (Tell City-Perry County Public Library), Rose Gibson, Linda Isbell, Cheryl B. Cossey, Leonard Copley, Lee Bilderback, Nora Schoppenhorst, Robert Martin, Dorothy Hall.

The Michigan District: Leona Krill Betts, Elaine Condon, Richard Gwinn, Albert Dean Schweinfurth, Tom Niethamer, Doris Plogsterd, Charlene Schaar, Marilyn Toner, Isabelle Wells, Elnora Zischke, Rhonda Casler (Defiance Public

Library), Bill Maneval, Tanya S. Brunner, Rev. John C. Park, Hermit Hoesman, Arlene Hatch, Janet Van Wyck, Rev. Geoffrey Hayes, Wanda Reinford (Goshen Public Library), Inga Kyler, Timothy A. Brennan, Lowell Kosloskey, Kelly Swartz (Public Libraries of Saginaw), Lisa Crouse, Esther Sinclair.

North Ohio District: Cleo Carpenter, Shirley Neiswonger, Rev. Ellen Phillips, Karen Romick, Jeanne Ritchie, Glenna Meckstroth, Mary Pendell, Gracelouise Sims Moore, Jude Wudarczyk.

A special thanks goes to Mary Ann Mayer who took my photos and prepared them for this book. I also appreciate the proofreading of Rev. Warren and Marilyn Montgomery and the patience of all those who had to listen to me rattle on about my passion for researching this subject.

Glossary of Terms

AMEN CORNER—"a place in some Protestant churches, usually at one side of the pulpit occupied by worshipers leading responsive amens of the congregation."[*]

APPOINTMENT—The church or churches that the Bishop appointed a pastor to serve.

CHARGE—The pastor's charge referred to the church or churches that the pastor served. *Two-point* or *three-point* charge means that there were two or three churches that were served by the same pastor.

CIRCUIT—Circuit is similar to *charge* but it to refers to the schedule or route that the pastor followed in visiting his churches.

CONFERENCE—Conference is the name given to the governing body of the Methodist church and also refers to the area of jurisdiction of that body. The conference is divided into districts.

DISTRICT SUPERVISOR ("D. S.")—The district supervisor is the administrator of a district.

E.U.B., U.B., E.R.—These are initials that stood for other Methodist-like denominations which eventually united with the Methodist Church when it became the United Methodist Church. E.R. was Evangelical Reformed, U.B., United Brethren and E.U.B. (Evangelical United Brethren), the union of the two afore mentioned denominations.

EPISCOPAL—This refers to the body or conference presided over by a bishop.

---

[*]. *Random House Unabridged Dictionary*, copyright 1997, by Random House, Inc. on Info please.

EPWORTH LEAGUE—Epworth League is the former name of the young peoples' group, now called United Methodist Youth Fellowship.

EXHORTER—The exhorter was often a layman or one who did not have all the credentials to be a full pastor. He exhorted by advising or strongly appealing to the people in the way an evangelist might do. A footnote in one church history also added that the exhorter's job was to "make sure the people stayed awake" and to use a "headknocker" to guarantee that.[*]

FRAUENVEREIN—This was the German term for the Ladies Aid Society.

LADIES AID—This society was made up of the women of the church. They raised money for missions, did a lot of the care of the church and parsonage, and were responsible for many dinners and other activities of the church.

LOCAL PREACHER—The local preacher was a layman from the community who preached when the regular pastor could not be there.

LOVE FEAST—There was a description of a Love Feast in a church history— "In the afternoon a love feast was held. After the passing of bread and water, testimonies were given interspersed by verses of appropriate hymns."[†]

MISSION—The conference sent one or more people to an area that did not have a church but had people who might be interested in organizing one. The missionaries preached, formed groups and eventually helped establish a church, if there was enough interest.

MITE SOCIETY—The Mite Society preceded the Ladies Aid as a group organized to do mission work for the church.[‡]

PREACHING POINTS—see "Charge"

PRESIDING ELDER ("P. E")—The presiding elder was the same as the district supervisor.

PROBATIONERS - These were people who wished to join a church and were in the process of being approved.

PROTRACTED MEETING—The term protracted meeting referred to a revival meeting which lasted for several days or weeks.

STATION—A church became a station when it "stood on its own" without any financial help from the conference. Also, the pastor of a station only served one church as opposed to a circuit with several churches.

SUPPLY—When a church was served by "supply" it was usually small and weak.

---

[*]. *History of the Spraytown Free Methodist Church*, 4.

[†]. Edward D. Grossman, *The History of St. Paul's Church*, 1944.

[‡]. The name comes from the story in the Bible about the widow's mite (Mark 12:41–44 and Luke 21:1–4).

Bibliography

BOOKS REFERRED TO THROUGHOUT THE MANUSCRIPT

Minutes of the Annual Conferences. various publishers, various years.

Golder, C., John H. Horst, J. G. Schaal, *Geschichte der Zentral Deutschen Konferenz*. Cincinnati, Ohio: Jennings & Graham, n.d.

Rudin, Theodore, Diaries. 1898 to 1944, authors collection.

SECTION ONE—CINCINNATI DISTRICT

Books

Aurora Sesquicentennial Historical Committee, ed. *Aurora Sesquicentennial*. Aurora, Ind.: 1994.

Barnes, DD, Rev. R. M. and Rev. W. W. Snyder, AM. "Grace Church." In *Historic Sketches of the M. E. Church in Madison, Ind*. Madison, Ind.: The Courier Co., Printer and Binders, 1906.

Casari, Robert B., Chillicothe Bicentennial Commission, Ross County Historical Society, et al. *Chillicothe, Ohio 1796–1996: Ohio's First Capital*. Jackson, Ohio: Jackson Publishing Co., 1995.

Centennial History of Butler County, Ohio. Indianapolis: B. F. Bowen, 1905.

Decatur County Historical Society. *Decatur County History*. Dallas, Tex.: Taylor Publishing, 1984.

Evans, Nelson W. *A History of Scioto County. Ohio*. Portsmouth: Nelson W. Evans, 1903.

Evans, Nelson Wiley and Emmons Buchanan Stivers. *A History of Adams County, Ohio*. West Union, Ohio: E. B. Stivers, 1990.

Hardesty, H. H. *Hardesty's Historical and Geographical Encyclopedia*. Toledo: H. H. Hardesty & Co., 1883.

History and Biographical Cyclopaedia of Butler County, Ohio, A. Cincinnati: Western Biographical Publishing Co., 1882.

History of Dearborn and Ohio Counties. Chicago: F. E. Weakley & Co., 1885.

History of Lower Scioto Valley. Chicago: Inter State Publishing Co., 1884.

History of Montgomery County, Ohio, The. Chicago: W. H. Beers & Co., 1882.

History of Ross and Highland Counties Ohio. Cleveland: William Bros. Publishers, 1880.

History of Wayne County, Indiana. Chicago: Inter-State Publishing Co., 1884.

Lake, D. J. *Atlas of Dearborn County, Indiana.* Philadelphia: Lake, Griffing & Stevenson, 1875.

Leffel, John C., ed. *History of Posey County.* Chicago: Standard Publishing Co., 1913.

McIntosh, W. H., and W. H. Beers & Co. *The History of Darke County.* Chicago: W. H. Beers & Co., 1880.

Meigs County Historical Society. *Meigs County, Ohio.* Paoli, Pa.: Taylor Publishing Co., 1979.

Morrow, Josiah. W. H. Beers & Co. *History of Brown County,* Chicago: W. H. Beers & Co., 1883.

Reifel, August J. *History of Franklin County, Indiana.* Indianapolis, Ind.: B. F. Bowen & Co., Inc., 1915.

Ripley County Historical Society. *Ripley County History.* Vol. 2. Osgood, Ind.: Ripley County History Book Committee, ca. 1993.

Ripley County History Book Committee. *Ripley County History 1818–1988.* Dallas: Taylor Publishing Co., 1989.

Smith, Alan F. *A Tale of Two Townships.* Vevay, Ind.: Venage Press, 1996.

Thompson, Carl N., comp. *Historical Collections of Brown County, Ohio.* Piqua, Ohio: Hammer Graphics, Inc., 1969.

Willard, Eugene B., ed. *Standard History of Hanging Rock Iron Region of Ohio.* Chicago: The Lewis Publishing Co., 1916.

Wilson, Frazier E. *History of Darke County, Ohio, from its earliest settlement to the present time: in two volumes.* Milford, Ohio: Hobart Publishing Co., 1914.

Zachman, Richard. *Historic Homes of Ripley.* 1976.

Church Histories and Pamphlets

"Anniversary Celebrations, Hyde Park Bethlehem United Methodist Church, 1981–1988." Cincinnati, Ohio: 1988.

Beck, M. A. "The Spring Grove Avenue Methodist Church, Cincinnati, Ohio." Nippert Collection, Cincinnati Historical Society Library Archives, Cincinnati, Ohio.

Booklet on history of Nast and Trinity Churches, Cincinnati, Ohio, 1985.

The Centennial of Methodism in Laughery Township (1845–1945). Pamphlet. Ind.

"Franklin Avenue United Methodist Church." Booklet published for the 150th anniversary, Portsmouth, Ohio, 1994.

Freeland, Harold L. *History of Adams Township,* Sunman, Ind.: 1950.

"History and Program, The Ninetieth Anniversary of the Salem Methodist Episcopal Church." Newport, Ky.: 1938.

"History of Epworth United Methodist Church." *History of Mt. Healthy Methodism.* Mt. Healthy, Ohio: 1989.

History of Methodism in Sydney, Ohio, A. Privately published, 1989.

"History of Van Buren Street Methodist Church." Nippert Collection, Cincinnati Historical Society Library Archives, Ohio.

"History" Salem Gemeinde and Salem United Methodist Church 1876–1982, Campbell County Historical Society, Ky.

Koerner, Mrs. J. J. "Our History," Auburn Methodist Church Sixtieth Anniversary 1950, Nippert Collection, Cincinnati Historical Society Library Archives, Ohio.

Langebrake, C. O., ed. "Chronology of Events in the History of Grace United Methodist Church." Waverly, Ohio: 1988.

Johnson, Ray C., and Lawrenceburg Historical Society. *History of Lawrenceburg, Indiana.* Lawrenceburg, Ind.: Lawrenceburg Historical Society, 1953.

Maag, K. "History of Grace Methodist Church." Hamilton, Ohio; 1961.

150th Anniversary, 1830–1980, New Palestine United Methodist Church. Anniversary booklet. New Palestine, Ind.: 1980.

"One Hundred Years...A Century of Christian Service." Centennial pamphlet for New Jersey Street Methodist Church. Indianapolis, Ind.: 1946.

Park, Clyde W. "Historical Statement." Nippert Collection, Cincinnati Historical Society Library Archives, Ohio.

Phillips, Herschel L. "Brookville United Methodist Church, 1883–1983." *177 Years of Methodism, 1806–1983.* Brookville, Ind.: Whitewater Publications, 1983.

Pope, Frances and Edna Holle. *Our Memorial Stained Glass Windows, Hyde Park–Bethlehem United Methodist Church.* Booklet. Cincinnati, Ohio: 1974.

Pope, William M. "The History of Immanuel United Methodist Church," 2551 Dixie Highway, 1984. Lakeside Park, Ky.

Schroetter, C. Albert. "The Story of Immanuel Methodist Church," in *One Hundredth Anniversary, Immanuel Methodist Church,* 1949. Covington, Ky.

Senior English Class of Piqua High School 1929. *Piqua as it is Today,* Piqua High School, Piqua, Ohio.

The Seventy-Fifth Anniversary of the First Methodist Church 1870–1945. Batesville, Ind.

Stinth, June. "Wheelersburg M. E. Church." In *History of Scioto County, Ohio,* Portsmouth Area Recognition Society, Dallas, Tex.: Taylor Publishing Co., 1986.

Wesenburger, Ruth. "A Brief History of Immanuel United Methodist Church formerly known as German Methodist Episcopal Church." In *The History of Immanuel United Methodist Church.* Covington, Ky.: 1997.

Zoar Methodist Church 1858–1983: 125 Year Celebration. Anniversary bulletin. Hanover, Ind.: Zoar, 1983.

Miscellaneous Sources

Baur, Theodore. *Historical Record.* Public Library of Cincinnati and Hamilton County, Cincinnati, Ohio.

"Brown Street Methodist Church Centennial Celebration Historical Reading." Lafayette, Ind., November 27, 1951.

Historic Lawrenceburg Foundation. Plaque on Zerbe Law Offices building, Lawrenceburg, Ind.

"The History of Brown Street United Methodist Church." Lafayette, Ind. http://gbgm-churches.gbgm-umc.org/brownstreetin/history (accessed 2003).

Mora, Maye Crary. "Meigs County's Early Religious Heritage." From a paper presented to Meigs County Pioneer and Historical Society by Return Jonathan Meigs Chapter, Daughters of the American Revolution, 1976.

Muth, Konrad. *German Methodist Episcopal Church.* 1962. Translated by Mario G. Pelli. The Archives of Indiana Methodism, DePauw University, Greencastle.

Recorder's Office, Georgetown, Brown County, Ohio.

Scott, Robert W. "The Religious Landscape of Southern Indiana in the Nineteenth Century," Indiana: myindianahome.net/gen/jeff/ records/church/religions (accessed 2000).

Sinks, Ruth. *History of Brown Street Methodist Church.* Centennial program. Lafayette, Ind.: 1951.

"Some Types of Early Buildings in Terre Haute–XXIV." Article. Community Affairs File. Vigo County Public Library, Terre Haute, Ind.

"Spring Grove Methodist Church." Church bulletin, 1959. Nippert Collection, Cincinnati Historical Society Library Archives, Ohio.

Untitled handwritten history of Spring Grove M. E. on church stationery. n.d. Nippert Collection, Cincinnati Historical Society Library Archives, Ohio.

Walley, Edwin C. *History of Third German Church.* 1934. Public Library of Cincinnati and Hamilton County, Cincinnati, Ohio.

PART TWO—LOUISVILLE DISTRICT

Books

Baird, Lewis C. *Baird's History of Clark County, Indiana.* Indianapolis: B. F. Bowen, 1909.

Clayton, W. W. *History of Davidson County, Tennessee.* Philadelphia: J. W. Lewis & co., 1880.

De la Hunt, Thomas James. *Perry County, A History.* Indianapolis: The W. K. Stewart, 1916.

Elliott, Joseph P. *A History of Evansville and Vanderburgh County, Indiana.* Evansville, Ind.: Keller Publishing Co., 1897.

Goodspeed Brothers. *History of Pike and Dubois Counties, Indiana.* Chicago: Goodspeed Bros. & Co., 1885.

Goodspeed Publishing Co. *History of Posey County, Indiana.* Chicago: The Goodspeed Publishing Co., 1886.

Griffing, B. N. and D. J. Lake & Co. *An Illustrated Historical Atlas of Henderson and Union Counties, Kentucky.* Philadelphia: D. J. Lake & Co., 1880.

Leffel, John C., ed. *History of Posey County, Indiana.* Chicago: Standard Publishing Co., 1913.

History of Vanderburgh County, Indiana. Madison, Wis.: Brant & Fuller, 1889.

History of Warrick, Spencer and Perry Counties, Indiana. Chicago: Goodspeed Bros. & Co., 1885.

Jennings County Historical Society. *Jennings County, Indiana, 1816–1999.* Paducah, Ky.: Turner Publishing Co., 1999.

Massac County Historical Society. *Pictorial History of Massac County. Illinois,* Metropolis, Ill.: The Metropolis Planet, 1993.

———. *Massac County, Illinois.* Paducah, Ky.: Turner Publishing Co., 1987.

May, George W. *History of Massac County.* Galesburg, Ill.: Wagoner Printing Co., 1954.

Noblitt, Loren. *The Composite History of Jackson County, Indiana, 1816–1988.* Paducah, Ky.: Turner Publishing Co., 1988.

———. *A History of Jackson County Churches, 1815–1997.* Brownstown, Ind.: A Heritage Publication, Jackson County Historical Society, 1997.

Pope County, Illinois, 1986: History and Families, 1816–1986, Pope County, Illinois. Golconda, Ill.: Pope County Historical Society; Paducah, Ky.: Turner Publishing, 1986.

Sweeney, Margaret. *Faction, Fiction and Folklore of Southern Indiana.* New York: Vantage Press, 1967.

Williams, L. A. & Co. *History of the Ohio Falls Cities and their Counties.* 2 Vols. Cleveland: L. A. Williams & Co., 1882.

Woolridge, John. *History of Nashville, Tenn.* Nashville: Publishing House of the Methodist Episcopal Church, South, 1890.

Church Histories and Pamphlets

Bartelt, William. *It is a Little Place.* Zoar, Ind., 1973.

Becker, Herman. Viola Hartman, and Laverne Seifert. *An Anchor in the Community.* St. John's Centennial celebration booklet. Caborn, Ind.: 1987.

Binder, Rev. August. *Churches: Posey County,* Mt. Vernon, Ind.: self-published, 1988.

"Calvary Methodist Church Centennial to be Celebrated in New Albany Sunday." March 8, 1945. Churches, New Albany Public Library, New Albany, Ind.

"Centenary." Leaflet from Centenary United Methodist Church, New Albany, Ind.

Claycamp, Harold. *History of Santa Claus Methodist Church and Camp Ground.* Depauw University United Methodist Archives, Greencastle, Ind.

"The German Methodist Church." *History of the United Methodist Church of Huntingburg, Indiana.* 1984.

Griffin, Frederick P. *Harrison County, Indiana Cemeteries, Vol. 3.* n.p.: 1971.

"Historical Sketch." In *Souvenir and Program The Centennial Celebration Market Street Methodist Church,* 1940, Nippert Collection, Cincinnati Historical Society Library Archives, Ohio.

"Historical Sketch of Salem Methodist Church." *Centennial Celebration 1846–1946.* Evansville, Ind.: 1946.

"The History of German Methodism in Louisville and Vicinity." Nippert Collection, Cincinnati Historical Society Library Archives, Ohio.

History of the Church. A history of Central Barren United Methodist Church. Central Barren, Ind., ca. 1970.

History of the Community Church from the 1840s to September 1970. History of Mt. Vernon church. Mt. Vernon, Ind.: 1970.

History of the Spraytown Free Methodist Church. Seymour, Ind.: Spraytown Free Methodist Church, 1983.

Hoelscher, Alice. *History of Fourth Street M. E., 1843 to 1933.* Evansville, Ind.: 1933.

One Hundred Twenty-Fifth Anniversary. Holland, Ind.: Holland United Methodist Church, 1981.

"Our Church History, 1892–1976." *First United Methodist Church.* Tell City, Ind.: The Swiss Printers, Inc., 1976.

Quebbeman, Frances. *Celebrate 125 Years Central Barren United Methodist Church.* Central Barren, Ind.: 1976.

Rockport–Spencer County Sesquicentennial. [Rockport? Ind.: Sesquicentennial Committee, 1968].

Roell, Mabel Schaaf. *The Santa Claus United Methodist Church Historical Record 1899–1999.* Santa Claus, Ind.: 1999.

St. Peters United Methodist Church. Church history. Posey County, Ind.: ca. 1994.

Summers, Catherine Kelley. *Harrison County, Indiana Churches.* Harrison County, Ind. 1989.

Topper, Richard. "Churches Yesterday & Today," *Mt. Vernon, IN 175th Birthday 1816–1991.* Souvenir booklet. Mt. Vernon, Ind.: ca. 1990.

Traupe, R. Gerald. *The Golconda Methodist Church*, 1955. Illinois Great Rivers Conference Archives, Pfeifer Library, MacMurray College, Jacksonville.

Wall Street United Methodist Church. 190th anniversary publication. Jeffersonville, Ind.: ca. 1997.

White Creek United Methodist Church, 1846–1984. Church history. Columbus, Ind.: 1984.

Miscellaneous Sources

Church Record Survey, Church History Summary, The Archives of Indiana United Methodism, Depauw University, Greencastle.

Emmanuel Cemetery, Clark County, Ind., www.rootsweb.com/~inccpc/emmanuelcemwood (accessed 2003).

Hoff, F. A. "Historical Record Santa Claus." Translated by Mario C. Pelli, 1968, The Archives of Indiana United Methodism, Depauw University, Greencastle, Ind.

Kasting, George. Notes. 1973. Seymour, Ind. (photocopy).

Minutes from meeting with District Superintendent. Boonville Public Library, Ind.

Mosby, James. "German Methodism in Perry County." *A Living History of Perry County,* website: www.perrycountyindiana.org/history/methodism (accessed about 2000).

Quarterly Conference minutes, August 11, 1968, Boonville Public Library, Ind.

Salem Cemetery. Vanderburg County, Ind., www.rootsweb.com/~invander/cemeteries/salem_umc/index (accessed 2003).

Shepherd, Bob. "A Brief Chronology of Methodist Temple," Evansville, Ind.: www.methodisttemplle.evansville.net/history (accessed 2000).

St. Andrews UMC, Cullman, Alabama, www.standrewumc.org/history (accessed 2003).

Part Three—Michigan District

Books

Aldrich, Lewis Cass. *History of Henry and Fulton Counties, Ohio.* Syracuse, N.Y.: D. Mason & Co., 1888.

Arnott, Catherine Mary, comp. *The History of Woodland Township 1837–1987.* [Ann Arbor, Mich.]: C. M. Arnott, [1987].

Baxter, Albert. *History of the City of Grand Rapids.* New York and Grand Rapids: Mussello Co., 1891.

Bay City Directory. Bay City, Mich.,1868–1869.

Bowen, F. F. and Co. *History of DeKalb County, Indiana.* Indianapolis: B. F. Bowen, 1914.

Clinton County Historical Society. *History of Clinton County, Michigan.* St. Johns, Mich.: The Clinton County Historical Society, 1980.

Danford, Ardath. *Perrysburg Revisited.* Perrysburg, Ohio.

Druse, Joseph L. *Pulpit and Prayer in Earliest Lansing.* Lansing, Mich.: The Historical Society of Great Lansing, 1959.

Evans, David S. and Lyle Blackledge. *A History of Okemos Methodist/Community Church.* Okemos, Mich.: Okemos Community Church, 1997.

Farmer, Silas. *The History of Detroit and Michigan.* Detroit: Silas Farmer & Co., 1884.

Gansser, Augustus H. *History of Bay County, Michigan.* Chicago: Richmond & Arnold, 1905.

Goodspeed, Weston Arthur. *County of Williams, Ohio: Historical and Biographical.* Chicago: F. A. Battey & Co., 1882.

Johnson, Crisfield and D. W. Ensign & Co. *History of Allegan and Barry Counties, Michigan.* Philadelphia: D. W. Ensign & Co., 1880.

Killits, John M. *Toledo and Lucas County, Ohio.* Toledo: The S. J. Clarke Publishing Co., 1923.

Page, H. R. and Co. *History of Muskegon County, Michigan.* Chicago: H. R. Page & Co., 1882.

Little Traverse Historical Society. *Historical Glimpses: A History of Petoskey.* Petoskey, Mich.: Little Traverse Printing, 1986.

Lowell Board of Trade. *Lowell: 100 Years of History, 1831–1931.* Lowell, Mich.: Lowell Ledger, 1931.

Lucas County Chapter of the Genealogy Society. *Lucas County Church Records Inventory.* Lucas County, Ohio: 1990.

Meek, Basil. *Twentieth Century History of Sandusky Co.* Chicago: Richmond-Arnold Publishing Co., 1909.

Muskegon City Directory. Detroit: R. L. Polk & Co., 1891–92, 1912.

Noble County History Book Committee. *The History of Noble County, Indiana.* Tex.: Taylor Publishing Co., 1986.

Proctor, Hazel and Ann Arbor Federal Savings. *Old Ann Arbor Town.* Ann Arbor, Mich.: Ann Arbor Federal Savings, 1974.

Shinn, William H., ed. *The County of Williams.* Madison, Wis.: Northwestern Historical

Association, 1905.

Smith, John Martin and DeKalb Sesquicentennial, Inc. *DeKalb County 1837–1987, sesquicentennial.* Auburn, Ind.: DeKalb Sesquicentennial, Inc., 1990.

Waggoner, Clark. *History of the City of Toledo and Lucas County, Ohio.* New York: Munsell & Co., 1888.

Warner, Beers & Co. *History of Defiance County, Ohio.* Chicago: Warner, Beers & Co., 1883.

Whitlock, Elias D., et al. *History of the Central Ohio Conference of the Methodist Episcopal Church.* Cincinnati: The Methodist Book Concern, 1913.

Woodville Historical Society. *A Sketch Book of Woodville, Ohio, Past–Present: To Commemorate the Woodville Village Sesquicentennial 1836–1986.* Woodville, Ohio: Woodville Historical Society, 1986.

Yates, Marion Roth. "The Swiss in Vergennes," *Vergennes Township Living History.* Edited by Eunice Vander Veen. n.p.: Vergennes Club, 1984.

Church Histories and Pamphlets

Balesky, Mrs. Fred. *The History of the Kochville Methodist Church.* Kochville, Mich.: 1932.

Beach, B. M. *History of the Emanuel M. E. Church near West Unity, Ohio.* Stryker, Ohio: Stryker Advance Print, 1908.

Bloir, Steven C, comp. *History of West Buffalo.* West Buffalo, Ohio, by the author, n.d.

Boughner, Floyd. *History of the First Methodist Church in Marine City, Michigan.* Marine City, Mich.: 1949.

Bueker, Henry. *Our One Hundredth Year at Kochville Methodist.* Kochville, Mich: 1957.

Chapman, Alida. *Looking Back,* Delhi Twp., Mich.: Delhi Township Bicentennial Commission, 1976.

Diamond Jubilee and Home Coming. Anniversary program, Zion M. E. Church. Toledo, Ohio: 1933.

Dibert, Charles W. *St. Paul-Trinity United Methodist Church: A History within a History.* Elmore, Ohio.: 1984.

Emanuel United Methodist Church. Church history, prepared under the pastorate of Rev. Harley Martin. Edgerton, Ohio: 1975.

Evangelist, The. Vol. 2. Nippert Collection, Cincinnati Historical Society Library Archives, Ohio.

Evansport United Methodist Church, 1874–1974. Centennial history and program. Evansport, Ohio: October 13, 1974.

From Hand to Hand and Heart to Heart for 125 Years. Evansport United Methodist Church. Evansport, Ohio: 1999.

Historical Note. Emanuel Church, Township Road K, Floral Grove Cemetery, Brady Township, West Unity, Ohio.

History of Pleasant Bend Church (no title). 1994. New Bavaria, Henry County, Ohio, Archives of Ohio United Methodism, Ohio Wesleyan University, Delaware.

History of St. Paul's United Methodist Church. Defiance, Ohio.

Justus, Judith P. "Friendly First Church." in *Timeline.* Perrysburg, Ohio: 1995.

Knepper, Mrs. W. H. *History of the Methodist Church, Edon, Ohio*. Edon, Ohio: 1943.

Kyler, Inge Logenburg. *Holt United Methodist Church Celebrating 150 Years of Fellowship: A Brief History.* Holt, Mich.: 2003.

Lane, Henry. *Bethlehem Methodist Church*. Flint, Mich.: 1960.

Maynard, Kevin. "Emanuel M. E. Church the Pride of German Emigrants." In *A Guide to Williams County's History.* Montpelier, Ohio.: Williams County History Society, 1995.

The Michigan Sesquicentennial Agency for Delhi Township. *A Michigan Sesquicentennial History of Delhi Township*. Ingham County, Mich. 1957.

Morgan, Larry, ed. *Salem United Methodist Church: A History.* Toledo, Ohio.: 1989.

One Hundredth Anniversary of the Alto United Methodist Church. Pamphlet. Alto, Mich.: 1974 .

One Hundred Twenty-five Years with Kochville United Methodist. Kochville, Mich.: 1982.

Robinson, Al, et al. *First Methodist Church Pigeon, Michigan, 1871–1996*. Pigeon, Mich., n.d.

Salem Grove United Methodist Church 1853–2003, Family—Friends—Tradition. Anniversary booklet. Grass Lake, Mich.: 2003.

60th Anniversary of the Stryker Methodist Church Structure. Stryker, Ohio: 1962.

South Monterey United Methodist Church. History and dedication program. South Monterey, Mich.: 1973.

Souvenir and Program of the Diamond Jubilee of the Roseville Methodist Episcopal Church. Roseville, Mich., 1924. Nippert Collection, Cincinnati Historical Society Library Archives, Ohio.

Tillman, Blanche. *Bethlehem Methodist Church to Celebrate 45th Anniversary Sunday.* Program. Flint, Mich.: 1964.

Werner, Henry J., Jr. "Emanuel —Centenarian." Centennial program. Toledo, Ohio: 1949.

Zion United Methodist Church. Historical pamphlet for the 128th anniversary celebration. Toledo, Ohio.: 1979.

Miscellaneous Sources

Betts, Leona Krill. Emanuel UMC, Edgerton, Ohio.

Condon, Elaine. Bethlehem German M. E., Flint, Mich.

Dale, R. D. Deed. Edgerton German Methodist Parsonage, Edgerton, Ohio.

"Emanuel and the Next Century," Toledo, Ohio, ca. 1950.

"Find-A-Church." Directory: Emanuel UMC, Edgerton, Ohio. Archives.umc.org/Find-A-Church Directory/ChurchDirectory (accessed in 2010).

Gwinn, Richard. *Ora Labora*. Caseville, Mich.

"History of St. Paul's United Methodist Church." Defiance, Ohio.

Interview with Paul D. and Rosa Krill and Hulda Valet, 1976. Emanuel German M. E., Edgerton, Ohio.

Koch, John C. South Bend, Ind.

Kochville United Methodist Church. www.gbgm-umc.org/kochville/programs, Kochville, Mich. (accessed 2009).

Lansing, Michigan, Seymour Avenue German M. E., www.gbgm-umc.org/firstumd/History (accessed 2009).

Liber 1, Emmet County Deeds, 1880. Petoskey, Mich.

Lindholm, J. One-page history of Valley Avenue Methodist, 1989. Grand Rapids, Mich.

Niethamer, Tom. Woodland, Mich., private collection.

Omo Zion United Methodist Church, "A Brief Look at Omo Zion Thru the Years." Lenox, Mich., www.omochurch.org (accessed in 2010).

Plogsterd, Doris. Hopkins, Mich., private collection.

Redeemer United Methodist Church, Dewitt, Mich., www.dewittredeemer.org/aboutus/churchhistory.html (accessed in 2010).

"Salem Methodist Church 90th Anniversary." Program. China Township, St. Clair, County, Mich.: 1941.

Schaar, Charlene. Dewitt, Mich., private collection.

Schweinfurth, Albert Dean. Francisco, Mich., private collection.

Toner, Marilyn. Edon, Ohio, private collection.

Wells, Isabelle. Ingham County Genealogical Society, Holt, Mich.

West Side United Methodist Church. Ann Arbor, Mich., www.westside-umc.org/history.htm (accessed in 2010).

Zischke, Elnora. Hopkins, Mich., private collection.

PART FOUR—NORTH OHIO DISTRICT

Books

Aldrich, Lewis C., ed. *History of Erie County.* Syracuse, N.Y.: D. Mason & Co., 1889.

The Auglaize County Historical Society. *A History of Auglaize County. Ohio.* Defiance, Ohio: The Hubbard Co., 1979.

Bauman, John. *Then and Now: a Family and Community History.* Henrietta, Ohio: 1964.

Caldwell's Illustrated Historical Atlas. Newark, Ohio: J. A. Caldwell, 1797–1880.

Crisfield, Johnson, ed. *History of Cuyahoga County, Ohio.* Cleveland: D. W. Ensign & Co., 1879.

Danbury map. *Combined Historical Atlas of Ottawa County, Ohio.* Mt. Vernon, Ind.: Windmill Publications, 1998.

Everhart, J. F. *1794 History of Muskingum County, Ohio.* Columbus, Ohio: F. J. Everhart & Co., 1882.

Gould, H. T. and J. W. Starr. *An Illustrated Atlas of Crawford County.* Bucyrus, Ohio: Gould & Starr, 1873.

Graham, Bernice. *Early Methodism in the Northwest Territory.* New York: Carlton Press Corp., A Hearthstone Book, 1996.

Hill, N. N. *History of Coshocton County.* Newark, Ohio: A. A. Graham & Co., 1881.

———. *The History of Licking County.* Newark, Ohio: A. A. Graham & Publishers, 1881.

History of Allegheny County Pennsylvania. Chicago: A. Warner & Co., 1889.

History of Crawford County. Chicago: Baskin & Battey, History Publishers, 1881.

History of Franklin and Pickaway Counties, Ohio. Cleveland, Ohio: Williams Bros., 1880.

History of Marion County, Ohio. Chicago: Leggett, Conaway & Co., 1883.

History of Tuscarawas County, Ohio. Chicago: Warner, Beers & Co., 1884.

Holy Pittsburgh Records: A Partial List of Early Churches and Synagogues. Pittsburgh: The Western Pennsylvania Genealogical Society, 1990.

Lane, Samuel A. *Fifty Years and Over of Akron and Summit County.* Akron, Ohio: Beacon Job Department, 1892.

Longaberger, Glenn. *Dresden, 1817–1957 Pioneer Days to Modern Ways.* Dresden, Ohio: Lindsey Printing, 1967.

Lytle, James R. *History of Delaware County.* Chicago: Biographical Publishing Co., 1908.

Maienknecht, Theresa and Stanley. *Monroe County, Ohio: A History,* Mt. Vernon, Ind.: Windmill Publications, Inc., 1989.

Meckstroth, Glenna. *Tales from Great-Grandpa's Trunk.* Wooster, Ohio: Wooster Book Co., 1998.

Monroe County Chapter of the Ohio Genealogical Society. *Monroe County, Ohio Families.* Dallas, Tex.: Taylor Publishing Co., 1992.

Moore, Gracelouise Sims, ed. *Tapestry of Faith.* Cleveland, Ohio: The Methodist Union of the Cleveland District of the United Methodist Church, Inc., 2003.

Peeke, Hewson. *The Centennial History of Erie Co.* Cleveland, Ohio: The Penton Press Co., 1925.

Romine, Trella H., ed. *Marion County 1979 History.* Dallas, Tex.: The Taylor Publishing Co., 1979.

Shepard, O. L. *The Story of Lakeside.* Lakeside, Ohio: Lakeside Association, 1923.

"Sixteen United Methodist Church." *Mansfield District Local Church Directory.* 1996.

Trinter, Betty. *The Way It Was.* Norwalk, Ohio: Ebert's Inc., 1976.

Williams History of Washington County. Ohio. Cleveland, Ohio: H. Z. Williams & Bro. Publishers, 1881.

Wolf, Carolyn Zogg, Julie A. Kraus, Sherry Fritschi, and Monroe County Historical Society. *Nine Communities of Monroe County.* Woodsfield, Ohio: The Society, 1984.

Church Histories

Bicentennial Anniversary, Fourth Street United Methodist Church. Wheeling, W.Va.: 1985.

Brunkhorst, Mamie Rymers. *History of Methodism in Erie Township.* La Carne, Ohio: 1952.

Church History. Henrietta, Ohio: 1952.

1845–1945 Centennial Program: The Church of the Cross. History. Cleveland, Ohio: 1945

Dennig, William, et al. *Time Turns the Pages of Church History.* Galion, Ohio: 1978.

Geissendoerfer, Lena and John Bauman. "The History of Henrietta Methodist Church." Henrietta, Ohio: 1978.

Hertzler, C. W. "When Emanuel Church Accepted the Immigrant 85 Years Ago." In *History of Methodism in Berea, 1843–1976.* Berea, Ohio: 1939.

"History." *Centennial Worship Service.* Kossuth-Zion UMC. Kossuth, Ohio: November 8, 1970.

"The History of the Church." *1845–1945 Centennial Program,* First German Church/Church of the Cross/Community of Living Hope. Cleveland, Ohio.: 1945.

The History of the Christ United Methodist Church: Bethany Church. Cleveland, Ohio: 1988.

History of Community of Living Hope United Methodist Church. Cleveland, Ohio: 2002.

History of Zion Church. Clarington, Ohio: Revised and updated June 1984.

Klebe, Albert E. *History of Central Methodist Church.* Wheeling, W.Va.: 1951.

McGrew, Caroline, ed. *75 Years of Celebrating Past Commitments & Future Dedication at Epworth Church.* Bucyrus, Ohio: 1993.

One Hundred Fifty Years of Methodism in Mansfield and Richland County. Mansfield, Ohio: n.d.

One Hundredth Anniversary. Bethel Methodist Episcopal Church. Clarington, Ohio: 1935.

Porter, Sue. *Livingston United Methodist Church.* History. Columbus, Ohio: 1981.

Powers, Rev. P. Raymond. "Why it was named Trinity Educational Building." In *Fifty Years in First Church.* Akron, Ohio: ca. 1955.

Schott, Ruth E. *One Hundred Years on this Corner,* First German/Prospect Street Methodist Church. Marion, Ohio: 1969.

Sesquicentennial Committee. *The New Knoxville United Methodist Church.* History. New Knoxville, Ohio: 1993.

Smith, George H. *One Hundredth Anniversary.* History. New Knoxville, Ohio: 1943.

"A Summary of the History of St. Mark U.M.C." Galion, Ohio: n.d.

Tropft, Clarence. *A Sketch of a History of Immanuel (German Sixteen) Church.* History. Galion, Ohio: 1960.

Weiss, Albert F. *History of the Church of the Cross.* Cleveland, Ohio: 1965.

Miscellaneous

Frobisch Church. Abandoned Church Listing, January 1971, Barnesville District, Ohio.

Alexander, Thurman F. Written description of Leith Run Methodist Church. Photo copy, Washington County, Ohio: June 1958.

Zion Methodist. Archives and History Commission, The, "Local Church History Survey," #10, 1982, United Methodist Archives, Ohio Wesleyan University, Delaware.

Leith Run/Grandview. "Local Church History Survey." 1982, United Methodist Archives, Ohio Wesleyan University, Delaware.

Bethel German M.E. Bill of Sale. Switzerland Township, Monroe County, Ohio, July 11, 1962.

Buzza, Richard. Copy of letter concerning disposition of Frobisch Methodist Church, June 1995, Monroe County, Ohio.

Carpenter, Cleo. Letter. September 2002, Monroefield, Ohio.

Christ United Methodist Church anniversary plate, 1974, Marietta, Ohio.

Chili church. Fresno Charge file, North-East Ohio Conference, Methodist Church, United Methodist Archives, Ohio Wesleyan University, Delaware.

———. Works Progress Administration Survey of State and Local Historical Records, 1936, Ohio Historical Records Survey, Church Records Form.

"The History of the First Methodist Church." Dover, Ohio, typed manuscript in United Methodist Archives, Ohio Wesleyan University, Delaware.

Neiswonger, Shirley. E-mail, August 15, 2002, Monroe County, Ohio.

Neuhardt, Franklin S., photocopy of letter to Rev. Richard Drake, July 1960, Cambridge, Ohio.

Phillips, Rev. Ellen. Letter, August 23, 1997, Columbus, Ohio.

Preface of "Cemetery Inscriptions of Ottawa County, Ohio," 1970–76, Ottawa County Chapter of the Ohio Genealogical Society, Ohio.

Prospect United Methodist Church, Marion, Ohio, www.gbgm-umc.org/prospectst (accessed July 10, 2009)

Report of Ladies Aid, Zion M. E., Cleveland, Ohio, 1926–27, United Methodist Archives, Ohio Wesleyan University, Delaware.

Schulz, W. H. Photocopy of hymn. Wheeling, W.Va.: 1938.

Young, Rev. Norman Carlysle, ed. "Braddock: Muhleman Memorial" Church Records: Western Pennsylvania Conference of the United Methodist Church, Pittsburgh, Pa., umchurchrecords.org.

Index

A

Ablett, Rev. Joseph 216
Ackeret Chapel (Reddington, Ind.) 99–100
Ackeret, Conrad 99
Ackerman, Rev. Louis 128, 140, 155, 159
Adams Street Church (Bay City, Mich.) 211–212
Adamson, Rev. 341
African American 28, 29, 47
   African Methodist Episcopal (New Albany, Ind.) 93
   school 139
Ahrens, C. 274
Ahrens, Rev. A. 32
Ahrens, Rev. William 56
Akron, Ohio 323–324
Alaiedon German M.E. Church (Mich.) 202
Albright, Father 284
"All Stars" of Portsmouth 78
Allegan German M.E. (Mich.) 175
Allegheny City, Pa. 351
Allegheny German M.E. (Pittsburgh, Pa.) 351
Allen Schoolhouse 199
Allen Temple African M.E. Church 259
Allinger, Rev. Carl (Charlie) 108, 147, 155, 290, 313
Allinger, Rev. Jacob 139, 140
Allinger, Rev. Louis 193
Altmann, John 190
Alto Parish Charge (Mich.) 181
Alto UMC (Mich.) 181, 182
Alto, Mich. 180, 181
American Civil War 47, 53, 73, 100, 165, 209, 293
American Legion Hall (Alto, Mich.) 181
Americans 341
Amherst, Ohio 267
Anderson, Bishop 308
Andre(e), Rev. William 64, 65, 69, 323, 325, 344
Angola, Indiana, Mission of the Ohio Conference 227
Ann Arbor Circuit (Mich.) 195
Ann Arbor, Mich. 185, 193, 197, 200
Apologete 6
Appalachian 28
Arlington Place Methodist Church (Indianapolis) 18
Armada, Mich. 190
Armory Ave. Church
   Cincinnati 103
Artz, Nadine 196, 197
Asbury Third Church (Cincinnati) 33
Ashland, Ohio 237, 286, 292
Assembly of God
   Piqua, Ohio 56
Auburn and Bryan Mission 227
Auburn and Kendallville Mission 227
Auburn Avenue German M. E. Church (Cincinnati) 32
Auburn German M.E. Church (Ind.) 234–235
Auburn, Ind. 228, 235
Auglaize Co., Ohio 313, 315
Auglaize County Fair 316

Aurora, Ind. 9, 10, 12
Ayersville, Ohio 227

B

Bach, Rev. 54, 55
Baechtold, Rev. J. J. 90, 140, 301, 344
Baer, Rev. John 80
Bahrenberg, Rev. J. H. 32
Bahrenburg, Rev. J. H. 334
Baker Schoolhouse (Ohio) 286
Baker, Rev. 232
Balduff, Rev. John 258
Baldwin, Donald 335
Baldwin, Shirley 335
Baldwin-Wallace College 34, 78, 162, 263, 352
Baltimore Station, Mich. 189
Balzer, Heinrich 190
Bancroft, Rev. W. E. 78
Bank, Mrs. 203
Bank, Rev. Henry 203, 210
Baptists 43, 182, 341
   Aurora, Ind. 10
   Lawrenceville, Ind. 10
Bare's, Jacob 328
Baresville, Ohio 271, 327, 331, 334
Baresville, Ohio, Circuit 327–329
Barnard Art Memorial (Madison, Ind.) 12
Barth, Rev. John 21, 22, 28, 165–166, 279, 284, 302
Barth, Rev. Philip 165
Barth, Rev. Sebastian 165
Bartruff, Pauline 203
Basaka family 157
Basel, Ohio 296
Basel, Switzerland 34
Batesville Circuit (Ind.) 3–10
Batesville, Ind. 3–4, 9
Bau, Rev. Hartmann 301, 352
Bauer Bros. 331
Bauer, Rev. Charles 17
Baum family 37
Bauman, Rev. 103
Bauman, Rev. F. F. 350
Baumann, F. J. 103, 301
Baumann, Mrs. 215
Baumann, Rev. C. 215, 216, 290, 301
Baumann, Rev. Nicholaus 266
Baumgart schoolhouse (Seymour, Ind.) 99
Baur 34
Baur family 134, 210
Baur, Alfred E. 242

Baur, Rev. A. C. 134, 162
Baur, Rev. Emil 209, 210, 351
Bax, H. 40
Bay City German M.E. Church (Mich.) 211–212
Bay City, Mich. 212
Bay Port, Mich. 209
Bayard Park Methodist (Evansville, Ind.) 130
Bayer family 353
Beal, B. F. 20
Beal, Brother 6
Beal, Rev. 344
Beaubien Street Church (Detroit, Mich.) 185
Beaver, Ohio 72
Becker, Rev. 128, 307
Becker, Rev. Friedrich 139, 140
Becker, Rev. Peter B. 47
Bedford Circuit (Ind.) 104, 110
Beeler, Conrad 179
Behrman, Alfred 105
Behrman, Walter 105
Belle River German Methodist Mission 190
Belle River, Mich. 190
Ben Israel Congregation 182
Benkenstein Hall (Cincinnati) 31
Benkenstein, Mr. 31
Benz, Brother 6
Berea Children's Home 299
Berea Circuit (Ohio) 267
Berea Orphan Home 313
Berea Orphanage 261, 306, 307
Berea, Ohio 21, 88, 261–??, 263, ??–264, 323, 352
Berg, Rev. George 264
Berlin German Methodist (Ohio) 325
Berlin, Ohio 325, 325
Berne, Mich. 210
Bertha, Miss 79
Bertram, Rev. Gustav 175, 177, 179, 180, 186, 210
Berville, Mich. 190
Best, Rev. Carl 334, 341
Bethany German M.E. (Cleveland) 259–260
Bethany M.E.
   Pomeroy, Ohio 69, 70
Bethel A.M.E. Church (New Albany, Ind.) 93
Bethel German M.E. (Ohio) 334–335, 337

Bethel, Ohio 334
Bethlehem German M.E. Church (Flint, Mich.) 203–204, 205, 206
Bethlehem German Methodist Church (Ohio) 303
Bethlehem M.E. Church
  Cincinnati 35–37
  Evansville, Ind. 131
Bethlehem, Ohio 302
Betts, Leona (Krill) 230
Beuchler (Biegler), Paul 111
Beuscher, Rev. 6, 29, 313, 314
Beyer, Rev. Herman C. 19, 261, 290, 301, 313
Biegler (Beuchler), Paul 111
Bier, Rev. John 67, 220, 286
Big Four Railroad 33
Biltimeier, Mr. 20
Bingham (Birmingham) Church (Pittsburgh, Pa.) 352
Birmingham (Bingham) Mission (Pittsburgh, Pa.) 352
Black's Chapel 120
Blair, John 220
Blake, Dr. Edgar 308
Blanchard Methodist (Cincinnati) 31, 38
Blanchard, Mr. 31
Blattler 334
Blesch, William 153
Block, John 140
Block, Katherine 140
Bloir, Helen 231
Bloir, Jack 231
Bloir, Steven 231
Bloomington, Ohio 302, 303, 305
Blue Grass Church
  Hookerville, Ind. 133
Blume, Rev. 302
Bobtown Church (Jackson Co., Ind.) 109
Boch, Rev. 290, 301
Bockstahler, Rev. 344
Bockstahler, Rev. C. W. 334
Bockstahler, Rev. J. J. 132
Bockstahler, Rev. Jacob 19, 94, 105, 121, 132, 290, 301, 333
Bockstahler, Rev. W. J. G. 124, 146, 161
Bockstaler, Rev. E. W. 330, 334
Bodmer, Rev. John R. 349
Boettcher, Julie 216
Bolin, Bob 145
Bollinger, Don A. 104
Bonn German M.E. (Ohio) 340
Bonn, Ohio 337, 338, 340, 343

Boonville Circuit (Ind.) 137–138
Boonville Mission (Ind.) 153, 157
Boonville Savings Association (Ind.) 138
Boonville, Ind. 132
Borcherding, Rev. J. 19
Borcherding, William 37
Borneman, Henry R. 19, 39, 78
Bos, Rev. 200
Bosse property 11
Boswell, Dr. C. M. 308
Bovard, Dr. W. S. 103
Bowers, Anna L. 343
Bozenhard, Rev. Karl 351
Braddock, Pa. 352
Bradford Circuit (Ind.) 97, 111–114
Bradford, Ind. 111
Bragsick (Brocksick) family 309
Brandywine Station, Ohio 294
Braun, Rev. Jacob 189, 210
Braun, Rev. John 129, 211
Braunhelm, Ohio 267
Breckinridge Street Church (Louisville) 87, 89, 91, 92
Bremer, Rev. 78
Brenzikofer, Charles 329
Brethren Church (Auburn, Ind.) 235
Breuhl, Mr. 31
Breunig, Rev. George A. 63
Brickner (Brueckner), Mrs. 78, 103
Brickner (Brueckner), Rev. Dr. William 67, 68, 78, 79, 103
Brinton Avenue Presbyterian Church 352
Broadway Church (Toledo, Ohio) 244
Brocksick (Bragsick) family 309
Brodbeck, Rev. Paul 56
Brodbeck, Stephen 72
Brodbeck, Vincent 73
Brokensword German M.E. (Ohio) 293–295
Brokensword, Ohio 286, 292, 293, 297
Bronnemann farm 188
Brookport, Ill. 167
Brookville, Ind. 9, 11
Brotherhood Temple Methodist Church 201
Brown Co., Ohio 81
Brown Street UMC (Lafayette, Ind.) 22–??, 24, ??–24
Brown, Mr. & Mrs. E. 309
Brown, Peggy Jean 289
Brown, Rev. Warren 178
Brueckner. *See* Brickner 78
Bruehl, R. A. W. 31

Brunersburg Circuit 226
Bucher, Dr. A. J. 6, 51, 103, 323
Buchs family 266
Buckhill Bottom German M.E.
  (Ohio) 327, 329, 332, 333
Buckhill Bottom, Ohio 327, 334
Bucyrus Circuit (Ohio) 286, 292, 293–302
Bucyrus German M.E. Church
  (Ohio) 294, 295
Bucyrus, Ohio 284, 286, 288, 296, 301, 302, 305
Buege, Frank 176
Buerkle, Rev. Carl F. 216, 297
Buhren, Rev. Ernst H. 255
Burke, Rev. 39
Burke's Chapel (Cincinnati) 27
Burkle family 72
Burkle, Rev. 290, 301
Burnips, Mich. 176
Burns, Bishop Charles Wesley 103, 104
Burrows, Dr. M. R. 50
Butler, Rev. Raymond 289
Buwalda, Rev. Dennis 201
Byron Center, Mich. 176

C

Caborn, Catherine 122
Caborn, Ind. 128
Caddell, Clifton 101
Calvary Chapel 94
Calvary Church
  New Albany, Ind. 92–94
Calvary Methodist
  Terre Haute, Ind. 24
Camp Wesley 307
Canal Dover Circuit (Ohio) 324–325
Canal Dover German Methodist
  (Ohio) 324–325
Canal Dover, Ohio 324–325
Cannelton and Tell City Circuit
  (Ind.) 138–141
Cannelton German M.E. (Ind.) 139
Cannelton Mission (Ind.) 140
Cannelton, Ind. 138
Captina Circuit (Ohio) 334–337
Captina, Ohio 341
Carpenter, Mrs. Cleo 339
Carson family 138
Carson, Charles 118
Cartwright, Peter 43
Caseville, Mich. 210
Catholics 34

Cedar Point, Ohio 270
Centenary Methodist 94
Center Church (Holt, Mich.) 201
Central Barren German M. E. (Zoar)
  (Ind.) 111–113
Central Barren UMC
  New Salisbury, Ind. 112–113
Central Barren, Ind. 111
Central Church (Huntingburg, Ind.) 144
Central German Church (Salem,
  Ohio) 231
Central German Conference 10, 12, 13, 18, 19, 22, 23, 33, 36, 38, 39, 47, 51, 57, 67, 68, 71, 73, 76, 80, 81, 91, 92, 97, 99, 102, 110, 112, 118, 119, 125, 130, 165, 166, 174, 177, 185, 187, 191, 199, 203, 228, 234, 238, 243, 246, 262, 264, 265, 283, 284, 288, 297, 306, 307, 313, 327, 337, 338, 352, 353
  Michigan District 171
Central Hower High School 324
Central Junior High 305
Central Methodist (Wheeling) 355, 356
Chapel on Read Street
  Evansville, Ind. 131
Chapline, William 354
Charity UMC (Flint, Mich.) 204
Charles 283
Charles, Anthony 11
Charlestown Circuit (Ind.) 96
Charlestown German Church (Ind.) 96
Charlestown, Ind. 93, 111
Charlie 269
Chelsea German Methodist Church
  (Mich.) 194
Chelsea, Mich. 193
Chester Circuit (Ohio) 68
Chester Methodists (Ohio) 68
Chester UMC
  Chester, Ohio 69
Chester, Ohio 68, 342
Chesterfield, Mich. 189
Chesterville, Ind. 11
Children's Home 88
Chili German Methodist (Ohio) 325
Chili, Ohio 325
Chillicothe Circuit (Ohio) 63–65, 67
Chillicothe, Ohio 57, 65, 72, 76, 279
China 20
Christ Church (Cleveland) 260
Christ UMC 289, 344

Index

Christian Church 81
   Aurora, Ind. 10
Christian Church (Mich.) 180
Christian German Agricultural and
   Benevolent Society of Ora
   Labora 209
Christian Science Church 234
Christian Unions 341
Christie Chapel 317
Christlich Apologete 286
Christman, Lee 339
Church of Christ
   Mt. Vernon, Ind. 118
Church of God (Goshen, Ind.) 237
Church of the Cross (Cleveland) 256,
   257, 259
Church of the Nazarene (Brookville,
   Ind.) 11
Church of the Shadow (Columbus,
   Ohio) 281
Cincinnati Board of Education 33
Cincinnati, Ohio 5, 27–39, 40, 47, 68, 77,
   79, 99, 146, 151, 165, 281, 284,
   309, 313
   Brighton district 31
   Mill Creek 32
   Mt. Auburn 29–31
   Texas area 28
   Walnut Hills 35
Circleville, Ohio 279, 285
Clarinda, Ohio 334
Clarington Circuit (Ohio) 334–337, 338
Clarington, Ohio 335, 337, 341
Clark Co., Ind. 97, 114
Clark Co., Wood Twp., Ind. 113
Clermont Co., Ohio 33
Cleveland West Side Church 258
Cleveland, Ohio 58, 60, 213, 255–261,
   324
Cochran, Rev. Ina L. 110
Cole Cemetery (Dillsboro, Ind.) 11
Coleman, Mrs. Mary 93
Collingwood Evangelical Church 247
Columbia Church (Ind.) 110
Columbus, Ind. 109
Columbus, Ohio 76, 279–285, 296
Community Church (Mt. Vernon,
   Ind.) 118
Community of Living Hope UMC 257,
   259
Corinne 269
Cornell farm 233
Cornell, R. C. 233

Cornerstone UMC (Portsmouth,
   Ohio) 75, 76, 79
Cortes, William 165
Corydon, Ind. 111, 113
Coshocton Co., Ohio 325
Covington Mission (Ky) 47
Covington, Ky. 43–45
Cozadd, Rev. Donald 177
Cramer, Dr. 39, 108
Cramer, Rev. M. 165
Cranston, Bishop Earl 19, 20
Crawford Co., Ohio 292
Crawford Twp., Ohio 325
Creslan, Ind. 10
Crown of Life Evangelical Lutheran
   Church 344
Cuba 266
Cullman, Ala. 166
Cumberland Presbyterian Church 168

D

Daescher, Rev. 334
Dale, Ind. 131
Dangel, Rev. 78, 79, 228
Dangle, Mrs. 23
Danker, Father 334
Danker, G. 327
Danker, George 341
Danville, Ohio 296
Davis-Reynolds, Rev. Sade 257
Dayton Circuit (Ohio) 56
Dayton, Ohio 39, 53–55, 57, 58, 60
Dearborn Co., Ind. 9
Decatur Co., Ind. 11
Deemer, Rev. 232
Defiance Circuit (Ohio) 226–227
Defiance German M.E. (Ohio) 226
Defiance, Ohio 219, 227
Delaware Circuit (Ohio) 302
Delaware German M.E. (Delaware,
   Ohio) 284
Delaware Mission (Ohio) 286
Delaware, Ohio 237, 279, 284, 296
Delker, Joseph 274
Dendel, Lizzie 177
Dennig, Mrs. W. J. 288
Denton, Rev. Douglas B. 257
Denzler family 19, 20
Dering (Doering), William 309
Detroit Conference 203
Detroit Third Church (Mich.) 182
Detroit, Mich. 185–187, 188
DeWitt Circuit (Mich.) 197, 198–200

DeWitt Methodist Church (Mich.) 199
Dickhaut, Rev. 45, 343
Diehl, Dr. 188
Diekmann, Dr. J. A. 108
Diem, Gottfried 190
Dieterle, Rev. Max 34, 56, 57
Diffendorfer, Dr. Ralph E. 50
Dillsboro, Ind. 10, 11
Disciples' Church (Ripley, Ohio) 80
Doering (Dering), William 309
Doering, Dr. 349
Dohrmann, Frederick 43
Donutt Church (Edon, Ohio) 232
Donutt, Rev. George 232
Dornbirer, Rev. 273
Dover, Ohio 285, 324–325
Dresden German M.E. (Ohio) 285
Dresden, Ohio 279, 285
Druckses family 17
Dryer, Chester 189
Dubois Co., Ind. 143
Duck Creek, Ohio 340, 343
Duke Lake (Duck Lake?), Mich. 178
Dumontsville, Ohio 279, 285
Duncan's Brewery 305
Dunkard Society (Edon, Ohio) 232
Dunn, John 118
Dunn, Mary 118
Duquesne 352
Duttweiler, Rev. Herbert 210

E

E. L. Gordon Methodist Church (Flint, Mich.) 204
E.U.B. Church 294
East Ohio Conference 262, 299, 340
   and History Commission 292
East Tenth Street Church (Indianapolis) 19
East Toledo German Methodist Mission 245
Ebenezer Berne Memorial Cemetery (Ora Labora, Mich.) 211
Ebenezer German M.E. (Boonville, Ind.) 137–138
Ebenezer Mission (Pigeon, Mich.) 210
Ebert, Jacob 335
Edelmaier, Rev. 6, 50, 79, 120, 128, 162, 188
Edgerton Circuit (Ohio) 227–234
Edgerton, Ohio 227, 231
Edon Methodist (Ohio) 232
Edon, Ohio 227, 233

Eighteenth Street German M.E. (Louisville) 89, 90–92, 97, 102
Eiselen, Dr. F. C. 103
Electronics' Research INC 138
Elkins, Virginia 196
Ellinger, Rev. 313
Elmore Circuit (Ohio) 237–239
Elmore, Ohio 200
Elyria, Ohio 267
Emannuel (Bucyrus, Ohio) 296
Emanuel Church (West Unity) 219
Emanuel German M.E.
   Edgerton, Ohio 228–231
   Ind. 138
   Toledo, Ohio 240–242
Emanuel M.E. Church 234
Emanuel Methodist Church (Mich.) 199
Emanuel UMC (Edgerton, Ohio) 231
Emanuel. See, First Church, Detroit, Mich.
Emmanuel Church
   Fishers Settlement, Pultight 113
Emmanuel German M.E. (Berea, Ohio) 261–264
Emmanuel UMC (Clark Co., Ind.) 97, 114
Emmich family 37
Emrich, Daniel 72
Enderis, Dr. 6, 78, 108
Engel, William 351
English Conference 202, 246, 288, 297
English Lutheran
   Goshen, Ind. 237
   Hamilton, Ohio 57
English M.E. Church
   Batesville, Ind. 4
   Galloway, Mich. 179
   Sidney, Ohio 56
English Methodist Church
   Akron, Ohio 323
   Bucyrus, Ohio 297
   Cincinnati 30
   Cleveland, Ohio 255
   Detroit, Mich. 186
   Galion, Ohio 287
   Goshen, Ind. 237
English Sixteen Church (Ohio) 286, 290
Ennis, Marilyn 216
Enochsburg, Ind. 11
Epworth UMC 297
   Bucyrus, Ohio 296, 300
   Cincinnati 39
Erie church 271
Espinoza, Rev. Modesto 258

Etna, Ohio 279, 285
Evangelical League of Christian
    Endeavor 247
Evangelical Maple Grove
    Campground 146
Evangelical United Brethren
  Cincinnati, Ohio 39
  Mt. Vernon, Ind. 120
Evangelicals 133
Evansport, Ohio 225
Evansville German Mission (Ind.) 117, 120, 137, 168
Evansville, Ind. 12, 128, 129–134, 168
Ewing, Samuel 63

F

F., Frank 269
Fairview German M.E. Church (Ohio) 80
Fairview, Ohio 80
Faith Covenant
  Madison, Ind. 13
Faith UMC
  Grand Rapids, Mich. 175
  Mt. Vernon, Ind. 120
Farmer's Retreat, Ind. 11
Father of German Methodist 27
Feldwish-Kuck farm 144
Fellers, Gottlieb 325
Fenneman, H. H. 143, 145
Fenneman, Harvey 161
Fenneman, Rev. Will 150
Ficken, Rev. John 350
Fidelity building
  Wheeling, W.Va. 355, 356
Fiedler, Rev. Gustav 202
Fifth Street M.E. Church (Lafayette, Ind.) 22
Findlay Street UMC (Portsmouth, Ohio) 76
First Church
  Batesville, Ind. 4
  Cincinnati 32
  Cleveland, Ohio 255–257, 259
  Columbus, Ohio 279–281, 282, 284, 285
  Detroit, Mich. 185–186
  Evansville, Ind. 129–131, 134
  Pittsburgh, Pa. 349–350, 352
First German M.E. Church 305, 306
  Ann Arbor 193–194
  Cincinnati 27–28
  Columbus, Ohio 279, 281
  Indianapolis 17–18, 20
  Lawrenceburg, Ind. 7–9
  Marion, Ohio 304–307
  New Albany, Ind. 93
  Newport, Ky. 47
  Seymour, Ind. 102
First M.E. Church 118
  Pennington, Ind. 5
First Methodist Church 324
  Berea, Ohio 263
  Columbus, Ohio 281
  Dover, Ohio 325
  Greenfield, Ohio 63
  Hamilton, Ohio 57
First UMC 238
  Lansing, Mich. 198
  Mt. Vernon, Ind. 117
  of Bucyrus, Ohio 299
  Portsmouth, Ohio 76
  Tell City, Ind. 140–141
Fischbach, Philippina (Metzgar) 53
Fischbach, Rev. B. C. 338
Fischbach, Rev. J. W. 342
Fischer, P. C. 343
Fisher Settlement, Ohio 267
Fishers Settlement, Ind. 111
Fishing Creek (Zoar) Church (Ohio) 239
Fiske, Mr. 56
Fitzgerald, Bishop 353
Five Corners Methodist Church (Holt, Mich.) 200
Flaccus, Ch. L. 351
Flat Rock Children's Home 299
Flat Rock, Ohio 267
Fleiner, Rev. 305
Flint Park, Mich. 204, 205, 206
Flint, Mich. 92, 203, 204, 217
Floerke, Rev. 132
Floerke, Rev. William 55
Floral Grove Cemetery (Ohio) 219, 220, 221, 227
Florida 150
Flory, Rev. Barb 201
Flower Creek, Mich. 178
Footlighters (Newport, Ky.) 49
Forest Run German M.E.
  Forest Run, Ohio 71
Forest Run UMC (Ohio) 71
Four Square Gospel Church 325
Fourth German M.E. Church
  Cincinnati 31
  Indianapolis 18–19
Fourth Street Church (Portsmouth, Ohio) 73

Fourth Street M.E.
    Evansville, Ind. 129–131
Fourth Street Methodist
    Evansville, Ind. 79
    Wheeling, W.Va. 354, 356
Francisco Circuit (Mich.) 195–197
Francisco German Methodist Church
    (Mich.) 195–197
Francisco, Mich. 193
Frank (grandfather of Ms.
    Meckstroth) 317
Frank, Mrs. Jacob 88
Franklin Avenue UMC (Portsmouth,
    Ohio) 74, 76, 77
Franklin Boulevard Methodist 258
Franklin Co., Ind. 11
Franklin County Senior Citizens (Ind.) 11
Fraternal Order of Eagles (Lawrenceburg,
    Ind.) 9
Free Methodists (Cannelton, Ind.) 139
Freeport Circuit (Mich.) 179–182
Fremont German M.E. (Indiana) 233–234
Fremont, Ind. 227
Freudiger 334
Freyhofer, Rev. J. Wesley 189, 264
Fritchie, Rev. G. H. 12
Fritsche, Louis 308
Froebisch, John George 340
Frost, Rev. Charles 257
Ft. Wayne, Ind. 242
Fulton Street Market (Grand Rapids) 176
Furnace Mission (Ohio) 65
Fusz, Rev. 131

G

Gabel, Charles 88
Gahn, Rev. Conrad 32, 258, 296
Galbreath, Elmer E. 80
Galena Street German Methodist Church
    (Toledo) 248
Galena Street Mission 241
Galion Circuit (Ohio) 285–292, 293
Galion, Ohio 284, 286, 287, 296
Galloway schoolhouse (Mich.) 179
Gares, John 220
Gares, Sarah 220
Garrett Biblical Institute 103
Garrett German M.E. (Ind.) 235
Garrett Post Office 235
Gatchel family 141
Gates Fourth Methodist Church
    (Columbus, Ohio) 283
Gehring, Christian 329

Geib, Rev. Philipp 325
Gelvin, Mrs. 6
Genheimer Church (Pine Grove, Ohio) 71
George 269
George Geyer Cemetery 315
Georgi, Dr. Hugo W. 51
Georgia 257
German 28
German Baptist
    Sidney, Ohio 56
German Conference 133, 178, 288, 324
German M.E. Church 3, 178, 343
    aka Emanuel (Mich.) 199–200
    Batesville, Ind. 3–4
    Bedford, Ind. 111
    Boonville, Ind. 137
    Brokensword, Ohio 293–295
    Brookville, Ind. 11
    Bucyrus, Ohio 295–300
    Chesterville, Ind. 11
    Chillicothe, Ohio 64
    Galion, Ohio 287
    Grand Rapids 173
    Hanover, Ind. 13
    Henderson, Ky. 168
    Holland, Ind. 145–150
    Holt, Mich. 201
    Ironton, Ohio 65–66
    Laughery, Ind. 5
    Lawrenceville, Ind. 10
    Madison, Ind. 12
    Mansfield, Ohio 292
    Milan, Ind. 10
    New Knoxville, Ohio 309–314
    New Palestine, Ind. 17, 21–22
    Pennington, Ind. 5
    Penntown, Ind. 9–10
    Piqua, Ohio 56
    Pomeroy, Ohio 69–70
    Portsmouth, Ohio 72–76
    Richmond, Ind. 56
    Ripley, Ohio 80
    Sidney, Ohio 56
    Switzerland Co., Ind. 14
    Terre Haute, Ind. 24
    Waverly, Ohio 64
    Wheeling, W.Va. 354–355
    Zoar, Ohio 286
German Methodist Church
    Dillsboro, Ind. 11
    Golconda, Ill. 167
    Greenville, Ohio 55–56
    Kendallville, Ind. 234

German Mission Society (Cincinnati) 33
German Ridge, Ind. 140
German Russians 203
German Village 282
German Wallace College 34, 261, 262
German-English M.E. Church (Cullman, Ala.) 166
Germans 341
Germany 51, 181
Gertrude 283
Geyer, Ohio 315
Geyer, Rev. John 68
Geyer, Rev. William 68, 69
Giesen 35
Giesen, Otto 39
Giesen, Rev. 187
Glass Workers Union Hall 247
Gleb, Valentine 257
Glotfelty, Rev. Alma 201
Goeschel, Herman 214
Goff, Sue 117, 118
Golconda Circuit (Ill.) 166–167
Golconda, Ill. 166
Golder, Rev. Dr. Christian 20, 31, 39, 69, 350
Gommel, Rev. John C. 11, 200, 258
Goshen German M.E. (Ind.) 236–237
Goshen, Ind. 236–237
Gospel Temple (Defiance, Ohio) 226
Grace M.E.
  Bedford, Ind. 110
  Hamilton, Ohio 59
  Madison, Ind. 12
Grace Methodist Church 49
  Hamilton, Ohio 57–58
Grace UMC
  Bedford, Ind. 110, 111
  Hamilton, Ohio 59
Graessle, Louise (Schneck) 102
Graessle, Rev. Andrew (Andreas) 88, 165, 315, 334
Graessle, Rev. Bernhard 315
Grand Rapids Circuit (Mich.) 173, 179, 180
Grand Rapids, Mich. 173, 179, 187
Grant, Ulysses 165
Grass Lake, Mich. 195, 197
Grassman, Charles 73
Greater Whitestone Baptist Church 261
Greathouse Methodist Church (Mt. Vernon, Ind.) 124
Green, Rev. Lewis 197
Greencastle, Ind. 24, 25

Greenfield, Ohio 63, 64
Greensburg, Ind. 12
Greenville Mission (Ohio) 56
Greenville, Ohio 55, 56, 57
Greenville/Piqua Circuit (Ohio) 55–57
Greer, Dr. Frank 19
Grell, Simeon 126
Grentszenberg, Rev. H. 73
Grettenberger, Louis 202
Grettenberger, Rev. George 202
Griver, Mrs. 79
Grob family 25
Grob, Rev. Theodore 24, 104, 313
Grosse Point, Mich. 185
Grossman family 129
Grossman, Rev. 128
Guenther, Rev. J. C. 301, 307
The Guesthouse B&B 238
Guinther, Abe 291
Gunnisonville, Mich. 199
Gustave, Rev. 188
Guth, Dr. George 29
Guth, Sophia 44
Guthrie, Wayne 19
Gutting, Frank 305
Gwinn, Richard 210

H

H., Julius 330
Haas family 157
Haas, O. C. 108
Haas, Rev. John 294, 297
Hahn, John Adam 126
Hahn, Nicholas 126
Hamilton Circuit (Ohio) 56
Hamilton, Ohio 38, 57–58
Hamline Chapel 8
Hamp, Brother 20
Hamp, Mrs. Fred 19
Hamp, Rev. F. A. 215
Hanaford, Samuel A. 32
Hanging Rock Iron Region (Ohio) 65
Hannibal German M.E. (Ohio) 328, 333
Hannibal UMC (Ohio) 328
Hannibal, Ohio 290, 300, 327, 330, 337
Hanning family 157
Hanning, Jim 160
Hanning, Mary Ellen 160
Hanover, Ind. 13
Hard Corners 230
Harmony U.M.C. 294
Harrer, Rev. 19, 301, 344
Harrison (Harris) Settlement (Ind.) 157

Harrup, Dr. R. W. 51
Hartmann family 35
Hartmann, Rev. John Martin 185
Hartmann, William 28
Hartshorn family 274
Harvey, Rev. M. S. 324
Hass, Jacob 118
Haueisen, John 264
Haueter, Mr. & Mrs. Felix 329
Haueter, Nina 329
Haueter, Rev. Otto E. 79, 203, 333
Hausser, Rev. G. F. 103
Hauswald, Jake 78
Hayn, Rev. W. F. 187
Heineman, Timothy 43
Heinlein, Rev. H. C. 288, 335, 336
Heitmeyer, Rev. Karl Frederick 126, 139, 143
Helen-Elizabeth 103
Heller, Rev. Frederick 138
Helser, Rev. John 96
Helwig home 341
Helzer's Settlement 96
Hemmer, Adolph 152
Hemmer, Ed 162
Hemmer, Louis 152, 156
Hemmer, Mrs. Herman 162
Hemmers, Adolph 151
Henderson Settlement, Ky. 229
Henderson, Bishop 78
Henderson, Bishop Theodore 50, 51, 73, 78, 145, 174, 188
Henderson, Ky. 132, 168
Henke, Rev. E. 6
Henke, Rev. H. 89
Henrietta German Methodist Church (Ohio) 264–266, 274, 333
Henrietta UMC (Ohio) 265
Henrietta, Ohio 264–266
Henry Street Church (Delaware, Ohio) 284
Herbolt family 40
Herion, Rev. John 335, 336, 339
Heritage UMC (Lafayette, Ind.) 24
Heritage United Methodist (Cincinnati) 39
Hermannsaue, Mich. 213
Herrlich, Max 22
Hertzler, Prof. 301
Herwig, Emma 255–256
Herzer, C. G. 239
Herzer, Rev. 290, 341
Hewitt Chapel 35

Hey, Rev. Theophil 201, 202
Higginsport, Ohio 80, 81
Highland, Ind. 131
Hill Grove, Ohio 343
Hiller, Rev. G. E. 20
Hinderer, Virginia (Wahl) 197
Hingeley, Dr. J. B. 50
Hinners & Albertson pipe organ 146
Hinners, Mr. 23
Hispanic 28
Hite, A. L. 81
Hitt, Charles W. 88
Hocking, Ohio 279, 285
Hoefner, Christov 220
Hofer, Rev. John 93
Hoff, F. A. 158, 159
Hoffman, Barbara 216
Hoffmeier, H. 159
Holland 79, 129, 156, 306
Holland Central German M.E. (Ind.) 145–150
Holland UMC (Ind.) 150
Holland, Ind. 133, 134, 145–152, 307
Holmes Co., Ohio 325
Holmes-Liberty High School 294
Holt Circuit (Mich.) 197, 200–202
Holt German M.E. Church (Mich.) 200–202
Holt Methodist Church 201
Holtkamp, Rev. 50
Holverstot property 304
Holzer (Helser, Hoelzer), Johannes 96
Hopkins Circuit (Mich.) 175–178
Hopkins German M.E. (Mich.) 177, 178
Hopkins, Mich. 175, 176
Hoppen, Rev. John 72
Horst, Dr. 128, 129
Horst, Rev. John 211
Horst, Rev. John H. 39, 44, 88, 291
House of God Testament Temple (Louisville) 89
Hoverman, Mr. 316
Howe, Irene 312
Huber family 108
Huber, Bro. 92, 107
Huber, Dr. John 103
Huber, Edmund 51
Hufnagel, Artus 133
Hufnagels 152
Hunefeld, Frank 148
Hunter, Rev. Alfred 216
Huntingburg Circuit (Ind.) 143–156

Huntingburg German M.E. (Ind.) 143–145
Huntingburg Lumber Co. (Ind.) 155
Huntingburg Mission (Ind.) 140, 143, 145, 153
Huntingburg UMC (Ind.) 144, 145
Huntingburg, Ind. 12, 128, 134
Hurd Schoolhouse 199
Hurst, Bishop J. J. 351
Hyde Park Bethlehem (Cincinnati) 36, 37
Hyde Park Methodist Protestant Church (Cincinnati) 37

I

Iberia UMC (Ohio) 292
Immanuel (Emanuel) German Methodist (Swan Creek, Mich.) 191
Immanuel Church
  Lakeside Park 45
Immanuel Evangelical Church (Cleveland) 257
Immanuel German M.E. Church 259
  Cleveland 259, 260
  Covington, Ky. 43–46
Immanuel Mission (Cleveland) 256
Immanuel Pentecostal Church (Cleveland) 259
Immanuel UMC
  Ironton, Ohio 66
Independence
  Evansville, Ind. 133
Independence, Ill. 167
Indiana Conference 12, 97, 99, 102, 105, 110, 120, 124
Indiana Conference Corporation 160
Indiana State University 25
Indianapolis, Ind. 17–21, 22
Infant of Prague Catholic Church (Bay City, Mich.) 212
Ingold, Charles 329
Ipswich, England 298
Ireland, Mr. 104
Ironton Circuit (Ohio) 68
Ironton, Ohio 65–66
Irving Circuit (Mich.) 179
Irving, Mich. 179

J

Jackson Co., Ind. 100
Jacobsmuehler, Hermann zur 351
Jacoby, Rev. Ludwig 43
Jahraus, Mrs. 77
James, Bishop 24, 63

Jefferson Street German Methodist (Louisville) 89, 90, 91
Jeffersonville, Ind. 12, 45, 94–95
Jend, Rev. Henry 174, 241, 344
Jennings Co., Ind. 102
Jennings County German M.E. Ind. 102
Jewett School (Kochville, Mich.) 216
Johannes, Rev. 151
John 56, 79, 151
Jones, Mrs. George H. 343
Jones, Rev. Hughey 58
Jung, Rev. 274

K

Kaetzel, Rev. 335
Kalamazoo, Mich. 177
Kaletsch, Rev. 29, 39, 162, 290
Kalmbach, George 187
Kargbo-Davis, Edward 264
Kargbo-Davis, Melrose 264
Kasting, George 101
Katterheinrich, Elmer 312
Katterheinrich, Noah 313
Katterheinrich, Norman 312
Katterheinrich, Wesley 314
Katterjohn, Frank 151, 152
Katterjohn, Herman 153
Katterjohn, Will 152
Katterjohn, William 153
Keller, Rev. Christoph 22
Kendallville Circuit (Ind.) 234–236
Kendallville, Ind. 228, 236
Kentucky Conference 47, 51, 87
Kenyon College 27
Kern, Rev. 290, 295, 344
Kessinger, Rev. Karl 44
Killion, Rev. O. E. 124
Kisling (Kiesting, Kiesling), Rev. John 11, 12, 21, 92, 99, 309
Kisling, Rev. John 99
Klebaattel, Rev. August 203
Klein, Rev. John A. 190, 255, 266, 274, 351
Klett, George 178
Klocksiem, Rev. O. C. 34, 325
Klotz, Rev. 314
Klotzbach, A. 256
Kluesner, Rev. John C. 314
Knauf(f), Rev. 50, 51, 103
Knoxville, Tenn. 166
Koch, John C. 234

Koch, Rev. Dr. John H. 50, 51, 78, 162, 338
Koch, Rev. Karl 325
Kochville German M.E. Church (Mich.) 214–217
Kochville Township Hall (Mich.) 216
Kochville United Methodist Church 216
Koeneke, Rev. Henry 68, 120, 137, 143, 340, 341
Koepke, Gustavus 214
Koerner, Gotlieb 230
Kokomoor, Fr. 159
Korea 343
Kosloskey, Lowell 182
Kossuth German M.E. (Ohio) 309, 315–318
Kossuth Zion Church (Ohio) 318
Kossuth Zion UMC (Ohio) 316–318
Krapohl, Gerhardt 215
Kratzville, Ind. 131
Kraus, Ferdinand 303
Krehbiel, Rev. Jacob 177, 189, 190, 197, 199, 200, 211, 213, 214, 274
Krieg, Friedrich 28
Krill, Paul D. 230
Krill, Rev. Henry 231
Krill, Rosa 230
Kruse family 39, 55, 157, 309
Kruse, Curtis 312
Kuck, Alice 312
Kuck, William 145
Kuehnle, Mrs. Margaret 299
Kunz, Bro. 146
Kunz, Ed 146

L

La Carne German M.E. (Ohio) 271
La Carne Post Office (Ohio) 271
La Carne, Ohio 267
La Carpe church 271
La Iglesia de Dios, Inc. 226
La Point UMC (Ohio) 271
Laas, Rev. G. 173
Laas, Rev. Gustav 173, 213
Lafayette, Ind. 22–24
Lageman, Rev. 5, 6
Lagemann family 307, 308, 309
Lake Erie 274, 284
Lake Shore Mission 267
Lakeside Park, Ky. 45, 46
Lakeside, Ohio 257, 274, 307
Lamy, John 79
Lamy, Rev. 34, 77, 79, 354

Langebrake, Elmo 155
Lansing German M.E. Church (Mich.) 197–198
Lansing, Mich. 197, 198, 200
Lantz, Rev. Fred 341
Lasalle Avenue Church. *See also,* Second Church, Detroit, Mich. 186
Laubscher, Christian 132
Laubscher, Mrs. Simon 132
Laughery Mission 9
Laughery, Ind. 5, 9
Lawrence Furnace Circuit (Ohio) 65, 67
Lawrenceburg Mission (Ind.) 3
Lawrenceburg, Ind. 7–9, 12
Lawrenceville Circuit (Ind.) 9–11
Lawrenceville German M.E. 350
Lawrenceville, Ill. 110
Lawrenceville, Ind. 10
Lawson, Rev. Dwight 204
Lebanon 266
Lee, Abner S. 182
Lees Run German M.E. (Ohio). *See also,* Leith Run 339, 341
Leger, Mr. 67
Lehman, Rev. 336
Leith Run (Lees Run), Ohio 337, 338
Leith Run Methodist Church (Ohio) 339
Lenz, Rev. Henry 196
Leonard, Dr. A. B. 20
Leveridge, Benjamin 287
Levi, Jane 216
Lewis, Bishop W. S. 162
Lexington, Mich. 189, 190
Liberty, Ohio 279, 285
Lich, Rev. Heinrich G. 31, 131
Liggett Chapel (Ripley, Ohio) 80
Lima Organ Company 312
Lima, Ohio 237
Lincoln Way M.E. Church (Bucyrus, Ohio) 292, 296
Lindner, Elisabeth 211
Link, Rev. Jacob J. 177, 178, 203, 206, 245, 313
Lint, Angeline 231
Lint, Samuel 231
Little Dutch Church Association 340
Livingston M.E. Church (Columbus, Ohio) 281
Livingston UMC (Columbus, Ohio) 280
Livingston United Methodist Church (Columbus, Ohio) 281, 284
London, Ohio 296
Lorain Co., Ohio 266

Lorain, Ohio 333
Lott School (Holt, Mich.) 200
Loudonville, Ohio 296
Louisville Art Glass Studio 125
Louisville, Ky. 29, 35, 79, 87–92, 99, 103, 125, 284, 314
Lowell, Mich. 179, 180
Lower Sandusky Mission (Ohio) 239
Luckey, George 238
Ludwig family 157
Lukemeyer, Rev. J. H. 127, 143, 144
Lutheran Church 203, 341
Lutherans 100, 137, 173, 178, 197, 214, 237, 273

M

M., John 283
M.E. Church (Pearl, Ohio) 325
Maag, Rev. Henry 58, 78, 128
Macomb Co., Mich. 190
Madison 13
Madison Avenue Methodist Church (Cincinnati) 36
Madison Circuit (Ind.) 12–13
Madison, Ind. 12, 13
Maentz, Rev. George H. 210
Magdanz 34, 354
Magly, Rev. P. F. 350
Maier, George 228
Maier, Mary 228
Maier, Mrs. Lena 124
Main Street Methodist Church (Huntingburg, Ind.) 144
Makley, Mary 179, 180
Malaga and Matamoras Mission 338
Malaga, Ohio 327, 338
Mansfield Mission 292
Mansfield, Ohio 284, 286, 290, 296, 301, 302
Mantz, Rev. H. 173
Manzer, Clara 288
Maple Street German M.E. Church (Jeffersonville, Ind.) 94–95
Marblehead Peninsula 274
Marietta Circuit (Ohio) 343
Marietta German M.E. (Ohio) 340, 341–344
Marietta, Ohio 68, 79, 338, 341–345
Marine City Circuit (Mich.) 189–191
Marine City, Mich. 21, 190
Marion Church 302
Marion Circuit (Ohio) 302–307
Marion Co., Ohio 302

Marion High School 305
Marion, Ohio 296, 302–308, 315
Market St. Church (Louisville) 284
Market Street Church (Hopkins, Mich.) 175, 177
Market Street German M.E. Galion, Ohio 287, 287–290
Market Street German Methodist (Louisville) 87–89
Marks, Rev. Bernard 298
Marrs Circuit (Ind.) 117, 120–129
Marti, Adam 215
Marti, Jacob 214
Marting, Henry 73
Marting, Rev. 301
Marting, Rev. A. L. 301
Marting, Rev. Dr. Albert L. 76, 78, 79, 262
Marting, Rev. Dr. John C. 35, 283, 313
Marty, Randolph 329
Mary's Chapel (Hannibal, Ohio) 328
Masons 178
Massac Co., Ill. 167
Matamoras, Ohio 338, 341
Matthai, Rev. Daniel 179, 241
Mavsety, Dr. 308
Mayer, Andrew 234
Mayer, Rev. John 58, 188, 283, 284, 309, 313
Mayers family 188
Maysville, Ky. 72
McCallum, Rev. Marvin 210
McConnell, Bishop Francis J. 74
McGowan, Rev. W. H. 124
McKeesport German M.E. (Pittsburgh, Pa.) 352
McKeesport, Pa. 352
Meckstroth family 309
Meckstroth, Glenna 316
Medina, Ohio 324
Meigs Co., Ohio 342
Melle, Dr. Otto 103
Messiner, Mr. 305
Methodist Cemetery (Batesville, Ind.) 4
Methodist Church of Berea 263
Methodist Episcopal Church, South (Nashville) 165
Methodist Temple (Evansville, Ind.) 130, 131
Methodists 341
Metropolis, Ill. 166, 167
Mexico 313
Meyer, John 20

Michigan Conference
　of the Methodist Episcopal Church 199
Middletown, Ind. 111
Midway, Ill. 167
Milan, Ind. 9, 10
Militzer, Mrs. 196
Militzer, Rev. R. C. 245
Miller, Bishop George A. 313
Miller, Charlie 78, 79, 108, 162, 283
Miller, Rev. 94, 95
Miller, Rev. Adam 7
Miller, Rev. Louis 51, 140
Miltonsburg, Ohio 334, 338
Mitter, Rev. George 20
Moeller, Rev. Dr. 6, 103
Monroe Co., Switzerland Twp., Ohio 334
Monroe Mission 341
Monroefield Circuit (Ohio) 338–340, 341, 343
Monroefield German M.E. (Ohio) 337, 338
Monroefield, Ohio 335, 336, 338
Montague Circuit (Mich.) 178
Montague, Mich. 173, 179
Monterey German M.E. (Mich.) 177
Moorman, Anthony 11
Morgan's raiders 100
Morlock, Dr. Christian 6, 103, 108, 126, 307
Mormons 178
Mt. Auburn German M.E. Church (Cincinnati) 29–31
Mt. Clemens Mission (Mich. 190
Mt. Clemens, Mich. 189
Mt. Healthy 57
Mt. Healthy German M.E. Church (Cincinnati) 37–39
Mt. Healthy UMC (Cincinnati) 38, 39
Mt. Pleasant German M.E. Church (Cincinnati) 37
Mt. Pleasant Mission (Cincinnati) 38
Mt. Vernon Circuit (Ind.) 117–120
Mt. Vernon German M. E. Church 117
Mt. Vernon German M.E. (Ohio) 329, 331, 333
Mt. Vernon, Ind. 117, 132, 134
Mt. Vernon, Ohio 296, 327, 338
Mud Creek Church (Ohio) 239
Mud Creek, Ohio 239
Mueller family 40
Mueller, E. E. 20, 21
Mueller, F. W. 103
Mueller, Rev. A. H. 108

Mueller, Rev. Dr. Fred W. 33, 50, 51, 103, 203, 256, 290, 294, 301, 307, 308, 316, 353
Mueller, William 215
Muhleman Memorial German M.E. (Pittsburgh, Pa.) 352
Muhlemann, Captain Charles 330, 352
Muhlemann, Minnie 330, 352
Mulberry Street Wesleyan Church (Chillicothe, Ohio) 63
Muskegon and White Hall Mission (Mich.) 178
Muskegon Circuit (Mich.) 178
Muskegon, Mich. 173, 178, 179
Musser, Dr. 162
Muth, Rev. Konrad 17, 24, 93, 94, 120, 137, 140, 143

N

Nachtrieb, Rev. 291
Nachtrieb, Rev. Christian 305
Naffe family 108
Naffe, Mrs. 107
Nagler, Rev. F. L. 28, 228, 323
Nashville, Tenn. 79, 165–166
Nast Memorial Church (Cincinnati) 27, 108
Nast, Dr. 43, 51, 63, 302, 305, 306, 308, 313
Nast, Dr. Albert 29
Nast, Rev. Dr. Wilhelm (William) 6, 7, 17, 22, 27, 28, 51, 57, 284, 285, 286, 296, 297, 328, 334, 349, 355
Nast-Trinity Church (Cincinnati) 27–28, 32
Nast-Trinity UMC (Cincinnati) 29
Native Americans 345
Neff, Gottlob 290
Neff, Rev. 286
Negroes 333
Neir, Rev. John 189
New Albany, Ind. 12, 92–94, 111
New Albany, Ohio 79, 129
New Bavaria, Ohio 227
New Bloomington, Ohio 304
New Haven, Mich. 189
New Jersey Street M.E. Church (Indianapolis) 18, 19
New Knoxville Circuit (Ohio) 309–315
New Knoxville German M.E. Church (Ohio) 309–314, 315, 318
New Knoxville UMC (Ohio) 310

New Knoxville, Ohio 56, 309–314
New Martinsville, Ohio 302, 338
New Matamoras, Ohio 339
New Mexico 317
New Middleton, Ind. 113
New Palestine UMC (Ind.) 21, 22
New Palestine, Ind. 17, 21–22
New Rochelle 77
New Salisbury M.E. (Ind.) 113
New Salisbury, Ind. 111
New Washington, Ohio 294
New Washington–Scioto Charge 294
New Winchester, Ohio 286
New York 354
New Albany, 150
Newark German M.E. (Ohio) 285
Newark, Ohio 279, 282, 285, 296
Newburgh German M.E. (Ind.) 138, 139
Newpoint, Ind. 9
Newport Mission (Ky.) 47
Newport, Ky. 43, 47, 50
Newport, Mich. 185, 189, 190
Nicholson, Bishop 6, 313, 314
Nicholson, Dr. 308
Nichter, Bonaparte 220
Niethamer, Tom 180
1913 flood 73
1937 flood 47, 74, 88
Nippert Memorial Methodist Church (Indianapolis) 18
Nippert, Alfred K. 19
Nippert, Rev. Ludwig (Louis) 17, 18, 21, 37
Nobs (the Knobs), Ind. 111
Nocka, Rev. William E. 6, 57, 294
North Holt Methodist Church (Mich.) 201
North Hyde Park Church (Cincinnati) 37
North Lake Methodist 196
North Lowell, Mich. 179
North Ohio District 294
North School (Holt, Mich.) 200
Northeast Ohio Conference 263
  Cambridge-Barnesville District 337
Norwalk, Ohio 267
Nothdurft, Rev. George 196
Nuelsen, Dr. 290
Nuhfer, Rev. Nicholaus 190, 286, 293, 296
Nusz, Rev. Gordon W. 210
Nye, William 284

O
O'Dell, Rev. Max 148

Oak Grove German M.E. (Ohio) 80
Oak Park Methodist Church (Bethlehem, Mich.) 203
Oborn, Dr. 162
Oborn, Dr. J. W. 161
Oceola, Ohio 286
Oetjen, Rev. John 30, 290, 308, 343
Ohio City, Ohio 258
Ohio Conference 3, 24, 57, 193, 228, 240, 255
  Angola, Indiana Mission 227, 228
  Cincinnati District 36
  of English-speaking Methodist churches 67
  of the Evangelical Church 246
  of the Evangelical Congregation 245
  of the Methodist Church 267
  of the Methodist Episcopal Church 66, 190
Ohio River 284
Ohio Wesleyan University 285
Ohio State University 283
Oil Creek German M.E. (Ind.) 140
Okemos M.E. Church (Mich.) 202
Old Folk's Home (Quincy, Ill.) 6
Old Milan, Ind. 10
Old Mission Church 298
Olin Mathieson Chemical Corporation 327
Olive Chapel 317
Omo, Mich. 190
Opp property 11
Ora Labora, Mich. 209–210, 351
Orange German M.E. (Ohio) 71
Oregon Twp., Clark Co., Ind. 97
Oriole Methodist Church (Ind.) 140
Oriole, Ind. 139, 140
Orr, Thomas 63
Otisco German M.E. (Ind.) 96–97
Ott, Bishop Donald A. 211
Otto Bros. 344
Otto, Mrs. (Andre) 344
Otto, Rev. 344
Our Lady of St. Carmel (Bay City, Mich.) 214
Our Saviour Lutheran Church (Goshen, Ind.) 237
Over the Rhine district 28
Overbeck, Frank 162

P
Pa 269

Park Avenue Mission (Pittsburgh, Pa.) 350–351
Patow, Mrs. 206
Patow, Rev. Karl 206, 217
Payne Chapel AME 58
  Hamilton, Ohio 58, 59
Peace Lutheran Church
  Galion, Ohio 288
Pearl, Ohio 325
Pelusi, Philip 350
Pendell, Mary (Marting) 262
Peninsula, Ohio 267
Pennington Church (Ind.) 5
Pennington, Ind. 5, 9
Pennsylvania 209
Pennsylvaniaburg Mission (Ind.) 3
Pennsylvaniaburg, Ind. 4, 9
Penntown, Ind. 4, 9–10
People's National Bank (Lawrenceburg, Ind.) 9
Peppertown, Ind. 11
Perm, Dr. J. Garland 50
Perry Co., Ind. 138
Perrysburg Circuit (Ohio) 248
Perrysburg German M.E. (Ohio) 238–239
Perrysburg, Ohio 220, 239
Petoskey German M.E. (Mich.) 182, 187
Petty, Rev. A. L. 350
Pfaffenberger, George 101
Phelps, A. M. 138
Phetzing, Rev. John 67
Philip, Rev. 201
Philippines 20, 58
Phillip, Rev. 50, 79, 307, 308
Phillipp, Paul 78
Phillipp, Rev. 51
Phillipp, Rev. P. C. 29
Phillips, Rev. Ellen 281, 282
Phillips, Rev. William 263
Pierson, Clarinda 334
Pigeon First UMC (Mich.) 211
Pigeon German M.E. Church (Mich.) 210–211
Pigeon River 210
Pigeon, Mich. 210–211, 351
Piketon, Ohio 72
Pilgrim Holiness Church (Hopkins, Mich.) 176
Pink, J. J. 20
Piqua, Ohio 55, 56, 193, 318
Pittsburgh, Pa. 35, 349–353, 354
Plains Church (Ohio) 292, 297
Plains, Ohio 286, 297

Pleasant Bend UMC (New Bavaria, Ohio) 227
Ploch, Rev. C. E. 132
Plogsterd, Doris 175, 176, 178
Pluddemann, Rev. Paul 79, 301, 302, 335
Plueddemann, Rev. Richard 47, 187, 350
Plummer, Mr. 293
Poland, Ind. 24, 25
Pomeroy Circuit (Ohio) 68–71
Pomeroy UMC
  Chester, Ohio 70
Pomeroy, Ohio 72
Pontiac, Mich. 185
Pope Co., Ill. 166
Port Clinton, Ohio 274
Port Huron, Mich. 189, 190
Portsmouth, Ohio 67, 68, 72–76, 77–79
Posey Co., Ind. 118, 120
Powers, Ill. 167
Powers, Rev. P. Raymond 324
Presbyterians 24, 219, 341
Price family 11
Price Hill, Ohio 43
Primera Iglesia Methodista Unida Hispana en Cleveland 258
Primes, Rev. Joseph 257
Prospect Street Church (Marion, Ohio) 304
Prospect Street M.E. Church 306
  Indianapolis 18
Prospect Street UMC
  Marion, Ohio 302, 304–307
Puerto Rico 20
Pullmann, Rev. Henry (Heinrich) 33, 35, 173, 174, 210, 211, 290, 301
Pultight, Ind. 111, 113, 114

Q

Quicks Road, Mich. 189, 190
Quincy Street Mission (Cleveland) 255, 259
Quincy, Ill. 6

R

R., Joe 270
Raab, Adam 175
Raab, Casper 175
Raab, Charles 176
Raab, Jacob 175, 176
Ramsey, Mary 13
Ramsey, Thomas 13
Raper Chapel (Cincinnati) 31
Rau, Mrs. 268

Reath, Marguerite 110
Red Bird Mission School 299
Reddington, Ind. 99
Redeemer UMC (Mich.) 199–200
Redford, Mich. 185
Redwill (Rethwelm) family 309
Reformed Church 203, 214
Reformed Church building 309
Refuge Church of God in Christ (Lawrenceville, Pa.) 350
Reimenscheider, Rev. Englehard 237
Reorganized Church of the Latter Day Saints (Ann Arbor) 193, 194
Republic, Ohio 267
Resurrection Fellowship (Grand Rapids) 174
Rethwelm (Redwill) family 309
Reusser, Rev. Godfrey 266
Reuter, Rev. George A. 215, 242, 267, 293
Rexroth, Miss 162
Ribbe, George 65
Ribbe, Peter 64, 65
Rice, Dr. 188
Richard's Schoolhouse, Mich. 189, 190
Richardson, Bishop Ernest G. 283, 284
Richmond, Ind. 55, 56, 57
Ridgeton, Ohio 293
Riechner, Rev. 205
Riemenschneider, Rev. Engelhardt 108, 220, 227, 228, 238, 266, 327
Riemenschneider, William 195
Riley Church (Mich.) 200
Ripley Co., Ind. 9
Ripley, Ohio 80
Rise, Rev. J. 334
Rixse, Albert 148
Robins, Miss 305
Rochester 236
Rockford Circuit (Ind.) 104
Rockford, Ind. 99
Rockport church 259
Rockport German M.E. (Cleveland) 257–258
Rockport, Ohio 255
Rodeheffer, Bro. E. A. 6
Roehm family 141
Roesner, Mrs. 338
Roessner, Rev. Elmer 6, 79, 103, 108, 140, 301, 334, 337, 338, 344
Rogatzky, Brother 33
Rogatzky, Rev. 29, 354
Rogatzky, Rev. M. Herman 31, 78, 295
Rogatzky, Rev. Oscar 51, 186, 210, 290, 297
Rogatzky, Rev. William 182
Rogers, Rev. Robert W. 112
Rogue, John 126
Rollman, Elizabeth 339
Rome (German Ridge) Methodist (Ind.) 140
Rome, Ind. 138
Roper, Rev. Jocelyn 39
Rose 269
Roser, Rev. 39
Roser, Rev. Elias 243
Roseville German Methodist Church (Mich.) 188
Roseville, Mich. 185, 186, 188, 190
Rosmarie 79, 162, 332
Roth Cemetery (Ind.) 138
Rothenberg School (Cincinnati) 33
Rothweiler, Rev. Jacob 28, 188, 195, 290
Round Knob, Ill. 168
Rousch, Rev. 307
Ruckheim, Rev. 215
Rudin family 150
Rudin, John 33, 133, 134, 331, 332
Rudin, Otillia (Weidmann) 33, 50, 56, 76, 77, 95, 103, 104, 148, 150, 151, 152, 158, 162, 205, 268, 332, 354
Rudin, Rev. Theodore 5, 19, 28, 33, 39, 50, 58, 67, 72, 76, 89, 91, 107, 120, 128, 133, 147, 155, 156, 187, 203, 204, 266, 267, 271, 273, 283, 289, 294, 300, 307, 327, 328, 329, 337, 340, 344
Ruekheim, Rev. H. 177
Ruff, Rev. Frederick 226
Ruff, Rev. Friedrich 234
Runkel, Rev. A. F. 206, 215, 217
Runkel, Rev. Emil 201, 228
Russelism 351
Rynkiewich, Dr. Michael 126

S

S., Fred 272
Saginaw German M.E. Church (Mich.) 213–214
Saginaw, Mich. 213
Sailer, Father 302
Sailer's Grove (Ohio) 335
Salem Church (Ohio) 231
Salem Circuit 133
Salem E.U.B. 247

Salem German M.E.
  Belle River, Mich. 190
  Cleveland 261
  Evansville, Ind. 131–133
  Hopkins, Mich. 175–176, 177
  Newport, Ky. 47–50
  Toledo 245–248
Salem German Methodist Church
  (Ohio) 303–305, 318
Salem Grove UMC 195
  Mich. 195–197
Salem Indian Mission 176
Salem Methodist Cemetery
  Evansville, Ind. 132
Salem Methodist Church 190
Salem Methodist Episcopal Church 309
Salem, Ohio 286, 302, 303
Salisbury, Ind. 113
Sanders, Charles 121
Sandusky Bay 267
Sandusky Circuit (Ohio) 266–274
Sandusky City Mission 267
Sandusky Co., Ohio 240
Sandusky, Ohio 19, 33, 34, 35, 55, 64, 94,
  268, 271, 331, 353, 354
Santa Claus Association (Ind.) 159
Santa Claus Methodist Church and
  Campground (Ind.) 159
Santa Claus, Ind. 19, 157–161
Santa Fe, Ind. 157
Sardis, Ohio 337
Sauer, Mr. & Mrs. J. H. 304
Sauer, Rev. George 100
Sauers, Ind. 100
Schaal, Dr. J. G. 51
Schaal, Mr. 269
Schaal, Rev. 295
Schaal, Rev. J. B. 28
Schaar, Charlene 199
Schaefer, Rev. 108
Schaenzlin, Rev. Fred 178, 188, 290, 313
Schall, Rev. J. G. 308
Schantzenbacher, Rev. 40
Schaub, F. 103
Schenk, Michael 196
Schertzer, Mr. 303
Schieber, Rev. 294, 295
Schimmelpfennig, Rev. 39, 44, 45
Schimmelpfennig, Rev. F. (father) 56, 315
Schmidlapp, John David 13
Schmidt family 67, 68
Schmidt, Joe 104
Schmucker, Peter 117

family of 157
Schmucker, Rev. Peter 12, 72, 87, 120,
  131, 185, 302
Schneck, Louis 101
Schneider (Snider), John 286
Schneider, Johannes (father) 285
Schneider, John 286
Schneider, Prof. 344
Schneider, Rev. 58
Schneider, Rev. Peter F. 240
Schnuerle, Rev. M. 123, 139
Schnur, George 123
Schoberth, Carl 215
Schoppenhorst family 161
Schoppenhorst, Nora 150
Schott family 230
Schreiber, Rev. 108, 284
Schreiber's Hall 22
Schreifer, G. 159
Schroetter, Albert 132
Schruff, Rev. 344
Schruff, Rev. W. A. 20, 34, 78, 79, 128,
  129, 188, 344, 353
Schuermause, Julia 203
Schulland (La Carne), Ohio 267
Schulz, W. H. 356
Schumann, A. F. 20
Schumann, Rev. Theodore 182
Schwandt, Rev. James P. 211
Schwaninger, Will 78
Schwartz, Frank 102
Schwarzkopf, Rev. 205
Schweinfurth, Albert 197
Schweinfurth, Rev. John 195, 213, 302,
  303
Schweitzer, Rev. C. J. 68, 71, 308
Schweizer, Frederick 242
Schwinn, Rev. George 234
Scioto Circuit 63
Scioto UMC 294
  Bucyrus, Ohio 295
Sebright, Christian 177
Sebright, Mary 177
Second Church
  Cincinnati 5, 28–29, 103, 151
  Cincinnati, Ohio 50, 78, 79
  Detroit, Mich. 186
  Evansville, Ind. 131
  Lawrenceville, Pa. 350, 351
  Louisville, Ky. 92, 102
  Pittsburgh, Pa. 352
Second German M.E. ??–258
Second German M.E. Church 258–??

Columbus, Ohio 280–282, 284
Indianapolis 18, 22
Second UMC (Grand Rapids) 175
Sedan German M.E. (Ind.) 235
Seddelmeyer, John 193
Sedelmeyer, Rev. 17
Seefeldt, August 237
Seemann, Martin 343
Seher, Mr. 34, 274
Sehnert, Rev. 225
Seif's Baker School House (Ohio) 286
Seiter, Daniel 302
Semple, Brent 31
Seventh Day Adventist
  Cleveland 256
  Galion, Ohio 288
  Jeffersonville, Ind. 94
  Louisville, Ky. 95
  New Albany, Ind. 93
Severinghaus, Rev. 283
Severinghaus, Rev. Charlie 79
Severinghaus, Rev. J. F. 153, 158, 162
Sevringhaus, Rev. 129
Seymour Avenue German M.E. (Lansing, Mich.) 197–198
Seymour Circuit (Ind.) 99–102, 110
Seymour Conference 103
Seymour Trinity Church 99
Seymour, Ind. 103, 108, 129
Shake, Rev. C. A. 108
Shank, Rev. Donald 337
Shelby, Ohio 284, 286, 292
Shell Oil 118
Sherwood, Marcus 123
Sherwood, Prudence 123
Sidney Mission (Ohio) 315
Sidney, Ohio 55, 56, 309, 315
Siegrist, Bill 313
Simpson Methodist Church of Pomeroy, Ohio 69
Sinclair, Esther 271
Singapore 266
Singer, David, Sr. 232
Singwald, Lewis 329
Sirkle, Lewis 126
Sixteen German M.E. (Marion Co., Ohio) 290, 290–292
Sixteen UMC (Marion Co., Ohio) 291
Slocum, Ohio 67, 68
Smith, Bishop H. Lester 263
Smith, Rev. 228
Smith, Rev. Albert 108
Smith, Rev. J. 351

Smithfield English M.E. Church 354
Snider (Schneider), John 286
Snow, Mich. 181
Snyder family 303
South Akron Mission (Ohio) 324
South America 266
South Indiana Conference 112, 159
South Lowell German M.E (Mich.) 180
South Lowell, Mich. 179, 181
South Monterey Methodist (Mich.) 177
South Portsmouth, Ky. 68
South Rockport, Ohio 257
Southwestern Indiana Conference 21
Spaeth, Christian 180
Speckman, Rev. Dr. Timothy A. 88, 190
Speckmann, Rev. J. C. 131, 132
Spencerville Circuit (Ohio) 315–318
Spencerville German M.E. (Ohio) 318
Spencerville Methodist Church 309
Spencerville, Ohio 315–316
Spraytown Church (Ind.) 109–110
Spraytown Free Methodist Church (Ind.) 110
Spring Grove German M.E. Church (Cincinnati) 31–32, 38
Spring, David 329
Springfield, Ohio 94
St. Andrew's UMC (Cullman, Ala.) 166
St. Clair Charge (Mich.) 191
St. Clair Mission (Mich.) 190
St. Clair, Mich. 185, 189, 190
St. John's Church 309
  Mich. 200
St. John's German M.E.
  Baresville, Ohio 328–329, 330, 331, 333, 334, 337, 338
  Evansport, Ohio 225
  Sauers, Ind. 100–101
  St. John's, Ohio 315
St. John's German M.E. (Baresville, Ohio) 332
St. John's UCC (Elmore, Ohio) 238
St. John's UMC
  Caborn, Ind. 121–122
St. John's, Ohio 315
St. Louis National League 78
St. Luke's A.M.E. (Bay City, Mich.) 214
St. Mark building 289
St. Mark's UMC
  Galion, Ohio 287, 288–289
St. Maurice, Ind. 11
St. Paul's Methodist Church 226
St. Paul's German M.E.

Cleveland, Ohio 258
Elmore, Ohio 237–238
Evansville, Ind. 126–128
Indiana 101
Mt. Vernon, Ind. 117–118, 119
Sandusky, Ohio 267
St. Paul's South Ridge Methodist (New Bavaria, Ohio) 227
St. Peter's German M.E. Reddington, Ind. 99–100
St. Peter's UMC (Ind.) 123–126, 128
St. Stephen's Evangelical Lutheran Church New Salisbury, Ind. 113
St. Stephen's Lutheran Church (New Bavaria, Ohio) 227
St. Stephens Cemetery (Midway, Ill.) 167
Stained Glass Theatre (Newport, Ky.) 49
Stair, Dr. 51
Staub, Rev. Brian 248
Steinbrecher, Otto 38
Stengel, Jacob 215
Steuben Co., Ind. 227
Stewart, John 299
Stief, Rev. 72
Stiefel, Dr. 162
Stiefel, Dr. Carl 162, 314
Stiles, Rev. Tom 149
Stoll, Rev. Daniel A. 140, 352
Storms, Dr. A. B. 78, 103
Storms, Dr. John 162
Stover, L. D. 288
Straub, Roman 237
Strauch, Rev. John 120, 123, 126
Strausberger, Peter 228
Strickler 291
Stryker Circuit (Ohio) 219–225
Stryker German M.E. (Ohio) 219–220
Stump family 17
Sussick, Charles 118
Swan Creek, Mich. 190
Sweet Leaf Primitive Baptist Church (Louisville) 92
Swiss Church (Henrietta, Ohio) 266
Swiss settlers 180
Switzerland 214, 327
Switzerland Co., Ind. 14
Switzers (Swiss) 331
Sycamore Creek United Methodist Church 201

T

Taft, William Howard 333

Taglauer, George 45
Tales from Great-Grandpa's Trunk (Meckstroth) 316
Tanner, Rev. 128
Tatgenhorst family 30
Tell City German M.E. (Ind.) 140–141
Tell City, Ind. 141
Tellejohn farm 153
Tennant, Rev. Wilson 201
Tenth Street M.E. Church (Indianapolis) 19
Terre Haute, Ind. 24–25
Texas, Ohio 302
Third German M.E. Church
 Cincinnati 29, 30, 32–33
 Detroit 186
 Indianapolis 18
Thirfield, Bishop W. P. 50
Thirty-second Street German Church (Detroit) 187
Thomas family 289
Thomas, Dale 231
Thompson, Dan 312
Thompson, Jeff 312
Thompson, Marian 313
Thompson, Mark 312
Thompson, Ray 313
Thomson, Ohio 267
Thonen, Gottlieb 329
Thornville, Ohio 296
Tiffin, Ohio 267
Toledo Mission (Ohio) 242
Toledo Trust Co. 244
Toledo, Ohio 203, 240–248
Toner, Marilyn 233
Trail Run German M.E. (Ohio) 339–340
Trail Run, Ohio 337, 338
Trefz, Rev. G. 232, 235
Treuschel, Rev. Karl 128, 212, 308
Trinity Church (Cincinnati) 27
Trinity Freewill Baptist (Cleveland) 259
Trinity German M.E. Seymour, Ind. 101–102
Trinity German Methodist (Akron, Ohio) 323–324
Trinity M. E. Church 267
Trinity Methodist 343
 Madison, Ind. 12
Trinity UMC Seymour, Ind. 102
Trist Church (Waterloo, Mich.) 197
Tropf 291
Troy, Ohio 292

Tuscola Street M.E. Church (Saginaw, Mich.) 213–214
Twenty-Fourth St. Church (Detroit, Mich.) 186

U
Uebele, Sister Julia 200
Ulmer, Daniel 237
Ulmer, Matilda 237
Uncle John 150
Union Church (Mt. Vernon, Ind.) 118
Union School 297
United Brethren 308, 341
   Brookville, Ind. 11
   Cleveland, Ohio 259
   Woodville, Ohio 238
United Methodist Church 247
   Holt, Mich. 201
   of Berea, Ohio 264
   of Pomeroy, Ohio 69
Upper Salem M.E. Church (Metropolis, Ill.) 167–168
Upper Salem, Ill. 167
Upper Sandusky, Ohio 298
utopian society 351

V
Valet, Hulda 230
Valley Avenue German M.E. (Grand Rapids) 174–175
Valley, Ohio 337
Vallonia Church (Ind.) 110
Van Buren Methodist Community Center (Dayton, Ohio) 54
Van Buren Street Church (Bay City, Mich.) 211–212
Van Buren Street German M.E. (Dayton, Ohio) 53–54
Van Wyck, Janet 180
Vanderburgh Co., Ind. 130
Venice German M.E. (Ohio) 272
Venice, Ohio 272
Verdin Company 146
Vermillion German M.E. (Ohio) 274–275
Vermillion, Ohio 264, 267, 274–275
Vogel, Rev. Christian 43
von Gunden, Johann 240
Vondielingen, Fred 101

W
Wagstaff, Joseph 220
Wahl, Rev. George 29, 200, 201, 335
Wakefield, Ohio 55
Walden, Bishop J. M. 33
Waldo, Ohio 303
Walker, C. A. J. 308
Wall Street UMC Jeffersonville, Ind. 94
Wallace, Rev. Ross 106
Waller, Charles 51
Walnut Grove church 317
Walnut Hills German M.E. Church (Cincinnati) 35–37
Waltersburg, Ill. 167
Wapakoneta, Ohio 313, 314
Ward, Joseph 335
Ward, William 342
Warne, Bishop 308
Warner, Dr. 297
Warrick Co., Ind. 138
Washington Co., Ohio 338, 339
Washington, Ind. 110
Waterloo Zion German M.E. Church (Mich.) 197
Waterloo, Mich. 193, 196
Wauas, Rev. Conrad 177
Waverly, Ohio 64, 67, 72, 76
Wawaka German M.E. (Ind.) 235–236
Wawaka, Ind. 236
Wayne Street M.E. Church Piqua, Ohio 56
Weber, George, Sr. 228, 230
Weber, Mrs. George 228
Weber, Rev. Phillip 293
Wehmann family 33, 35
Wehmann, Emma 33
Wehmann, Ida 33
Weidmann, Rev. John C. 19, 20, 21
Weigle, Rev. Hal 162
Weiler, Pearl 88
Weiler, Rev. 128, 129, 162, 313, 344
Weiler, Rev. William 140, 234
Weiler, Theodore 51
Weiss, Mrs. Carl 119
Weiss, Rev. Edwin 193
Weitkamp, Dan 151
Weitkamp, Henry 162
Weitz Chapel (Williams Co., Ohio) 232–233
Weitz, Adam 233
Wellemeyer, Rev. Alfred 77, 79, 148
Wells, Isabelle 202
Wenckebach, Rev. 340
Wendell, Opal 247
Werner family 77

Werner, Rev. Ernst 5, 51, 78, 79, 128, 133, 186, 228, 231
Werremeyers family 150
Wesler, C. H. 8–9
Wesley Chapel
  Batesville, Ind. 4
  Higginsport, Ohio 80–81
Wesley Hall (Covington, Ky.) 45
Wesley Methodist Church 258
Wesley UMC
  Cincinnati 33
  Portsmouth, Ohio 76
West Cullman M.E. Church (Ala.) 166
West Michigan Conference 182, 201
  Kalamazoo District 177
West Park Methodist (Cleveland) 259
West Side Church
  Evansville, Ind. 133
West Side Methodist Church (Ann Arbor) 193
West Union Circuit (Ohio) 76, 80
West Union, Ohio 72
West Unity Circuit (Ohio) 226
West Unity Emanuel German M.E. (Ohio) 220–225
West Unity, Ohio 219, 221
West, Rev. E. Parker 298
Western 6
Westside Independent Baptist Church (Cleveland) 261
Wetzel, George 102
Wetzel, S. 159
Wheelersburg M.E. Church (Ohio) 67
Wheeling, W.Va. 79, 290, 301, 330, 334, 354, 355
White Creek Church (Ind.) 104–109
White Creek Circuit (Ind.) 104–110
White Creek UMC (Ind.) 105, 109
White Creek, Ind. 104–107, 108
White Hall (Muskegon), Mich. 173
White Hall Mission (Mich.) 178
White River, Mich. 178
Whitecreek UMC (Ind.) 107
Whitneyville, Mich. 181
Wibbeler, Adolph 152
Wibbeler, Rev. Ben 148
Widmer family 37
Wiedler, Mr. 64
Wienefeld family 55
Wild Fowl Bay 209
Williams County Historical Society 231
Williams Schoolhouse (Ohio) 286, 290
Williams, Dr. F. H. 73
Williams, Francis 285
Wingerter, Glen 92
Winkenhofer, Mrs. George 106
Winkenhofer, Rev. 108
Woehrman family 108
Woehrman, Rev. Frank H. 108
Woodland Dance Hall 256
Woodland German Methodist (Mich.) 179–180
Woodland, Mich. 179
Woods, Hiram 118
Woodville German M.E. (Ohio) 238
Woodville, Ohio 239
World War I 5, 18, 24, 35, 47, 94, 124, 144, 155, 159, 193, 214, 215, 291, 296
  anti-German sentiment 4, 147, 237, 243
  hysteria 283
World War II 37, 48
Worthington Children's Home 306, 317
Worthington, Ohio 296
Worthman, Rev. Dietrich 312, 336, 337, 352
Wuerfel, Rev. 308
Wulzen family 60
Wulzen, Rev. H. E. 58, 90, 127
Wunderlich, Rev. Ehrhard 324, 350
Wurfel, Rev. Paul 187
Wyttenbach Settlement (Ind.) 157
Wyttenbach, Rev. Christian 3, 157, 351

Y

Yaussey family 329
Yaussey, Rev. G. 301
Yokel, Hettie 132
York Street Church (Cincinnati) 32
Young, Dr. 323
Youngstown, Ohio 289, 324
Ypsilanti German Methodist Church (Mich.) 194
Ypsilanti, Mich. 193

Z

Z., Ed 272
Zanesville, Ohio 285
Zarwell 313
Zarwell, Rev. A. F. 9
Zarwell, Rev. John 22
Zenor, Henry 118
Zenor, Percilla 118
Zerbe Law Offices 9
  Lawrenceburg, Ind. 7

Zierer, Edward 6, 7
Zion ("the Sinks," Detricks M. E.)
    (Ind.) 113
Zion Church
    Edgerton Circuit, Ohio 232
    Midway, Ill. 167
Zion German Lutheran Church 267
Zion German M.E. 315
    Cleveland, Ohio 260
    Columbus, Ohio 280
    Irving, Mich. 179
    Lowell, Mich. 180–181
    Ohio 335–337
    Toledo, Ohio 242–245
Zion German Methodist Church
    Macomb Co., Mich. 190
    Mich. 189
    Ohio 302

Zion Methodist Church
    Slocum, Ohio 67
Zion UMC 242, 261
    Pennington, Ind. 5
Zion, Ohio 302, 335
Zischke, Elnora 176
Zoar Church
    Crawford Co., Ohio 286
    Fishing Creek, Ohio 239
    Oil Creek, Ind. 140
Zoar German M.E.
    Mt. Vernon, Ind. 118–120
Zoar UMC
    Hanover, Ind. (photo) 13
    Holland, Ind. 152–156
    Madison, Ind. 13
Zwahlen, Rev. John 309, 311, 334, 354

About the Author

Barbara Dixon, a retired elementary school teacher, became interested in her German heritage at the age of ten when she discovered the German words to "Silent Night" in a songbook. Her mother, Rosemarie Brown (whose first language was German) and her grandmother, Otillia Rudin, helped her learn the words.

Forty years later, Barb's mother showed her the diaries that her father, Theodore Rudin (a German Methodist pastor) had kept for forty years. Barbara became intrigued with these and so for several years Rosemarie mailed her four or five diaries from Florida and when she was done reading them, Barbara mailed them back and waited for the next set. After retirng, Barbara typed out copies of all the diaries to share with relatives.

Barbara then became interested in learning more about the German Methodist Episcopal church, locating all the churches and learning their histories up to the present. To aid in research, she enrolled in a German class at a senior center in Hamilton, Ohio, taught by a retired high school German teacher. Then she embarked on an odyssey of research trips to locations all over Ohio, Indiana, lower Michigan as well as Pittsburgh, Wheeling, southeastern Illinois and northern Kentucky. As her husband, Roy, says, "We toured all the inner city slums of all the major cities in the area." The couple also traveled numerous country roads searching for many of the elusive churches that time forgot. The result is this book.

Barbara and her husband raised two talented daughters, Tara, an author and veterans advocate, and Gini, an environmental engineer at Cape Canaveral, and live in Loveland, Ohio, with their two adopted cat daughters.